I0125533

Routledge Revivals

The Other Languages of England

The 'other' languages of England — those which originated in South and East Asia, and Southern and Eastern Europe — are now important parts of everyday life in urban England. First published in 1985, this book gives detailed information about which languages are in widespread use among children and adults, patterns of language use in different social contexts, the teaching of these community languages inside and outside of mainstream schools, and the educational implications of this linguistic diversity for all children in England. The authors argue that this continued and widespread bilingualism is a valuable potential resource for both the speakers and society as a whole.

The Other Languages of England

Linguistic Minorities Project

Xavier Couillaud, Marilyn Martin-Jones, Anna Morawska, Euan Reid, Verity Saifullah Khan and Greg Smith

Routledge
Taylor & Francis Group

First published in 1985
by Routledge & Kegan Paul

This edition first published in 2017 by Routledge
2 Park Square, Milton Park, Abingdon, Oxon, OX14 4RN
and by Routledge
711 Third Avenue, New York, NY 10017

Routledge is an imprint of the Taylor & Francis Group, an informa business

© 1985 University of London Institute of Education

All rights reserved. No part of this book may be reprinted or reproduced or utilised in any form or by any electronic, mechanical, or other means, now known or hereafter invented, including photocopying and recording, or in any information storage or retrieval system, without permission in writing from the publishers.

Publisher's Note
The publisher has gone to great lengths to ensure the quality of this reprint but points out that some imperfections in the original copies may be apparent.

Disclaimer
The publisher has made every effort to trace copyright holders and welcomes correspondence from those they have been unable to contact.

A Library of Congress record exists under LC control number: 8424874

ISBN 13: 978-1-138-24224-1 (hbk)
ISBN 13: 978-1-315-27861-2 (ebk)
ISBN 13: 978-1-138-24235-7 (pbk)

DEDICATION

We wish to dedicate this re-issued volume to our late colleague and friend, Anna Morawska, who died in 2014.

It is also dedicated to all bilingual and multilingual people in England, in the United Kingdom and around the world and to those who respect and value linguistic diversity.

PREFACE

The publication in 1985 of *The Other Languages of England* was a key moment in the development of sociolinguistic research on multilingualism in the United Kingdom (UK). It contributed significantly to the debates about linguistic and cultural diversity taking place at the time. This re-issued volume presents research that was conducted as part of the Linguistic Minorities Project, which was funded by the Department of Education and Science. The project director was Verity Saifullah Khan and the co-investigators were Marilyn Martin-Jones, Anna Morawska, Euan Reid, and Greg Smith. The research was commissioned in 1979, under a Labour government, but carried out during the first Thatcher-led Conservative government. A knowledge exchange project – Language, Information Network Coordination (LINC) – was funded alongside the Linguistic Minorities Project by the European Commission. The director of that project was Xavier Couillaud.

The Linguistic Minorities Project was the first major sociolinguistic research project focusing on multilingualism to be carried out in the UK. It included the development of systematic ways of conducting language surveys in schools (the Schools Language Survey and the Secondary Pupils Survey), and the design and conduct of more detailed sociolinguistic survey work in Bradford, Coventry and London with adults and with organisers of 'complementary' schools and classes (the Adult Language Use Survey and the Mother Tongue Teaching Directory). The research was designed and carried out in the absence of any prior sociolinguistic survey work of this kind or any national census data (at the time, there was no language question in the census for England, in contrast to the data gathering arrangements for the census in other regions of the UK).

The Adult Language Use Survey contributed significant new knowledge at the time to the sociolinguistics of multilingualism in England. Nineteen local surveys were carried out with speakers of a range of languages from South and East Asia and from Eastern and Southern Europe. With additional funding from the European Commission for the LINC project, the findings of these local sociolinguistic surveys were disseminated back to local linguistic minority groups in each research context. The aim of this extensive survey and knowledge exchange work was to "create a solid basis for more detailed case studies in the future" (Linguistic Minorities Project, 1985: 15). Unfortunately, in the new political climate of the mid-1980s, we were not able to pursue these intentions,

In addition to presenting and discussing the findings of this extensive school and community-based research on multilingualism, *The Other Languages of England* also set the research within a wider policy context. Firstly, it made reference to the 'mother tongue debate' taking place in the UK at the time when the project was first funded, a debate prompted partly by a European Communities Directive (EC, 1977) regarding provision within national education systems for the teaching of the languages of linguistic minorities.

Secondly, the volume made reference to wider debates taking place at the time about linguistic and cultural diversity, in education and in civil society more generally. An earlier policy discourse about the need to 'integrate' newcomers into the nation was challenged and dominant discourses about cultural homogeneity were unpacked. And, thirdly, the volume also raised concerns about the discriminatory ideologies about language circulating at the time.

Over three decades later, we see significant resonances between the dominant discourses circulating in England in the late 1970s and early 1980s, and contemporary discourses about language and migration. We see the return of the trope about 'integration of newcomers', partly through European Union policy. As Martin-Jones (2015: 259) points out: "In the light of the most intensely discriminatory discourses circulating in the twenty first century, reference to 'integration' now indexes – for some – a relatively moderate politics of inclusion". Across Europe, and in the United Kingdom over the last two decades, we have seen a significant retreat from the pluralist multiculturalism of the previous decades (Fekete, 2009; Lantin and Titley 2011). The impact of the outrages of 9/11 in the United States, and the 2005 terror attacks in the UK has been a growing concern with security and Islamic radicalisation that has fed into strategies of counter-terrorism and assimilationist preoccupation with social cohesion that have undermined a commitment to human rights and a political capacity to embrace diversity (Husband and Alam, 2005; Kundani, 2007). Thus, we have seen the rise of more explicit forms of language-based discrimination and exclusion (Blackledge, 2005) and increasing contemporary manifestations of racism and linguistic xenophobia, including objections to the public use of languages other than English.

When we consider the sociolinguistic landscape of England depicted in this volume, we see that there have been major changes, largely due to the increase in the intensity and complexity of transnational migration, particularly since the accession of Eastern European and Baltic countries to the European Union. Thus, for example, in the 2011 census, (which included a language question for England) Polish was recorded as being the most widely spoken language for the UK as a whole, after English and Welsh, surpassing the South Asian languages which were at the centre of public attention in the 1980s.

There have also been major changes in sociolinguistic research on multilingualism since 1985. Two processes have coincided: Firstly, there has been an epistemological shift towards ethnographic approaches which incorporate critical, poststructuralist and postmodern perspectives on language in social life, and there has been a significant turn to discourse. (Rampton, 2006; Heller, 2007, 2011; Blackledge and Creese, 2010; Martin-Jones et al., 2012; Martin-Jones and Martin, 2017). Secondly, over the last two decades, there has been an intense focus on the social, linguistic and cultural changes ushered in by globalisation, by transnational population movements, by the advent of new communication technologies and by the changes taking place in the political and economic contours of different regions of the world. The analysis of these developments has been powerfully shaped by the post-1980s impact of the postmodern turn in social and sociolinguistic analysis and the consequent sensitivity to the intersectionality and contingency of processes of identification.

These epistemological shifts have led to a rethinking of the relationship between language and society and of the multilingual realities of the late modern era (Blommaert, 2010; Blommaert and Rampton, 2011; Duchêne and Heller, 2012). Thus, for instance, researchers have turned their attention "from stability to mobility"

(Heller, 2011: 5-6) and from a focus on 'communities' to 'contact zones' (Pratt, 1991), such as those in local urban neighbourhoods, in adult education classes, in schools or in local workplaces. There has also been an unpacking of the notion of 'language' as a fixed and bounded entity (Makoni and Pennycook, 2007) and greater attention to communicative repertoires and to the communicative resources available to speakers. Blommaert (2010) has, for example, called for a "sociolinguistics of mobile resources" – a sociolinguistics that takes account of the way in which such resources get evaluated across the hierarchically ordered scales of social life.

The text of *The Other Languages of England* anticipated some of these conceptual changes, in the use of terms such as "multiple identities", in the representation of bilingualism as "a social process" characterised by considerable vitality (Husband and Saifullah Khan, 1982), and in the insistence that boundaries of languages, of cultures and of social groups are not fixed but are the outcomes of social action. One particularly far-sighted recommendation in the volume relates to the call for more research to be done by researchers who are bilingual themselves and for research in multilingual teams.

We welcome the re-issue of our 1985 book and we hope that it can contribute to the recalibration of contemporary debates and to the necessary reassertion of the principle of respect for otherness and for speakers of 'the other languages of England'.

Verity Saifullah Khan, Xavier Couillaud, Marilyn Martin-Jones, Euan Reid and Greg Smith

December 2016

References

Blackledge, A. (2005) *Discourse and power in a multilingual world.* Amsterdam: John Benjamins

Blackledge, A. and Creese, A. (2010) *Multilingualism: A critical perspective.* London: Contiuum.

Blommaert, J. (2010) *The sociolinguistics of globalization.* Cambridge: Cambridge University Presss.

Blommaert, J. and Rampton, B (2011) Language and superdiversity. *Diversities* 13 (2): 1-21.

Duchêne, A. and Heller, M. (eds.) (2012) *Language in late capitalism: Pride and profit.* New York: Routledge.

European Communities (1977) Council Directive on the education of the children of migrant workers. 77/486. Brussels: EC.

Fekete, L. (2009) *A suitable enemy: Racism, migration and islamophobia in Europe*. London: Pluto Press.

Heller, M. (ed.) (2007) *Bilingualism: A social approach. Basingstoke*, Hamphsire: Palgrave Macmillan.

Heller, M. (2011) *Paths to post-nationalism: A critical ethnography of language and identity*. Oxford: Oxford University Press.

Husband, C. and Saifullah Khan, V. (1982) The viability of ethnolinguistic vitality: some creative comments. *Journal of Multilingual and Multicultural Development*, Vol. 3 (3), 351-366.

Husband, C. and Alam, Y. (2011) *Social cohesion and counter-terrorism: A policy contradiction*. Bristol: Policy Press.

Kundani, A. (2007) *The end of tolerance: Racism in 21ˢᵗ century Britain*. London: Pluto Press.

Lantin, A. and Titley, G. (2011) *The crises of multiculturalism*. London: Zed Books.

Makoni, S. and Pennycook A. (eds.) (2007) *Disinventing and reconstituting languages*. Clevedon, Avon: Multilingual Matters

Martin-Jones, M. (2015) Afterword. In J. Simpson and A. Whiteside (eds.) *Adult language education and migration: Challenging agendas in policy and practice*. Abingdon, Oxfordshire: Routledge.

Martin-Jones, M., Blackledge, A. and Creese, A. (eds.) (2012) *Routledge Handbook of Multilingualism*. Abingdon, Oxfordshire: Routledge.

Martin-Jones, M. and Martin, D. (eds.) (2017) *Researching multilingualism: Critical and ethnographic perspectives.* Abingdon, Oxfordshire: Routledge.

Pratt, M-L. (1991) Arts of the contact zone. *Profession* 91. New York: Modern Language Association.

Rampton, B. (2006) *Language in late modernity.* Cambridge: Cambridge University Press

The Other Languages of England

Linguistic Minorities Project

Routledge & Kegan Paul

London, Boston, Melbourne and Henley

First published in 1985
by Routledge & Kegan Paul plc

14 Leicester Square, London WC2H 7PH, England

9 Park Street, Boston, Mass. 02108, USA

464 St Kilda Road, Melbourne,
Victoria 3004, Australia and

Broadway House, Newtown Road,
Henley on Thames, Oxon RG9 1EN, England

Set in Press Roman
by Hope Services, Abingdon, Oxon.
and printed in Great Britain
by T. J. Press (Padstow) Ltd
Padstow, Cornwall.

© *University of London Institute of Education 1985*

No part of this book may be reproduced in
any form without permission from the publisher,
except for the quotation of brief passages
in criticism

Library of Congress Cataloging in Publication Data

The other languages of England.
(Language, education, and society)
Bibliography: p.
Includes index.
1. Linguistic minorities—England.   2. Education,
Bilingual—England.   I. Linguistic Minorities Project
(Great Britain)   II. Series.
P119.315.086   1985   404'.2'0941   84-24874

British Library CIP data available

ISBN 0-7100-9929-0 (c)
ISBN 0-7102-0417-5 (p)

Contents

Tables

Figures

Maps

General Editor's preface

Simply a list of some of the questions implied by the phrase *Language, Education and Society* gives an immediate idea of the complexity, and also the fascination, of the area.

How is language related to learning? Or to intelligence? How should a teacher react to non-standard dialect in the classroom? Do regional and social accents and dialects matter? What is meant by standard English? Does it make sense to talk of 'declining standards' in language or in education? Or to talk of some children's language as 'restricted'? Do immigrant children require special language provision? How can their native languages be used as a valuable resource in schools? Can 'literacy' be equated with 'education'? Why are there so many adult illiterates in Britain and the USA? What effect has growing up with no easy access to language: for example, because a child is profoundly deaf? Why is there so much prejudice against people whose language background is odd in some way: because they are handicapped, or speak a non-standard dialect or foreign language? Why do linguistic differences lead to political violence, in Belgium, India, Wales and other parts of the world?

These are all real questions, of the kind which worry parents, teachers and policy makers, and the answer to them is complex and not at all obvious. It is such questions that authors in this series discuss.

Language plays a central part in education. This is probably generally agreed, but there is considerable debate and confusion about the exact relationship between language and learning. Even though the importance of language is generally recognised, we still have a lot to learn about how language is related either to educational success or to intelligence and thinking. Language is also a central fact in everyone's social life. People's attitudes and most deeply held beliefs are at stake, for it is through language that personal and social identities are maintained and recognised. People are judged, whether justly or not, by the language they speak.

Language, education and society is therefore an area where scholars have a responsibility to write clearly and persuasively, in order to communicate the best in recent research to as wide an audience as possible. This means not only other researchers, but also all those who are involved in educational, social and political policy-making, from individual teachers to government. It is an area where value judgments cannot be avoided. Any action that we take – or, of course, avoidance of action – has moral, social and political consequences. It is vital, therefore, that practice is informed by the best knowledge available, and that decisions affecting the futures of individual children or whole social groups are not taken merely on the basis of the all too widespread folk myths about language in society.

Linguistics, psychology and sociology are often rejected by non-specialists as jargon-ridden; or regarded as fascinating, but of no relevance to educational or social practice. But this is superficial and short-sighted: we are dealing with complex issues, which require an understanding of the general principles involved. It is bad theory to make statements about language in use which cannot be related to educational and social reality. But it is equally unsound to base beliefs and action on anecdote, received myths and unsystematic or idiosyncratic observations.

All knowledge is value-laden: it suggests action and changes our beliefs. Change is difficult and slow, but possible nevertheless. When language in education and society is seriously and systematically studied, it becomes clear how awesomely complex is the linguistic and social knowledge of all children and adults. And with such an understanding, it becomes impossible to maintain a position of linguistic prejudice and intolerance. This may be the most important implication of a serious study of language, in our linguistically diverse modern world. This book on *The Other Languages of England* is a major publication which reports some of the most important sociolinguistic research to be done in Britain in recent years.

There is widespread ignorance of the most basic facts of linguistic diversity in Britain, and many readers will be surprised simply by the large number of languages which are used in different areas of England. Much of the information presented here has not been available at all before in any systematic form, and it is only recently that we have started to have answers to questions such as: Which languages are spoken in Britain? By how many people? Are the children and grandchildren of immigrants retaining these languages or switching to an exclusive use of English?

One very important feature of the research, which sets new standards for subsequent work, is the central place given to the immediate practical spin offs of their varied research methods. The researchers have aimed throughout to make meticulously gathered information accessible to those who need it: teachers, educational planners, social workers, linguists and other social scientists, and members of the linguistic minorities themselves. Dissemination was an integral part of the research programme, and the book discusses what effect such work can have on the people who participate in the research process. (This book is, in fact, only one, rather traditional, means of dissemination: the dissemination project attached to LMP is also using several other ways of making the work available to those who can use its findings. This includes not only other articles and reports, but teaching materials, questionnaires, posters and a video.) All too often, social and linguistic research is done without recognising from the outset that research can affect and change what is being studied. This book provides discussion of this moral and political issue.

On the basis of systematic information on the languages used in certain areas of England, the book contributes to clear discussions of issues of great social importance, including educational planning, and forms of discrimination and racism. Overall it provides a strong case for regarding widespread bilingualism among users of a wide range of languages, not as a problem, but as a valuable resource for the individual speakers and for British society. It also provides substantial new data for researchers interested in theories of individual bilingualism and societal multi-lingualism.

The work of the Linguistic Minorities Project is already widely known and respected. This book will quickly establish itself as an essential source of information for anyone concerned with linguistic minorities in Britain and elsewhere.

Michael Stubbs
Nottingham

Preface

The other languages of England are all those languages apart from English that are ignored in public, official activities in England. They are the languages that constitute unrecognised social skills among a large proportion of our urban population. It is the predominance of the English language and the related assumption that monolingualism is the norm that makes them seem 'other'. In reality, the languages of the different linguistic minorities are now part of everyday life in multilingual England, and valuable social and economic resources for the country as a whole. To go on seeing them simply as 'other' is to reinforce the view that being bilingual is a problem – for the speaker and for the society.

The aim of this book is twofold: first, to provide information about patterns of language use and language teaching among South and East Asian and Southern and Eastern European linguistic minorities in some areas of England; second, to consider the educational implications of linguistic diversity for all school children whether they are presently bilingual or monolingual.

The book has been written in the hope of attracting a wide readership beyond the traditional academic disciplines to which it is most closely related. We have tried, therefore, to minimise the use of unnecessarily technical terminology, and discussion which presumes familiarity with ongoing academic debates.

The book has its own internal logic, and we would encourage all readers to work through from beginning to end. However, for those who can only give limited time to it, we recommend one of two alternative routes:

1   For those most interested in the school-based educational issues, Chapters 1, 2, 7, 8 and 9, with the addition of Chapter 6, which raises crucial questions about the boundaries and responsibilities of 'the school system'.

2   For those most interested in bilingualism in society, Chapters 1, 2, 4, 5 and 6, with the addition of Chapter 3, for a discussion of the contribution of sociolinguistic research to this field.

We hope that all readers will start with Chapter 1 and end with Chapter 10, and that all those interested in the wider questions posed by sociolinguistic or educational research may benefit from reading Chapters 3 and 7 respectively.

Acknowledgments

This book is the product of collective writing following four years of collective team work. Instead of insisting, as so many lone authors must do, that the opinions expressed are the sole responsibility of the author, each of us can with some justification disown the overall text! The taxing procedures involved in the production of this book have taught us a lot about ourselves and, we hope, about our subject. We hope that what was at times an excessively laborious way of working has enriched rather than diluted our contribution to this field of enquiry. If we have prepared a solid foundation on which others can build we will have fulfilled one of our main objectives.

First and foremost, we want to thank colleagues who participated in so much of our work: Michael Morawski, the assistant programmer, and our administrative and secretarial assistants, Christine Dean, Carrie Harvey, Jenny Norvick, Deloris Reviere, Bernadette de Soyza, Judy Tasker and Mee Lian Yong. Their contribution, in coordinating a busy team, often working in another city, keeping our spirits up and taking on tasks such as supervising coders and design of publications, has been central.

If the data and issues that are explored in this book are of value to the wide audience we anticipate, this is in large measure due to the experience we gained in the course of the project. So, our most sincere thanks must go to all those who supported and often guided us during the field research, in particular the fieldwork co-ordinators, Safder Alladina, Xavier Couillaud, Shamim Nasser and Lorenza Raponi, and the 150 bilingual interviewers from Coventry, Bradford and London. The language consultants, calligraphers, survey consultants and community contacts are too numerous to mention by name. We are greatly in their debt and believe that they still have much to contribute to these issues. Similarly we want to thank nearly 2,500 people who were interviewed in the ALUS survey, the hundreds of mother tongue organisers and teachers who gave even more of their time, and the thousands of pupils who participated in the schools surveys.

All of the teachers, administrative staff, advisers and education officers with whom we collaborated have had some familiarity with research projects before, and have some institutional support to follow up the implications and to re-use the research instruments. This is not the case for many mother tongue teachers who were particularly co-operative in offering their own time, with little chance of any immediate change in their working conditions. It is with this in mind that we must also thank the National Council for Mother Tongue Teaching for their extended contribution to the development of the Mother Tongue Teaching Directory Survey. This has been devised so that they can promote the survey throughout the country, and establish a data bank at the Centre for Information on Language Teaching and Research.

Our final thanks go to the three chairmen of our project, Henry Widdowson, Harold Rosen and Jagdish Gundara, the members of our Academic Advisory Committee (including our overseas advisers), members of the Steering Group, the Department of Education and Science who funded our project, and also the Commission of the European Communities for funding the LINC project which continued actively to disseminate our work.

1
Introduction

This book is about the other languages of England — what these South and East Asian, Southern and Eastern European languages are, who speaks them and for what purposes. It is also about the significance these languages have for their speakers and for society as a whole. The research discussed in the ten chapters that follow derives above all from our interest in the educational implications of linguistic diversity which is so much a feature of everyday life in England today.

There are many bilingual adults in England who altered their patterns of language use when they moved from their homelands and migrated to England. In future, however, there will be increasing numbers of British-born bilinguals who learn their 'mother tongue' from their parents, relatives and friends, and use it in local community-based activities alongside the English which they learn and use at school. The extent of environmental support these young people experience for their languages will depend, of course, on how many people use these languages around them, who these people are, and what purposes the languages serve. There is likely to be a great difference, for example, in the degree of exposure to Greek for a teenager living in North London, as compared with that available in Panjabi for a teenager living in a small provincial town. The former will have access to many activities in Greek beyond the home, whereas the latter may have very few in Panjabi.

The opportunities bilingual adults have to use their other-than-English languages depend on their patterns of social interaction, which are influenced in large measure by the local labour market. Their British-born bilingual children grow up with two or more languages, using them differentially in a range of situations and settings. These languages are learnt, informally at first, through the processes of language socialisation of the home, kin, the peer group and the local community. Then, from about the age of five onwards, the more formal processes of language learning offered by the local state school, and in some cases also by local community-run classes, are introduced.

If we are to understand the impact of language learning on the overall educational development of pupils in our schools, we need to understand how these processes influence the different elements in a child's linguistic repertoire. (Here we are talking about the non-standard vernacular and standard varieties of English for so-called monolingual pupils, and these varieties of English as well as vernacular and standard varieties of other languages for bilingual pupils.) Most important of all, we need to analyse how the learning of the two or more languages is inter-related in different contexts and over time. For example, increasing numbers of pupils attend mother tongue classes organised outside the regular state school system. In some of these classes English is rarely used; in others it is the medium of instruction for teaching the language still commonly referred to as 'the mother tongue'.

This book is offered as a starting point in a relatively new area of research, and we hope that both researchers and educational practitioners will use it to work out the implications of our findings for their own areas of interest. There are many social scientists and professionals working in the field of ethnic relations who need to recognise the significance of language use in the transmission of culture and the distribution of economic and political resources. There are also many educationalists who are so busy facing the immediate, practical questions posed by linguistic and cultural diversity in their classrooms, schools or local education authorities, that they have little time to pause and reflect on the impact of bilingual language acquisition on general educational development and opportunities in adult life. Those of our readers who live the daily reality of being bilingual in England may find that the book hardly begins to convey the richness that their linguistic and cultural skills offer or the difficulties that they may impose on them. We hope, however, that our decision to present different perspectives on bilingualism among a range of minority populations will help them place their experience in its wider setting.

The organisation of this book reflects our wide perspective on the educational issues relating to mother tongue teaching in England. The last section of this chapter indicates the reasons for our focus on a wide range of linguistic minorities, and the difficulties associated with it. By way of introduction to the linguistic minorities in England whom we did study, Chapter 2 presents some brief profiles, then discusses them in the context of the three cities where the Linguistic Minorities Project (LMP) carried out most of its work.

Chapter 3 places the project and its focus of enquiry in its academic context. Our predominantly sociolinguistic perspective has a particular relevance for the educational debates arising from the presence of large numbers of bilingual pupils in the state school system. Chapter 7 looks more specifically at these language and education issues and acts as a link between accounts of the two community-based surveys in Chapters 5 and 6, and the two school-based surveys in Chapters 8 and 9.

Chapter 4 discusses the sampling and fieldwork procedures which provided the foundation for the most complex of our four surveys, the Adult Language Use Survey. Indirectly, Chapter 4 indicates the value of much of the additional data which we amassed through the creation of our sampling frames, the development and piloting of a standardised bilingual questionnaire in different languages, and the recruitment and collaboration of bilingual interviewers from the local linguistic minorities. In Chapter 5, we present the basic information about patterns of language use in eleven linguistic minorities in three cities. Each of them could, of course, profitably be given a separate chapter, and this material was treated more fully by the ESRC follow-up project, Community Languages and Education, 1983-5. Against the background of social interaction and patterns of language use described in Chapters 4 and 5 for some linguistic minorities, we move on to look at one particular form of minority institution which aims to counter the general trend of language shift to English by the younger generation. The findings of the Mother Tongue Teaching Directory Survey discussed in Chapter 6 fill out the picture to include reference to the full range of languages taught in the three cities in which we worked. (A partial picture of community-run provision for mother tongue teaching emerged from ALUS.) This chapter presents a picture of a parallel school system running alongside, but often unconnected with, the official state school system. We discuss the role of these mother tongue schools and classes in the local linguistic minorities and as a challenge to the state school.

Chapter 7 considers some of the educational implications of bilingualism for adults, and of the language socialisation process experienced by many bilingual children in state schools. It places these personal experiences in the context of the recent historical development of language education for minority children and of education for a multicultural society. Having also sketched in the background of the constraints on communication between minorities and the state school system, and between the official and unofficial school systems, we prepare the ground for an account in Chapters 8 and 9 of the two school-based surveys. Chapter 10 summarises some of the contributions of our research and suggests developments for future research and practice.

One of the reasons we chose a very broad scope for our work was that there was almost no previous research about the use of languages like Bengali, Greek, Panjabi, or Polish in England. Even the numbers of people using a language other than English in daily life are not known, although this has not prevented speculation about the probable changes in the numbers of speakers and about differences in language loyalties between the generations. The very basic data we collected in different areas of the country about the proportions of pupils reporting some degree of bilingualism surprised many of the professionals involved in these children's education. Up to 30 per cent of the children surveyed by LMP in 1980-1 reported spoken skills in a minority language, and a consistent 40 to 50 per cent of these pupils also reported some literacy skills in a minority language – both figures considerably higher than many had estimated. Knowledge of the distribution and sociolinguistic characteristics of different linguistic minorities helps also to inform the debate about which minority languages could be taught in the state school system and which varieties are most appropriate for different purposes (Reid, (ed.), 1984).

This book outlines a conceptual framework and offers an empirical base for exploring bilingualism as a social process. The sociolinguistic profile of Britain has undergone far-reaching changes in the post-war era: it is still changing. To explain these changes, within an historical and political framework, we must begin by looking at the socio-economic factors which explain the arrival in England of speakers of languages other than English: languages such as Bengali, Cantonese, Greek, Italian, Panjabi, Polish, Turkish and Ukrainian (see Chapter 2). The changing status in the wider society of what are now seen as 'minority languages', and their patterns of use within particular local populations, are also related closely to the socio-economic position of the minorities in question. This position influences relations with the dominant majority, as well as with other linguistic minorities.

Many researchers have written about the economic and political factors which affect the life chances of members of ethnic minorities. They have demonstrated, for example, how the structures of discrimination are reinforced by the values and concepts which pervade economic and social processes. Nor is it difficult to see how social and political values influence the distribution of resources within the school in England. So it should be no surprise that the prevailing attitudes to linguistic minorities in our society are affected by implicit assumptions about the social value of other cultures and, most significantly from the point of view of this book, by underlying conceptions of what 'cultures' and 'languages' are and how different languages and cultures are related. Both ethnic terms and linguistic labels are, of course, culturally conditioned, and linguistic categories are much more problematic than is often assumed (Le Page and Tabouret-Keller, 1982). Discussions have started too about the changing form of some of the languages — for example, the increased influence of English on the vocabulary and even the grammar of North Indian languages spoken by young bilingual people in England (Agnihotri, 1979; Rampton, 1981). Much of this speculation has taken place with very little reference to the sociolinguistic situation of the speakers of these languages.

The social and linguistic skills of many members of linguistic minorities — especially those singled out as black or brown by members of the dominant culture, be they of West Indian or South Asian origin — are generally perceived to have little economic, political or social value for the society at large. This essentially negative attitude to ethnic minorities focusses on *their* culture, but in fact tells us much about dominant cultural assumptions. It is assumed by the dominant majority that through contact with the English culture these minorities should and will inevitably assimilate culturally and linguistically. But members of linguistic minorities in England are full members of English society, although they are characteristically defined by the dominant group as ethnic or 'racial' minorities (Wallman, 1978). There is also often the assumption of a one-to-one fit between language and culture. For example, if 'they' adopt our culture, then 'they' won't need their language or their own culture; and if 'they' use our language, they must have accepted our values. Such simplistic inferences are not uncommon in societies where the one-language one-nation ethos has predominated. They provide the foundation for the view that bilingualism — at least among ethnic minorities — is bound to be problematic for the individual and for society as a whole.

A book about the other languages of England is therefore indirectly a book about the dominant language and values in England. It is a book about the social worlds of the speakers of these other languages, nearly all of whom now also know and use English and have developed a particular relationship to it. It is also a book about the potential speakers of these other languages, including those 'once-bilinguals' who have lost their skills, and those English-speaking monolinguals who could learn and use skills in other languages in their multilingual environments. So it is about attitudes and choice. You may be bilingual and have few opportunities to use languages other than English. You may alternatively know very little of your parents' 'mother tongue', but be motivated to seek out a place to learn it. You may be monolingual English, with no intention of recognising other people's rights to use their own language in public. Or you may be monolingual English but with a wish to learn the language used in your neighbours' houses or by your workmates.

By presenting bilingualism as a normal feature of social life, and an individual and societal resource, we hope to show how monolingual perspectives and policies in the field of education reinforce the prevailing view of bilingualism as a problem. To put these issues in perspective we focus on several areas of England where bilingualism is the norm for a large proportion of the population.

Although in most of this book we use without qualification common and widely accepted language names like 'English' and 'Panjabi', it is important always to bear in mind that, whether we are speaking of English or another language, there is usually a considerable distance between the 'high' literary varieties of a language taught in school and the varieties in day-to-day use. Looking at language use among adolescents in the East End of London or in Bradford, for example, we need to differentiate between the prestigious Southern British Standard on the one hand, and Cockney or Yorkshire English on the other. In addition to these varieties of English many adolescents of Bangla Deshi origin in the East End of London speak Sylheti and have a working knowledge of Bengali, and many adolescents of Pakistani origin in Bradford have literacy skills in Urdu and oral skills in Panjabi. In each of these cases it would be helpful to know the value of particular languages or varieties, as well as their communicative and symbolic significance. Some varieties may be used very rarely, or used only for specific purposes. Yet, although linguistic skills in a language may be minimal, they may still have a very important symbolic value (related to religion, for example, or have a communicative function related to literacy. Both of these may encourage further learning. Other languages or varieties are widely used in areas of high concentration of their speakers and, despite sometimes being stigmatised as low-status languages by outsiders, the internal bonds of solidarity and mechanisms of boundary maintenance may ensure their perpetuation as a symbol of in-group membership and rejection of the values of outsiders (Milroy, 1980).

This book does not add to existing research on the sociolinguistic description of English, but it does add other perspectives to studies looking at low-status varieties of English or at English as a world language. This is because the position of minority languages in England is in part to be explained in terms of the dominance of standard English in Britain.

We should remember in this connection that the social mechanisms restricting the use of minority languages, and the value accorded to them, are often the same mechanisms which maintain the dominance of standard English in Britain and in other parts of the world. It is of course powerful institutions such as the school system or the media which are the instruments of social reproduction, and control the cultural transmission of knowledge. Both overt institutional policies and covert organisational practices may reinforce the low or marginal status accorded to minority language use and teaching in a society. Even the concepts and terms which might encourage higher status are lacking in British English usage. We have no concept of biculturalism like that reflected in the North American hyphenated identity of 'Italian-American', for example. The notion of multiple identities provides a more open approach to the complex and flexible processes of ethnicity, by linking general and specifically 'ethnic' identities with other social identities. It is quite possible to be at the same time, for example, Italian, Bussesi, English, Bedfordian, working-class, female, and student, but there seems to be a reluctance in the current dominant ideology to accept the reality of such multiple identities.

The English spoken by many bilinguals in England is often different from that spoken by their monolingual peers. It may be a form of 'Panjabi Leeds English' or 'Greek London English' reflecting the new social reality of its speakers, and their use of particular discourse strategies such as code-switching skills. Some would go as far as to suggest that new varieties are emerging which cannot be adequately described solely by reference to either contributing language (Le Page, 1978). And there are also a few reported cases of English monolingual children incorporating features of the language varieties of their peers into their own English-based repertoires (Hewitt, 1982).

Both bidialectal and bilingual speakers adapt their language use according to the institutions and networks they belong to, and according to whom they are with. The ways in which they draw on their linguistic repertoires convey different aspects of their social identity. In the formal school situation, however, many pupils have little real choice about which languages or varieties they can use. Although there is increasing agreement among educationalists that teachers should make use of the full range of the cultural and linguistic resources their pupils bring to school, without encouragement the pupils may no longer even offer all of these resources. They are quick to interpret messages about appropriateness and value, and if similar messages accumulate over time they may gradually lose their non-English linguistic resources altogether.

This personal loss is also a loss for our society which goes far beyond the curtailment of educational potential for the individual, or the personal damage inflicted by interrupting children's development. The subordination of a language is a subtle way of ignoring a people, and in the context of England it is another means of restricting the social and intellectual horizons of English monolinguals.

The context of the project

The Linguistic Minorities Project (LMP) was set up in September 1979, funded by the Department of Education and Science (DES) originally for three years. At that time the main interest of the DES was to discover the extent of bilingualism among the school population, and the scale of mother tongue teaching provision available. The policy-orientation of the Department led them to emphasise the need for the Project to work with a large number of local education authorities (LEAs). Underlying their emphasis on information from as many different areas as possible was a recognition of the great diversity of situations in different parts of the country, and the belief that local policy-makers were more likely to reconsider their attitudes and policies if they recognised in our findings a situation similar to their own.

The LMP research team argued successfully that an understanding of the fundamental educational implications of bilingualism ought also to involve studies of language use beyond the school and among the adult population. The impact of language policies at school could only be understood in the context of language use in the full range of social activities. Patterns of language use in the family and in the locality were bound to influence the degree of mother tongue retention in future school populations. It was therefore necessary, we argued, to investigate such questions as when and where minority languages were being used; how important they were to the speakers concerned; whether there really were many opportunities to use languages other than English; what kind of formal mother tongue teaching was arranged by the local population; whether many parents knew about the possibility of introducing mother tongue teaching in the state school system, and, if so, whether they supported the idea; whether their children felt confident enough to talk about or use their mother tongue on the premises of their local state school; what proportion of them were attending local community-run language classes in the evenings or at weekends.

Although we acknowledged the value of working in different regions of the country and of developing a sizeable data-base, we were also keen for our research to explore in more depth and in a smaller range of settings the relationships between patterns of language use and social factors. If we were successful in this, then interested policy-makers and educationalists, we suggested, would be able to develop those implications relevant to their own context. Even though we knew the uninterested or hostile were unlikely to be influenced by either quantitative or qualitative findings, we hoped these findings would make it more difficult for them to ignore or reject the issues we raised.

When our research project began in 1979, the 'mother tongue' debate, as it had come to be called in England, was only just beginning on a national scale (CILT, 1976). For several years there had been lively local discussions in many regions, where ethnic minorities, and sometimes teachers' associations, had mounted campaigns for the introduction of mother tongue teaching in some LEA schools. Some policy-makers genuinely felt they could not change their policies on language teaching in local authority schools, or even support community-run initiatives outside the schools, without some idea of the numbers and more understanding of the issues involved. Others no doubt felt that a request for further information might enable them to avoid taking a position on the issue for some time longer.

The terms of the debate changed rapidly over the following few years, partly because of continuing demands to local authorities from minority parents, the change of government in 1979, the economic recession and changing patterns of ethnic relations. However, one of the main reasons for the build-up of minority pressure even before 1979 was the appearance and initial rejection of a draft Directive from the European Communities on the education of the children of migrant workers. The national discussions which ensued clearly indicated a poor level of understanding about the issues involved and a lack of commitment to resolving them among people of different political persuasions. A new version of the Directive, which considerably weakened the individual's right to support for mother tongue from the state education systems, was accepted by the member states in 1977 (EC, 1977). The article of the Directive relating to the support for the mother tongue was so heavily qualified by the introduction of such phrases as 'take appropriate measures to promote' and 'in accordance with their national circumstances and legal systems', that its legal force seemed almost entirely undermined.

In 1978 the DES set up a 'Mother Tongue and English Teaching Project' in several primary schools in Bradford. It was in the same year that they decided to fund the Linguistic Minorities Project. In 1981 the European Communities also supported, in collaboration with the Inner London Education Authority, the Schools Council Mother Tongue Project, intended to produce actual teaching materials and strategies. Our own project was not therefore intended to lead directly to an improvement in the resources available for mother tongue teaching, as some frustrated campaigners were ready to remind us. Nor were we asked to contribute to discussions on the conceptual or psycholinguistic aspects of the debate, since these were intended to be covered by some of the related projects just referred to.

There were two particularly interesting developments during the course of LMP. First, the scope of the debate in both published articles and in teachers' meetings began to broaden notably. From a discussion focussing rather narrowly on the specific needs of bilingual children at secondary school level calling for their mother tongue to be taught as a modern language, there is now more interest in the possibility of primary school children having some of their early learning experiences through the medium of their first language or of developing literacy in their mother tongue. Second, a range of very different initiatives has been taken in the mother tongue field by local education authorities. While some authorities remain resistant to requests from local linguistic minorities, others have responded by appointing peripatetic or school-based mother tongue teachers themselves, or financially supporting community-run mother tongue schools. A more recent development is in the provision of bilingual support staff within multilingual classrooms. And, reflecting parallel trends in the wider arena of education for a multilingual society, more attention is now being given to educating monolingual teachers and pupils about linguistic diversity (Houlton and Willey, 1983), in an effort to counter the ghettoisation sometimes involved in the system of 'withdrawal groups' whether for tuition in English as a second language, or for mother tongue teaching (Levine, 1981).

Some of the local political and social conditions which have stimulated these developments will become clearer when specific contexts are discussed later in the book. LMP and its affiliated project LINC (Language Information Network Coordination) may already have made some impact on the regions where the researchers did detailed work. But an assessment of the actual and potential contribution of LMP to policy evaluation should not be made until the project has been situated in a wider framework. Three levels, closely interrelated, need to be distinguished in any attempt to contextualise our work — Europe, Britain and England.

The EC Directive on the education of children of migrant workers is an example of an attempt at legislative reform which may in fact reinforce resistance to change (see Appendix 1). Some of those who are against British membership of the European Communities see the Directive simply as an example of economically motivated legislation designed to make it easier to repatriate migrant workers and their families. Others resent the Directive from the standpoint of a general resistance to interference by Brussels in the details of social legislation. The member states of the European Communities all in fact have to deal with very similar issues related to migrant workers, there being today approximately twelve million people of migrant worker origin in the most industrialised countries of North-Western Europe. The movement of populations into the industrial centres of Europe was predominantly economic in motivation, and was encouraged only so long as it suited the receiving countries' developing economies. Faced with economic recession and the arrival of an increasing number of dependent family members, these countries have discovered the social costs of labour policies which assumed that these workers were temporary and alien visitors: alienation, segregation, scapegoating are only the most obvious.

The changing responses of the school systems of the different European countries provide a good indicator of how these migrant populations have been perceived. In Germany, for example, educationalists have only comparatively recently begun to acknowledge that theirs is a country of permanent settlement, and that they should not assume that the children of migrants will want to return eventually to the country of origin of their parents (Castles, 1980). In France, the arrival of a socialist government in 1981 led to much more discussion about intercultural education and the rights of national minorities, both indigenous and non-indigenous (Giordan, 1982). Much can be learned from a comparison between the situations of the descendants of migrant workers in different European states.

The British dimension to which the work of LMP needs to be related must include reference to the position of indigenous linguistic minorities. This is the case for several reasons, only two of which will be mentioned here. The historical development of indigenous ethnic relations tells us a lot about the power of English speakers to undermine the political base of regional cultures. However, the rise of an indigenous language movement in Wales, for example, is a reminder that linguistic change is not inevitably a one-way process towards English. In other words, these is in Britain local experience to draw on which illustrates some of the positive, and negative, effects of educational and social legislation on language. As by now some non-indigenous linguistic minorities have been in Britain for three or four generations, it is becoming difficult to maintain a clear distinction between these 'indigenous' and 'non-indigenous' categories. The work of LMP was restricted to England, with only very occasional references to Gaelic or Welsh arising in three of its four surveys. But the Project has been struck by how little contact there still is between researchers and practitioners working in bilingual areas and school systems, even between England and Wales. Many of the newer minorities in England could benefit from the Welsh experience and expertise.

Another feature of the British context which has indirectly had a powerful effect on patterns of bilingualism in England is recent immigration legislation. Changes in immigration policies have influenced patterns of settlement and, with the 1981 Nationality Act, have legitimised the institutional and individual racism based on colour which is endemic in British society. Immigration policies obviously affect the physical movement of people, but in their contribution to the general political climate, they can also influence people's sense of affiliation or belonging. Insecurity generated by powerlessness and an imposed identity can lead to the fostering of closer links with countries of origin: visits to or from the homeland, and regular correspondence, are two important means for British-born bilinguals to maintain language skills. Interest in the learning of community languages other than English (see Figure 6.1) is generated not only by outside factors, then, but also by the increasing signs of rejection bilinguals may feel emanating from within British society.

British-born children of migrants may have greater access to the English language and culture than their parents, but they may be subject to similar social and economic exclusion which restricts their personal opportunities and defines their minority status (Saifullah Khan, 1982b). It is within the context of ethnic relations in England that we can understand why many bilingual pupils lose their mother tongue skills while they attend school, and why some try to re-learn them in late adolescence. Ethnic relations are reactive processes in which dominant and subordinate cultures compete for restricted economic, social and political resources. The political imbalance between the cultures in contact determines the distribution of knowledge and other cultural resources. This process is not static, language use being affected by changes in political and economic relations. Language shift (see p. 119) may also reflect changing perceptions of the relationship between language and culture. Many migrant parents assumed that their languages would be learned by their children as an inevitable part of their cultural baggage. As they experienced their children's preference for greater competence in English, however, some parents began to appreciate for the first time the fundamental role of their languages in the transmission of cultural and religious values. Youngsters from bilingual families are now creating the new emergent cultures of British-born bicultural youth and, in the process, language is becoming for some a far more salient, articulated marker of in-group identification.

In England itself the Linguistic Minorities Project coincided with the years of the most overt demonstrations of ethnic conflict seen in the post-war period. By the late 1970s the extent of white racist activities was notably increasing, already well organised in at least one area of East London where we worked, and coming to an ugly head in Coventry some months after we completed our main surveys. The economic and social causes underlying these developments, and the street rioting which erupted in 1981, have been discussed by others (Hall, 1978). It is important, however, to stress that these conflicts were used by some politicians, and by much of the media, to reinforce the popular belief in a 'race problem' caused by the presence of 'coloured migrants' in England. The attention of the dominant majority was focussed on people of Afro-Caribbean and South Asian origin, significantly the two largest groups of minorities in England of ex-colonial origin. In response, both these very heterogeneous populations became more united and more organised. Some were particularly forceful in their criticism of the proposed 'ethnic' question in the 1981 National Census, which would have been in effect a colour question. At a time when further immigration restrictions, and the 1981 British Nationality Act, were under discussion, any enquiry which might have produced data capable of misuse by public authorities, understandably came under severe scrutiny from minority organisations.

It was within this context that LMP carried out its work, shielded in some ways by the fortunate fact that language had not emerged to any great extent as an issue in 'race' or 'community' relations in England. This is in marked contrast to many other parts of the world, including of course near neighbours Wales and Belgium. Having sketched the context of LMP's work, we move on to describe some of the implications of its content.

The content of the project

The context for the Project just outlined, and the time and other resources available to the team, were the major influences on the methodology and scope of our work. It was soon clear that our research should explore language use in local linguistic minorities, as well as the amount and range of mother tongue teaching in state and community-run mother tongue schools. We were equally clear about our commitment to those who would provide us with this information, although we were not so sure at that stage of how we could best reciprocate their co-operation or ensure that our research findings would be accessible to them.

From the initial response to our project, it was obvious too that we needed to remind people that the linguistic minorities of England were not solely South Asian minorities. And we were acutely aware of the danger of reinforcing another widespread assumption by the existence of our project: many people still saw bilingualism as a problem.

It was not an easy task to counter the generally held stereotypes which fed the problematic and assimilationist perspective, and the view of bilingualism as a problem. For example, we sometimes came face to face with the view that it was bilingual pupils who 'had' the problems, and that being bicultural or bilingual was inherently confusing and detrimental to overall educational development. It might have been simpler, too, without the specifically 'minority' label attached to the project.

However, from the outset we adopted procedures and terminology in our research to counter this assumption. We argued that bilingualism was to be seen as a personal and societal resource which should be the concern not only of bilingual members of our society, but of all those who were interested in developing the social and economic resources of the country. These arguments needed to be seen in relation to another fundamental perspective. Although our research was certainly looking into an issue that was in detail new in England, for educationalists there were potential repercussions on perennial issues about the educational development of children. Discussion about home-school liaison and parental involvement in schools, language across the curriculum, 'language awareness', education for a multicultural society, and anti-racist education, all share an ultimate concern to ensure that children can develop their full potential and thereby extend their educational and social horizons.

In the absence of any substantial previous research, it was valuable at this early stage to expose the scale of the language dimension by comparing the situation of a wide range of different linguistic minorities, rather than focussing on a more thorough analysis of only one or two. Since the relatively short time span did not allow us to study changes over time, we chose to take 'snapshots' of the situation in a wide range of local minorities and school systems at particular points in time.

The inclusion of three sociolinguists in the LMP interdisciplinary team reflected its initial intention of avoiding a purely demographic and short-term policy-related exercise, and of moving beyond self-report surveys to observational studies of language use. As with so many research projects, the final outcome was a compromise between the two. Taking seriously the policy interests supporting our project, we agreed that one of the four surveys (the Schools Language Survey, SLS; see Chapter 8) should be designed to investigate the range of linguistic diversity throughout an education authority, and that this survey should be carried out in five or six LEAs. But we also agreed that such a basic policy-related exercise was to be supplemented by a more sociolinguistic research exercise which would involve documenting bilingual and monolingual school pupils' own perceptions of languages around them and their own patterns of language use. This Secondary Pupils Survey (SPS) and the other two community-based instruments, the Mother Tongue Teaching Directory (MTTD) Survey and the Adult Language Use Survey (ALUS), were to be carried out only in a few areas, with the intention that the data from the different surveys would be complementary and create a solid basis for more detailed case studies in the future.

The background and development of each of these research instruments is described in detail in the chapters which follow. Their findings are only a small part of the contribution we hope LMP will leave for future researchers and practitioners. As a pilot project breaking new ground, our main aims were to contribute to debates relating to language and education in the context of ethnic relations, and to develop and assess the value of varied research methods.

Our research methods were often developed without any of the usual background information, such as census data, that many research projects can start from. Each survey presented unexpected challenges, and the time involved in dealing with them meant that in the end we were never able to go beyond survey techniques which involved the respondents reporting on their language use. However, the painstaking assessment of the difficulties we faced provided us with a rich source of supplementary data, which we were often able to take account of in subsequent developments. The experience of conducting both the Schools Language Survey and the Secondary Pupils' Survey also illustrates how the preparations for the methodical administration of research in schools can provide invaluable insights into the institutional constraints affecting educational innovation.

From the very beginning of this work, we were acutely aware of our responsibilities as social science researchers. We were particularly conscious of the increasing criticism from teachers, and of the disillusionment of many minorities with research projects set up with public funds. There were two main criticisms which we felt were justified and deserved a response: first, that research was often used as an excuse for not taking practical steps to improve the situation on the ground and, second, the minorities were wrongly singled out as the cause of a problematic situation which should be elaborately defined before beginning to be remedied. The situation already outlined in the last section shows that LMP was itself very much part of the wider context it was studying. The political and economic constraints within which it worked could easily have minimised the pedagogic impact of the research. Since we were part of the academic educational establishment, the limitation to the usual dissemination processes would have involved information reaching an extremely restricted number of educational policy-makers and advisers, rather few teachers, and even fewer members of linguistic minorities not working in the field of education.

While acknowledging that the team's academic interests and policy-related funding had to be given due weight, we nevertheless sought ways of making a more immediate impact. After considering a range of possibilities, we managed to set up a related project with the specific task of disseminating information on LMP's aims, research methods and findings, and of assessing the impact of this dissemination on the research process. The Language Information Network Coordination Project, funded by the Commission of the European Communities and known as LINC, was set up with the intention of reaching a wide audience, yet to be fully defined. It was to pay special attention to the institutional constraints, conflicts and misunderstandings influencing communication between the dominant ethnic majority and subordinate ethnic minorities in the field of education.

LINC initially focussed on processes of education in the context of ethnic relations. This involved looking at the distribution of linguistic and cultural resources in the local authorities. LINC also assessed the distribution of information and understanding about these resources among different categories of people — parents, teachers, local authority staff, etc. While it is evident that the policies of the state school system influence language learning, use and attitudes, there are other, subtle processes which influence the distribution of knowledge. We did not simply want to ask how much is known, for example, by teachers about bilingual pupils or by minority parents about educational opportunities, but were interested also in a more fundamental question about the availability of knowledge and how it was interpreted by the different participants involved in the research cycle.

LINC aimed therefore to build in an appreciation of the dynamic relationships our research has begun to explore. It was also to show that dissemination need not be a one-way process from researcher to practitioner. An active and ongoing involvement in dissemination from the beginning of the research, building upon existing contacts and insights, can feed back into the definition of objectives and research methods. In fact the funding body for the LINC project, the EC Commission, was interested in ensuring three things in particular: (i) that members of ethnic minorities had access to basic knowledge about the school system and about their rights, (ii) that the state education system might have immediate access to the information gathered through research in a way which would help the implementation of the EC Directive on the education of the children of migrant workers, and (iii) that information on research methods and findings about linguistic minorities would circulate between the different member states.

The Commission agreed that the LINC project offered a rare opportunity to assess the different strategies for what we called 'active dissemination' (see p. 343). LINC's main aim was to consider the effectiveness of these strategies with reference to different target publics. These were progressively defined for each area surveyed, according to socio-professional categories, and re-grouped across categories according to our assessment of their 'degree of interest'. Active dissemination goes on to assess what information is most needed by whom, and how the recipients can better process and utilise it. It also assesses who is not interested or is positively antagonistic, and how best to reach them. Its main objective is to ensure that the findings of the research project can be taken over and utilised by all those pupils, parents, teachers and policy-makers to whom it is potentially relevant.

This book is one form of dissemination. In it we have chosen to present some findings of each of our surveys to what we hope will be a wide audience of researchers in different parts of the world, other professionals and a wide range of other people interested in bilingualism in our society.

Boundaries and definitions of linguistic minorities

Any attempt to construct a universally valid definition of 'linguistic minorities' is beset with difficulties. Both elements in the term contain definitional problems. Nonetheless we chose to use it as the most concise way of expressing concern with both language and majority-minority relations, yet without implying a particular theoretical framework from 'race' or 'ethnic' relations research, and without committing ourselves to any assumptions about the existence of 'groups' and 'communities'.

As there are some neighbourhoods in certain cities where 'linguistic minorities', or even a single 'linguistic minority', form the numerical majority of the local population, we should make it clear from the beginning that the quantitative connotations of the term 'minority' are to be interpreted with reference to the population of England as a whole. Furthermore, our conception of linguistic minorities incorporates the dimension of relative powerlessness, which distinguishes subordinate minorities from the dominant majority in terms of their access to economic, political and cultural resources. The starting point for a definition of a specific linguistic minority is that it is a category of people who share a language which is not the language of the dominant majority − in the British context, English. This, of course, does not exclude the possibility that migrants also have some knowledge of English, or even developed skills in that language. Many migrants from the Indian subcontinent, for example, knew English before they came to England, since it continued to play an important role within India, Pakistan and Bangladesh after Independence.

The difficulties in operationalising the concept of linguistic minority, and the sometimes arbitrary decisions that were necessary in particular cases during our research, will soon become evident. A definition based on 'sharing a language' is clearly using a minimal criterion of belonging. It may include people who identify with a given language or the collectivity in which it is used, without themselves possessing a wide range of linguistic skills, or even regularly speaking or fully understanding the language. On the other hand, people who use the language in question without necessarily identifying with the linguistic minority would also be included. The definition is a social one, delimiting the set of people for whom a 'language' (in this sense a symbolic entity that they themselves define) has either affective or communicative significance. It is a definition which to a large extent must rely on subjective information provided by members of the minority in question, rather than on criteria of actual linguistic behaviour adopted by researchers.

In defining linguistic minorities in this way we presuppose to some extent that the language in question has already been defined according to 'commonsense' criteria, and normally accepted without too much dispute by both minority and majority members of the society. This usually means that the language is a national or regional standard language, already described and codified by grammarians and accepted as a medium of education and official communication by some national or regional government. It is this kind of standard language which is usually the 'taught mother tongue' in Illich's terms (Illich, 1981), the target for formal language teaching, where a different variety may still play a greater role in defining a local or an in-group identity.

The impossibility of giving a satisfactory definition of a linguistic minority in purely linguistic terms derives from the difficulty of settling two crucial issues on the basis of linguistic data alone. First, the boundaries of particular languages cannot in reality be easily established. The study of variation within language, of linguistic change, and of bilingual repertoires has led sociolinguists to the conclusion that it is not possible in the real world to see languages simply as fixed structures or systems 'in which everything hangs together' (Meillet, 1921). A language does not exist in the abstract, but only in the context of social interaction between speakers, and different varieties, dialects and languages often do not have clear-cut boundaries at all (Le Page and Tabouret-Keller, 1982; see also pp. 43-4). In particular, speakers of Creole languages, or those individuals growing up in situations of language contact, often do not have a label recognised by linguists for the variety they speak. There are also, for example, unresolved debates among linguists and among speakers of the languages, in England, as in the Indian subcontinent, about the linguistic discreteness of Kutchi from Gujerati or Sindhi (Shapiro and Schiffman, 1981), or of Sylheti from Bengali. In both these cases, our sampling procedure among adult populations in England, and the groupings we used for the summary presentations of our school-based data, treated speakers of the related languages as single linguistic minorities. However, we were made forcibly aware at several stages that the implicit assumptions about linguistic and cultural homogeneity were far from acceptable to all.

Second, the issue of who is to be counted as 'a speaker' of a given language is not always easy to resolve. Does a person who uses a single word or phrase of a given language qualify as a speaker, or must a speaker be someone who exhibits more or less 'complete fluency', or who regularly uses the language for communication? This problem is especially difficult in the case of linguistic minorities where the process of language shift or the creation of a mixed code is under way. And, for example, many British-born young people who have a very limited range of skills in a minority language, nevertheless still regard it as their 'mother tongue'.

These issues will be discussed further in Chapter 3. They have been introduced here in order to lead into a discussion of the role of language in the social process of ethnicity, some understanding of which is essential if we are to appreciate the social context in which linguistic minorities in England lead their daily lives.

Much of the discussion about the process of ethnicity centres around the concept of ethnic boundaries (Barth, 1969). A boundary is revealed where a category of people perceive a dichotomy between 'us' and 'them', and structure their behaviour accordingly. Such boundaries are not necessarily accepted as valid by every section of society, nor need they be permanently fixed (Wallman, 1979). They may be 'marked' symbolically by a large number of separate variables, or by a smaller cluster of factors which are highly correlated together.

Language is only one of the possible set of such 'ethnic markers'. Religion, skin colour or other physical features, nationality or dress can all be used as ethnic markers. One of the difficulties in defining linguistic minorities in England is that the language variable, of course, is not always perfectly correlated with any of the other markers, nor is it relevant in every context in which a differentiation between 'us' and 'them' is made.

To illustrate this lack of fit between various ethnic markers we can look at the example of some of the South Asian populations who live in England. In terms of nationality – which does not necessarily correspond either with birthplace or country of origin of the family – there are 'Indians', 'Pakistanis', 'Bangladeshis' and 'British', for example. The language ('taught mother tongue') of Indians could be Gujerati, Bengali, Urdu, Hindi or Panjabi. Pakistanis may speak, for example, one or more of Panjabi, Pushtu, Sindhi or Urdu. Only for Bangladeshis is it usually said that there is a single language, Bengali, but even that is only the case if we ignore the difference already referred to between Sylheti and Bengali. In some cases there is a closer correlation between religion and nationality: most Pakistani nationals, for example, are Muslims. Linking language and religious affiliation, there is a high degree of probability that Urdu speakers in England will be Muslims and that Hindi speakers will be Hindus, but Gujerati and Bengali speakers may be either Hindus or Muslims, while Panjabi speakers may be Sikhs, Muslims, Hindus or Christians. The complexitities of these inter-relationships of nationality, national origin, language and religion illustrate why it has proved so difficult to devise a technically adequate 'ethnic question' for use in the British National Census.

Even if we are willing for certain purposes to take the language other than English as a significant primary boundary marker, we need to be aware that it can be used in two distinct ways to separate 'us' from 'them'. The first way is when the name of the language, or the literary tradition that goes with the standard language, carries a strong symbolic value for the people in question. In such cases it is quite common for two groups, which in practice communicate through their vernacular with a high degree of mutual comprehensibility, to deny that they speak the same language. Such is the case in the division between Hindi and Urdu. In the spoken form linguists and even native speakers find it quite difficult to tell the two varieties apart (Mobbs, 1981). The earlier use of the term 'Hindustani' to describe the common spoken form reflected this situation. However, the association of Islam with Urdu, written in a Perso-Arabic script, and of Hinduism with Hindi, written in the Sanskrit-derived Devanagri script, has made the name of the language an important ethnic boundary marker. This was given official recognition in 1947 after the partition of undivided India into India, and West and East Pakistan.

In contrast the standardisation and reification of a single national language can make the very name of the language a strong symbol of national or even pan-national identity. For example, 'Arabic', which stretches from Morocco to Iraq despite the low degree of mutual intelligibility between some spoken varieties; and 'French', which commands loyalties across a francophone area including parts of Belgium, Switzerland and Canada, and areas of Africa as well as France itself.

A second way in which language can be used as a marker of ethnic identity is where the emphasis is on the use of particular items or forms of language. The most striking example is a biblical story where a single phonological variant, the use of '*s*' or '*sh*' in pronouncing the word 'Shibboleth', was sufficient in itself to establish membership of one of two tribes of Israel, with fatal consequences to the tribe which had just lost the battle (Judges 12: 6). Even today an individual variant such as postvocalic '*r*' or glottal stop in English, or more commonly the differential use of several linguistic variables, can mark the social boundary between 'us' and 'them', and distinct urban working-class varieties of English are retained in most urban centres in Britain (Trudgill (ed.), 1978). Although the varieties in question may be given different names, they may not always be regarded as different languages, unless and until the ethnic or social boundary they symbolise becomes so important as to demand the creation of a new 'language'. Thus, for example, the development of London Jamaican as a language of resistance amongst black teenagers (Hewitt, 1982).

A further important definitional problem is that the criteria for membership of a linguistic, or any other, minority can be defined from both inside and outside the population, and the perceptions of group boundaries held by the monolingual majority may be quite different from those held by members of a bilingual or multilingual minority. An outsider might refer to an 'Arabic' linguistic minority for general classificatory purposes, but such a grouping would include widely disparate people. For example, there would be not only Arabic-speaking Moroccans of migrant worker origin like most of those settled since about 1970 in the Paddington area of London, and old-established Yemeni Arabic-speaking populations like those in Birmingham and parts of Newcastle, but also the affluent Saudi Arabic-speaking annual 'migrants' living in some of the most expensive parts of London. These populations are unlikely to have any sustained social contact between each other, and may have little in common besides their language allegiance. In certain situations and for certain purposes linguistic criteria for social differentiation could be extremely important to them, but in many day-to-day circumstances their religious (Islamic, Christian, Bahai) or national (Moroccan, Yemeni, Saudi) affiliation is of greater importance.

A different kind of example is the Panjabi-speaking population of England. In the first place many people within the monolingual English majority might not make the categorisation at all on the basis of language, but put them all together with Gujerati and Bengali speakers under a general category of 'Asian' or 'Pakistani'. Even when the finer distinction according to language is made, the majority perception of the category 'Panjabi' is still unlikely to coincide with the ethnic boundary categories most significant to members of the Panjabi-speaking population. Members of this population all originated from a single region in the North West of the Indian subcontinent, which until 1947 had a single government (see Map 2.1, p. 46). Some Panjabi speakers have been settled in East Africa for several generations. However, within this area of the Panjab three great religious traditions and associated literary traditions are found, which provide the most significant boundaries in terms of educational policies and script choice. At a lower level caste or kin-group membership, sub-ethnic and dialect loyalties, as well as religious sects, may provide other focal points. The Panjabi case is discussed in more detail later in the book (see pp. 45–7 and 143). In this case the members' 'internal' perceptions of the national, religious and linguistic boundaries directed our decision to recognise two distinct populations for the purposes of sampling and analyses in the Adult Language Use Survey: 'Panjabi (U)', those of predominantly Pakistani origin whose language of literacy is Urdu, and 'Panjabi (G)' for those of predominantly Sikh Indian origin who now teach the Gurmukhi script for literacy purposes. Figure 1.1 attempts to set out the inter-relationships between linguistic, national and religious affiliations for Panjabi speakers.

The case of a general 'Chinese' classification shows similar complexities in respect of boundaries, at least as perceived by the outsider. The 'Chinese'-speaking minority in England includes people with origins in Hong Kong who are Cantonese mother tongue speakers, as well as others who are Hakka mother tongue speakers and have Cantonese as a second language. In addition to these there are 'ethnic Chinese' refugees from Vietnam who speak Cantonese as well as Vietnamese, and students and professionals from Malaysia and Singapore who speak English and some combination of Hokkien, Cantonese and Mandarin. In many ways these groups have little in common, although in certain circumstances they too might be drawn together on the basis of a common geographical, literary and cultural heritage.

Figure 1.1 Spoken and written languages in Panjab

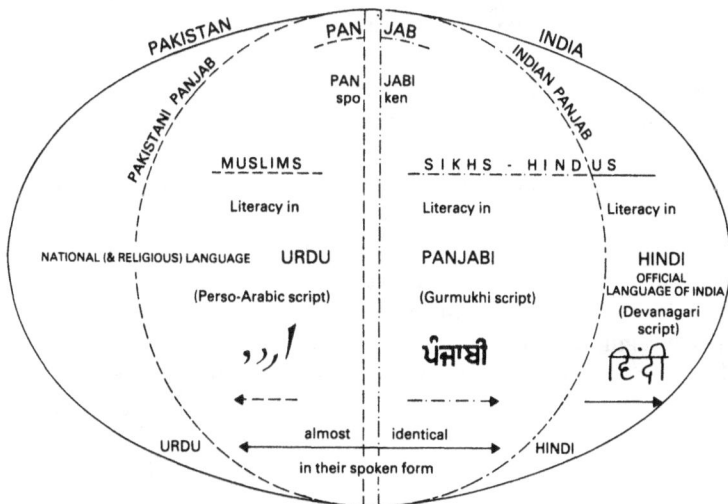

We ourselves chose to use the general term 'Chinese', because, although our Adult Survey was constructed around and usually presented in the spoken Cantonese language, our preliminary fieldwork had also shown us that there was a more significant presence of bilingual Cantonese-Hakka speakers than we had expected, and in one city our respondents were drawn entirely from the refugee population from Vietnam. Although these interviews were carried out in Cantonese, we did not want to prejudge whether the speakers would identify more strongly with one language than with the other.

The work we undertook in our Schools Language Survey also illustrated the mismatch between majority and minority perceptions of language boundaries, and the multiple criteria on which ethnic boundaries are based. Teachers were asked to record whatever labels the pupils volunteered, in most cases names of a language or a dialect, but also in some cases their national or religious affiliation. Some younger children do not know the name of the language other than English that they speak, and many were surprised that it should suddenly be of interest in a context where it had hitherto been ignored. We found, too, that older pupils might know the name of their language, but in the school environment offered the 'outsiders' classification (see p. 322). Many monolingual teachers in England do not know the names of their pupils' languages and some assume there is a one-to-one fit between language and culture or language and nationality.

These examples led us to the conclusion that for the purposes of research the boundaries of a linguistic minority needed to be defined with reference to the particular objectives of the specific survey, and that this might involve a compromise between the outsiders' and the insiders' perceptions. The cases mentioned show that there is an ongoing process of negotiation, and that there may not even be agreement from within a 'linguistic minority', because of the speakers' different social backgrounds and because situations and perceptions change.

The lack of fit between minority and majority perceptions of linguistic boundaries is particularly evident in multilingual populations in England. For example, Gujerati speakers in England include some migrant adults who are bilingual Gujerati-English speakers, and others who are multilingual in, for example, Gujerati, Urdu and English, or Gujerati, Hindi, Swahili and English. Yet in social and educational terms there are good reasons, in England, to group such speakers as a single 'Gujerati' linguistic minority. Less easy to resolve are the cases of multilingual offspring of marriages between members of two different linguistic minorities, such as, for example, Polish/Italian/ English trilinguals.

In some of these difficult cases, one of the other-than-English languages may be identified by its speakers as the most important spoken language – because it is the language of the home, or because it is the language of the country of origin or because of religious affiliations. In these situations it may be justifiable to allot those speakers to that linguistic minority rather than the other. There are many cases, however, where both spoken languages other than English are equally important or relevant for different purposes. These examples suggest that, while the notion of a linguistic minority is a convenient heuristic device, in some cases the allocation of multilingual speakers to one minority rather than another can distort the subjective reality of the individuals concerned.

Dialect speakers are also liable to draw boundaries at a point different from members of the majority society who are locked into perceptions based on national standard languages. In the case of Italian, some observers would identify all those of the same national origin as Italian speakers. However, the ethnic and linguistic differentiation within Italy, which is sharply represented in the different migrant populations, may be retained in England. While not denying that they are members of an Italian minority in England, some of the older residents in particular will say that they do not speak Italian ('lingua italiana'), but specify instead the name of their 'dialect' (Tosi, 1984a; see also p. 59). Other 'Italian'-speaking respondents in our Adult Survey, when asked to name the languages they knew, said that they spoke Italian, then added the name of their dialect as another language they knew. There is least likelihood of agreement about dialect and standard, among members of a linguistic minority, if linguistic differences reflect the socio-economic stratification of society in the country of origin. Such is the case with Italian and Bengali.

The difficulty of defining the boundaries of linguistic minorities is added to by the rapid social changes which follow migration, and by the new social structural position of the immigrant population. Of course, boundaries also change over time and according to context. In cases where there is extensive individual bilingualism, it may be better to define linguistic minorities with reference to a shared bilingual repertoire, rather than with reference to a single language. However, it is likely that in the situation experienced by many migrant populations and their British-born offspring, there will not even be a repertoire which is shared by every individual, only a repertoire which is available to the minority as a whole and from which individuals will draw their own linguistic resources. Migrant adults from Pakistan may be Panjabi-English bilinguals and also users of Urdu, which is the case too for their children in certain parts of the country. Other children from the same linguistic minority may be almost monolingual in English and only 'potential speakers' of their 'mother tongue'. Children from Cantonese- and Hakka-speaking families may learn to speak both, or only one of the two; some, over time, may lose their command of both. Language loss, experienced during speakers' lifetimes, may affect the different non-English components of their repertoires in very different ways. On the other hand, some members of bilingual families are receptively bilingual and may in fact 'restore' their active use of their 'mother tongue'. They may begin by using mainly the minority language, move to using mainly English or a mixed code, then later take steps to improve their command of either their 'mother tongue' or a related 'community' language, e.g. Mandarin in the case of the Chinese minorities.

Actual patterns of language use will shift over time, with the result that the content and balance of any collective linguistic repertoire will not remain fixed. The number of non-English-speaking monolingual adults living in England is probably decreasing, but there is still a large number of children who have limited command of English before they start school. This redistribution of linguistic resources between one generation and the next, rather than during the lifetime of a speaker, is the process usually referred to as language shift. Of course, minority institutions may be able to foster the maintenance or revival of a minority language, or a third language may come to be used as a lingua franca in preference to either English or the original minority language, or as a symbolic marker of a broader ethnic identity, e.g. in Britain, Cantonese for speakers of a range of regional Chinese languages, or Hindi-Urdu for speakers of different South Asian languages.

If they were migrants themselves, members of linguistic minorities spend at least part of their life interacting in the wider society, and if they were born here they belong to the wider society (Gesellschaft) in which many of their role relationships bring them into alliances or conflicts with the majority. This means that there may be frequent crossing and renegotiating of some of the ethnic and linguistic boundaries. Only in a traditional self-sufficient society (Gemeinschaft), where individuals are typically related in dense multiplex networks of kinship and economic interdependence, can boundaries remain stable for long periods. The renegotiation of such boundaries may be manifested linguistically by new patterns of language use and by code-switching, and socially by the emergence of multiple ethnic identities. An individual may, for example, think of herself or himself primarily as an English-speaking pharmacist in the context of the work place, and as a Polish-speaking Catholic at Mass each Sunday, and act accordingly without the situation becoming in any way problematic.

The problems we have outlined concerning the definition of linguistic minorities show that it is a formidable task to define the collectivities of minority language speakers in England. However, most of the problems occur because of the inevitable fuzziness of social boundaries in complex modern multi-ethnic societies. Even then the difficult cases are the exception rather than the rule. For most people the ethnic markers of language, religion, ancestry and nationality closely correlate, and neatly fit patterns of identity, affiliation, network interaction and participation in institutional life.

The very fact that numerous linguistic minorities have already organised some of their institutions to support language maintenance suggests that language is already a highly salient marker of ethnicity (see Chapter 6, p. 265). Because of this, and the importance of such languages to the educational debate, there is a case for defining 'linguistic minorities' for some purposes in terms of their sharing a taught minority language.

It would appear that this definition is largely 'culturally' based, and therefore subject to the criticism that we have failed to take account of broader political and socio-economic factors. In fact this is not the case, since our analysis of the situation of the linguistic minorities takes place in the context of an understanding of the processes of labour migration. The definition and renegotiation of linguistic and ethnic boundaries are influenced to a large extent by the relationship of the subordinate minorities to the local economic structure, and to the socio-economic structure of the country of origin. The patterns of language use and the desire for language maintenance are set in a context where an uneven distribution of power and economic resources in education, in housing, and in employment are the major factors constraining change.

We would argue, therefore, that the use of the term 'linguistic minorities' enables us on the one hand to maintain an interest in the social and economic factors which have traditionally been the focus of the field of ethnic relations, while introducing the new and critical variable of language. On the other hand it enables us to avoid some of the difficulties of more narrowly linguistic ways of looking at language, based on the assumption of a well-defined single variety of a language shared by all speakers who engage in mutually comprehensible communication.

It was important for us, before discussing our four surveys later in the book, that we should have to illustrate that what may be desirable in theory is not necessarily feasible in practice. A project of such wide scope could not investigate in great detail all the minutiae of linguistic and social data which might interest the range of disciplines which intersected in our work. Our decision to ensure coverage of a range of languages meant that we gave priority to quantitative methods such as sociolinguistic surveys which focussed on language use as reported by individuals, rather than to the observations of language use in social interaction.

The fact that each of the instruments designed by LMP had its own focus and methods meant that our working definitions of linguistic minorities needed to differ according to our detailed purposes and were inevitably set up on the basis of different criteria and sometimes by different people. For example, in the Adult Language Use Survey the set of potential respondents was defined by the researchers, usually on the basis of 'ethnic' criteria such as family name or membership of a community organisation. The set of actual respondents, on the other hand, was defined by negotiation between the interviewer and the person on the doorstep, in response to a preliminary discussion as to whether they spoke the language in question. In the Mother Tongue Teaching Directory Survey the boundary between linguistic minorities was defined on the basis of which languages were taught by schools in the community-run or statutory sectors. If, for example, a school taught Chinese to children from Hakka, Cantonese and Hokkien language backgrounds together, it had defined its linguistic minority as the broader category of 'Chinese'. In the two school surveys the researchers only became fully aware of the boundary problems after the data had been collected. The Schools Language Survey relied on teachers' perceptions, our written guidelines and the pupils' answers to define groups of pupils with the same or different languages. The Secondary Pupils' Survey, on the other hand, gave pupils much more freedom to place themselves inside or outside one of the linguistic minorities, although their decision was obviously affected by the atmosphere of the classroom and the influence of teacher and peer group.

It is perhaps impossible in the end to construct a definition which is theoretically coherent and at the same time has sharp enough boundaries to deal with every case in a clear-cut way. Chapter 3 will take up some of the sociolinguistic issues in more detail, but first in Chapter 2 we will sketch in the sociolinguistic background to some of the main linguistic minorities in England, and we will also situate them in the context of the cities of Coventry, Bradford and London, in the Midlands, North and South of England respectively.

2
History and background of linguistic minorities in England

The first step towards an understanding of the sociolinguistic position of linguistic minorities in England is to look at the historical and political developments which have determined the relationship between the people who speak the minority languages and the dominant majority.

Most members of linguistic minorities in England are people who arrived in England between 1940 and 1975 and their descendants. The populations and the languages can be broadly classified along two intersecting dimensions, as well as along a time axis. First, linguistic minorities can be distinguished according to the main reason for the original migration and settlement: some came primarily as political refugees, while others came as part of the migrant labour force recruited during the post-war period of reconstruction and expansion in British industry. The second dimension concerns places of origin, which can be broadly divided between ex-colonial Third World countries and European countries. This dimension corresponds roughly with distinctions of 'race' and skin colour, which during the period in question have been the main categories implicitly used in the political debate about immigration policy. Schematically the main linguistic minorities can be placed as in Figure 2.1.

The linguistic minorities of Cypriot origin are the most difficult to fit into this schema, since they originate from an ex-colony not generally regarded as a Third World country, and until the early 1970s came mainly as labour migrants. However, people arriving from Cyprus since the war of 1974 can be regarded as refugees. Also excluded from this schema are those who came as students, e.g. from African countries and from Malaysia or Singapore.

This neat schema cannot of course represent fully the interaction between the economic and political factors behind the migrations. Nor does it explain the subsequent social structural position of most members of linguistic minorities in England.

Figure 2.1 A typology of recent migrations to Britain

	Migrant labour	Political refugees
Ex-colonial	Bengali, Panjabi, Gujerati, Hong Kong Chinese (West Indians) (1960–75)	East African Asian (1968–73) Vietnamese Chinese (1979–82)
	Greek and Turkish Cypriots (1960–75)	
European origin	Italians (from 19th century, but most since 1950) Portuguese, Spanish (from 1960)	Polish, Ukrainian and other East European (1945–50)

The political refugees from Eastern Europe faced particular problems of adjustment on arrival in England, which were often ignored. Yet it is significant that many arrived before the issues of immigration and 'race' (seen in terms of black–white relations) were so closely related in popular discourse (Husband, 1977). Their public invisibility may have facilitated individual social mobility, to the extent that by 1981 in the cities in which we worked many of the Polish and Ukrainian speakers in our samples were in higher-status housing and occupation than the average for linguistic minorities as a whole. (See Table 5.10.)

The East African political refugees arrived much later, in the 1960s and early 1970s, and came from a relatively privileged background, compared with most South Asian migrants from the Indian subcontinent, in fact from the middle of the 'colonial sandwich'. However, their visibility and ex-colonial status produced particular social and psychological hardships, on top of their restricted opportunities and loss, in many cases, of material wealth. The stark contrast with life in East Africa may well have fostered the greater political consciousness which led to some of the major industrial disputes involving workers from this background, e.g. Grunwick, Imperial Typewriters.

But the historical and political dimensions are equally important in our understanding of the labour migrations from ex-colonial and Southern European countries. These migrations were defined in terms of a severe 'labour shortage' during the post-World War Two period of economic expansion. An alternative economic and political strategy would have involved greater investment in the renewal of industrial equipment, and an improvement in the wages of the lowest paid indigenous industrial workers, which would have meant a lower immediate return on capital. However, the 'colonial' solution was still open to Britain, so that migrants were recruited from colonies and ex-colonies to the metropole. The countries of the British Empire had previously been a source of cheap raw materials, and now they provided a source of cheap labour.

The available unskilled jobs were essentially those that the English did not want to do − for example those with unsocial hours, or poor conditions and wages. Workers settled in cheap housing close to their work, and thus the condition of run-down inner city areas of many British cities became associated in the public mind with the arrival of the outsider, 'alien' people. By the early 1960s there was increased pressure from local authorities and public opinion to restrict immigration. The announcement of more and more restrictive immigration legislation in the 1960s had the immediate effect on each occasion of actually increasing the flow of migrants from South Asia and the West Indies, since it stimulated a 'beat the ban' rush among workers and their families. By the early 1970s a mythology about the presence of 'black people' was being increasingly accepted and used by anti-immigration organisations, and even by the so-called 'respectable' media. This was in spite of the fact that there was a virtual stop to 'coloured' immigration except for the benefit of very specific sectors of the employment market, for family dependants and fiancé(e)s of people already settled, and for a restricted number of British passport holders from East Africa.

During the late 1970s the economic recession, and the international 'reorganisation' of the market economy between North and South by transnational corporations, contributed to high rates of unemployment in certain sectors of the British economy. This hit members of ethnic minorities disproportionately hard, as they were concentrated in unskilled and semi-skilled jobs. These were often in declining or 'restructured' industries where people were increasingly subject to both blatant and subtle forms of institutionalised racism. The 1970s also saw − and this was surely no coincidence − the increase in fascist organisations, and overtly 'racial' conflict in the streets. There were also increasingly explicit statements by senior Conservative politicians about the need to defend the 'British way of life', suggesting that it was quite legitimate to feel a serious threat of being 'swamped' by people of a different culture (Sivanandan, 1982).

Particularly since Britain's entry into the EC in 1973, there has been a change in the source of cheap labour away from the ex-colonial countries and towards the Mediterranean periphery. This followed the example of our neighbours in industrialised Northwest Europe, and as with France and Germany, for example, the countries of emigration were not confined to the other EC member states. Just as Germany's largest minorities include Turks and Yugoslavs, and France's Algerians and Portuguese, so Britain already has many Moroccans, Spaniards, and Portuguese. Again, like our EC partners, the jobs available to such migrants are the least secure, lowest paid and in many cases, least unionised – in catering and hotel work, in cleaning and in hospital domestic work.

One of the characteristics of the development of the debate about 'race relations' in England has been the playing of the 'numbers game'. The attempt in the mid-1960s to introduce a policy of 'dispersal' of 'immigrant' school children was often rationalised in terms of the maximum desirable proportion of non-English-speaking children in any class or school. And much of the immigration legislation itself used the spurious argument that lower proportions of immigrants in any area would minimise prejudice and hostility towards them. Another characteristic of the debate which we have already mentioned is the preoccupation in England with the so-called 'coloured' minorities. The focus in public discussion on statistics and on visible minorities has contributed to the confusion over categories, and to the very emotive nature of many of the contributions to the debate about ethnic record-keeping, the need for monitoring the 'underachievement' of certain minorities or for positive discrimination policies.

It will be evident in the discussion of our approach to sampling (see Chapter 4, p. 162) that the lack of comprehensive ethnic or language statistics meant that a lot of our time had to be devoted to dealing with this lack, in order to carry out ALUS (see Chapter 1, p. 15). It should become clear from the present chapter that the total numbers of a linguistic minority at a national level are of little relevance in terms of language use and language maintenance at the local level. However, the local demographic situations do relate to economic opportunities, and to exclusion from economic opportunities, sometimes overtly on the basis of language skills.

Since the status of a language is so closely bound up with the perceived status of its speakers, it is important that we present in the pages that follow a series of population profiles, and some estimates of the overall numbers of speakers of particular languages, and that the reader bears these in mind when considering the local detail which follows in the forthcoming chapters.

Another reason for providing national sketches before the specific local details of the cities where we worked, is that the local figures may become out of date more rapidly. This is especially so in areas of high unemployment which may lead to movement out of the area or to a change in occupation within the same city.

The statistics from the 1981 Census which are most commonly quoted in discussions of the social position of ethnic minorities in England are based on the number of people recorded as living in households where the head of the household was born in the New Commonwealth or Pakistan. This category is a euphemism for those countries in South Asia and the West Indies which sent most 'coloured immigrants' to Britain, and is carefully constructed to exclude the less politically problematic migrants from the 'Old' (i.e. 'white') Commonwealth countries like Australia, Canada and New Zealand. Once again this categorisation for the presentation of statistics reflects the preoccupation with skin colour and 'race' in political discussion. It is the only even partially relevant census statistic widely available, given the decision not to include a specific 'ethnic question' in 1981. For our sociolinguistic and educational purposes it would be more useful to have the figures referring to birth place under headings for each separate country. However, even such figures would give a very poor indication of the size of any linguistic minority, for two main reasons. Firstly, the British-born are excluded, although in some linguistic minorities they may by now constitute over half the total population. Secondly, national origin alone does not indicate the particular language involved, especially in the case of the multilingual countries with which we are concerned.

According to the 1981 Census the population of England was 45.8 million, of whom 3.1 million were born overseas. Nearly a third of the overseas born were living in London. The demographic structure of the general population in terms of age and sex is given in Figure 2.2, in order to provide a comparison with the data from ALUS on the nineteen local linguistic minorities.

Profiles of the main linguistic minorities in England

We go on now to give an outline sketch of the social, economic and linguistic background of the eleven linguistic minorities who were the focus of our Adult Language Use Survey. First we look at the national picture, with illustrative data from ALUS. Then we describe the local situation in the three cities where we carried out research. Here for convenience we group the linguistic minorities into four categories, South Asian, East Asian, East European and South European.

Figure 2.2   Population of England – 1981 Census

Total Population 45.8 million

		Males			Females	
Age groups						
Scale	2m	1m	0		1m	2m
85+	•	•	*	****	•	•
80–84 years	•	•	**	*****	•	•
75–79 years	•	•	*****	*********.		•
70–74 years	•	•	********	**********		•
65–69 years	•	•	**********	************		•
60–64 years	•	•	***********	************		•
55–59 years	•	•	*************	**************		•
50–54 years	•	•	*************	************		•
45–49 years	•	•	*************	************		•
40–44 years	•	•	*************	************		•
35–39 years	•	•	***************	***************		•
30–34 years	•	•	*****************	*****************		•
25–29 years	•	•	****************	***************		•
20–24 years	•	•	****************	*****************		•
15–19 years	•	•	********************	********************.		•
10–14 years	•	•	********************	*******************		•
5–9 years	•	•	***************	**************		•
0–4 years	•	•	*************	************		•

The South Asian linguistic minorities in England

Speakers of Panjabi, Gujerati and Bengali

.All of these linguistic minorities have their geographical origins in the
Indian subcontinent and come from a background where there has been
considerable contact with the British in the colonial and post-colonial
context. The major phase of primary migration to England took place
between 1955 and 1970, when young men from a number of regions
of India, Pakistan and Bangladesh (then East Pakistan) came to Britain
as unskilled migrant labour. When the unrestricted right of entry for
Commonwealth citizens was taken away by the immigration legislation
of the 1960s and 1970s, more wives and families joined the male
workers in the UK. By 1980 the majority of households in these
minorities consisted of reunited families, although there remained a
small number of all-male households and many families which included
recent arrivals, especially in the populations of Pakistani-Panjabi and

Bangladeshi origin. The demographic profiles which result from the particular circumstances of migration show a high proportion of children and young people, with most households in our surveys containing at least one child.

The major exceptions to this pattern are the East African Asians, most of whom arrived with British passports between 1968 and 1973 as political refugees. They came most notably from Kenya and Uganda, as a result of the Africanisation policies of those countries, and the majority were Gujerati-speaking, mainly Hindus and some Muslims. There were also many Panjabi-speaking Sikhs, Muslims and Hindus. The demographic profiles resulting from the forced migration of whole families is very different from that of the migrant labourers from related linguistic backgrounds in the subcontinent.

As a result of the migrations from the Indian subcontinent and East Africa, there existed in England as a whole in 1981 a population of well over 1 million people of South Asian origin. Because of the absence of specific 'ethnic' and language questions in the census in England, and the difficulties of definition mentioned earlier, it is impossible to give a more precise estimate. However, the 1981 Census records 378,712 people who were born in India, 179,723 born in Pakistan and 46,868 born in Bangladesh, together with 190,689 people who gave their birthplace as East Africa of whom it is likely that a very high proportion were of South Asian origin. In order to illustrate in more detail the demographic patterns in the separate local linguistic minorities we now present some of the relevant data from the ALUS, in the form of population pyramids.

The people in the households of Bengali-speaking respondents in both Coventry and London (Figs 2.3a and 2.3b) are predominantly young. (We include under 'Bengali-speaking' in this section speakers of Sylheti: for fuller discussion see p. 44.) There is scarcely anyone over the age of 65 and a large proportion of children aged under 11. In the older age cohorts in Coventry, and in all adult age cohorts in London, the men outnumber the women. These facts reflect a pattern of male labour migration in the late 1960s and early 1970s with the women arriving more recently.

The household members of Gujerati-speaking respondents (Figs 2.4a and 2.4b) are most numerous in the 16–30 age group. (We include under 'Gujerati-speaking' in this section speakers of Kutchi: for fuller discussion see p. 44.) The age structure of the over-30 age range is somewhat less distinct. The demographic pattern reflects a mixture of migration patterns, beginning with primary labour migration direct

Figure 2.3.a Bengali speakers in Coventry

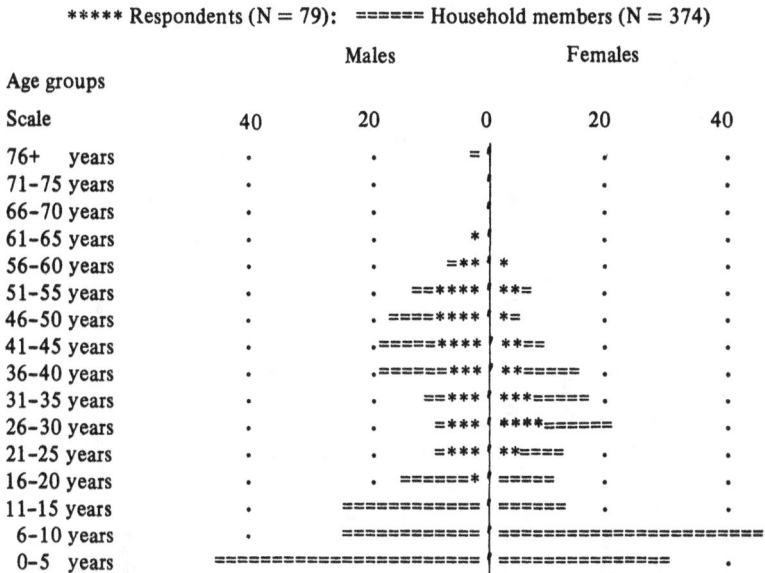

***** Respondents (N = 79):   ====== Household members (N = 374)

```
                           Males              Females
Age groups
Scale            40       20       0        20        40

76+   years      .        .       =|        '         .
71-75 years      .        .        |        .         .
66-70 years      .        .        |        .         .
61-65 years      .        .      * |        .         .
56-60 years      .        .    =** | *      .         .
51-55 years      .        .  ==**** | **=    .         .
46-50 years      .       . ====**** | *=     .         .
41-45 years      .     .=====**** | **==    .         .
36-40 years      .     .======*** | **=====  .        .
31-35 years      .        . ==*** | ***=====  .       .
26-30 years      .        .   =*** | ****======  .     .
21-25 years      .        .   =*** | **=====    .      .
16-20 years      .        . ======* | =====      .     .
11-15 years      .    ============= | ======    .      .
 6-10 years      .      ============ | ================== =====
 0-5  years   ===================== | ==============   .
```

Figure 2.3.b Bengali speakers in London

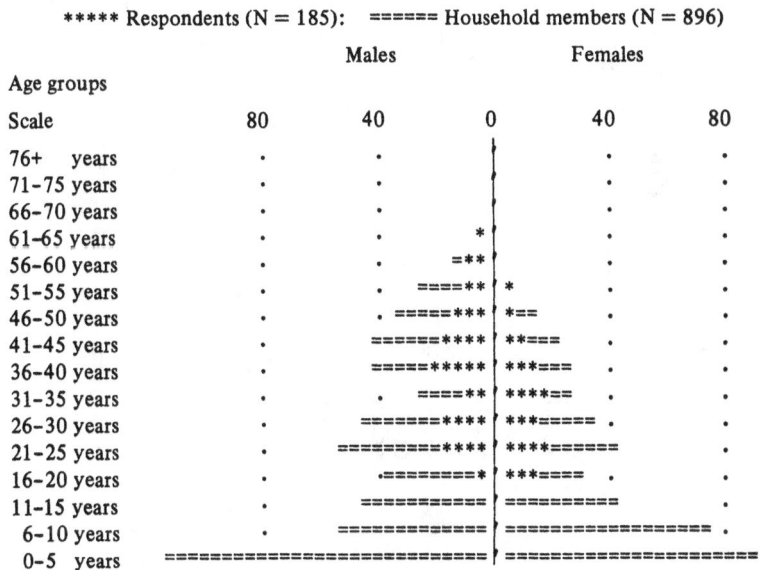

***** Respondents (N = 185):   ====== Household members (N = 896)

```
                           Males              Females
Age groups
Scale            80       40       0        40        80

76+   years      .        .        |        .         .
71-75 years      .        .        |        .         .
66-70 years      .        .        |        .         .
61-65 years      .        .      * |        .         .
56-60 years      .        .    =** |        .         .
51-55 years      .        .  ====** | *      .         .
46-50 years      .        . =====*** | *==    .        .
41-45 years      .    ======**** | **===    .         .
36-40 years      .    =====***** | ***===    .        .
31-35 years      .        . =====** | *****=    .      .
26-30 years      .     =======**** | ***======  .      .
21-25 years      .   ==========**** | ****======    .  .
16-20 years      .     .========* | ***=====   .      .
11-15 years      .    ============ | =========         .
 6-10 years      .    ============ | ==================  .
 0-5  years   ==================== | ======================
```

Figure 2.4.a Gujerati speakers in Coventry

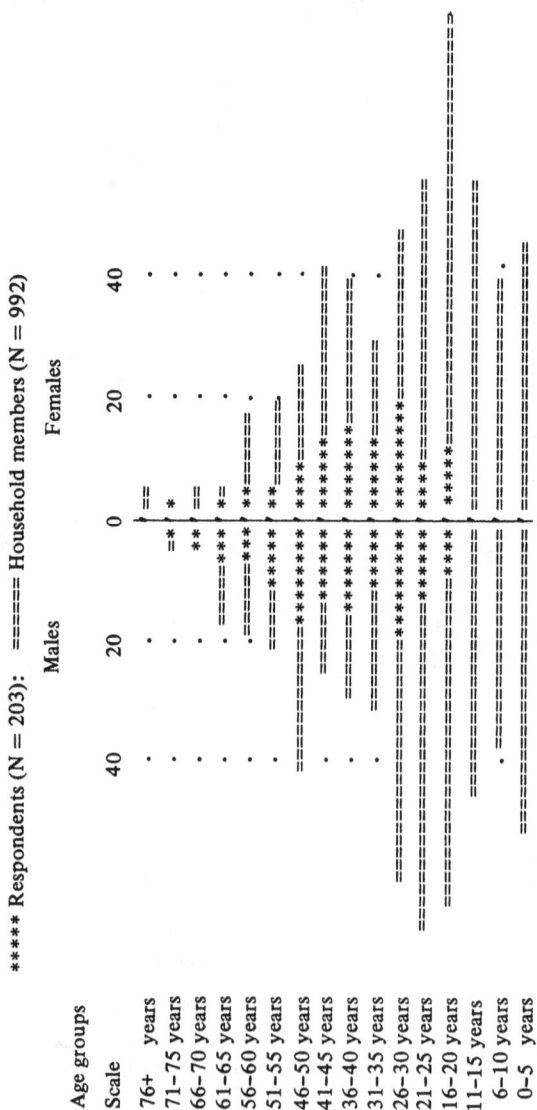

***** Respondents (N = 203):   ===== Household members (N = 992)

Males   Females

Age groups

| Scale | 40 | 20 | 0 | 20 | 40 |

76+   years
71–75 years
66–70 years
61–65 years
56–60 years
51–55 years
46–50 years
41–45 years
36–40 years
31–35 years
26–30 years
21–25 years
16–20 years
11–15 years
6–10 years
0–5   years

Figure 2.4.b Gujerati speakers in London

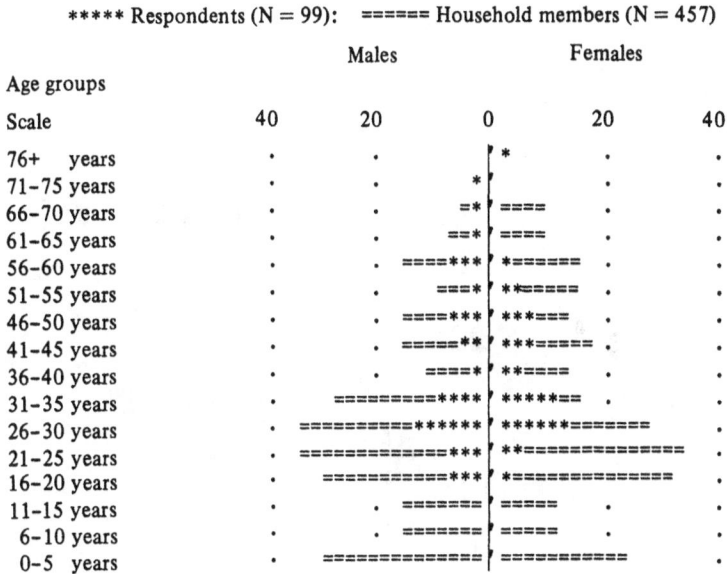

***** Respondents (N = 99):   ====== Household members (N = 457)

	Males			Females	
Age groups					
Scale	40	20	0	20	40
76+ years	.	.	*	.	.
71-75 years	.	.	*	.	.
66-70 years	.	.	=*	====	.	.
61-65 years	.	.	==*	====	.	.
56-60 years	.	.	====***	*=======	.	.
51-55 years	.	.	===*	*=====	.	.
46-50 years	.	.	====***	***====	.	.
41-45 years	.	.	====**	***=====	.	.
36-40 years	.	.	====*	**=====	.	.
31-35 years	.	=========****	******	******==	.	.
26-30 years	.	==========******	******========	.
21-25 years	.	=============***	**==============	.
16-20 years	.	============***	*===============	.
11-15 years	.	.	=======	=====	.	.
6-10 years	.	.	=======	=====	.	.
0-5 years	.	==============	===========	.

from India in the early 1960s, followed by the migration of whole families of refugees from East Africa between 1968 and 1973. In fact 69 per cent of London and 58 per cent of Coventry Gujerati-speaking respondents appeared to have some connection with one of the East African countries.

The household members of Panjabi(G)-speaking respondents in Coventry and Bradford (Figs 2.5a and 2.5b) are very young overall, with a large proportion of children of 10 years and under. (For a discussion of the distinction between Panjabi(G) and Panjabi(U), and an explanation of the abbreviations, see pp. 45-7.) In both cities there are higher numbers in the households in our samples in the 46-50 age group. These are most likely to be the migrants of the early 1960s who reached the UK in the period leading up to the 1962 Commonwealth Immigration Act. It is more difficult to explain the quite large numbers in the 25-40 age group, unless we assume they are the children of the early migrants who were born in India before their parents migrated, and who later joined their families.

The household members of Panjabi(U)-speaking respondents in Coventry and Bradford (Figs 2.6a and 2.6b) show a similar age structure

Figure 2.5.a Panjabi(G) speakers in Coventry

***** Respondents (N = 200):   ===== Household members (N = 1025)

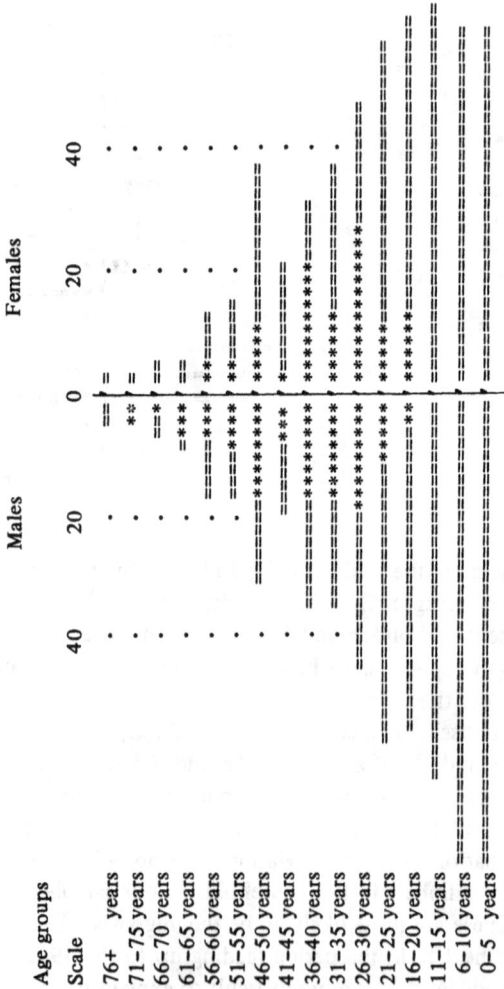

Males   Females

Age groups

Scale

40   20   0   20   40

76+   years
71–75 years
66–70 years
61–65 years
56–60 years
51–55 years
46–50 years
41–45 years
36–40 years
31–35 years
26–30 years
21–25 years
16–20 years
11–15 years
6–10 years
0–5   years

Figure 2.5.b Panjabi(G) speakers in Bradford

```
***** Respondents (N = 98):  ====== Household members (N = 529)

                              Males              Females
Age groups

Scale           40          20         0          20          40
76+   years      .           .         *  =        .           .
71-75 years      .           .         *           .           .
66-70 years      .           .        =*  ==        .           .
61-65 years      .           .       ===*  =        .           .
56-60 years      .           .       =**  *=        .           .
51-55 years      .           .       ==**  *==       .           .
46-50 years      .           .     =====**  ***===     .          .
41-45 years      .           .       ===*  **=======  .          .
36-40 years      .           .     ==***  *****==     .          .
31-35 years      .        =======*****  *****=====.      .
26-30 years      .       ==========*****  *****=======
21-25 years      .  ===============*****  *****============ .
16-20 years      .     ===============**  *===========    .
11-15 years      . ==================  ===========     .
6-10 years    ===================  =============     .
0-5   years   ===================  ====================
```

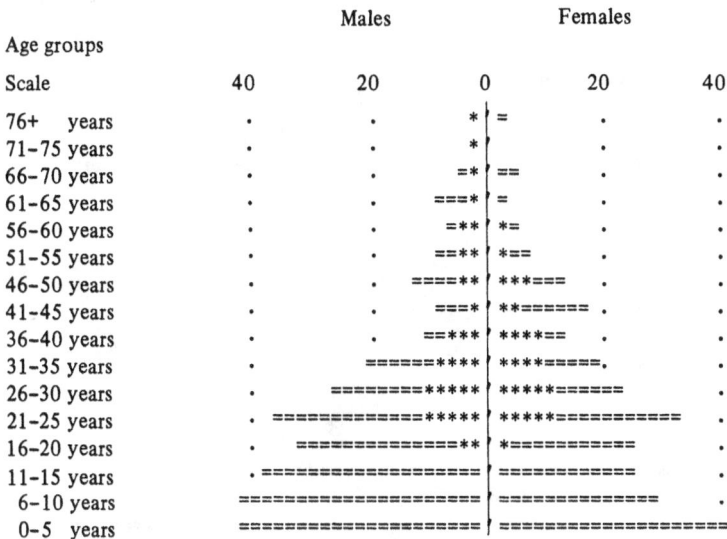

to the Panjabi(G)-speaking ones, although the gender imbalances are more striking. There are more males than females in the over 40 age groups, and also among children in the 11-16 age group.

The distribution of the populations of South Asian origin across the country is largely a result of the employment opportunities which existed in the 1950s and 1960s, and of the process of chain migration in which information about specific localities, and personal contacts in these localities, played an important part. The major areas of settlement were the conurbations of Greater London, the Midlands, Yorkshire and Lancashire. Panjabi-speaking Muslims are strongly represented in Bradford and the Lancashire towns in the textile industries, and to a lesser extent in Birmingham, parts of East London and many other towns. Panjabi-speaking Sikhs and Hindus together probably form the most numerous minority, and are widely dispersed across the country. The main areas of settlement are Southall and Newham in London; Birmingham, Wolverhampton, Coventry; Leeds, Bradford, Huddersfield; Peterborough, Bedford, Gravesend and a number of other smaller towns. Members of this minority tend, especially in the Midlands, to be employed in heavy industry and engineering factories. Gujerati speakers,

Figure 2.6.a   Panjabi(U) speakers in Coventry

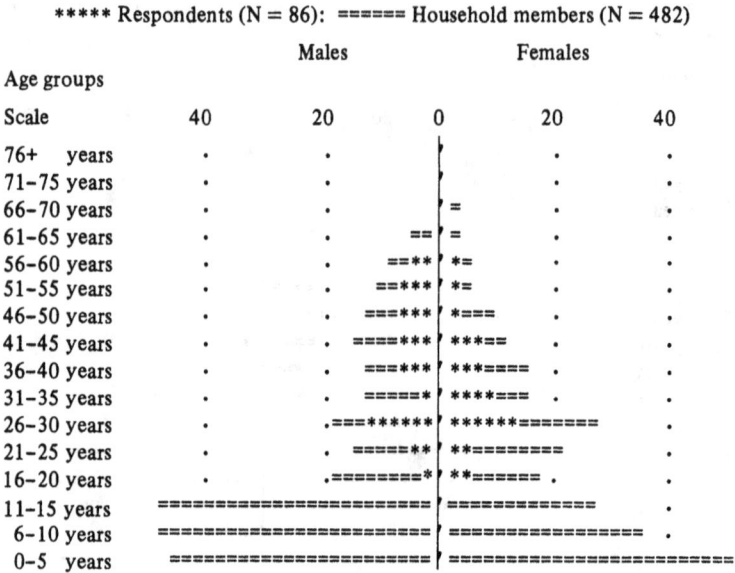

```
***** Respondents (N = 86):  ====== Household members (N = 482)
                        Males              Females
Age groups
Scale           40      20       0       20      40
76+   years      .       .       |        .       .
71-75 years      .       .       |        .       .
66-70 years      .       .       =        .       .
61-65 years      .       .     == |=       .       .
56-60 years      .       .   ==** |*=       .       .
51-55 years      .       .   ==***|*=       .       .
46-50 years      .       .  ===***|*===     .       .
41-45 years      .       . ====***|***==     .       .
36-40 years      .       . ===***|***===     .       .
31-35 years      .       .  =====*|****===    .       .
26-30 years      .      .===******|******========
21-25 years      .       . =====**|**========
16-20 years      .      .=======*|**======= .
11-15 years  =======================|============ .
 6-10 years  =======================|=============== .
 0-5  years   ======================|========================
```

Figure 2.6.b   Panjabi(U) speakers in Bradford

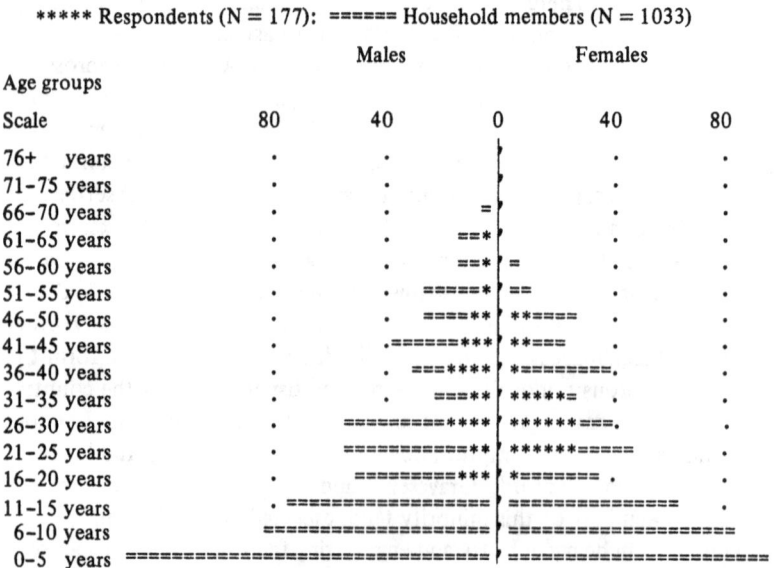

```
***** Respondents (N = 177):  ====== Household members (N = 1033)
                        Males              Females
Age groups
Scale           80      40       0       40      80
76+   years      .       .       |        .       .
71-75 years      .       .       |        .       .
66-70 years      .       .       =|        .       .
61-65 years      .       .     ==*|        .       .
56-60 years      .       .     ==*|=        .       .
51-55 years      .       .  =====*|==        .       .
46-50 years      .       .  =====**|**=====     .       .
41-45 years      .      .=======***|**====      .       .
36-40 years      .       . ===****|*========.     .
31-35 years      .       .  ====**|*****=    .       .
26-30 years      .   ===========****|******===.      .
21-25 years      .   ============**|******=====    .
16-20 years      .   ============***|*======= .    .
11-15 years      . =================|============= .
 6-10 years   =================|=================
 0-5  years ====================|========================
```

including the East African Asians, are to be found in large numbers in Leicester, Coventry, East and North West London and in the northern textile towns. For Bengali speakers the major settlements are in East London, where many work in the clothing industry, with smaller numbers in Birmingham, Manchester, Bradford, Coventry and several other towns. Other South Asian linguistic minorities who have settled in small numbers in particular localities include Hindi speakers in several cities, Malayalam and Tamil speakers in parts of London (as secondary migrants from Malaysia and Singapore), and Pushtu speakers in Bradford and Birmingham.

There has been considerable previous research among the South Asian populations in Britain. Much of it has concentrated on issues of discrimination faced by these 'visible' minorities in the fields of housing, employment and education. Often they have been studied alongside people of Caribbean origin who have settled in similar neighbourhoods. As a result even such substantial studies as Rex and Moore (1967), and D. Smith (1977), etc., have not usually distinguished between the linguistic and ethnic minorities within the South Asian population, although other studies by social anthropologists have focussed on specific minorities in a particular local setting, for example Panjabi speakers of Pakistani origin in Bradford (Saifullah Khan, 1977b), in Manchester (Werbner, 1981) and in Rochdale (Anwar, 1979); Panjabi-speaking Sikhs from India and East Africa in Bradford (Singh, R., 1979) and Leeds (Ballard, 1973) and in Southall (Brah, 1978); Sikhs from East Africa in West London (Bhachu, 1981); and Gujerati speakers from India in London (Tambs-Lyche, 1980) and in Leicester (Michaelson, 1979).

The language background

The outstanding feature of the language background of all South Asian linguistic minorities is the wide range of related languages, varieties and dialects, that exists throughout the subcontinent, coupled with the high level of multilingualism involving regional languages, official languages and English (Pattanayak, 1981; Pal, 1969). The Indian subcontinent is the home of two major language 'families', the Dravidian group in the South and the Indic in the North. For 3,000 years the two groups have developed alongside each other, and there has been much mutual influence, involving borrowing of lexical items and phonological and grammatical structures. Both language 'families' exist in traditional rural South Asia as dialect continua, where forms of speech vary gradually and almost imperceptibly from one village to the next (Shapiro and Schiffman, 1981).

Language standardisation through the spread of education, literacy and the media is a relatively recent development in South Asia. In India, for example, the policy of linguistic states, each with a single regional standard language, has only developed since independence (Das Gupta, 1970). Although regional languages have become highly salient as markers of ethnic identity, and command a high level of loyalty which often leads to political mobilisation, for many rural people the gap between vernacular and standard is so wide as to make learning the standard almost like learning a second language. In addition to the official language of their own state, most educated Indians will learn the official language Hindi, and English as a language of wider communication for use both inside and outside India. There is already a tradition within India of linguistic and sociohistorical descriptions of contact between South Asian languages and English (Khubchandani, 1979; Bhatia, 1982).

Apart from the small number of Malayalam and Tamil speakers already mentioned, the Dravidian languages are scarcely represented in England. The majority of speakers of South Asian languages here have origins in rural areas of North India, Pakistan and Bangladesh, and use one of the local rural vernaculars as the home language. They may also use one of the standard regional languages – especially for formal purposes, including those involving the use of written language. And they are likely in the first place to express their language loyalty in terms of the standard taught language rather than the home language. Thus, for example, some people originating from Sylhet in Bangladesh who speak Sylheti, are likely to name their language as 'Bengali', and to seek 'mother tongue' teaching in that national language. A few are beginning to campaign to raise the status of Sylheti, pointing out the existence of an earlier Sylheti literature in a distinct script, and suggesting that classes for children in England should use and teach Sylheti in addition to Bengali, or even as an alternative to it.

In some cases the boundary between language and dialect is more complex still. For example, Kutchi (sometimes spelled 'Kachchi' in English orthography) is usually characterised by linguists as a dialect or a variety closely related to Sindhi, one which may have developed out of contact between earlier varieties of Sindhi and Gujerati (Shapiro and Schiffman, 1981). However, because of their family origins in Gujerat State, and education through the medium of Gujerati, many Kutchi speakers in England will describe themselves as speakers of a variety of Gujerati. At present they are likely to welcome the provision of Gujerati 'mother tongue' classes for their children, although, like Sylheti speakers, they may be expected to campaign at some stage for improved status for their language.

The problem of language naming is of particular interest with reference to speakers of Panjabi and Urdu. In all of the areas in which LMP worked, the interpretation of data relating to bilingual families who have their origins in the Panjab has been the most complex sociolinguistic issue we have had to face (see Figure 1.1 in Chapter 1). In order to understand the problem it is necessary to appreciate something of the sociohistorical situation in Northern India and Pakistan, and in families from those backgrounds who now live in England.

Before the partition of the subcontinent in 1947, the whole of Panjab was part of a single state, and the majority of the population spoke one of the local dialects of Panjabi as a mother tongue. Even today there is a high degree of mutual intelligibility between the spoken forms of Panjabi used on either side of the Indo-Pakistan border, which gradually give way to varieties closer to Hindi as one moves south. For this reason many linguists refer to a large part of the north of the subcontinent as the 'Hindi-Urdu-Panjabi' area or dialect continuum (Khubchandani, 1979). However, as religious divisions became institutionalised in the creation of the new nations of India and Pakistan, language became more closely associated with national and religious identity. Urdu, a language based on the speech of educated Muslims of Northern India, and written in the Perso-Arabic script, was declared to be the national and official language of Pakistan, although most native speakers of Urdu to be found within the borders of the country were migrants and refugees. Almost all education, official business and literacy in Pakistan are conducted in the medium of Urdu. Most Pakistani migrants to England came from Panjab, or adjoining districts of 'Azad' Kashmir. They speak local dialects of Panjabi as their home language, but may regard Urdu as their 'mother tongue' and use it as their language of literacy. It is these speakers whom we refer to as 'Panjabi(U)' (= Panjabi speakers likely to use Urdu for formal purposes). In a similar way many Muslim Gujerati speakers of the migrant generation want their children to learn to read and write Urdu for religious purposes, alongside or instead of Gujerati.

On the Indian side of the border two standard languages are widely used. The official language of India is Hindi, which in its spoken form is mutually intelligible, indeed almost identical, with the spoken form of Urdu. However, Hindi is strongly associated with the Hindu religion,

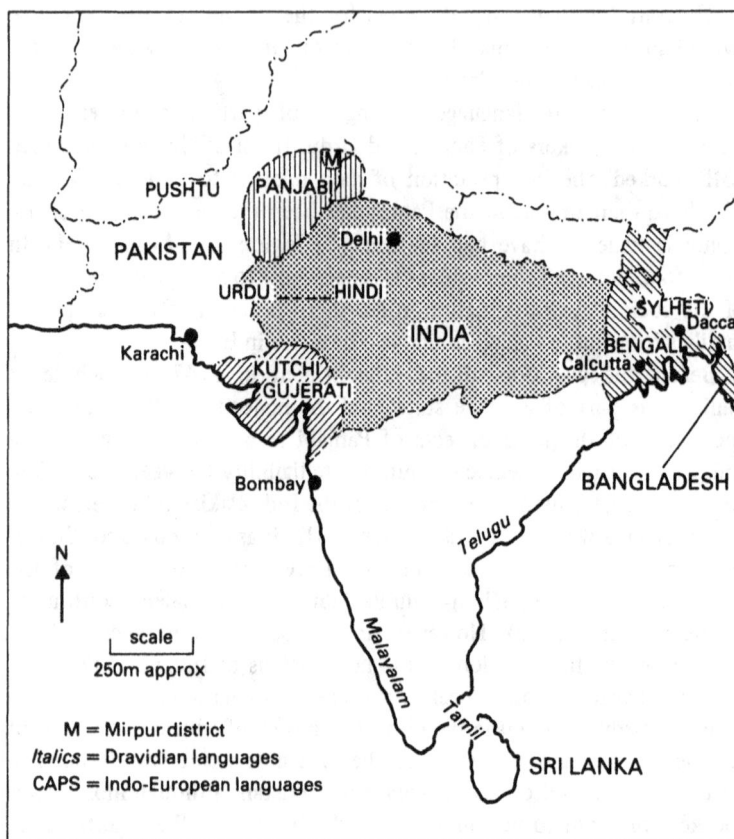

Map 2.1 Sketch map of the Indian subcontinent showing the regions of origin of the main South Asian languages

and in formal styles is strongly influenced by Sanskrit, the classical language of the main Hindu scriptures. Hindi is normally written in the Devanagri script, which is derived from the script used for Sanskrit, and is different from the Perso-Arabic Urdu script. This situation is a typical incidence of what has recently been described as digraphia (Dale, 1980).

When the linguistic basis for the division into states became more and more obvious, each state having its own standard language and script, the Indian part of the old province of the Panjab presented particular difficulties. Eventually the state was divided into two in the 1960s, the southern part, in which Hindus are in the majority, becoming the state of Haryana, where Hindi is the official language. In the northern part, which now bears the name Panjab, the official language became Panjabi. This variety is strongly associated with the Sikh religion and is written in a script known as Gurmukhi, developed by the scribes who first wrote down the Sikh scriptures in the sixteenth century. Sikhs living in the Indian Panjab and elsewhere will speak Panjabi as a home language, write it in the Gurmukhi script and regard it as their 'mother tongue'. It is these speakers whom we refer to as 'Panjabi(G)' (= Panjabi speakers likely to use the Gurmukhi script for formal purposes). They may use Hindi as a second language or lingua franca, and older people may know both spoken and written Urdu, since this was the medium of education in the region before 1947. Hindus originating from this region will speak Panjabi, and may know how to write it in the Gurmukhi script, but are more likely to know spoken and written Hindi and exhibit loyalty to Hindi, rather than Panjabi, as both their official language and 'mother tongue'.

The result of the sociolinguistic history of this area of South Asia is that most families in England with origins in the Panjab, whether in India or Pakistan, and whether they are Muslim, Sikh or Hindu by religion, will use spoken varieties which are likely to be mutually intelligible. Furthermore, languages such as Hindi and Urdu continue to serve the function of lingua franca among speakers of different South Asian languages in Britain. However, Muslims, Sikhs and Hindus would normally expect tuition in their distinct languages of literacy, e.g. Panjabi in the Gurmukhi script for the Sikhs, Panjabi in the Gurmukhi script or Hindi for Hindus originating from the present Indian state of Panjab, and Urdu for Muslims from the Pakistani part of Panjab. Therefore, for purposes of planning educational support, it is probably desirable to make a distinction between three linguistic minorities.

Two other factors in the linguistic background of South Asian linguistic minorities are important. In Muslim minorities in particular, a great value is still attached to calligraphic skills (Martin-Jones, 1984). Calligraphy is an art form in itself, and can be an important means of subjective expression and discipline, because of reverence for the Islamic scriptures and because pictorial representation has been discouraged under Islam. One of the goals of Urdu and Arabic instruction in Britain today is to pass on some of this calligraphic tradition to the younger generation.

Secondly, Panjabi and Gujerati speakers brought up in East Africa who have now settled in Britain came from a very different

sociolinguistic setting from those who came directly from the subcontinent. The South Asian minorities in East Africa have had a long
history of language maintenance and of community-run schooling in the
'mother tongue' for their children, alongside the mainstream English-
medium schooling which many of them experienced in those countries
(Martin-Jones, 1984).

A multilingual repertoire was considered to be the norm for many
people who grew up in the East African context. For example, Neale
(1974b) observed among Kenyan Asians whom she studied, that
different members of the linguistic minority drew in different ways on
an elaborate communicative repertoire which required a working
knowledge of at least four languages: Gujerati, Hindi, Swahili and
English. In the Zambian context Datta (1978) reported that the sociolinguistic repertoire of the predominantly Gujerati-speaking minority
was somewhat different. Gujerati and Hindi were widely known and
used, but knowledge of English varied according to age, since the
younger generation received their schooling for the most part through
the medium of English. In both African countries however, the use of
South Asian 'mother tongues' was supported by radio broadcasts from
the subcontinent, by family contacts with South Asia, and by regular
screening of the very popular Indian films, mostly in Hindi-Urdu.

The East Asian linguistic minorities in England

Speakers of Cantonese, Hakka, Hokkien and Vietnamese

Most of the people of East Asian origin who now live in Britain are of
Chinese ethnic background, although there are a small number of people
of Malay, Indo-Chinese and Japanese origin in various parts of the
country.

There have been sizeable minorities of Chinese origin in Britain
since at least the early part of the twentieth century, particularly in
dockland areas of East London and Liverpool (Watson, 1975). A wave of
migration from Southern China in this period led to the establishment of
communities of overseas Chinese in many parts of the world. However,
the settlements in which our adult survey was carried out are largely
the result of later migrations – the exception being a few people in the
London sample who were resident in Tower Hamlets, and who came
from families long established in England. The majority of respondents
in our London and Coventry Chinese samples originated in Hong Kong

(particularly the New Territories), and had come to settle in the UK within the previous twenty years. Many of them were employed in the catering trade, working either in Chinese restaurants or takeaways (Watson, 1977), and in London in particular there is also a large number of people of Chinese origin who have come to the UK to further their education. Many of this last group are from Malaysia or Singapore, although there are also substantial numbers from Hong Kong. The most recent group of migrants, who are represented by the Bradford ALUS respondents and a minority within the London ALUS sample, are recent political refugees from Vietnam (Jones, 1983).

With such a varied range of migration histories within this minority in Britain, there is obviously a rich variety of social and ethnic backgrounds. Even the migrants from Hong Kong are by no means a homogeneous ethnic group. Most have origins in the rural New Territories rather than in urban Hong Kong itself. Some − in fact, the majority of our Coventry sample − have the Hakka language as their spoken vernacular. The Hakka ('k'echia' or 'guest') people are believed to have originated in Northern China, migrated southwards several hundred years ago, and can now be found settled in widely dispersed pockets in most parts of Southern China and in a number of villages in the rural areas of the New Territories. The Cantonese mother tongue speakers ('pun-ti' people) are indigenous to Southern China. Economic and political pressure in the 1950s and 1960s caused many people from rural parts of Southern China to move from the People's Republic to the expanding urban areas such as Hong Kong and Macao. So for many Cantonese speakers the move to Britain was a second stage of migration.

Refugees from Vietnam are for the most part 'ethnic Chinese', most of them speaking Cantonese as their 'mother tongue' (sometimes with a quite distinctive accent). Many of them have been educated through the medium of Vietnamese, and a few have had contact with French and English as the language of recent occupying powers. Those settled in Britain from Singapore and Malaysia are from Cantonese and Hokkien speaking backgrounds for the most part. However, educational policies in those two countries have tended to promote the learning of English and Mandarin in the case of Singapore, and Malay in the case of Malaysia, with the result that significant language shift away from Cantonese and Hokkien has already taken place among the educated classes. In the course of our research we also came across a number of families of Chinese ethnic origin who had migrated to England from the Caribbean, after their families had been established there for three or more generations. Most of them had little or no knowledge of any of the Chinese languages.

It had been estimated that there were around 60,000 people of Chinese origin in the UK (Chin and Simsova, 1981; Watson, 1975). The major concentrations of speakers of Chinese languages were thought to be in London (27,000), Liverpool (4,000), Birmingham (2,700), Glasgow (2,000) and Manchester (2,000). (These local figures, which include British born children, are estimates made by Chin and Simsova in 1981 on the basis of analysis of telephone subscribers and 1971 Census data. In the light of the 1981 Census data more recently made available, they are probably under-estimates, although the proportions between cities are likely to remain the same.) The remainder are widely scattered around the country, a tendency which has arisen because of the limited market for Chinese food in individual localities.

At the time of the 1981 Census 52,000 people born in Hong Kong, 15,000 born in the People's Republic of China, 12,000 born in Vietnam and 29,000 born in Singapore were usually resident in England. Even if not all of these people are 'Chinese-speaking', the fact that children born in the UK to parents of Chinese origin were not counted under this heading in the Census means that a total figure of perhaps 150,000 is not unrealistic for this linguistic minority as a whole.

It appears that the population of Chinese origin in England is relatively young, probably the result of migration patterns in which young men were the pioneers in the 1960s, and were followed by their wives some years later. The peak years for migration from Hong Kong were 1960 to 1962 (Watson, 1975). The demographic profiles of the members of respondents' households in the three 'Chinese' ALUS samples seem to confirm this pattern (Figs 2.7a, 2.7b and 2.7c), although the small numbers involved in Coventry and Bradford make detailed interpretation somewhat risky. In London, however, there is a large number, of males especially, in the 16-25 age cohorts. Since there are relatively small numbers in their parents' generation (40-55) this pattern is probably a reflection of the large numbers of students and young professionals in the London Chinese sample.

The language background

Ninety-five per cent of the population of China are speakers of one of a family of languages known as Han-yu (Chinese). The two thirds of the population living in the northern part of the People's Republic speak varieties in broad terms mutually intelligible with the Peking standard

Figure 2.7.a 'Chinese' speakers in Coventry

***** Respondents (N = 43): ====== Household members (N = 213)

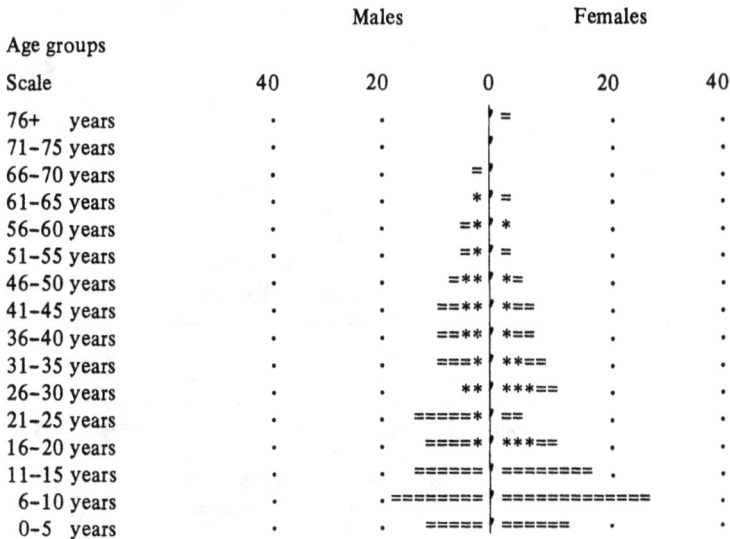

	Males		Females	

Age groups

Scale	40	20	0	20	40
76+ years	·	·	=	·	·
71-75 years	·	·		·	·
66-70 years	·	·	=	·	·
61-65 years	·	·	* =	·	·
56-60 years	·	·	=* *	·	·
51-55 years	·	·	=* =	·	·
46-50 years	·	·	=** *=	·	·
41-45 years	·	·	===** *==	·	·
36-40 years	·	·	===** *==	·	·
31-35 years	·	·	===* **==	·	·
26-30 years	·	·	** ***==	·	·
21-25 years	·	·	======* ==	·	·
16-20 years	·	·	====* ***==	·	·
11-15 years	·	·	====== ========	·
6-10 years	·	· ========= =============	·
0-5 years	·	· ===== ======	·	·

Figure 2.7.b 'Chinese' speakers in Bradford

***** Respondents (N = 50): ====== Household members (N = 244)

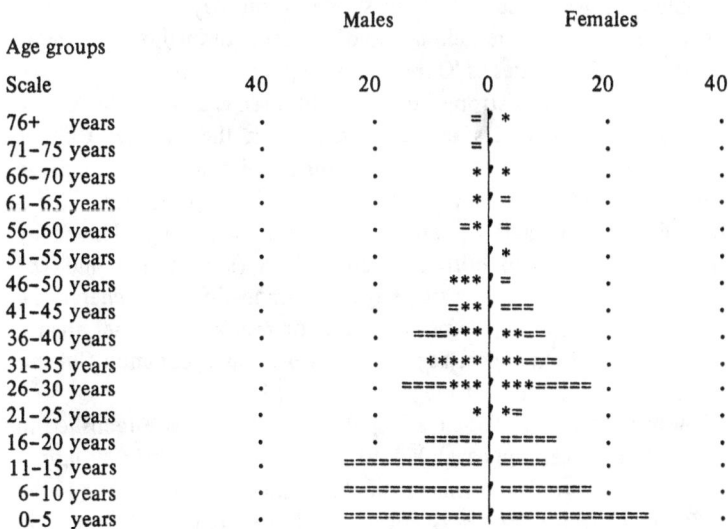

	Males		Females	

Age groups

Scale	40	20	0	20	40
76+ years	·	·	= *	·	·
71-75 years	·	·	=	·	·
66-70 years	·	·	* *	·	·
61-65 years	·	·	* =	·	·
56-60 years	·	·	=* =	·	·
51-55 years	·	·	*	·	·
46-50 years	·	·	*** =	·	·
41-45 years	·	·	=** ===	·	·
36-40 years	·	·	===*** **==	·	·
31-35 years	·	·	***** **===	·	·
26-30 years	·	· ======*** ***====== ·
21-25 years	·	·	* *=	·	·
16-20 years	·	·	===== =====	·	·
11-15 years	·	============ ====	·
6-10 years	·	============ ======== ·
0-5 years	·	============ =============	·

Figure 2.7.c 'Chinese' speakers in London

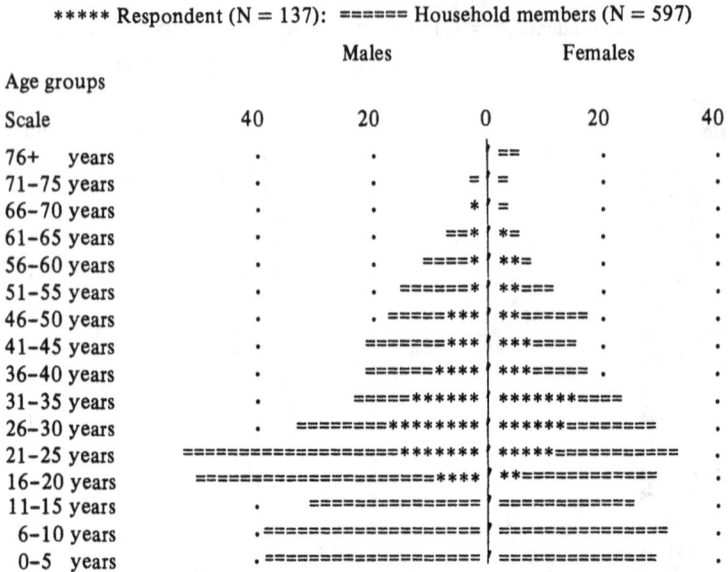

***** Respondent (N = 137): ====== Household members (N = 597)

```
                              Males                    Females
Age groups
Scale          40        20        0        20        40
76+   years     .         .      |==         .         .
71-75 years     .         .      = =         .         .
66-70 years     .         .      * =         .         .
61-65 years     .         .    ==* *=         .         .
56-60 years     .         .   ====* **=         .         .
51-55 years     .         .  ======* **===         .         .
46-50 years     .         . ======*** **======= .         .
41-45 years     .       ========*** ***===== .         .
36-40 years     .       =======**** ***====== .         .
31-35 years     .     =====******* *********====         .
26-30 years     .  ===========******** ******==========         .
21-25 years   ====================******* *****============         .
16-20 years   ====================****   **============         .
11-15 years     .    ===============   ===========         .
 6-10 years     . ================   ==============         .
 0-5  years     . =================   ==============         .
```

variety referred to quite widely in the West as Mandarin. In the south of China a number of related varieties are used. These, which include Hakka, Hokkien and Cantonese, are sometimes referred to as 'dialects' of Chinese. However, since in their spoken form they are distinct from each other and from the Peking-based standard, throughout this book we refer to such varieties as 'Chinese languages'.

There is a long and strong literary tradition in China, and literacy in the traditional characters is highly valued. In the overseas Chinese communities too there has been a centuries-old tradition of language maintenance and of literacy teaching in each new generation. This is reflected, perhaps, in the relatively high rates of literacy claimed by Chinese respondents in both SLS and ALUS (see pp. 335 and 188 respectively). Traditionally a single system of non-alphabetic characters, each representing a single meaning unit or morpheme rather than a sound unit or phonological segment, was used as a common Chinese script for all the regional languages.

However, when the People's Republic of China was established in 1949, the political upheaval led to a new sociolinguistic situation. There are now two rival forms of standard Chinese (Hsu, 1979): (1) the traditional Taiwan or overseas norm, mostly referred to as 'Guoyu' in its spoken form (which is based on a conservative Peking variety) and modern 'Baihuawen' (vernacular or colloquial writing style) in its written form; and (2) the mainland norm, known as 'Putonghua' or Modern Standard Chinese. The written form has been reformed and simplified since 1956 under the auspices of a 'Language Academy' in the People's Republic. There are 2,000 simplified characters which cover all the common lexical and grammatical items and which form the core of Modern Standard Chinese. At the same time the 'pin yin' system of romanised spelling is being developed. The term 'Mandarin' is a European coinage first used in the nineteenth century to refer to 'Guanhua', the language spoken by the Mandarin scholars. With the establishment of the Republic in 1911 and the dissolution of the Mandarin hierarchy, the term 'Guanhua' was abolished. 'Mandarin' is, however, still loosely used to refer to either 'Guoyu' or 'Putonghua'.

According to Hsu, literacy in Chinese is undergoing a process of redefinition:

> The Chinese language is at present going through a transitional period during which two major norms, while being mutually exclusive in their primary spheres of influence, can under certain circumstances actually coexist. (1979: 117)

Besides these two major norms described by Hsu, other mixed varieties of the written language have developed in other regions, such as Hong Kong, Singapore and Malaysia, where the writing system is widely used and taught. In the population in England, where, as we have seen, the common spoken languages are Cantonese, Hakka and to a lesser extent Hokkien, Mandarin and Vietnamese, the influence of Hong Kong literacy practices is predominant. This involves the use of the traditional overseas norm of the common script for Chinese languages, with certain adaptations for Cantonese grammatical forms and lexical items specific to Hong Kong.

Bilingualism and multilingualism are common amongst the Chinese in Hong Kong. Cantonese is recognised as the standard and official language of the colony. However, English has equal official status and is widely used in governmental and commercial circles (Luke and Richards, 1982). Educated bilingual adults often use both languages, with systematic code-switching between them (Gibbons, 1979). Education at primary level is in Cantonese, with English medium available mostly for the elite. At secondary level both Cantonese-medium and English-medium schools are available in Hong Kong, although more and more parents are opting for English. So those who speak Hakka at home may be trilingual in Hakka, Cantonese and English, even before they come to Britain.

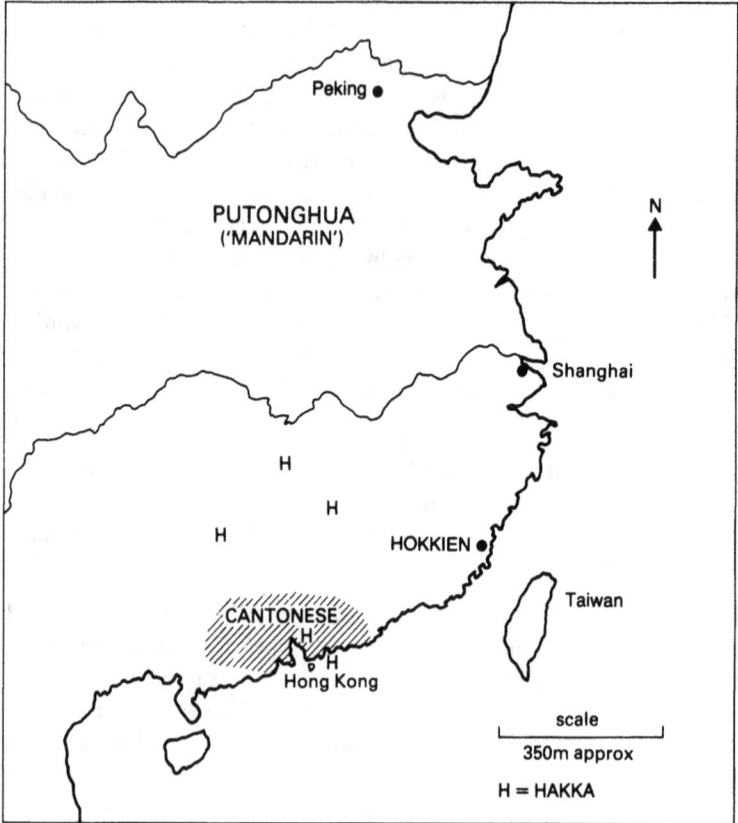

Map 2.2 Sketch map of China showing the regions of origin of Chinese languages

The South European linguistic minorities in England

Since 1945 large numbers of people from the less developed southern periphery of Europe have migrated in search of work to the urban centres of many North West European countries. The UK has received a lower proportion of South European migrants than, for example, West Germany or France. However, significant numbers of Italian, Portuguese, Spanish and Cypriot people have settled in England. In this section we shall deal with the Italian-, Portuguese-, Greek- and Turkish-speaking linguistic minorities who were surveyed in the ALUS.

Speakers of Italian

There has been an Italian presence in Britain for several centuries, with trading, banking and cultural links going back to before the Renaissance. By 1861 there were approximately 2,000 Italians living in London, in the Clerkenwell area which came to be known as 'Little Italy', and there have long been small groups of scholars, musicians, craftsmen and merchants living in various parts of the capital. There was also a seasonal migration of peasant farmers from Northern Italy, who took on subsidiary trades during the long Alpine winters. Then in the nineteenth century Mazzini found political refuge in London, along with some other Republican exiles. During his time in London Mazzini founded an Italian school in 1841, and a 'Society for the Advancement of Italian Workers' which still exists today, now known as the Circolo Mazzini Garibaldi. The second half of the nineteenth century also saw the establishment of St. Peter's, the Italian church in Clerkenwell, and of the Italian hospital (King, 1979).

From the mid-nineteenth century until the first decade of this century there was a significant increase in migration from Northern Italy. The size of the Italian population in England and Wales increased more than threefold: from 6,504 in 1881 to 20,332 in 1901 (Sponza, 1980; King, 1979). The Aliens Order of 1905, and subsequent legislation in 1919, marked the end of this period.

The turn of the century was a time of rapid growth and considerable prosperity in the service and catering industries, and after 1911 café life flourished in London and elsewhere in Britain. The Italians were the first to move into this sector and some became very successful entrepreneurs: the large Forte catering and hotel business, for example, had its beginnings in small-scale ice-cream sales in Dundee. The period of prosperity for Italians at the beginning of this century was shattered by World War Two, when the Italian-speaking minority were classified as 'aliens', and many were interned in detention camps on the Isle of Man, or were deported to Australia or Canada. Others returned to Italy.

The post-war period has been characterised primarily by migration from the south of Italy, from regions such as Campania, Calabria and Sicily, and since 1945 approximately 180,000 Italians have come to work in Britain (King, 1979). Initially this migration was encouraged by the Italian and British governments to meet increasing labour demands in Britain's expanding industries: recruitment offices were set up in Naples and Palermo (Crisp, 1980). However, the initial officially sponsored recruitment later developed into a pattern of chain migration from these same areas of Southern Italy.

The relative proximity of Italy makes it possible for families settled here to maintain links with their place of origin. Many Italians make plans to retire in Italy, and travel back and forth is a common feature of British-Italian family life.

As a result of this period of migration, new settlements of Italians were established, principally in the South Midlands, but also in the North and South East of England. From 1951 onwards, it is estimated that 15,000 Italian men were recruited for the brick industry, based principally in Bedford, but also in towns such as Peterborough, Loughborough and Bletchley (King, 1979). A further 10,000 Italians, mostly from Sicily, found employment in the horticultural industry in the Lea Valley just north of London. During the 1950s and early 1960s Italian workers were also recruited into the South Wales steelworks, and in 1951, the National Coal Board recruited 2,500 Italian miners. However, as a result of British trade union opposition, many of these miners either returned to Italy or found work in Belgian mines (Crisp, 1980).

Women workers were also recruited on a fairly large scale under the 'Official Italian Scheme'. About 2,000 Italian women aged between 18 and 40 came to work in cotton and wool mills, in rubber and pottery industries, and as domestics in hospitals, until the scheme was phased out in 1951 (Crisp, 1980). Another dimension of migration in this period was the arrival in Britain of 'war brides', some of whom married former Polish army combatants based in Italy. Since the immediate post-war period, the pattern of employment for many Italian migrants has changed. Some women, in particular, have found work in newer industries (Crisp, 1980). Many Italian men have opted for self-employment, particularly in the catering industry, opening restaurants, coffee bars, fish and chip shops or running ice-cream vans. Others have started small tailoring, hairdressing or grocery businesses. In 1969 2,800 firms in Britain were registered as Italian-owned, and approximately 8 per cent of the population of Italian origin in Britain are self-employed (King, 1979). (In the older-established Glasgow settlement 85 per cent of the Italians are self-employed (Colpi, 1979).)

The 1981 Census recorded a total of 89,085 Italian-born residents in England. Official Italian statistics, which also include children born in Britain of Italian parents, estimate the total Italian population (of the UK) at about 140,000 (Palmer, 1977). The Italian Catholic Mission Census puts the overall figure at over 200,000 (King, 1979), with 85,300 living in the South East of England, 47,000 in the Midlands, 15,000 in Scotland and 23,000 in Wales. A closer look at these figures shows that the greatest concentration of Italian settlement is in three areas, Greater London and the Lea Valley, Bedfordshire, and the Huntingdon and Peterborough districts. Figures 2.8a and 2.8b show the ALUS respondents and their households in Coventry and in London.

The household members of Italian-speaking respondents in both Coventry and London are concentrated in two age bands in each case. The people between 46 and 60 in Coventry represent the migrant generation who arrived in the 1950s; in London the corresponding group is some five years younger. In consequence the children of these migrants appear as a bulge in the 16-25 age group in Coventry and in the 11-20 group in London.

The Italian language and dialects

Italy is situated in the centre of the large area of Southern Europe which historical linguists and dialectologists describe as the Romance

Figure 2.8.a Italian speakers in Coventry

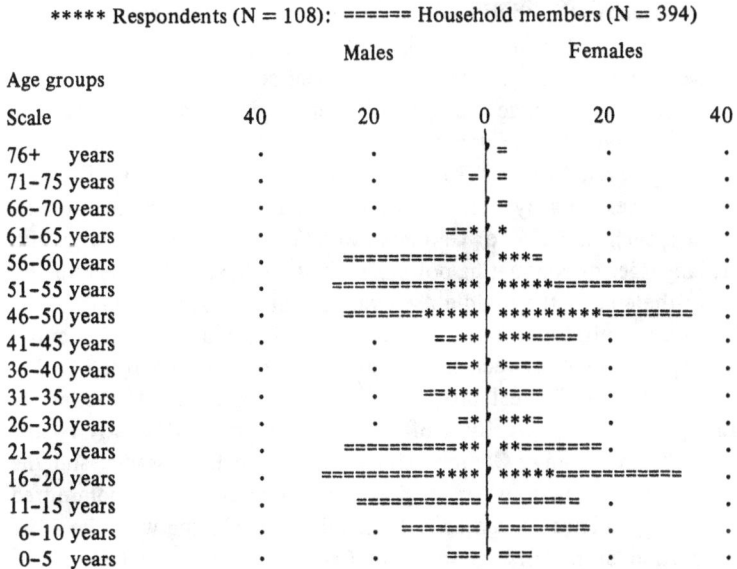

```
***** Respondents (N = 108):  ====== Household members (N = 394)

                        Males                    Females
Age groups
Scale            40       20       0        20        40

76+   years      .        .       |=        .         .
71-75 years      .        .     = |=        .         .
66-70 years      .        .       |=        .         .
61-65 years      .        .    ==*|*        .         .
56-60 years      .    ===========**|***=     .         .
51-55 years      .    ===========***|****=========    .
46-50 years      .    =======*****|********========    .
41-45 years      .        .   ==**|***====    .        .
36-40 years      .        .   ==* |*===        .        .
31-35 years      .        .  ==***|*===        .        .
26-30 years      .        .    =* |***=        .        .
21-25 years      .    ===========**|*=========.         .
16-20 years      .    ==========***|****============     .
11-15 years      .      ===========|======= =   .        .
6-10 years       .        .  =======|======== .         .
0-5   years      .        .   === |===       .         .
```

Figure 2.8.b Italian speakers in London

***** Respondents (N = 94): ====== Household members (N = 367)

```
                                Males                 Females
Age groups
Scale              40        20        0        20        40

76+   years         .         .        *|        .         .
71-75 years         .         .        *| ==      .         .
66-70 years         .         .        *| =       .         .
61-65 years         .         .        =| *       .         .
56-60 years         .         .      ===| *=====   .        .
51-55 years         .      ====*******| ***===     .        .
46-50 years         .       .=======**| ****=========      .
41-45 years         .       ======*****| ****=======       .
36-40 years         .         . ===**| **====     .        .
31-35 years         .         .    =*| ****=      .         .
26-30 years         .         .  ==**| **==       .         .
21-25 years         .         . ====*| *=======   .         .
16-20 years         .     ==========**| ***=========       .
11-15 years         .    =============| ================   .
 6-10 years         .         . =======| =======   .        .
 0-5  years         .         .    ===| ===       .         .
```

dialect continuum. Under the Roman Empire various local varieties of Latin became widely established as the vernaculars of Western Europe, and written Latin continued to be an important language of wider communication for fifteen hundred years. However, with the fall of the Roman Empire, and the period of reduced communication in Europe which followed, contact between different regions was much reduced, and the different local varieties of 'Vulgar' (= popular) Latin tended to diverge even further. These different varieties were also influenced to varying extents by contacts with the indigenous languages of their regions, such as Celtic or Germanic varieties in France, and later with the languages of conquering powers, such as Arabic and Moorish Spain.

By the end of the Middle Ages varieties at the extreme edges of the Romance continuum were too divergent for mutual intelligibility, although contact between neighbouring districts, even across political boundaries, was no real problem. Written communication was largely through a conservative form of Latin, and maintained mostly by the clergy of the Roman Catholic church. With the Renaissance and the rise of political nationalism, regional varieties began to be committed to writing and were eventually standardised, beginning with the 1492 publication of the first grammar of Castilian Spanish. In Italy it was in Florence that vernacular literature appeared earliest, with Dante as one of the first authors to write in the Florentine dialect. Other cultural centres in Italy, such as Venice, also produced influential writers and local standard languages. It was only after the whole of the Italian peninsula, Sardinia and Sicily came under a single government in the middle of the nineteenth century, that the Florentine or literary Italian standard began to be more widely accepted as the national language, 'la lingua italiana'. Other Italian varieties were demoted to the status of 'dialetti' − a status still resented by many of their speakers today.

The development of a public education system slowly spread the use of the national language throughout Italy, although in the rural regions, among the older generation, it is still very much a second language, used fluently only by the well-educated for reading, writing and wider communication. The development of travel, internal migration and the mass media in particular are currently extending the use of standard Italian throughout Italy. However, neither Italians who migrated to the UK in the immediate post-war period nor their children have had the benefit of such exposure. They tend to know only the local rural variety of the region of origin, with important consequences for the 'mother tongue' classes organised here (Tosi, 1984a).

The language classes organised and financed by the Italian government provide a focal point of Italian community life in England, but it is of course standard Italian that is taught in these classes. Northern and southern 'dialetti' are spoken throughout the country, although the patterns of migration and settlement described earlier have led to a preponderance of southern varieties in many areas, for example of Sicilian in the Lea Valley, and of dialects from the Naples region, the extreme south and Sicily in the Bedford area. The full range of linguistic diversity that exists in Italy, and is reflected in the sociolinguistic background of families living in Britain, is rarely reflected in the teaching in these classes.

Speakers of Portuguese

The most significant period of migration from Portugal to Britain was during the 1960s. Individuals and families came in search of work here, some as a result of economic hardship in Madeira. The mainland Portuguese, however, came mostly to earn enough for the extras which their salaries in Portugal could not buy − land, a house, a car, etc. The number of people of Portuguese origin living in Britain at the time of our Survey was estimated to be over 30,000, the Portuguese-born in the 1981 Census amounting to nearly 16,000.

The date of the main period of migration means that this population was predominantly middle-aged by 1981. The demographic profile of the ALUS respondents and their households given in Figure 2.9 bear this out. The household members of Portuguese-speaking respondents in London are concentrated in the 31-55 years age groups, with relatively few children in the households. The children that do appear are concentrated in the 16-20 age group. Amongst the older people there are more women than men, but otherwise there are approximately equal numbers. Younger men of 16-25 are under-represented as respondents, and in fact interviewers field reports made clear that although Portuguese speakers in this age group do exist, they were very rarely found at home, perhaps because of their often long and unsocial hours of work.

About two-thirds of Portuguese speakers in England are based in the Greater London Area, with smaller numbers in towns to the west of London, in the North of England and in some holiday resort areas. Outside London the most important settlement has been in Jersey and

Figure 2.9 Portuguese speakers in London

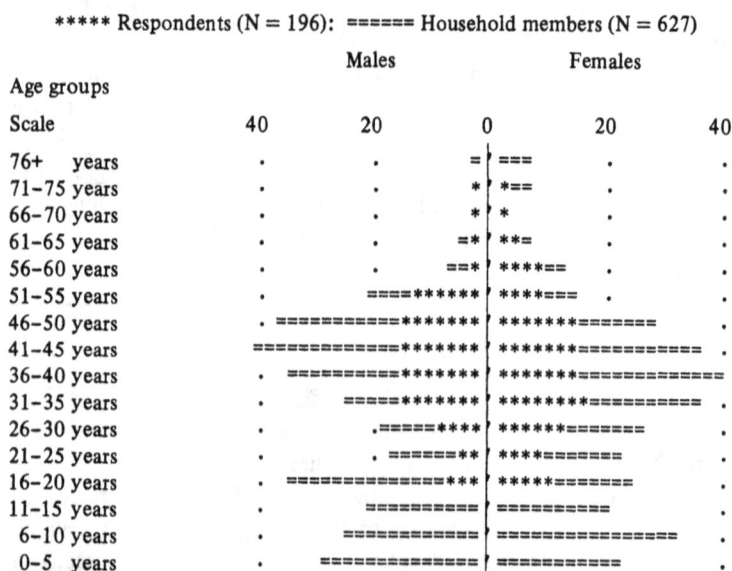

```
***** Respondents (N = 196):   ====== Household members (N = 627)
                            Males                    Females
Age groups
Scale         40        20         0        20        40
76+   years    .         .        =| ===      .         .
71-75 years    .         .        *| *==      .         .
66-70 years    .         .        *| *        .         .
61-65 years    .         .       =*| **=      .         .
56-60 years    .         .      ===| *****==   .         .
51-55 years    .    ====*******| *******===   .         .
46-50 years    . ============*******| *******========    .
41-45 years =============*******| *******============  .
36-40 years  . ==========*******| *******==============
31-35 years    . ====*******| ********============  .
26-30 years    .  .====*====**| *****====*====
21-25 years    .   . =======**| ***========
16-20 years    . ==============***| *****=========
11-15 years    .     ==========| ==========    .
 6-10 years    .    ===========| ===============
 0-5  years    .     ===========| ===========    .
```

Guernsey, with over 2,500 permanent residents, mainly from the island of Madeira. There is also an estimated seasonal migration of up to 3,000 workers coming in every year to the Channel Islands between March and October. Until the mid-1960s there was a preponderance of women in this migrant labour force. Some found work in hotels in London's West End or in resort areas, but the majority went into hospital and domestic services as cleaners, cooks and maids. By the mid-1970s the male-female ratio had evened out, but the pattern of employment remained the same. A survey carried out by the Portuguese Consulate in 1976 found that 55 per cent of Portuguese men worked in the hotel and catering industries – as waiters, porters and barmen – and in hospital and domestic work – as porters, janitors, cleaners and chauffeurs; 66 per cent of women were still also employed in these sectors. In the late 1970s the number of arrivals dropped significantly, because far fewer work permits have been granted since 1975.

Since workers in the hotel and catering industry only had an average weekly wage of around £70 in 1980, they were often forced to find additional employment on a shift work basis to supplement their income. This left little time for meeting people outside their own community, or for learning English outside the workplace. Most Portuguese workers are in Britain to save money to send back to Portugal, and many aspire to return home to buy a house or some land. Portuguese banks offer attractive tax-free interest rates, and benefit considerably from handling remittances sent back by workers in Britain, France and elsewhere.

Ties within the Portuguese minority in Britain are very close, especially in London districts such as Ladbroke Grove and Camden Town. Local social gatherings and music festivals are organised by about half a dozen Portuguese associations. The Portuguese Catholic church is also involved in social and welfare activities, as are the various voluntary associations and community groups.

Language and education are central concerns for parents in Portuguese-speaking families in Britain. In the case of some rural migrants they are seen as particularly important because they have had few educational opportunities themselves. Many therefore send their children to language classes organised by the Portuguese Consulate, and in 1979 there were approximately 700 children enrolled in these classes. Parents also make frequent visits to Portugal with their children, and some children are left in Portugal with relatives to consolidate or complete their education in Portuguese.

The Portuguese language

Portuguese like Italian, developed out of the Vulgar Latin of the late Roman Empire, Portugal being situated at the western edge of the Romance dialect continuum. And like Spanish, Portuguese was heavily influenced by the Arabic of the Muslim settlers in the Iberian peninsula. By the twelfth century Portugal had become an independent kingdom, and the local variety of Romance became a national language. Linguistically it was very close to Galician, the regional variety of Spanish spoken in North-western Spain. Because of the political division of the Iberian peninsula, Galician is usually treated as a variety of Spanish. In any case, for educated speakers today, Portuguese is to some extent mutually intelligible with Spanish.

In the fifteenth and sixteenth centuries Portugal became the leading European sea power, and established trading stations and colonies throughout the world. As a result Portuguese came to be spoken in many parts of the world, and influenced many other languages with which it came into contact. Outside Portugal itself, the main centres where Portuguese is still spoken in the twentieth century are Brazil (with 125 million speakers), Mozambique, Angola and Guinea Bissau, with smaller outposts in the Atlantic Islands, Goa and East Asia. The Brazilian and metropolitan varieties of Portuguese are distinct to much the same degree as American and British English, and other local varieties also exist. However, for the Portuguese in Britain the Lisbon-based standard is accepted as the norm for educational purposes.

Speakers of Greek and Turkish

When discussing the migration history and distribution of speakers of Greek and Turkish in Britain, it is convenient to treat them together for some purposes. This is so, firstly, because most of the speakers of these two languages in Britain, in contrast to Germany or Scandinavia for example, have their family origins not in mainland Greece or Turkey, but in Cyprus. There are therefore many similarities in their cultural backgrounds, as well as in their situation in the United Kingdom. Secondly, the Census and other official statistics often provide information on a 'country of birth' basis, which offers no way of distinguishing between Greek-speaking Cypriots and Turkish-speaking Cypriots.

Cyprus became an independent republic within the British Commonwealth in 1960, having been under British control for less than a hundred years. This followed three centuries of Ottoman Turkish rule.

The population at the time of independence was just under 600,000, approximately four-fifths Greek-speaking, one-fifth Turkish-speaking, with smaller Armenian and Maronite communities and a substantial continuing British presence. It is generally thought that the proportions of Greek and Turkish speakers within the UK population correspond roughly to that ratio (Oakley, 1979; Anthias, 1983), but there are estimates for the total population of Cypriot origin, including British-born, which range from 100,000 (Oakley, 1979), to 170,000 (Anthias, 1983). Since the Cyprus-born residents alone in the 1981 British Census amounted to more than 82,000, it seems likely that the higher estimates are more accurate when the British-born are taken into account.

The settlement from Cyprus can be seen in three main stages (Alkan and Constantinides, 1982): a small pre–World War Two migration; the major migration between 1945 and 1962, followed by a sharp reduction after the 1962 Immigration Act; and the most recent major movement after the Turkish intervention in Cyprus of 1974. Both Greek and Turkish Cypriots have settled mostly in the Greater London area (about 70 per cent of the Cyprus-born in the 1981 Census), earlier in the boroughs of Camden, Islington and Hackney, more recently in Haringey and in Enfield, with smaller numbers south of the Thames. The timing of the main migration results in a population made up predominantly of the original migrants, now middle-aged, and their children, now in their teens and twenties. Figures 2.10 and 2.11 for our London respondents and their households bear this out.

The household members of Greek-speaking respondents appear to be concentrated in two age bands, between 41 and 55 years and between 11 and 25 years. Presumably the first group are the primary migrants of the early 1960s, and their, on average, slightly younger wives. The younger group must be their children, who for the most part were born and raised in London.

The household members of Turkish-speaking respondents in London are also concentrated in the 41–50 age groups, representing the migrants of the early 1960s, and in the 16–25 age groups. However, there are also sizeable numbers in their thirties and of younger children. Among people over the age of 50 men considerably outnumber women.

Oakley (1970) reported that in the early stages of migration in the 1950s and 1960s, Greek Cypriots were working in the service sector in catering, in hotels, in the clothing and shoe manufacturing industries, in hairdressing and in grocery retailing; Turkish Cypriots seem to have followed a similar pattern. The economic activities of Cypriot women in particular have changed quite radically since migration. In the villages

Figure 2.10 Greek speakers in London

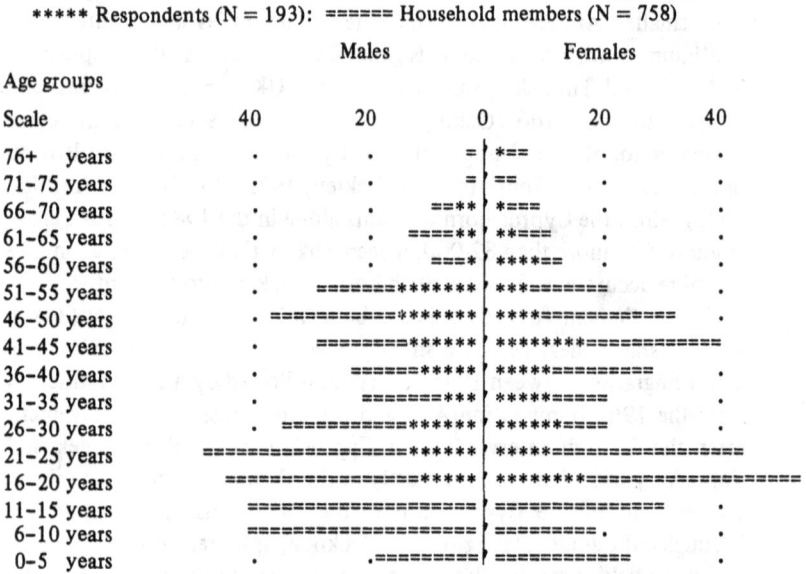

```
***** Respondents (N = 193):  ====== Household members (N = 758)
                        Males                Females
Age groups
Scale           40       20       0       20       40
76+   years      .        .      = ! *==      .        .
71-75 years      .        .      = ! ==       .        .
66-70 years      .        .   ===** ! *===    .        .
61-65 years      .        .  =====** ! **===  .        .
56-60 years      .        .    ===* ! *****==  .       .
51-55 years      .   =======*******! **========          .
46-50 years      . ============*******! ****===========   .
41-45 years      .   ==========*******! ********=============
36-40 years      .    ======******! ****==========     .
31-35 years      .    ========***! *****=====      .
26-30 years      .  ===========*******! *****=====      .
21-25 years   ==================*******! *****=================
16-20 years   ==================*****! ********================
11-15 years    =====================! ==============    .
6-10 years     ==================== ! ========= .        .
0-5   years      .    .=========! ============       .
```

Figure 2.11 Turkish speakers in London

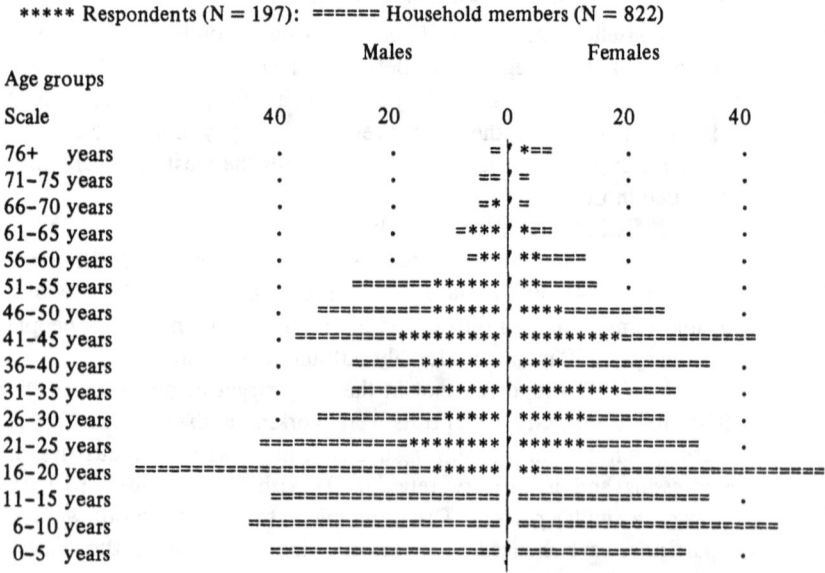

```
***** Respondents (N = 197):  ====== Household members (N = 822)
                        Males                Females
Age groups
Scale           40       20       0       20       40
76+   years      .        .      = ! *==      .        .
71-75 years      .        .      == ! =        .        .
66-70 years      .        .      =* ! =        .        .
61-65 years      .        .    =*** ! *==      .        .
56-60 years      .        .     =** ! **====    .        .
51-55 years      .    =========*******! **=====    .       .
46-50 years      .   ===========*******! ****=========   .
41-45 years      . ==========*********! ********=============
36-40 years      .    ======*******! ****==============    .
31-35 years      .    =========*****! *********=====
26-30 years      .  ==============*****! ******======    .
21-25 years    ===========*********! ******==========    .
16-20 years   =========================*****! *==================
11-15 years     ==================== ! ============== .
6-10 years     ==================== ! ===================
0-5   years      ================== ! ==============      .
```

of Cyprus, most women's work was confined to the household and fields, whereas in Britain a substantial number are employed in the clothing industry, either as machinists in small family-run factories, or as outworkers sewing clothes at home, at piece-work rates. Anthias (1983) describes more recent developments in the garment trade. She indicates that it is difficult to assess the size of this workforce, as female labour is for the most part unregistered.

From 1967 onwards, many more Cypriot men became self-employed and diversified into different types of small businesses – estate agencies, small building firms, travel agencies; others worked as interior decorators or painters (Leeuwenberg, 1979). These small businesses often provide goods and services primarily for other Cypriots (Constantinides, 1977), but there are still comparatively few Cypriots in professional occupations such as teachers, social workers, lawyers, accountants and architects.

The long hours of work involved in running small businesses, in sewing at home, or in working in a restaurant leave little time for leisure. For most Greek-speaking families, like many other members of linguistic minorities in England, what leisure time there is may be spent visiting relatives or close friends.

Religious observance among the Greek Cypriots is associated with Greek Orthodox Christianity, and the Orthodox church in Britain has long been under the control of the church in mainland Greece. The clergy are still largely from mainland Greece, although there are now some Cypriot priests in London.

Over the years a range of very different community organisations, welfare agencies, and political associations have emerged within the Greek-speaking minority in the London area. Some of the voluntary associations were formed specifically to cater for the needs of Greek Cypriot children growing up in Britain, notably the Greek Parents Association, started in the 1950s to arrange provision for the teaching of Greek to children. Today this organisation runs in the region of 100 classes throughout the North London area. Support for the teaching of Greek also comes from the Cyprus High Commission, the Greek Orthodox church and in some instances from the LEAs.

There is an equivalent range of Turkish Cypriot associations in London, although Muslim organisations do not appear to play a major role. Within the Inner London boroughs, the language censuses of ILEA schoolchildren carried out in 1981 and 1983 have shown that among the minority languages only Bengali has more speakers than Turkish. This fact is reflected in a growing interest and activity in the educational field.

The language background

Both before and after Cyprus became independent in 1960, the interdependence of Greek and Turkish speakers in Cyprus was hardly reflected in the patterns of schooling and of language-learning. Members of the minority Turkish community were much more likely to know Greek than Greeks were to know Turkish, of course, given the 4:1 ratio of Greeks to Turks on the island as a whole. Knowledge of English at this stage was confined mostly to the minority in direct contact with the colonial administration, and latterly with the British armed forces. The 1960 Independence Constitution, however, set up two separate 'communal chambers', which among other functions controlled educational provision, but neither of the new schools systems set up by the communal chambers included the teaching of the other main island language in their curricula. There was, in fact, considerable emphasis on the respective national links with, and cultures of, mainland Greece and Turkey. The continuing cultural and linguistic separation is thought by some to have contributed to the eventual de facto partition of the island in 1974: it certainly led to a greater use of English for intercommunal contacts, by the younger generation at least. People of Greek and Turkish Cypriot origin continued their economic interdependence in Britain (Ladbury, 1977). The quite widespread knowledge of Greek among Turkish speakers in London (see Table 5.1) is, however, probably more a reflection of the older Cyprus-based pattern of relationships than of the situation in London in the 1970s and 1980s.

Not surprisingly, given their geographical and latterly political separation from the 'mother countries', and their different history of language contacts, the varieties of both Greek and Turkish spoken in Cyprus, and subsequently in Britain by those of Cypriot origin, are significantly different from the mainland standard languages. And, as is usual in such situations, other people's perceptions of the inferiority of the non-standard variety influence the speakers' own assessment of it. For example, it is reported that Turkish Cypriots sometimes admire the 'clean' pronunciation of mainlanders from Istanbul or Ankara, in contrast to their own speech (Ladbury, 1977).

The Turkish language

The related languages referred to by linguists as the 'Turkic' group are spoken by around 100 million people in the world, most of them living in an arc stretching from the Balkans through Soviet Central Asia to the borders of China. These languages share a very similar agglutinative structure, and are to some extent mutually intelligible. About 50 million speak a Turkish whose standard form is based on the speech of the educated elite of Western Turkey.

Until the break-up of the Ottoman Empire after World War One, Turkish was written using the Arabic script, and Persian and Arabic lexical content was also very high. However, as part of Ataturk's westernising reforms in the 1920s, there was a switch to a modified Roman alphabet for written Turkish, and moves were made to replace non-Turkish loan-words with Turkic equivalents – a 'purification' process which has apparently recently been stepped up again (CILT, 1983).

These processes are in part simply the linguistic reflection of the move to a more narrowly nationalistic position after the end of the multilingual and multinational Ottoman period. But they are also part of a process of linguistic democratisation, an attempt to create a written standard language more easily accessible to less educated people. The gap between the language of the sophisticated Istanbul elite and that of the Anatolian peasant-farmers was very considerable by the late Ottoman period: Ataturk's reforms went some way to closing it.

The Greek language

The sociolinguistic history of Modern Greek has some interesting parallels with that of its near non-Indo-European neighbour, Turkish. Modern Greek is of course the descendant of Classical Greek, through New Testament Koiné and Byzantine Greek. It is now spoken by some 12 to 13 million people, 10 million of them in Greece itself, another half-million in Cyprus.

As part of the struggle to establish a pan-Hellenic identity after freeing itself from Ottoman rule in the early nineteenth century, katharevousa ('purified') Greek was created, and adopted by the newly independent kingdom as the medium for all official writing and public speaking. Katharevousa was a consciously archaising and literary form of Greek, drawing heavily on the classical language in lexis and grammar, as well as in the writing system. There was, and was intended to be, some distance between this form of Greek and the various demotic ('popular') varieties used in different parts of the Greek-speaking world – which until the early 1920s included quite extensive settlements in Anatolia. Katharevousa and demotic were in fact one of Ferguson's classic cases of diglossia (Ferguson, 1959).

But even before the end of the nineteenth century, the unbroken tradition of writing poetry in demotic had been extended to literary prose. The language question became a central political issue, with support for demotic associated with liberal and modernising ideologies, for katharevousa with conservative and nationalistic forces. This was demonstrated most clearly, perhaps, during the period of right-wing military rule from 1967 to 1974, when katharevousa was reinstated by military decree to its exclusive official status, only to lose that position again after the restoration of democracy. Language legislation in recent years has seen the adoption of Athenian demotic as the basis for a national written and spoken standard.

A recent article on the role of demotic quotes a student leader's denunciation of katharevousa as 'the old-fashioned medium of an educated elite . . . archaic and tediously demanding'. This same critic also speaks of its 'freakish diction . . . antiquated rhetorical devices and . . . insufferable verbosity', and demands more use of 'the popular Greek idiom, which [can be] handle[d] and comprehend[ed] without having to sweat over syntax and grammar books' (Dimitropoulos, 1983).

Cypriot Greek has incorporated many features as a result of the very extensive contact with a series of other languages during its varied history – in particular with French and Italian during a period of Frankish rule, and with English during its most recent colonial period. However, although there are some lexical and phonological differences in the dialect used informally by many speakers with Cypriot connections, like their fellow-Hellenes in Greece itself they now look to Athenian demotic Greek as their standard language.

The Eastern European linguistic minorities in England

Speakers of Polish

Nearly a third of all ethnic Poles live outside Poland (Davies, 1981), and there are Polish institutions in almost thirty countries on all continents (Kalendarz Dziennika Polskiego, 1984). The 6½ million Polish-Americans are not only the largest single Polish community abroad, but also one of the largest ethnic minorities of the USA (Davies, 1981). Although it is numerically not very large in comparison, the Polish minority in Britain, estimated at between 100,000 and 150,000, has become the political centre of worldwide Polish emigration. A historical background sketch should make clear why this is so.

The Nazi-Soviet Pact of August 1939 contained a secret protocol which foreshadowed the territorial division of Poland into German and Soviet 'spheres of influence'. The German invasion of Poland on 1 September 1939 led to the British and French declaration of war on Germany two days later, which as far as the fate of Poland was concerned was little more than a diplomatic gesture. The Soviet invasion on 17 September hastened the collapse of Polish resistance and prevented many Polish units from escaping abroad (Ciechanowski, 1980). However, before the Soviets sealed Poland's southern borders tens of thousands of military and civilian Poles escaped, and 80,000 of them continued the fight against the Germans under French command. After the collapse of France 27,000 Polish military personnel and 3,000 diplomatic staff arrived in Britain, and the First Polish Corps under British command was formed. 'In the Battle of Britain 1940, Polish pilots accounted for some 15 per cent of enemy losses, thus contributing significantly to the salvation of Great Britain' (Davies, 1981).

Meanwhile, in eastern Poland, the USSR carried out massive forced deportations of the population to concentration camps, to hard labour camps or into penal exile, 'simply because the Polish nation was seen as the inveterate enemy of its Russian masters. . . . By the time that the Amnesty was granted in 1941 (for crimes that had not been committed), almost half of the one-and-a-half million Poles deported in the previous years were already dead' (Davies, 1981).

By June 1940 the Polish Government set up in France had transferred to London. The Allied Powers had given it full official recognition, but were unwilling publicly to recognise the Soviet role in the outbreak of the war and the destruction of Poland. Following the German invasion of the USSR in 1941, the Soviet leaders established diplomatic relations with the Polish Government in London. 'The USSR stated its readiness to form a Polish army in Russia [and] to grant an Amnesty to all Polish internees. . . . The suspension of blatant injustices was presented to the world as a magnanimous Soviet "concession"' (Davies, 1981). General Anders, freshly released from Lubianka prison in Moscow, was given the task of creating from the released internees the Polish Army in the East. The Polish Army did not receive promised support and supplies, and when the Soviets had withheld its rations, 100,000 troops of Anders's army were allowed to evacuate to the Middle East, taking with them also some 35,000 Polish women and children (Anders, 1949; Davies, 1981). The Second Polish Corps of the British Eighth Army was eventually formed from those evacuees, and by the spring of 1944 there were nearly 200,000 Poles fighting with the British forces.

In April 1943 the Soviets broke off diplomatic relations with the Polish Government in London, and created the 'Union of Polish Patriots' on Soviet territory. This pro-Soviet group in July 1944 became the forerunner of the 'Polish Committee of National Liberation' and later of the Provisional Government. Though as yet unrecognised by the British and the Americans, it was de facto taking over the administration of Polish territory as it was liberated from the Germans. Between 1939 and 1945 the Polish borders, which had often been disputed before, were moved bodily westward (see Map 2.3), essentially as a deliberate Soviet policy (Davies, 1981).

At the end of the war the Western Powers withdrew their recognition of the Polish Government in London. However, the Polish corps of the British Army was not forced to return to Soviet-dominated Poland or to the eastern Polish provinces now incorporated into the Soviet Union.

Of the 250,000 members of the Polish forces in the West in 1945, about 200,000 came to Britain between 1945 and 1947 (Czaykowski and Sulik, 1961). Not all of those settled permanently in Britain. A certain number, in spite of everything, went back to Poland, others re-emigrated to the USA, Canada or Australia. Of those who stayed 114,000 joined the Polish Resettlement Corps, created in 1947 to facilitate the settlement of Poles and to channel help to them in matters of education, employment and housing.

Two other groups arrived with the Polish units – 2,000 survivors of the German concentration camps and over 21,000 prisoners-of-war, among them units of the Home Army taken prisoner after the Warsaw uprising of 1944. The ex-military personnel were joined by about 33,000 civilians, family members of the military personnel, and by about 14,000 European Voluntary Workers of Polish nationality, from the Displaced Persons' Camps in Germany. Most of the early post-war settlement took place in the areas where the different units of the Polish forces had been stationed during the war. For those who arrived later there were more than forty Polish Resettlement Corps camps, and a number of European Voluntary Workers' hostels. They were organised throughout Britain, where accommodation was available and labour needed.

By 1960 almost all the camps had been closed down, and by 1976 there remained only one, owned and run by a Polish organisation (Patterson, 1977). In fact, the regional settlement patterns had more or less crystallised by 1961, with London as by far the largest Polish settlement, numbering perhaps 30,000 to 35,000. Birmingham and Manchester had   some 4,000-5,000 each, Bradford about 3,000.

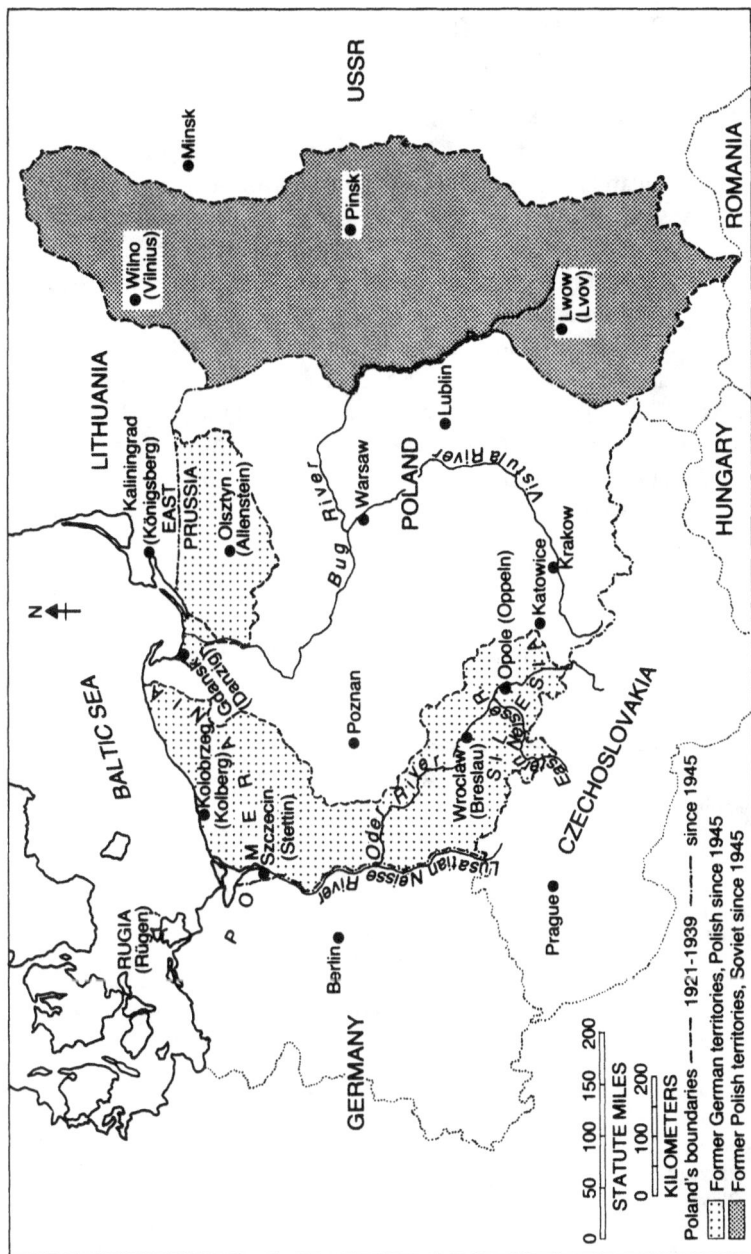

Map 2.3 Poland's boundaries before and after World War II

Wolverhampton, Leeds, Nottingham, Sheffield, Coventry, Leicester and Slough each had between 1,500 and 3,000. 'By 1976 the main residential changes were occurring inside and not between settlements' (Patterson, 1977).

The imbalance in the ratio of males and females among arrivals in the 1940s was acute: until 1955 females constituted around 25 per cent of the population. From 1956, after an improvement in East-West relations, some relatives were allowed to join their menfolk in Britain, and a small but constant trickle of 'new immigrants' from Poland started, at least three-quarters of them female. This resulted in a slight increase in the proportion of females among Poles in Britain, the 1961 Census giving their proportion as 31 per cent (unequal death rates among males and females has also contributed to the imbalance). Between 1950 and 1971, according to the 1971 Census, about 13,500 people born in Poland became resident in this country, and from 1972 to 1975 another 2,600 (mostly females) settled in Britain. This later influx has to some degree improved the earlier sex ratio imbalance, but it has not been entirely eliminated.

Figure 2.12.a Polish speakers in Coventry

```
***** Respondents (N = 168):  ====== Household members (N = 471)
                              Males                    Females
Age groups
Scale          40        20        0        20        40

76+    years    .         .       =*   *=        .         .
71-75 years     .         .        *   *=        .         .
66-70 years     .         .  =*****   *====       .         .
61-65 years     .    ====*******   *=            .         .
56-60 years  ======= ***************   ***=============      .
51-55 years    ===========********** ********=============
46-50 years     .         .  ====** ****=================
41-45 years     .         .   ==*  **======    .         .
36-40 years     .         .   =*   ****==    .         .
31-35 years     .         .    *   *=       .         .
26-30 years     .         .  ===***** *****===    .         .
21-25 years     .         .  ======** **=====    .         .
16-20 years     .    ===========**** ****=============    .
11-15 years     .         .  ======== ===========
6-10 years      .         .   ===== ====      .         .
0-5   years     .         .    ==   ==       .         .
```

Figure 2.12.b Polish speakers in Bradford

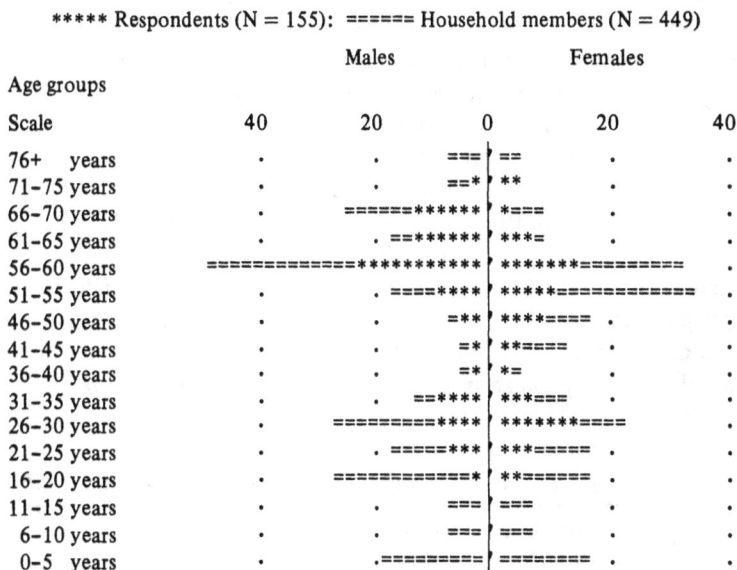

```
***** Respondents (N = 155):  ====== Household members (N = 449)
                              Males              Females
Age groups
Scale          40        20         0        20        40

76+   years     .         .       === | ==      .         .
71-75 years     .         .       ==* | **      .         .
66-70 years     .     ======****** | *===        .         .
61-65 years     .         . ==******* | ***=      .         .
56-60 years  ===============********** | ******=========     .
51-55 years     .         . ====**** | *****=============  .
46-50 years     .         .   =** | ****=====  .         .
41-45 years     .         .    =* | **=====    .         .
36-40 years     .         .    =* | *=         .         .
31-35 years     .         .  ==**** | ***=====   .         .
26-30 years     .     ==========**** | *******====   .
21-25 years     .         . =====*** | ***=====  .      .
16-20 years     .     =============* | **=====  .      .
11-15 years     .         .     === | ===       .         .
 6-10 years     .         .     === | ===       .         .
 0-5  years     .         .=========| ========  .         .
```

These demographic patterns appear clearly among the respondents and their households for our Adult Language Use Survey in Coventry and Bradford. The largest number of people in both cases are aged over 50, with the men being on average slightly older than the women of their generation. In Coventry the Polish speakers appear to be younger than those in Bradford by five years or so on average. There is scarcely anyone in the mid to late thirties age group. The bulge in the 16–30 age group represents the children of the migrants and refugees of the late 1940s, while there are signs in Bradford at least of increasing numbers of under-fives (the third generation).

There are no comprehensive statistics available on the occupational structure of the Poles who settled, but data referring to 84,000 members of the Polish Resettlement Corps tell us that more than a fifth of them were in various non-manual occupations. Of those in manual occupations the biggest group (9,000) was employed in the building industry, 8,200 in agriculture and 7,300 in mining (Czaykowski and Sulik, 1961). Of professionals who qualified in Poland it was mostly doctors, dentists, pharmacists and engineers who were practising in Britain by the end of the 1950s. By 1958 there were 600 Polish doctors and 80 dentists, and about 2,000 engineers and technicians. For other professions, such as lawyers and architects, requalification was more difficult, but a certain number did succeed. According to the terms of the resettlement over 10,000 younger Poles received grants for higher or technical education in Britain between 1947 and 1960. The majority of the older pre-war Polish intelligentsia became occupationally declassed, employed in manual or semi-manual jobs or setting up small businesses. Many compensated for this loss of status by involvement in the social and political organisations of the Polish community (Patterson, 1977).

According to data from the 1966 Census, 65 per cent of Polish-born people in Britain were economically active, which was higher than for immigrants of all nationalities (60 per cent) and higher than for the total population of Britain (47 per cent). The occupational status in 1966 of persons born in Poland who were in employment as compared with the British population as a whole is shown in Table 2.1 (Castles and Kosack, 1973).

Table 2.1 Occupational status of people in employment in Britain, 1966

Occupational Status	Polish-born men N = 69,000	Polish-born women N = 16,000	All men N = 15,574,000	All women N = 8,595,000
Non-manual	21.5%	31.8%	32.3%	51.9%
Manual	77.7%	67.2%	65.6%	47.1%

According to statistics of the Polish Resettlement Corps from 1948, the religion of nearly 86 per cent of Poles seeking settlement in Britain was Roman Catholic, 4 per cent Greek Catholic, 4 per cent Greek Orthodox, 4 per cent Protestant and almost 2 per cent Jewish. This differs substantially from the picture in pre-war Poland itself, where only 65 per cent were Roman Catholic, 10.5 per cent were Greek Catholic, 12 per cent Greek Orthodox, 2.5 per cent Protestant and 10 per cent Jewish (Patterson, 1977). The way in which the Second Polish Corps was created from the released Soviet internees was one of the factors responsible for this difference. 'Soviet officials insisted on treating all Polish citizens of Ukrainian, Byelorussian, Lithuanian or Jewish nationality as if they were Soviet subjects' (Davies, 1981), meaning that they did not benefit from the 'magnanimous Amnesty'. The 1984 *Polish Daily*'s Diary lists addresses of fifty-one Polish Parish Houses, or Polish Catholic Centres as many of them are called, in forty-four different towns and cities of Britain, including eight in London. One hundred and fourteen Catholic priests are listed. Almost a hundred Polish organisations of every description operate in Britain. The majority of them belong to the Federation of Poles in Great Britain, which to a certain extent co-ordinates their activities. The largest and most influential is the Polish Ex-Combatants Association (Stowarzyszenie Polskich Kombatantow, SPK), a world-wide organisation with branches in twenty-four countries of the Western World:

> In Britain and elsewhere the SPK has for thirty years fulfilled a wide and expanding variety of functions. As well as preserving the feeling of war-time comradeship and purpose, it provides financial and legal assistance, cultural facilities and social activities for its members. Since about 1970 the SPK has increasingly assumed the stance of a permanent Polish exile institution in relation not only to the exile community but to Poland itself. The report presented at the Tenth SPK World Congress in London in November 1976 referred to the resurgent opposition in Poland by workers, intellectuals, and the Church to the Communist regime. It also stressed the need for the SPK and the whole political *emigracja* [i.e. all those who had emigrated for political rather than economic reasons] to serve their countrymen at home with material assistance and continuing ideological support for national independence and Polish culture. (Patterson, 1977)

An increasingly important part of the activities of SPK is providing assistance to local branches for the running of Polish Saturday Schools, in co-operation with the Polish Educational Society Abroad, and frequently also with local Polish Parishes. In 1975 there were eighty-eight Polish Saturday Schools throughout Britain, teaching pupils Polish language up to 'O' and some even to 'A' level, and also Polish history, geography and culture. The tradition of these schools goes back to 1943, when the Polish army in the Middle East organised classes for youngsters evacuated from the USSR with Anders's army. The SPK also promotes and assists financially the Polish Scout and Guide movement, and the Association of Polish Sports Clubs.

The large modern headquarters of the Polish Social and Cultural Association, opened in 1974 in Hammersmith, London, houses major exile voluntary organisations, and educational and cultural ventures. It includes the Polish Library, with 60,000 volumes in Polish and another 40,000 in other languages, and is the showpiece of the Polish community in Britain.

The Polish language

The Polish language belongs to the western branch of the Slavic subgroup of the Indo-European family of languages. It is written in the Roman alphabet, not using 'q' or 'v' except in words of foreign origin, but employs several diacritics and two-consonant combinations to give a very consistent sound–symbol relationship.

Polish is the mother tongue of almost 35 million people in Poland and is also spoken by substantial numbers of Polish-Americans, in Canada, in Australia, in the USSR and in many countries in Western Europe and Latin America. It is closely related to the other West Slavic languages, Czech and Slovak, and more distantly to Slavic languages such as Russian, Ukrainian and Serbo-Croat. The large number of lexical borrowings from languages such as German, French, Italian and English, are evidence of the strong cultural ties with Western Europe.

Speakers of Ukrainian

Approximately 30,000 Ukrainians settled in Britain after World War Two. Between the world wars the eastern part of the Ukraine formed the Ukrainian Soviet Socialist Republic, which had a total population of some 25 million. The western Ukraine, whose inhabitants included nearly 5 million Ukrainians, was then part of the Polish Republic (see Map 2.3).

Comparatively tolerant government in the Soviet Ukraine in the 1920s gave way in the 1930s to brutal collectivisation of agriculture and nationality purges, which led to millions being deported to Siberia (Pearson, 1983). The oppressive nature of the Soviet regime made almost any change seem better, and so the German invasion of 1941 was initially welcomed by most of the Ukrainian population. German army units made up of Ukrainians, like the 'Nightingale' and 'Roland' batallions, were formed, and at least 200,000 Ukrainians joined the SS. Yet the Nazis did not want equal partners, they wanted slaves: millions of Ukrainians were transported to Germany itself to serve as industrial and agricultural workers, thereby releasing Germans for the Russian front. By 1944 two-thirds of all 'Eastern Workers' in Germany were Ukrainians, and at the end of the war many found themselves overtaken by the Allied forces.

Undoubtedly, some of these Ukrainians were among the more than 5 million Soviet nationals repatriated to the Soviet Union by the end of September 1945. Those who were not shot dead on arrival on Soviet

territory, were sent straight to Siberia (Tolstoy, 1977; Tolstoy, 1981).
More than 2 million of these people were repatriated from German,
Austrian and Czechoslovak territory in the US and British zones of
occupation, and a further quarter of a million from the rest of Western
Europe and Scandinavia (Proudfoot, 1956). It can be assumed that in
general most Ukrainians had no wish to be repatriated, but although in
principle the repatriation was not supposed to be forced, few were
given any real choice.

Of those who successfully asserted that they were not Soviet
nationals, almost 20,500 Ukrainians from the Displaced Persons' Camps,
23 per cent of them women, were admitted to Britain between 1947
and 1950 as European Voluntary Workers. In addition 8,400 Ukrainian
prisoners-of-war were brought to Britain from Italy in 1947, and by the
end of 1948 had been given civilian status as European Voluntary
Workers (Isaac, 1954). The conditions of entry as European Voluntary
Workers limited the kind of employment that could be undertaken, at
least for three years after arrival. For men it was agriculture (45 per
cent), coal-mining (17 per cent) and domestic service (8 per cent), for
women domestic service (40 per cent) and the textile industry (27 per
cent cotton and 15 per cent woollen industry).

In the mid-1950s up to half of the Ukrainians in Britain were still
living in various kinds of hostels, a high proportion of them engaged
in agricultural work. The East Midlands and the North of England
accounted for nearly half, with the rest spread in smaller numbers
through the rest of the country.

The household members of Ukrainian-speaking respondents in
Coventry have a similar demographic profile to the Polish speakers,
with most of them being over 50, women of that generation being on
average five or more years younger, and their children mainly in the
16-25 age group. Again this might be expected, given the timing and
nature of migration in the late 1940s.

The Ukrainian language

Ukrainian is one of the East Slavic languages, closely related to Russian
and Byelorussian in particular, and more distantly to other Slavic
languages such as Polish and Serbo-Croat. It is written in an alphabet
which draws on both Roman and Cyrillic traditions. There are some
35 million speakers of Ukrainian, mostly in the Soviet Union, but with
at least half a million in North America and smaller numbers elsewhere,
including Britain. Many of the older British Ukrainians were born in

Figure 2.13 *Ukrainian speakers in Coventry*

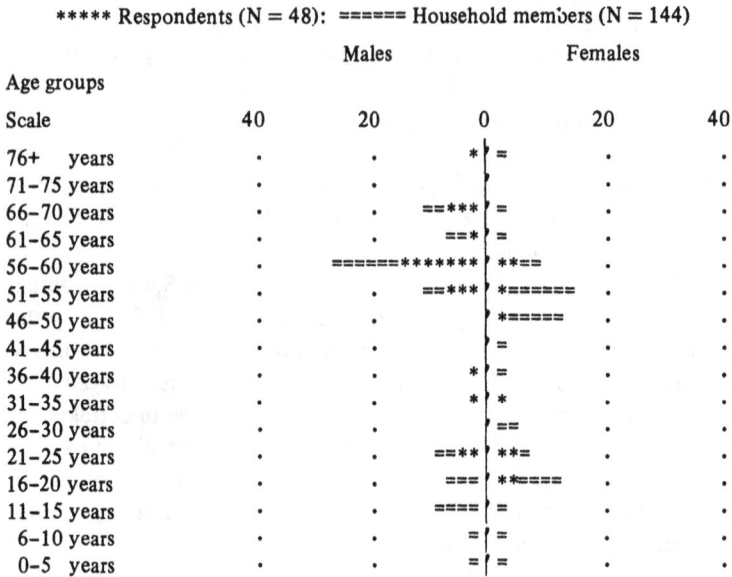

***** Respondents (N = 48): ====== Household members (N = 144)

	Males			Females	
Age groups					
Scale	40	20	0	20	40
76+ years	·	·	* =	·	·
71–75 years	·	·		·	·
66–70 years	·	·	==*** =	·	·
61–65 years	·	·	==* =	·	·
56–60 years	·	======*******	**==	·	·
51–55 years	·	·	==*** *=======	·	·
46–50 years	·	·	*=====	·	·
41–45 years	·	·	=	·	·
36–40 years	·	·	* =	·	·
31–35 years	·	·	* *	·	·
26–30 years	·	·	==	·	·
21–25 years	·	·	==** **=	·	·
16–20 years	·	·	=== **====	·	·
11–15 years	·	·	==== =	·	·
6–10 years	·	·	= =	·	·
0–5 years	·	·	= =	·	·

territory which was then part of Poland, and have some knowledge of Polish: some even use Polish spelling conventions for their names.

The context of three cities

The three cities in which LMP carried out most of its work exemplify the situation of linguistic minorities throughout the country. There are common factors in the economic and social settings in Coventry, Bradford and London, yet there are also local differences which make each city unique for its mixture of languages, and for the housing, employment and educational resources available to the people living there.

The pattern of settlement of all the recent linguistic minorities has largely been determined at the regional level by employment opportunities. The result has been that they have been concentrated to a large extent in unskilled work in the heavy industrial sector in the West Midlands, and in the declining textile industry in West Yorkshire and Lancashire. In London and the South East, employment is in a wider range of industries, notably the clothing trade in North and East London in the case of Bengali, Turkish and Greek speakers, the retail trade in small shops in the case of the Gujerati speakers, and various industrial and service sectors for speakers of other languages.

These patterns have been greatly influenced by structural changes in industry and by the pressures of local labour markets, coupled with institutionalised discriminatory practices which have tended to exclude minorities from many of the better jobs. In most cases the process of chain migration and the practice of recruitment by personal recommendation has further increased the level of segregation on the shop floor (Brooks and Singh, 1979). For members of many minorities an alternative route to 'prosperity' in the face of rising unemployment is the establishment of small businesses. Thus the 'ethnic sector' of local economies has developed rapidly, often drawing on contacts and resources within the minority for financial backing and material supplies, and in many cases also for labour and custom.

However, the distribution of languages at the neighbourhood level within each city seems to be related much more closely to housing patterns. With certain exceptions families of recent migrants are rarely to be found in the public rented sector of the housing market, but have become established as owner-occupiers in the central areas of cities, where property is relatively cheap and close to major workplaces. The details of the employment, housing and social situations of minorities vary considerably from city to city, and to illustrate this we shall look at our three cities in more detail.

Coventry

Coventry in 1981 had a population of 310,000, and was administered as a Metropolitan District within the West Midlands Metropolitan County. Coventry developed as an industrial town during the late nineteenth and early twentieth centuries, with engineering, textiles and other manufacturing as the key industries. During the Second World War the city centre was devastated by German bombs, but a period of prosperity in the 1950s and 1960s enabled massive redevelopment and rebuilding to take place. The modern shopping centre, the cathedral, the ring road, and a number of modern public buildings in the city centre all date from this period. There are modern housing estates both on the outskirts of the city and in some of the inner areas. However, many of the inner residential areas to the north and east of the city centre consist of the original terraced housing built at the turn of the century.

The prosperity of Coventry and the rest of the West Midlands region in the immediate post-war years was built to a large extent on the development of the vehicle manufacturing industry and the associated engineering factories. British Leyland and Talbot both have large works in the city, as do such components firms as Lucas. The other major employers are GEC in electrical engineering and Courtaulds in textiles, and there are also many smaller firms. During the post-war years the work conditions and wage levels offered in expanding industries led to the increasing use of migrant labour to fill the less desirable jobs, and it is from this period that most of the settlements of linguistic minorities in the city date. During the late 1970s and early 1980s the recession hit the motor industry particularly badly, and the rates of unemployment in the West Midlands generally by the time of writing had reached nearly 20 per cent. In Coventry itself 17 per cent of the economically active males aged over 16 were described in the 1981 Census as 'seeking work'.

The 1981 Census also showed that 276,000 out of Coventry's total population of 310,000 were born in the UK, 12,600 in the Irish Republic, 9,800 in India, 1,600 in Pakistan, 400 in Bangladesh, 2,700 in East Africa, 2,000 in the Caribbean, about 500 in Commonwealth countries in the Far East and about 1,000 in the rest of the Commonwealth. A further 5,300 were born elsewhere overseas. Country-by-country breakdowns were not available for Europe from the 1981 Census, but the 1971 Census recorded 1,255 born in Poland and 731 in Italy. In 1981 the number of people living in households where the head of household was born in the New Commonwealth and Pakistan, a figure which includes many British-born children of migrant parents, was nearly 30,000: this figure, of course, does not include the European linguistic minorities mentioned earlier.

The first of the major linguistic minorities to settle in Coventry in the post-war period were the Polish and Ukrainian speakers who arrived in the late 1940s and early 1950s. They came to Coventry because of the disruption caused in Eastern Europe by the Second World War, either as political refugees, servicemen demobilised from the Free Polish forces who had served in campaigns in the Middle East and Italy, or under the European Voluntary Workers scheme. They found work in a number of local industries at a time when the local economy was expanding, under work and wage conditions hardly acceptable to indigenous workers. By the end of the 1950s they had established a number of institutions like the Polish Parish, the Polish School, two Polish clubs, the Ukrainian Association and the Ukrainian Church. Italian migration took place at about the same time, and among the first to arrive were the single women who were recruited to work at the Courtaulds factory. A number of war-brides also settled in the Coventry area with their English, Irish or Polish husbands, and even today there are probably more Italian women than men in the older first generation of migrants. By the early 1980s some Italians in Coventry were self-employed, for example in catering, hairdressing or tailoring, although the majority remain in manufacturing industry.

By the late 1950s, migrants from different parts of South Asia and the Caribbean began to settle in Coventry, finding work in the less skilled jobs in heavy industry and to some extent in transport services. In the early 1970s there was an important addition to the South Asian populations when considerable numbers arrived from East Africa. A small number of Chinese also arrived and settled in the 1960s and 1970s to work in catering, most of them from Hong Kong.

Sikh Panjabi speakers of Indian origin (essentially our 'Panjabi(G)' category: see p. 47) formed the largest linguistic minority in the city by the 1980s. The total numbers were approximately 8,000 adults and 4,200 school-age children, according to the estimates we made by using distinctive Sikh names on the electoral registers and data from our own 1981 Schools Language Survey (see LMP/LINC, 1983; and Chapter 8). A small proportion of these people had come to England from East Africa rather than direct from India. There was also a sizeable number of Muslim Panjabi speakers of Pakistani origin (our 'Panjabi(U)' category: see p. 45), perhaps 1,000–1,500 adults and 500 school-age children. Smaller numbers of Hindu Panjabi speakers and Hindi speakers who may also originate from the Panjab were also to be found: for example in our Schools Language Survey nearly 200 children said they spoke Hindi at home. There was a population of Gujerati speakers including roughly 3,000 adults and 1,200 school-age children, of whom over half (58 per cent of our Adult Survey respondents) seemed to have some connection with East Africa. There was also a population of about 800 Bengali speakers, mostly originating in Bangladesh, and around 300 of Chinese origin, of whom two-thirds were Hakka speakers from Hong Kong. The European languages were also well represented, with an estimated 1,500 people of Polish origin, 300–500 of Ukrainian origin and around 600–800 of Italian origin.

Our method of arriving at these totals for the South Asian linguistic minorities involved a comparison of census figures on country of birth, with totals derived from our own studies of distinctive ethnic names on the electoral register. These last were undertaken in co-operation with Coventry City Council's Planning and Architecture Department, in preparation for the sampling for our Adult Language Use Survey (ALUS – see Chapters 4 and 5). For the other linguistic minorities we took account of local estimates given by people active in community work, together with census data and the name analysis of electoral registers and telephone directories undertaken by us, again in preparing a sample frame for ALUS. The details of this approach to estimating South Asian and Polish minorities, and the uncertainties associated with it, are described elsewhere (Smith, 1982a).

The inner city area to the north of the city centre, the Foleshill 'railway triangle', was the main area of settlement for the various South Asian groups. Studies of the electoral wards of Foleshill and St Michael's fill out the detail of the pattern of settlement for the Panjabi(G), Gujerati and Panjabi(U) speakers (Smith, 1982b; Winchester, 1974) (see Map. 2.4).

Our detailed studies of the Coventry electoral register showed how the distribution of some of the largest linguistic minorities has been affected by the type of housing available. For example, in the polling districts of one particular ward which we knew to be dominated by municipally owned blocks of flats, fewer than 10 per cent of the names on the register were South Asian, while in the adjacent polling districts containing substantial numbers of old terraced houses in private owner- ship, the proportion of South Asian names was as high as 30 or 40 per cent. In the outlying parts of the city which we knew to be modern council estates, South Asian names were hardly to be found at all. In fact there were probably more people of South Asian origin among house-owners in the modern southern suburbs of Coventry than there were among council tenants in the city.

So far as the distribution of the separate South Asian linguistic minorities in Coventry is concerned, we discovered from our work on the electoral registers some important features of the settlement. Firstly it emerged that the largest concentration of Panjabi(U) households in 1981 was in three or four polling districts around the Eagle Street mosque. The housing in this area is some of the cheapest in Coventry, but the presence of a strong network of Muslim compatriots, speaking the same language and coming from the same areas of origin, also explained concentration in this locality.

There is also a small cluster of Panjabi(U) speakers settled in a single polling district on the western edge of the city centre, but the rest of

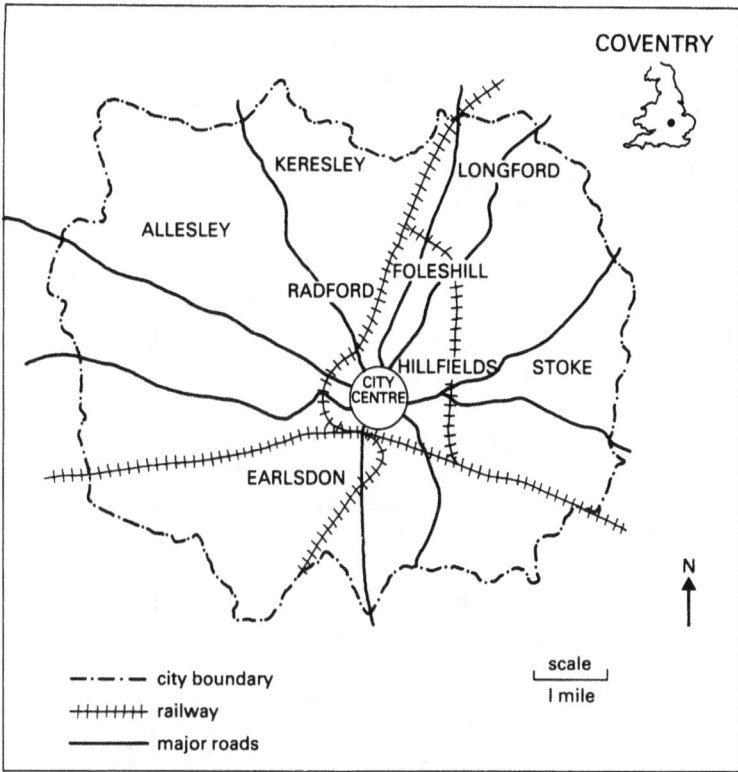

Map 2.4 Sketch map of Coventry showing neighbourhoods where ALUS was carried out

this linguistic minority shows a settlement pattern in line with the general South Asian population. The major settlement is in the Foleshill ward and there are a few scattered households in other parts of the city.

The large Panjabi(G) linguistic minority is concentrated in the north of the city, the focal neighbourhood being in the polling districts at the northern end of the 'railway triangle'. There up to 39 per cent of the population belong to this local linguistic minority. Thirty-five per cent of the Panjabi(G) speakers live in Zone One at the northern end of the triangle in Foleshill, another 16 per cent in the Hillfields area at its southern end, while a further 30 per cent live in a ring of four or five wards immediately surrounding the triangle. The remaining 18 per cent live scattered through the rest of the city. Not surprisingly, almost all the gurdwaras and other community institutions for this minority are to be found in the two central zones. (See Chapter 4 for an explanation of 'zone'.)

The Gujerati speakers' focal neighbourhood is the Hillfields area, and its extensions in a more dispersed settlement pattern are to the east rather than to the north. The central zone, containing 31 per cent of the Gujerati names, is spread across the base of the 'railway triangle', and the Hindu temple, where most of the Gujerati speakers worship, is also found here. The secondary zone for Gujerati speakers spreads out to the east from Hillfields into Stoke, and north to include the rest of the 'triangle': here 38 per cent of the Gujerati-speaking population live, alongside the Panjabi(G) and (U) speakers and other local people. The rest of the Gujerati speakers are scattered round the outlying parts of the city.

One important feature of the Gujerati-speaking population is that although it is predominantly Hindu, there is also a small number of Muslims, living mostly in a small area in Hillfields. Our names analysis of the electoral register had led us mistakenly to include these households in the Panjabi(U) sample, but our interviewers discovered that they, and most of their neighbours, were Gujerati-speaking, and that they had a small 'madrassa' (school) in one of the streets.

The other linguistic minorities are more widely dispersed. The more scattered distribution of the Chinese speakers is related to the location of their catering businesses, since many of them live 'over the shop'. The predominantly Muslim Bengali speakers are to a great extent concentrated in the cheapest housing and in the southern part of the triangle, near the Eagle Street mosque. The Polish and Ukrainian speakers are probably more widely dispersed than the other linguistic minorities. However, in the early days of the settlement they were more concentrated in the inner areas such as Hillfields and Foleshill, and the Polish church and Ukrainian Club are still to be found there. The Italian speakers have moved into the suburban housing in the north and north east of the city as their economic position has improved, and this is the area where the Italian Catholic church is situated. Those families who have not achieved the same economic success have remained closer to the inner city area, in the red brick Victorian houses.

In these housing patterns it is possible to see how the structural discrimination inherent in the housing market has interacted with the pattern of chain migration and kinship networks to produce a high degree of residential concentration. The detailed settlement patterns cannot be explained simply in terms of the type and cost of housing involved, and its relationship to social class. The fact that it is possible

Table 2.2 ALUS in Coventry: main demographic features

Language	Bengali	Chinese	Gujerati	Italian	Panjabi(G)	Panjabi(U)	Polish	Ukrainian
(1) Estimate of total population	600	300	4,500	600	15,000	2,000	1,500	300
(2) Number of households with member interviewed	79	43	203	108	200	86	168	48
(3) Numbers of people in the respondents' households	374	213	992	394	1,025	482	471	144
(4) % of respondents who were female	38	47	49	58	47	49	39	29
(5) % of people in respondents' households aged below 17	49	43	30	22	41	53	14	11
(6) % of people in respondents' households aged over 50	7	8	11	24	8	6	44	53
(7) % of households in owner occupation	75	61	91	96	98	94	92	88
(8) % of households in council housing	14	12	6	2	0	1	7	10
(9) % of males aged 17–65 at work outside home or in family business	72	72	74	82	78	73	80	78
(10) % of females aged 17–60 at work outside home or in family business	13	43	42	67	39	11	57	63
(11) % of people in respondents' households brought up overseas	51	56	56	49	45	41	54	60

to identify clear focal neighbourhoods for each linguistic minority in Coventry suggests that there is some preference for living close to other people of the same linguistic, ethnic and religious background who experience similar socio-economic pressures.

The preponderance of Panjabi-speaking Sikhs in the city means that they have a very strong and varied community life in comparison with some of the smaller linguistic minorities. It also means that in the Coventry context the language label 'Panjabi' almost always suggests Panjabi written in the Gurmukhi script. The Muslim Panjabi speakers may therefore be more reluctant than in Bradford, for example, to refer to their own spoken language as Panjabi, and would tend to use the label 'Urdu' as a way of marking clearly the ethnic boundary between themselves and Sikh Panjabi speakers.

At the time of our work in Coventry the Local Education Authority in Coventry was responsible for a total of 163 schools and 53,000 children. The school system was structured in the most common pattern for England and Wales, with children moving from primary schools to secondary comprehensive schools at the age of 11. Coventry had established a reputation for a progressive approach to multicultural and community education over recent years. At least ten of the secondary and twenty-two of the primary schools were designated as 'community' schools or colleges, where the facilities of the building were made widely available outside schools hours – fourteen of them for mother tongue teaching. Coventry established a Minority Group Support Service in 1977, and from there a team of specialist teachers of English as a second language worked on a peripatetic basis, and materials and in-service training related to multicultural education were provided. A post within the Minority Group Support Service as co-ordinator for mother tongue teaching was created in the late 1970s. Children had, in fact, been taking public examinations in, for example, Panjabi, Urdu, Gujerati, Polish and Ukrainian for some time before that.

Bradford

The Metropolitan District of Bradford had a population in 1981 of 454,000 people, and formed part of the Metropolitan County of West Yorkshire. The West Yorkshire conurbation lies in the eastern foothills of the Pennines, and was developed as a major urban and industrial area during the eighteenth and nineteenth centuries. The wool textile trade was located in the region because of the climate, the material resources easily available, and Bradford's central position in the industrial North.

It has remained the major industry in Bradford to the present day. The stone-built terraced streets which line the hillsides, and the textile mills with their high chimneys in the valleys below, remain the dominant feature of the urban landscape. Bradford city centre boasts a number of Victorian gothic buildings which testify to the former high prosperity of the town. A number of other industries have been introduced in recent years, and the financial and services sector has developed, for example in tourism, and with the location of the headquarters of a number of major building societies in the area. However, the textiles industry remains one of the largest employers, and is particularly significant in explaining the economic position of linguistic minorities within the city.

During the last thirty years the textile industry in West Yorkshire has been exposed for the first time to major competition from overseas producers. In the 1950s and early 1960s the industry was able to respond to this competition by investment in more technologically advanced machinery. However, because of the capital-intensive nature of the new processes, profitability could only be ensured by keeping the mills running twenty-four hours a day. This had serious implications during a time of national labour shortage. Mill work was generally hard and poorly paid (10 per cent below the average for manufacturing industry as a whole) and often regarded as women's work, so the employers began to recruit from further afield. Thus a migrant labour force came to Bradford, especially from Pakistan, and undertook most of the permanent night-shift work and many of the heavier unskilled jobs in the industry.

However, this 'cheap labour' solution has proved to be a temporary palliative, and has failed to halt the decline of the textile industry. Besides the other factors contributing to this decline, the textile industry faced competitors from overseas. In some countries in Asia, textile industries have developed with modern technology and lower labour costs. Capital investment has failed to counteract the ageing process that has seriously affected the industrial infrastructure of the city. The deep recession of the 1980s has had the effect in Bradford in the last few years of many mills closing, with 15,000 people losing their jobs between 1977 and 1980. As a result of the international redistribution of labour and production, and of these local factors, the male un-employment rate stood at over 20 per cent in some of the inner city wards at the time of the 1981 Census, and in the Bradford Metropolitan District as a whole 13.5 per cent of the economically active males over the age of 16 were 'seeking work' (Census 1981).

Bradford has experienced immigration and the settlement of linguistic minorities from early on in its industrial development. Some of the mill-owners and workers in the last century were German, and there is still a German church in the city centre. A large number of Eastern Europeans and of Italians arrived in the city in the post-World War Two period, and were also largely employed in textiles. In the same period small numbers of Panjabi-speaking door-to-door salesmen came to live in the town, and developed contacts in the textile industry where they bought the goods they sold. But it was in the late 1950s and early 1960s that large numbers of Panjabi-speaking Muslims from Pakistan came to settle in the inner city area. The fact that some of their own countrymen were already there encouraged the process of chain migration, and opened up access to employment and housing. Other people from South Asia and the Caribbean arrived in similar circumstances and took up similar employment. Only the most recent immigrants or the smaller linguistic minorities in Bradford have found economic opportunities outside the mills. For example, there are a few Greek Cypriot and Chinese catering businesses. The people who have settled in Bradford most recently — the fifty or so families of refugees from Indo-China — have still to establish their role in the economic life of the town.

The 1981 Census provides some demographic information related to the linguistic minorities found in Bradford. The total population of the Metropolitan District stood at 454,198 people, a decrease of less than 1 per cent from 1971, when the average decrease for urban areas in England was much steeper, and the population as a whole was significantly younger than the national average. Of the overseas-born, 17,668 people gave Pakistan as their birthplace, 6,379 India, 1,305 Bangladesh, 1,733 East Africa, 1,812 Caribbean Commonwealth countries, 716 Commonwealth countries in the Far East, and 3,592 European countries. Again, of course, these last figures do not include British-born speakers of other languages, although some approximation of these for some of the languages at least may be gleaned from the fact that 50,442 people lived in households where the head of the household was born in the New Commonwealth or Pakistan.

When the LMP fieldwork for the surveys was being undertaken in 1980 and 1981 the only census information available was nearly ten years out of date and was, for the reasons referred to earlier, of little use for obtaining precise information about language. We learned, however, that a number of Bradford-based researchers had already used for demographic work a method of manually analysing ethnically distinct names on the electoral register. Singh (1978) had estimated the Sikh population in Bradford, which is approximately equivalent to our 'Panjabi(G)' speakers (see p. 47); the local Community Relations Council had produced figures for the major religious groups, and the city's Corporate Policy Unit had used these, together with statistics from the Area Health Authority and from the education department, in making demographic projections for the South Asian community as a whole (Bradford M.D. Council, 1979).

If we take the figures produced by the Bradford Community Relations Council (CRC) for South Asian names as a whole, we obtain a total of 20,894 South Asian names on the electoral register in the three constituencies making up Bradford City (a smaller unit than Bradford Metropolitan District, representing the boundaries of the old Bradford prior to local government reorganisation in 1974). There were approximately 2,500 Sikh names, and around the same figure for Gujerati, Bengali, and Hindi names taken together. In addition we estimated that there were at least 15,000 Muslim adults of Pakistani origin living in Bradford. Many were from the Mirpur district of the Pakistani part of Kashmir, and used the Mirpuri dialect of Panjabi as their home language. Most of the other adults of Pakistani origin came from other districts of the Pakistani Panjab such as Jhelum, Sialkot, Multan and Attock (former Campbellpur) and spoke a local dialect of these regions. Apart from the Pathan minority, who were speakers of Pushtu, almost all the people of Pakistani origin in Bradford therefore fell into the linguistic minority we have labelled 'Panjabi(U)' (see p. 45) and clearly constituted the largest local linguistic minority. It was much more difficult to arrive at reliable figures for most of the other linguistic minorities in Bradford, and we do not offer any estimates here.

The figures for adults derived from electoral registers matched quite closely the data for children in Bradford schools obtained from LMP's own Schools Language Survey. Given that there were very few bilingual children reported in schools outside the old Bradford City boundary, except in Keighley, we can be confident that of the 14,000 bilingual children in Bradford Metropolitan District schools in 1981, a very high proportion lived in the Bradford City area. Of approximately 12,000 speakers of one of the South Asian languages mentioned in the Schools Language Survey, around 8,000 gave Panjabi or Urdu, 1,200 Gujerati, 400 Bengali, 400 Pushtu. Other languages with over 100 school-age speakers were Italian, Polish, Ukrainian and Chinese (LMP/LINC, 1983).

It is on the basis of the electoral register information that we constructed our sampling strategy for ALUS, and that we make the following comments about the residential distribution of the various minorities.

For a number of reasons the geography of linguistic minority settlements in Bradford was more complicated than that of Coventry. Firstly, Bradford's hilly topography meant that patterns of land use were somewhat constrained and residential areas tended to have fixed natural boundaries. There was no well-defined 'natural' limit where the suburbs met green fields, since Bradford Metropolitan District had developed outwards in ribbons up the valleys, and merged through a string of small urban villages into the rest of the West Yorkshire conurbation. The administrative boundary of the Metropolitan District included within it some isolated moorland farms and hills, while on its eastern side it was a purely arbitrary line, dividing indistinguishable areas of suburban Bradford from suburban Leeds.

Nonetheless, the distribution pattern of the various linguistic minorities was broadly similar to that in Coventry, with the South Asian minorities largely concentrated in the older terraced, owner-occupied housing near the city centre. There were increasing numbers of prosperous families living in the suburbs and outlying villages, and a very small number of South Asian households on the peripheral municipal estates.

There was a similar pattern of focal zones for the separate linguistic minorities (see Map 2.5). The Panjabi(G) speakers were concentrated in the eastern part of the city. Seventy per cent of the Sikh names on the electoral register were found in Zone One and nearly 40 per cent of them in the single ward of Bradford Moor; 25 per cent of them were in another five wards to the west and south west of the city, and only 5 per cent were distributed around the remaining areas. The distribution of the Panjabi(U) names complemented and overlapped with that of the Panjabi(G) names, in that the focal area was the western and south western side of town. There 65 per cent lived in our Zone Two, while 18 per cent lived in Zone One on the east of the town. The remaining 17 per cent were scattered around the outlying areas. The key wards for these names were Manningham and University, where 32 per cent and 44 per cent of the electorate had South Asian names, less than 4 per cent of these names being Sikh (Singh, 1978).

Other South Asian linguistic minorities whom we did not survey include speakers of Gujerati, Bengali and Pushtu. During fieldwork for the various surveys we came upon geographical clusters of households from each of these minorities, which again highlights the importance of close ethnic networks when migrants are excluded from wider access to

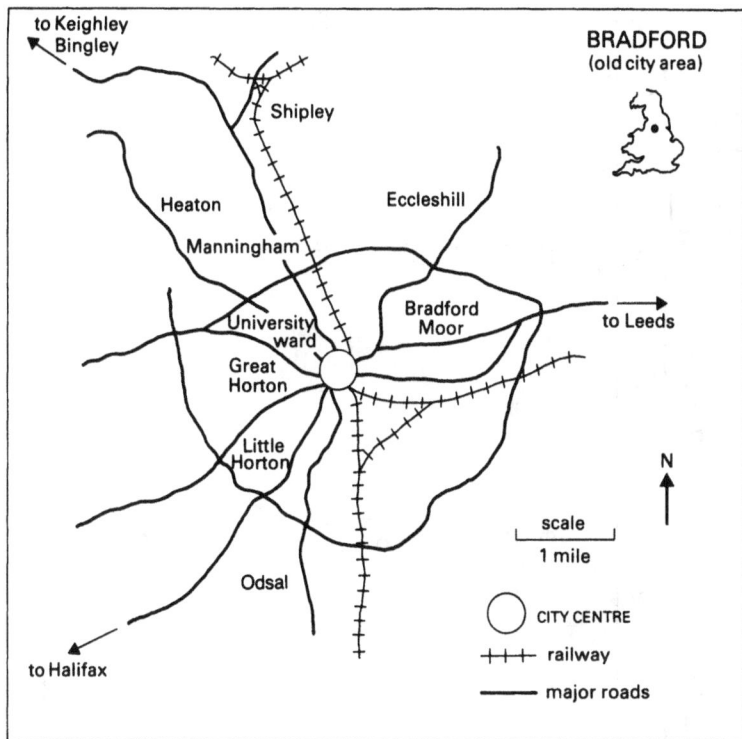

*Map 2.5 Sketch map of Bradford showing neighbourhoods where
ALUS was carried out*

employment, housing and other amenities. Gujerati speakers, for
example, had settled in Bradford in considerable numbers — 1,000 or
more families — and their focal area seemed to be the Great Horton
ward.

It became apparent during the survey fieldwork that the population
turnover in certain neighbourhoods of inner city Bradford was rapid,
especially in the University and Manningham wards. Many of the worst
areas of housing were being demolished for redevelopment, and many
families of South Asian origin had recently been rehoused. This means
that the pattern of distribution reported here for 1981 has already
changed significantly.

The Polish speakers were more widely distributed across the city.
In the early years of their settlement the majority lived in the inner city

Table 2.3 ALUS in Bradford: main demographic features

Language	Chinese	Panjabi(G)	Panjabi(U)	Polish
(1) Estimate of total population	250	6,000	37,000	2,000
(2) Number of households with member interviewed	50	98	177	155
(3) Number of people in the respondents' households	244	529	1,033	449
(4) % of respondents who were female	32	48	51	48
(5) % of people in respondents' households aged below 17	51	42	50	14
(6) % of people in respondents' households aged over 50	7	8	5	45
(7) % of households in owner occupation	0	99	96	93
(8) % of households in council housing	28	0	1	6
(9) % of males aged 17–65 at work outside home or in family business	9	72	61	70
(10) % of females aged 17–60 at work outside home or in family business	9	42	1	61
(11) % of people in respondents' households brought up overseas	87	42	43	51

areas, and many remain there to this day. Many had moved out to the medium-priced owner-occupied areas around Heaton and Shipley to the north of the city centre. Relatively few lived on the peripheral council estates or in the most prosperous suburbs and commuter villages. Other people of Eastern European origin had probably followed a pattern of settlement and relocation similar to that of the Polish speakers. The Chinese refugees from Vietnam had been allocated homes mostly on the municipal estates, or in property owned by housing associations. Usually ten or twelve families lived in close proximity within only a few streets of one another.

At the time of our surveys, the Bradford Local Education Authority was responsible for 175 primary schools, 62 middle schools, 26 upper schools and 20 special schools. Bradford had a more complex pattern than many LEAs, because its boundaries included areas which had formerly had different transfer ages between stages of schooling. Some had the major break between primary and secondary school at 11 – the most common pattern in England as a whole – and some of Bradford's schools are still organised in that way. However, most now fall into the three-tier system, at first schools for 5- to 9-year-olds, middle schools for 9- to 13-year-olds, and upper schools for 13- to 18-year-olds. 'Language Centres' for second language speakers in Bradford were started formally in the early 1970s, part of a widespread pattern of provision nationally, which was justified in terms of making possible concentrated language teaching by specialists to homogeneous groups of learners (see Chapter 7). By 1982, a decision had been taken to close these centres progressively, give up the system of withdrawal groups within ordinary schools, and adopt an overall policy of providing ESL teaching within the framework of the mainstream classroom. In multilingual reception classes additional nursery nurses are being employed to help with linguistic adaptation, and in multilingual schools additional ESL teachers are being attached to school staff, to work in several classes with the main class teacher.

In the early 1980s Bradford's Multicultural Education Service was being expanded considerably to meet the need for a comprehensive advisory staff covering multilingual and multifaith education, and for resource materials and in-service training to back up the Council's anti-racist equal opportunities programme.

London

As the largest city in Britain, and because of its special position in the socio-economic and governmental structure of the nation, London is unique in terms of the numbers and variety of linguistic minorities living there. Out of a total population of 6.6 million for the GLC area in 1981, the census suggests that more than a fifth lived in households where the head of the household was born overseas. As for language diversity, the 1981 Language Census catalogued some 131 different languages spoken by school children in Inner London alone (ILEA, 1981).

Rather than attempt an overview of the position of linguistic minorities in the capital as a whole, we will confine ourselves mainly to the two London boroughs in which most of our Adult Survey work was conducted, with some reference to the populations with which we worked when we crossed the boundaries of those boroughs.

Tower Hamlets

Immediately to the east of the City of London lies the London Borough of Tower Hamlets, with about 140,000 residents in 1981. The area includes the traditional 'East End', for the last two centuries one of the poorest districts in the capital and one with few physical amenities. The main economic activity of the area until recently was connected with the docks of the Port of London. The import and export trade, and the industries which processed the raw materials arriving from all parts of the world, called for a large force of unskilled heavy labour. Other industries such as furniture-making and garment manufacture also flourished further away from the river. The proximity of the docks and the need for labour has attracted immigrants to the area since at least medieval times, including the Huguenots in the seventeenth century, the East European Jews and Chinese at the turn of the century, and in recent years the Bangladeshis. The dockland area has also been the 'jumping off place' for seamen of many different nationalities, who have gone on to become the first link for their compatriots in the chain of migration.

During the last half-century there have been massive changes in the shape of the East End. During the war much of the area was destroyed by German bombers, and since the war massive slum clearance and redevelopment has taken place. By the early 1980s very few of the old Victorian terraced streets remained, and their place had been taken by modern municipally owned dwellings, mostly high-rise flats and maisonettes. Almost all the housing stock in the borough was owned either by Tower Hamlets Borough Council or by the Greater London Council. Out of 52,976 households in the borough at the time of the 1981 Census, 43,421 were situated in property owned by the two councils. A massive fall in the population of the area during the last fifty years followed the movement of thousands of families to outer London, Essex and the New Towns all round London. Employment opportunities have declined as the focus of shipping activity has moved down the River Thames to Tilbury, and many industries have chosen to relocate outside London. Today the docklands area has become a priority area for the central government's programme for renewal of the inner cities, and a special Docklands Development Corporation has been created in order to speed up the redevelopment of industry in the district.

For educational purposes, Tower Hamlets constitutes Division 5 of the Inner London Education Authority (ILEA). Largely because of the very high proportions of children from poorer families in its schools, ILEA is one of the highest-spending education authorities in the country. It is noted for the very comprehensive range of services it provides, in particular in connection with its multilingual school population. These facilities include one of the earliest 'language services', with a staff of peripatetic ESL teachers which is increasingly being integrated into mainstream school-classes. There is also a biennial 'language census' which assembles data on both home languages and needs in ESL for all ILEA's pupils. The 1981 Language Census showed that 5,308 of school age children in Tower Hamlets spoke home languages other than English — at 21.7 per cent of the relevant age groups, the highest proportion for any ILEA division. Sixty per cent of these children were Bengali speakers.

Another major educational facility provided by ILEA, and situated in the borough, is the Centre for Urban Educational Studies (CUES). This was set up in the early 1970s with a major emphasis on language education for linguistic minority children, and turned its attention increasingly by the late 1970s towards support for mother tongues as well as for English as a second language. With close links to the Multi-ethnic Inspectorate, CUES has been responsible in important ways for the evolution of a positive policy towards bilingualism in the Authority's schools, culminating in the appointment in 1983 of two advisers working within the Modern Language Inspectorate, with specific responsibilities in this field.

Children in Tower Hamlets go to local infants and junior schools from the age of 5 to 11 and then move to larger, comprehensive schools. ILEA has recently initiated a number of schemes in Tower Hamlets at school and adult education level in connection with the teaching of Bengali and teaching through the medium of Bengali.

Haringey

Haringey is a borough in North London which had a population in 1981 of 202,700. It stretches from Highgate and Muswell Hill in the west to Tottenham in the east. The western areas of the Borough are mostly owner-occupied, middle-class neighbourhoods; housing in the central area is of the less expensive owner-occupied type with some private rented terraces built before the First World War and with many multiply-occupied dwellings; and the eastern part consists largely of working-class council estates. It is a largely residential area, with many of the inhabitants employed in Central London rather than in Haringey itself. In 1971, for example, only 40 per cent of workers who lived in the borough were employed locally.

At the time of our research Haringey was one of the most linguistically and ethnically diverse areas to be found in England. In the 1981 Schools Language Survey 30 per cent of the children were reported as bilingual, and there were eighty-seven identifiably different languages: half these children were speakers of either Greek or Turkish (LMP/ LINC, 1983).

The main minorities were people of Greek and Turkish Cypriot origin, especially in the Harringay ward area, those from the different Caribbean islands particularly in the Wood Green area, and people of Jewish origin in the Stamford Hill area. Speakers of Bengali, Gujerati, Italian, Portuguese, Spanish, Chinese and West African languages were also found. The 1981 Census reported 12,129 residents who were born in the Caribbean New Commonwealth, 11,910 born in the Mediterranean New Commonwealth, 3,556 born in India, 2,657 born in East Africa, 694 born in Bangladesh and 667 born in Pakistan.

As an outer London borough, Haringey is responsible for its own educational system. At the time of the Survey this catered for more than 32,000 children, in eighty-one primary schools for 4- 11-year-olds, fourteen secondary schools for 11- to 18-year-olds, and five special schools. An 'English Language Resource Centre' had been established in 1970 to support specialised teaching of English as a second language, and the team of over thirty peripatetic teachers based there followed a policy of working alongside class teachers. This policy had been adopted completely in the primary sector, and was almost complete in the secondary schools too, although some teaching of withdrawal groups

Table 2.4 ALUS in London: main demographic features

Language	Bengali	Chinese	Greek	Gujerati	Italian	Portuguese	Turkish
(1) It was not possible to obtain satisfactory estimates of the total populations for London.							
(2) Number of households with member interviewed	185	137	193	99	94	196	197
(3) Number of people in respondents' households	898	597	758	457	367	627	822
(4) % of respondents who were female	41	45	51	50	54	56	45
(5) % of people in respondents' households aged below 17	44	33	25	23	30	24	30
(6) % of people in respondents' households aged over 50	5	9	16	14	16	12	11
(7) % of households in owner occupation	22	37	86	77	62	10	84
(8) % of households in council housing	65	37	8	16	32	28	9
(9) % of males aged 17–65 at work outside home or in family business	82	60	76	77	87	94	76
(10) % of females aged 17–60 at work outside home or in family business	11	37	43	44	75	73	32
(11) % of people in respondents' households brought up overseas	53	58	52	70	42	69	48

persisted. In addition, there was a Multicultural Support Group in Haringey, started in 1979, which worked with schools on general curriculum and in-service training. Overall, the LEA was committed to a policy based on a positive attitude to the bilingualism of so many of its pupils.

The following section of this chapter extends where necessary the national picture offered earlier. But in some cases, where the linguistic minority in question was situated largely in the capital, there is little to add to the account given earlier.

Bengali speakers in London

On the basis of local information we estimated originally that about 75 per cent of all Bengali speakers in London lived in Tower Hamlets. In fact, the 1981 Census shows that fewer than half of the 22,102 persons born in Bangladesh and living in the GLC area were in Tower Hamlets. The rest are widely spread around the capital, with the largest number in the borough of Camden (1,281 at the time of the 1981 Census).

The Bangladeshi population in Tower Hamlets is predominantly Muslim, poor and has little experience of formal education. Most of the men and some of the women work in bad conditions in the garment-making trade, and unemployment is high. In addition, Bengali speakers in the East End often experience particularly acute hostility from the local English population. This has come to the surface in numerous acts of racial harassment and violence, and is articulated at its most extreme by political groups such as the National Front and the British Movement.

Although the 1981 Census reports that 6,464 males and 3,344 females living in the borough were born in Bangladesh, there are other sources which suggest that a figure of around 14,000 for the total population of Bengali speakers is not unreasonable. The 1981 ILEA Language Census already referred to recorded 3,201 Bengali-speaking children in schools in Tower Hamlets, a figure which had almost doubled since the previous Language Census in late 1978. Although part of the increase may have been accounted for by changes in the wording of the ILEA Census questions, the major factor is that many wives and children had arrived from Bangladesh in the previous years to be reunited with the male members of their families.

Bengali speakers in Tower Hamlets live for the most part in council housing in the Spitalfields and Shadwell neighbourhoods. They have little choice, for in Tower Hamlets fewer than 2 per cent of the houses are owner-occupied, and Bengali speakers cannot usually afford them. Most of the housing, in fact, is municipally owned. The Spitalfields Survey (SHAPRS, 1981) suggests, however, that Bengali speakers are under-represented in council housing, in that they form only 28 per cent of council tenants although they comprise 47 per cent of the ward population. There is also strong evidence to suggest that, even where they are council tenants, Bengali speakers are the object of discrimination by the housing authorities in that they are over-represented in the oldest and worst types of council property. The rest of the housing in the Spitalfields ward of Tower Hamlets is privately rented and has very poor amenities. The current housing situation of Bengali speakers can be explained by the fact that, when the local settlement developed, the predominantly male population settled in some of the worst of this privately rented housing. When, in the process of redevelopment, some of this housing was condemned and demolished, the local authority had a legal duty to rehouse the former tenants. Thus an increasing proportion of Bengali speakers came to live in council property.

Because of racist attacks, some Bangladeshi organisations resisted the official policy of dispersal to estates throughout the borough, and matters came to head in the 'ghettos' dispute of 1978 (SHAPRS, 1981). Since that time the housing authorities have had a de facto policy of 'safe estates' and do not attempt to persuade Bengali speakers to accept housing outside of them. The result is a high level of ethnic segregation and encapsulation.

Given the unique circumstances of the Bengali speakers in Tower Hamlets, we felt that it was important to draw part of our sample from another, contrasting area. Haringey was chosen partly because of the convenience of working in a borough where other teams of interviewers would be working, and we attempted to conduct about a quarter of the Bengali interviews there. As the 1981 Schools Language Survey in Haringey (see p. 330) had identified more than 200 Bengali-speaking children, and the 1981 Census counted 694 people born in Bangladesh, it was likely that there would be more than 100 Bengali households in the borough. A large proportion of the Bengali speakers in Haringey were Indian Hindus rather than Bangladeshi Muslims, and included people with professional and other non-manual occupations. Most of them were living in the southern part of the borough, usually in owner-occupied terraced houses. They therefore complemented the sample drawn from Tower Hamlets.

'Chinese' speakers in London

Speakers of Chinese languages in London as a whole numbered about 27,000 in 1980, according to Chin and Simsova (1981). Although they are widely scattered, the focal area for the Chinese is the Soho area in the centre of London. This is, however, more of a business and recreational centre for Chinese all over London than a major residential zone. The boroughs with the highest numbers of speakers of Chinese languages are Westminster, Camden, Barnet, Ealing, Lambeth, Wandsworth, Brent, Haringey and Kensington, each with an estimated Chinese-speaking population of over 1,000. In Tower Hamlets there has also been a Chinese settlement based on Limehouse for several generations. Other Chinese speakers, mainly from Hong Kong, have opened restaurants and take-aways in scattered locations throughout the borough. More recently seventy families of refugees from Indo-China have settled in the borough. Haringey also has a large number of Chinese speakers, many of those in the catering trade originating from Hong Kong. Others are students and professionals, often with origins in Singapore or Malaysia, living in the borough but working or studying in other parts of London.

Gujerati speakers in London

There are Gujerati speakers in most parts of London, and it is probable that at least half of them are of East African origin, with much of the immigration having taken place in the late 1960s and early 1970s. The largest population is located in the London borough of Brent, especially in the Wembley area. Other major settlements are found in Newham in East London, and Croydon and Wandsworth in South London. Traditionally many East African Gujerati speakers have worked as shopkeepers and small businessmen, and there are certainly some in London who have re-established their businesses since migration.

In Haringey there are probably around 500 families concentrated in the north of the borough, in the Bounds Green and Bowes Park areas. They live mainly in owner-occupied, mid-priced terraced or semi-detached housing. Most of them are Hindus, although there is a small number also of Muslim and Ismaili Gujerati speakers.

Greek and Turkish speakers in London

More than two-thirds of the predominantly Cypriot Greek- and Turkish-speaking linguistic minorities in Britain live in the Greater London area.

As indicated earlier, the initial settlement was principally in Islington, Camden and Hackney, with some Cypriots also settled south of the Thames, mainly in Lambeth and Southwark. Although the number of Cypriots in Islington has always been higher than in Camden, it was Camden that became the focal area for Greek speakers. All Saints, the Cypriot church, was founded in Camden and it was here that the Greek Cypriot theatre workshop 'Teatro Technis' was later established.

Already in the mid-1960s nearly half of the Greek-speaking Cypriots were owner-occupiers (Oakley, 1970). In the London area, those who could afford to buy a small Victorian terraced house began to move northwards from the areas of initial settlement to outer London boroughs, notably Haringey. One of the focal points of this urban migration was the Green Lanes area, a neighbourhood noted for its Cypriot grocery shops, cafés, bakeries, restaurants and other small businesses. There was little doubt that the major concentration of Greek Cypriot settlement in the early 1980s was in Haringey, but estimates of the total numbers in the borough varied enormously. According to the 1971 Census, the total number of Cypriot-born residents was 17,594, but this figure, of course, includes both Greek and Turkish speakers. (A corresponding figure for the 1981 Census was not available at the time of writing.) Leeuwenberg (1979) claimed that if the second generation was included, the total population of Cypriot origin was more likely to be close to 20,000, with about 15,000 of these being Greek speakers. Alkan and Constantinides (1982) put the overall figure for Greek and Turkish Cypriots together in Haringey at 30,000 to 35,000.

A second, more recent trend in the northward migration within London has been for younger Greek speakers to settle even further out, in the boroughs of Enfield, Barnet, Brent and Waltham Forest. In the 1971 Census the Cyprus-born population of Enfield was reported to be just over 4,000, and Alkan and Constantinides in 1982 estimated that the overall numbers of the population in Enfield with origins in Cyprus had reached about 10,000.

The Turkish speakers have lived alongside the Greek speakers in North London without overt friction, despite the far from happy inter-communal relationship in Cyprus. There are many similarities between housing and employment patterns, but on the whole the Turkish speakers are less well off, and more of them are to be found in the poorer housing in the east of Haringey, and scattered eastwards into Hackney. The ratio of Turkish speakers to Greek speakers in the 1981 Haringey school population was about 30:70 (LMP/LINC, 1983).

In Hackney in the same year the proportions were roughly reversed, and in Inner London as a whole Turkish-speaking pupils were the second most numerous linguistic minority identified in both 1981 and 1983 Language Censuses (ILEA, 1981 and 1983).

Italian speakers in London

About a third of the people of Italian origin in Britain live in the Greater London area (King, 1979). The 1981 Census suggested that 30,750 Italian-born persons were living in the GLC area. Despite the overall increase in the Italian population of London in the last hundred years, there is today little evidence in the Clerkenwell area of the 'little Italy' of the nineteenth century. Italian families have become widely dispersed throughout the metropolis, the London boroughs with the greatest concentrations being Islington, Camden, Westminster, Lambeth and Enfield. In 1971 there were 3,590 people of Italian birth living in Islington (which includes Clerkenwell), and of the other boroughs mentioned each had over 2,000 people born in Italy. The Italian minority in the Islington, Camden, and Westminster areas of Central London consists mainly of people descended from the earlier migrants who originated in Northern Italy.

Generally speaking, within the Italian linguistic minority there has been a preference for home ownership, and many families have moved out towards the suburban areas of North London as their economic position improved. Highbury was often the first stage, followed by Finchley in the outer London borough of Barnet. Many Italian speakers are still employed in catering or other service sectors.

Portuguese speakers in London

Over three-quarters of the total population of Portuguese speakers in Britain live in the Greater London area. According to the 1981 Census the total number of persons born in Portugal resident in Greater London was 10,872, of whom only 4,766 were male and 6,106 female. These figures, of course, do not include younger Portuguese speakers born in the UK. The Portuguese-born residents were then mostly concentrated in the Inner London boroughs (8,114 people) rather than in outer London, the greatest concentration being in the boroughs of Westminster and Kensington, which include the Ladbroke Grove and Portobello Road neighbourhoods. The other London boroughs with large numbers of Portuguese residents were Lambeth, Camden, Hammersmith and Fulham, and Brent.

This pattern of settlement within London is largely a result of the employment opportunities available to Portuguese migrants. As pointed out earlier in the chapter, many men and women work in the hotel and catering industries and in janitorial and cleaning services in the large London hospitals. There is also a longer-established settlement of Portuguese speakers in the Whitechapel area of Tower Hamlets, many of them employed in the local hospital service as nurses, porters, cleaners and cooks. In the Ladbroke Grove and Portobello Road area another common source of employment is in domestic service in the wealthier private homes of South Kensington, Mayfair and Belgravia.

Map 2.6 Sketch map of London showing the boroughs and neighbourhoods where ALUS was carried out

Portuguese women work as maids, cooks and housekeepers, and men as door porters and chauffeurs.

Many of those who work in domestic service are provided with live-in accommodation. Others have qualified for council housing. However, for the most part the Portuguese migrants live in poor-quality privately rented housing in inner city areas, often in situations of multi-occupancy and overcrowding. There is one street in West London where the majority of inhabitants are of Portuguese origin, with about sixty families in small flats in a single terrace. The poor living conditions of these flats have recently been the subject of lengthy legal proceedings, and it now seems as though improvement work will eventually be carried out.

A minority of the Portuguese migrants have been able to save enough money to buy their own homes and move out, especially to the outer London borough of Brent to the northwest: there are individual Portuguese families living in Queen's Park, Harlesden and Wembley, for example.

3
Bilingualism and society

In the opening chapters of this book we discussed, among other things, the definition of the term 'linguistic minority'. In the second chapter we gave sketches of the language backgrounds of some of the linguistic minorities found in England, and described them in three urban settings. In this chapter we deal with the factors that are important in determining whether a language has minority status, and with some of the issues that have emerged in the sociolingustic study of bilingualism and minority languages over the last few decades.

As we consider it important to remind our readers of issues deriving from a wider perspective on societal bilingualism this chapter refers to Britain as a whole, rather than England alone, and it also mentions studies in other parts of the world. We delay the presentation and discussion of our survey findings to present important themes which readers should bear in mind when they assess the detail of our survey findings later in the book.

This chapter has particular relevance for the following two, which provide a description and discussion of the patterns of language use among a range of linguistic minorities in England: Chapter 4 outlines the research methods adopted in response to the particular contexts described in the last chapter; Chapter 5 presents some of the basic findings of our survey of adult language use. In Chapter 6 we look at one important institutional aspect of language use and maintenance found among linguistic minorities − 'mother tongue teaching'. After this consideration of language use in its social context we move on in the latter half of the book to consider some of the educational implications for our multilingual society.

In our opening chapters we stressed that to understand the concept of minority language we needed to appreciate the position of speakers of such languages in relation to speakers of the dominant language. The spread of English as a world language, and its contribution to the powerfully monolingual character of English ethnicity, need not be elaborated here (Fishman, Cooper and Conrad, 1977; Saifullah Khan, 1983). In such a national context the status of every minority language is likely to be lower than that of English, yet the majority response has not been quite the same towards different minority languages spoken in England.

When discussing a specific linguistic minority or minority language, its particular status will reflect the power imbalance and degree of perceived cultural distinctiveness between speakers of the dominant and of the subordinate language. The status of a minority language is based, not on any inherent characteristics of the language, but rather on the status of the people who use it, and on the past and present power relations between Britain and the other countries where the language is used (see pp. 30 and 48). Languages are only 'minority languages' because they are perceived as such by the dominant majority, and treated as such in social institutions such as the school system and the media. The relative prestige of a minority language, in other words, is closely bound up with the socio-economic and legal position in Britain of the linguistic minority in question.

Perceived cultural differences distinguishing the speakers of the languages other than English also influence the status accorded to the minority language by outsiders. The 'visibility' of other characteristics of the speaker, such as physical difference or dress, may exacerbate the stigma often associated with the minority language. Indeed, phenotypical difference may be so salient as a marker of ethnic or 'racial' affiliation that there may be practically no conflict overtly on the basis of language. But even when minority language use is restricted to the private and unofficial spheres of social activity, as is the case among many linguistic minorities in England, the likelihood of there being minority organisations which use and teach the language is high. Initial accommodation by minority language speakers, to expectations about the more or less exclusive use of English in the new country, may in fact in the longer term encourage a more organised resistance to linguistic or cultural assimilation. The mother tongue teaching provision organised out of regular school time is an obvious example of such resistance.

Between 1945 and 1975 the largest labour migrations which responded to the economic needs of post-war England were of people from Commonwealth countries who initially had legal rights of settlement and citizenship. The languages of these mostly non-European and ex-subject peoples were perceived as having a far lower status than any of the European languages. And despite the relatively high prestige enjoyed by languages such as Italian, Spanish and Classical Greek in the British education system, largely for historical reasons, the arrival of South European migrant workers in the 1960s did little to encourage an expansion of the teaching of these languages in LEA schools to either monolingual or bilingual members of the society (see Chapter 7). The bilingual children of these workers were not perceived as a resource for the predominantly monolingual schools. Nor was the opportunity offered by the presence in Britain of these Spanish- or Italian-speaking pupils seen by majority parents in the same light, for example, as the presence of French-speaking pupils in the French Lycée in London. The South European like the South Asian pupils were perceived simply as the children of economic migrants with a low socio-economic and cultural status, despite the rights of at least some of them as children of EC citizens.

The following section will outline several key factors likely to influence the general classification of minority languages by the dominant majority. But it should be borne in mind that the status of a language may be seen in a different way by the speakers of a language themselves. For example, Urdu and Chinese are generally valued highly by their speakers in England (especially first-generation migrants), in part because of their established literacy traditions. Nevertheless, these same languages may be generally perceived by English monolinguals as having low status.

In a situation of dominant–subordinate relations, minority speakers' perceptions of the dominant definition of the status of their minority language can have a powerful influence on their own evaluation of its worth. This reactive assessment may lead to a heightened sense of its lower status, especially by youngsters whose mother tongue has been dislocated from the social and economic base of their country of origin. Alternatively the reaction may be one of rejecting the dominant view, involving conscious statements of pride in the language or its associated culture, and of collective action to resist its loss.

The subjective interpretation of minority language status by minority language speakers may of course be influenced by the setting. Particular languages or language varieties may be perceived as having particular value for certain settings or with certain categories of people, for example in religious institutions, or with professionals such as doctors or teachers. Bilinguals living in an implicitly monolingual society may come to accept a functional or contextual division of the languages in their linguistic repertoire. But then of course different varieties of the same language often also have different statuses and functions. The difference in English, for example, between Southern British Standard and 'Scouse' (from Merseyside) is mirrored in the different statuses accorded by many Italians, including Sicilians, to standard Italian and to Sicilian.

In discussing the status of a minority language, then, it is important to look at it both from the outsider's and from the insider's point of view, and to acknowledge that any mismatch between the two evaluations may itself be an important factor in the changing status of a language. While acknowledging this complexity we shall, nevertheless, look first in this chapter at the factors influencing the status accorded to minority languages by the dominant group in our society. We do not claim to provide an exhaustive account of these factors, believing it is more important at this stage to understand how some of them interrelate in specific cases.

After discussing the scope and limitations of the two survey approaches we used in our community-based surveys (see Chapters 4-6), we move on in this chapter to discuss several other sociolinguistic concepts used in studies of societal bilingualism. While we do not attempt a comprehensive review of sociolinguistic research on bilingualism, it is important that the reader has some idea of the ground which our project did not cover. Some of the issues referred to suggest important areas for future research, and alternative approaches from those used by us.

As the book progresses, the reader will be able to appreciate how our research methods developed in response to the particular issues we were interested in, as well as in response to the politics and practicalities of our fieldwork situation. In neither of the community-based surveys discussed in this first part of the book could we be too ambitious, because of the lack of all but the most basic background data as a foundation for our enquiries. Our concern was to develop research strategies which would be appropriate for the complex multilingual urban settings in England in which we were working. Our adaptation of existing survey methods provided us with a solid foundation of data for future research, and the opportunity to have an immediate impact. Many of the challenging issues mentioned in the next sections call for observational research, and for longitudinal studies. While we were able to work with teams of initially untrained bilingual interviewers, future studies of this kind in bilingual populations in England will depend upon the existence of academically trained bilingual researchers from the linguistic minority in question.

Factors influencing the position of minority languages

There are several key factors which influence the status accorded to minority languages in the wider society and which are interrelated in a complex way with patterns of bilingualism. A number of researchers have tried to specify the main factors which influence language maintenance and shift (Kloss, 1968; Fishman, 1972b; Haugen, 1972). The concept of 'ethnolinguistic vitality', in particular, has enjoyed some currency recently (Giles, Bourhis and Taylor, 1977). It may have been useful as a heuristic device, but without an appropriate theoretical base it has limited application (Husband and Saifullah Khan, 1982). Giles, Bourhis and Taylor argue that the vitality of ethnolinguistic groups can be assessed by monitoring three categories of structural variables: status, demographic and institutional support variables. But a careful examination of the different variables in their taxonomy exposes their ambiguous status, and the difficulty of assessing the authors' claim that the more status a linguistic community is recognised to have on these dimensions, the more vitality it could be said to possess as a collective entity.

In contrast, some of the earlier sociolinguistic literature defined the status of minority languages in the context of the boundaries of national states (Stewart, 1966; Fishman, 1966b). Sociolinguistic typologies were devised to classify states according to the degree of linguistic diversity which characterizes them. In the late 1960s Fishman distinguished, on the basis of primarily demographic criteria, between

(1) 'linguistically heterogeneous polities', where no single language is spoken natively by 85 per cent or more of the population, and where a significant minority is present among the remaining 15 per cent; and

(2) 'linguistically homogeneous polities', where 85 per cent or more of the population are native speakers of a single language and in which no significant linguistic minority is present. (Fishman, 1966b)

Static typologies cannot, of course, take into account historical processes, nor keep up with changing demographic factors in the spread of bilingualism, such as immigration from within and beyond the nation state. Patterns of immigration of the kind experienced by Britain in the post-war period can significantly, and quite rapidly, change the sociolinguistic profile of a particular country. Fishman's criteria are also problematic because they do not take account of varieties of a single language, nor is there any indication of how long a language has to be spoken in a particular setting before it can be regarded as an indigenous language.

As we mentioned in Chapter 1, even in terms of numbers of speakers a 'minority language' can, of course, be the language of the majority in a particular localised community within a nation state. Examples of this include Basque in parts of France and Spain, Welsh in Gwynedd in North West Wales, and French in Quebec. Particular neighbourhoods in large metropolitan areas may be in a similar position: for example, Puerto Rican Spanish in Harlem or, formerly, Yiddish in several Eastern European cities and in major Western cities such as New York. We have already seen in Chapter 2 how situations like this now also obtain in various neighbourhoods in British cities (see p. 78).

The ascription of minority status to a language purely on the basis of numbers of speakers within a whole state, or even within a city, fails also to take into account crucial questions about who the speakers of the minority language are, and what political, economic and historical relationship there is between speakers of the dominant language and speakers of the minority language. Some minorities may be politically dominant, as was the case with the Normans after they took political power in much of England in the eleventh century, or Swedish speakers in Finland between at least the seventeenth and the mid-nineteenth century (Reuter, 1981). Haugen (1981) refers to such instances as 'elite minorities', and contrasts them with 'non-elite', or 'submerged', minorities. But even this characterisation does not take full account of the distribution of power and control within the modern nation state. In Britain, English is the overwhelmingly dominant language of literacy in education, in the media, in the workplace, in government and in all public dimensions of British life. The ability to read and write English is regarded as the crucial measure of educational achievement and, as such, it serves as one of the prime means of discrimination in access to employment, and to social and medical services.

The status of minority languages in Britain today, whether we are talking about Welsh, Panjabi or Greek, has to be defined with reference to the present status of English both as the dominant language in the United Kingdom, and as an increasingly important language of wider communication in most parts of the world. Minority languages in England only have a legitimised place within institutions such as the home, the temple, the church, the mosque or the local minority association, with a few also having found a place within ethnic sectors of the economy, for example catering in most parts of the country, small clothing factories in London.

Each minority language in Britain has its own particular range of functions and history of contact with English (Saifullah Khan, 1980a). Languages such as Hindi and Urdu for the most part serve the function of lingua franca among speakers of different South Asian languages in Britain, rather than being languages of the home for many speakers. But there are also broad historical similarities among many of the languages. For instance, the relationship between English and many minority languages in Britain today, both new and old, is embedded in a long history of colonisation, with English as the language of rule. This is the case for all those languages and varieties spoken in Britain by speakers of Cypriot, Caribbean and South and East Asian origin. The detailed sociolinguistic history of many of these newer linguistic minorities in Britain still needs to be documented. Some detailed historical accounts of the position of indigenous minority languages and dialects in Britain have already been produced (McKinnon, 1977; Durkacz, 1983; Romaine and Dorian, 1981; Trudgill, 1984).

A sociolinguistic history of a particular linguistic minority will, of necessity, include reference to the functions that the spoken language has had in different settings and for different sections within a local linguistic minority: older and younger, men and women. In settings where speakers use more than one language, some account is needed of the relative status of the two languages in the communicative repertoire of the linguistic minority.

The sociolinguistic study of the newer linguistic minorities in Britain today also needs to be informed by some understanding of the historical development of language education in the cultural setting of the country or countries of origin: such study would have to include discussion of the traditional definition of literacy instruction and the development of formal schooling, as well as of the language conventionally used as medium of instruction. Some documentation is also needed of the extent to which literacy instruction has been associated with the teaching of grammar and the codification of the languages.

Intricately tied to the history of schooling is the development and use of writing systems. The incidence of digraphia in the social history of a particular minority language is likely to have a considerable influence on traditional beliefs and attitudes about the relationship between the spoken and written language and, in turn, on patterns of literacy instruction and use. Dale defines digraphia as 'the use of two (or more) writing systems for representing a single language (or varieties thereof)' (Dale, 1980). Examples of digraphia from the South Asian context have particular relevance for the study of the uses of literacy in Britain among linguistic minorities from the subcontinent. And we have already mentioned the value of calligraphy, especially for Muslim minorities in Britain (see p. 47).

Besides some of the social, political and historical factors outlined so far, another crucial factor to take into account is the role of ideology in the definition of the status of minority languages. In many parts of the world both cultural and linguistic diversity have long been characterised by the dominant group as socio-political 'problems'. The use of minority languages is often associated with power differences, and in Britain the intolerance towards linguistic minorities has its roots in the period of internal and external colonial expansion. It is reflected in policies that have shaped English education over several centuries. For the Celtic minorities in Britain, the persistent denial of their language rights had far-reaching consequences, as documented in the notorious 'Blue Books' on language education in Wales (Khlief, 1980), or in the Statutes of Iona concerning education in the Gaelic-speaking Highlands of Scotland (Romaine and Dorian, 1981). The rise of English to linguistic sovereignty in the British Isles, backed up by the standardisation and the codification of the language by grammarians and lexicographers from the sixteenth century onwards (Leith, 1983), formed the basis of an ideology which spread to other areas of the world during the colonial era. As Romaine and Dorian (1981) have pointed out, intolerance of linguistic diversity is not limited to the predominantly monolingual institutions and attitudes found in England. In the anglophone world as a whole, there has been little enthusiasm for what Lambert (1972) described as 'additive' bilingualism. Language education practice in Britain in the post-World War Two period continued to be dominated by a broadly assimilationist outlook (see p. 282). Even the goal of many so-called 'bilingual' programmes for children from linguistic minorities in the USA is transitional bilingualism, with English as the only eventual medium of education.

Sociolinguistic surveys and censuses

The description of the status of a language in terms of political, social and historical factors is a research tradition that goes back at least as far as the work of linguists such as Weinreich (1953) and Schmidt-Rohr (1963), who tried to account for the differential status of languages in contact. This is the area of study that has come to be known by some as the sociology of language. Two broad empirical approaches have been adopted within this field of research: the language census and the sociolinguistic survey. Some examples of settings where these approaches have been tested out are reviewed in this sector of the chapter. LMP adopted both of these approaches in its work in the three urban areas of England where most of the work was carried out.

Systematic collection of language statistics has come to be recognised as an essential prerequisite to language planning and language legislation in a number of very different multilingual settings, including the South Asian subcontinent, Canada, the USA, Wales and Scandinavia. Questions about language are often included in a national population census, although sometimes only for certain regions of a country, as in the case of the United Kingdom. Or the census or survey may be specifically designed for a particular population, such as school pupils in a specific urban area, for example the Inner London Education Authority Language Censuses of 1978, 1981, and 1983 (ILEA, 1979, 1981 and 1983), and the New South Wales survey, (New South Wales, 1980). In some censuses and surveys, a question about literacy may also be added, as for example in the 1971 Census for Wales, or the LMP Schools Language Surveys (LMP/LINC, 1983).

The methodological issues arising from the analysis of language census returns have now been well documented (Bellin, 1982; Clyne, 1976; De Vries, 1974, 1977, 1981; De Vries and Vallee, 1980; Khubchandani, 1979; Lieberson, 1966, 1969; Ambrose and Williams, 1981). De Vries (1981) has drawn attention in particular to the issues that arise out of different formulations of census questions to do with language. He draws his examples from the Canadian census, and points to the implications of these methodological problems for obtaining accurate estimates of language maintenance and shift over time. Longitudinal language data from different censuses is essential to gain some insights into demographic trends within specific bilingual populations, as in Finland (De Vries, 1974, 1977), the USA (Waggoner, 1981), or in Wales (Bellin, 1982; Ambrose and Williams, 1981).

However, in the absence of data on opportunities for language use, language censuses of adult populations at best provide a broad social and geographic picture of reported language and literacy skills, without telling us anything about the social processes involved in patterns of language use in different spheres of activity. In some censuses a question about language choice in the home is included, but, as De Vries points out 'this narrow choice provides no measure of language use in other domains, such as the economy. For purposes of language planning, these other domains may be much more important than the home' (De Vries, 1981, p. 17).

The basic distinction between a census and a survey, of course, is that while censuses aim at complete coverage of a population, and are limited in the number of questions that can be asked, a survey involves more detailed questioning of representative samples of people within the population. The results obtained are intended to form the basis for generalising about the target population.

> Sociolinguistic surveys gather information about the social organization of language behavior and behavior toward language in specified populations. Because such behaviors encompass multitudinous phenomena and because populations vary in size, complexity, and basis of organization, sociolinguistic surveys vary widely in the questions which they ask, the ways in which they answer them, and the uses for which their results are intended. (Cooper, 1980, 114)

A sociolinguistic survey approach to the study of bilingual or multilingual populations is not only designed to obtain a broad profile of the social distribution of language and literacy skills. It also elicits self-report data on patterns of language use and language attitudes. This approach has now become a well-established research procedure for work in settings characterised by a long history of indigenous bilingualism. Two examples of this type conducted in the British Isles are a survey of language use on the Isle of Harris (McKinnon, 1977), and a recent survey of patterns of language use with children carried out among Welsh-speaking mothers in Wales (Bellin, Harrison and Piette, 1981).

Other sociolinguistic surveys of much wider scope have been carried out in other parts of the world in multilingual settings. One of the most extensive in recent years was the Survey of Language Use and Language Teaching in East Africa carried out between 1968 and 1971 in five different countries (Ethiopia: Bender, Bowen, Cooper and Ferguson, 1976; Kenya: Whiteley, 1974; Tanzania: Polomé and Hill, 1980; Uganda: Ladefoged, Glick and Criper, 1972; and Zambia: Ohannessian and Kashoki, 1978). With specific reference to the work on the East African survey, Polomé (1982) has recently defined the empirical goals of what he calls 'macrosociolinguistics' as follows:

> [To encompass] numerically sizeable communities, such as ethnic groups, or, in the case of the East African Language Survey, whole

nations, and [to try] to provide extensive quantifiable data on their broader characteristics, such as percentages of mother tongue speakers claiming various numbers of second languages, or self-assessed degrees of proficiency in various languages in a definite set of social contexts. (Polomé, 1982, p. 269)

Other surveys that have been carried out in predominantly anglophone settings have dealt with patterns of language use among immigrant and ethnic minorities. Fishman was one of the first researchers in North America to turn his attention to this area of work with the Language Resources Project, which led to a seminal publication in the emerging field of the sociology of language: *Language Loyalty in the United States* (1966). Haugen (1969) has also documented the bilingual experience of linguistic minorities of Scandinavian origin in the USA. More recently, in Canada, a Survey of Non-Official Languages was carried out among those ethnic minorities where languages other than French and English are spoken (O'Bryan, Reitz and Kuplowska, 1976), and surveys of Spanish speakers (Arce, 1982) and of minorities in Montana (Beltramo, 1981) were carried out in the USA.

Any quantitative data on patterns of reported language use collected in this way need to be interpreted and analysed in the light of a much broader qualitative understanding of the social, political and economic context. Polomé (1982) sets out the prerequisites for conducting sociolinguistically oriented surveys in the following terms:

To study a language in its social context on a country-wide scale, it is necessary to have a comprehensive knowledge and understanding of the country and its people, of its economy, of the fabric of the nation, of the historical development of its policies and government administration, as well as of its education system. (Polomé, 1982, p. 266)

Le Page has spelt out in some detail the kinds of background information his team collected for the Sociolinguistic Survey of Multilingual Communities in Belize and St Lucia (1978). Under the first heading, general background information, there are seven major topics, and the other headings range from anecdotal accounts by members of the community to in-depth family studies, a children's questionnaire and one for the family as a whole.

As was argued earlier, in a multilingual setting characterised by immigrant bilingualism some knowledge and understanding of the sociolinguistic history of the different languages and their speakers is a fundamental prerequisite. Some researchers working in bilingual settings have expressed particular dissatisfaction with 'macro' level approaches which combine sociolinguistic description on the basis of survey data, with typological analyses of nations and the linguistic communities within them (Williams and Roberts, 1983). They have called for more explanatory accounts of language use in bilingual communities, which would take into account the economic and historical bases of linguistic inequality.

Although, therefore, we recognised that a survey is sometimes 'an examination which obtains breadth of observation at the expense of depth' (Cooper, 1980), we decided to design our sociolinguistic survey instrument around the central question of 'who speaks what to whom and when'. Each sociolinguistic interview carried out as part of the LMP Adult Language Use Survey focusses on the patterns of language use between the individual respondent at home and other household members. Where appropriate, it also considers language in the workplace, with neighbours, and with other contacts including members of local community organisations. Our standardised questionnaire had to cover a range of social activities and types of contact likely to be common to respondents coming from eleven different linguistic minorities.

The major limitation of surveys of language use is their dependence on information about linguistic behaviour reported by the respondents, not information gathered by observation. Some researchers would argue that such 'self-report' studies are of particular value because they represent the choices that would be made in idealised situations with particular interlocutors, whereas observation would show that actual patterns of language use might be much less clearcut. Whether self-report techniques for eliciting information do in fact also tell us anything about real behaviour depends partly on the relationship between interviewer and respondent (for example, informal and supportive as compared with formal and distant), and partly on the openness and flexibility built into the questions.

Although self-report data is the most obvious outcome of large sample surveys, some sociolinguists are careful to supplement it with other sociolinguistic material, including more unstructured or informal interviews, and with actual 'micro-linguistic' data collected both during interviews and in casual or informal encounters (Gold, 1980; Labov, 1966; Le Page, 1978).

A wider societal analysis of the economic, historical and social bases for discrimination against minority languages necessarily involves 'a general theoretical framework dealing with the structure of language and its relations to society and individuals. Success at this stage depends not only on a correct methodology but also on having an adequate general theoretical framework' (Hudson, 1980, p. 147). The following sections question whether we should accept theories or theoretical paradigms which may not be able to handle all the uses or forms in which language may manifest itself over time in a given linguistic minority (Romaine, 1982). The preoccupation of many sociolinguists with internal linguistic variation has been at the expense of developing a coherent model for the analysis of language use in complex and changing multilingual settings.

One clarification which is fundamental if we are to avoid confusing different levels of abstraction in the development of such a model is the distinction between 'language use' and 'language choice', terms which are sometimes used as if they were interchangeable. The patterns of language use which we present in Chapter 5 are derived from a survey based on self-report data gathered from individuals. We describe there what a large number of people say they do — which may differ in individual cases from what they actually do — but we cannot explain why people act as they do without relating them to the wider social processes in which speakers are actively involved. By relating the data about reported use to that on reported skills, and in some cases to that on reported options, we can build up a picture of the likely social constraints on individual language choice in particular linguistic minorities.

The whole concept of language 'choice' is in fact grounded in an individualistic notion of 'free' choice as influenced by setting, audience, topic, etc. Important work has been done in this connection on communicative competence and choice (e.g. Hymes, 1974; Ervin-Tripp, 1968), but any discussion of the selection of appropriate language or alternation of varieties within a particular bilingual population has always to bear in mind the inequalities and conflicts that are faced by bilinguals in the processes of acquiring and using their different languages, especially if they belong to a linguistic minority.

The factors influencing language choice in individual interactions are not only those of the wider sociocultural context and range of options, and the more specific details of setting, topic, participants, etc. They also include an understanding of speakers' attitudes to the different varieties of their own repertoires, and their perceptions of their interlocutors' perception of them as individuals. Use of a particular language or variety in a particular context may as easily be intended to signal social distance as to indicate social solidarity.

The ethnography of communication is based, as its name implies, on detailed observational studies of linguistic behaviour, and on the identification and analysis of communicative events. On the other hand, many sociolinguistic surveys include language attitude measures (Agheyisi and Fishman, 1970; Cooper and Fishman, 1974; Shuy and Fasold, 1973). Our sociolinguistic survey concentrated on attitudes about provision of language teaching and language maintenance for the respondent's language (see p. 149). But, as already argued, general questions about attitudes to specific languages are inevitably confounded with attitudes towards the users of those languages. Moreover, studies of language attitudes cannot describe and explain linguistic *behaviour*. Responses are also liable to be influenced by the context and style of questioning. This kind of research, and the more experimental work asking a smaller number of individuals from specific linguistic minorities to evaluate recordings of speech or speech guises (Giles and Powesland, 1975; Lambert, 1972), is really looking at inter-group judgments and stereotypes.

Thus language attitude studies incorporated into survey techniques raise many serious methodological problems (see p. 215). But language attitudes and perceptions are of course fundamental in influencing patterns of use. In a minority language situation it is just as crucial to know about the attitudes of people who do not know the language, because many of the attitudes of minority language users are influenced by those held by the dominant majority. And the language attitudes of members of linguistic minorities themselves clearly must have a major influence on the maintenance of a first language among children in many bilingual minorities. 'The phenomenon of parents helping their children to learn the "correct" language [whether standard minority, or dominant English language], so as not to be stigmatized later in life and so as to advance socially, is widespread.' (Grosjean, 1982, p. 123; our addition in brackets).

We will return to some of these issues in the latter part of this book. To conclude this discussion, we should note that the Non-Official Language Survey in Canada was commissioned at the same time as a Majority Attitudes Survey (Berry, Kalin and Taylor, 1977). Unfortunately we could not incorporate a comparable study of majority attitudes within our brief, but, as later chapters of this book illustrate, we received important qualitative feedback on dominant views about bilingualism and linguistic minorities through the carrying out of our surveys (see pp. 314 and 359).

The power of majority attitudes and practices is one of the reasons why, in the case of attitude studies within minority language settings, answers should not be taken at face value (see comparison with MTTD Stage 2). It may be misleading to use data about language maintenance and teaching provision without a complementary understanding of the information available to respondents in relation to actual options, their legal rights and their understanding of the importance of language in educational development.

Language maintenance and shift

The first two chapters of this book pointed to the importance of historical, political, demographic and socio-economic factors in the maintenance of minority languages in England. Density of geographical settlement, time of migration, relationship to the local labour market and social mobility were mentioned in many of the examples cited. There are also different kinds of majority and minority institutional support, such as radio and television programmes in minority languages, minority language press, community-run schools and churches. (See discussions in Chapter 7.) But, as Grosjean argues even about his own list of factors affecting language maintenance and language shift, 'some of these factors are ambivalent, in that they may favour either maintenance or shift'.

> For example, if a minority group is small, it is easier for the leaders of the group to control it and hence to favour language maintenance, but at the same time fewer people and funds will be available for maintenance institutions such as ethnic press, schools, clubs, and so on. (Grosjean, 1982, p. 108)

Factors affecting language maintenance may be fundamental external forces influencing the economic, political and social resources of a linguistic minority. There may also be factors emerging from within the minority; and, in a situation of contact between cultures, this 'internal' response is often a reaction to outside pressures. Similarly, the process of 'language shift' is a reflection of power relations in a society producing a redistribution of social and linguistic resources from generation to generation. It should be clearly distinguished from 'language loss', which occurs during the lifetime of an individual, although of course language loss reflects and contributes to language shift.

Language shift refers to the habitual use of one language being replaced by the habitual use of another (Gal, 1979). The shift to the second language — English in the context of England — involves the gradual disappearance of the first. Sometimes language shift is also called 'language displacement', and it frequently occurs when a nation state is established or when a group of people migrate to another land.

Language shift is particularly rapid in countries of massive immigration like the USA. In this case it is possible to illustrate quite dramatic language shift through the very careful use of demographic data from censuses and surveys carried out over a long period of time. The US data on mother tongue or non-English language background needs to be treated with some caution, not least because of the history of migration and settlement patterns, of differences in the form of question and presentation of data, and of political factors influencing people's decision to claim a language as their mother tongue. It is difficult to measure language shift when it is not the same population that is being counted. Waggoner, reporting US Census data, points out that in 1940

> Nearly 5 million persons reported that their mother tongue was German; persons of German language background were nearly a quarter of all White persons claiming non-English mother tongues; Italian and Polish were the second and third largest groups; Spanish claimants were fourth; Yiddish and French had more than a million claimants each. (1981, p. 490)

whereas in 1970

> Nearly 8 million persons reported Spanish as their mother tongue; Spanish mother tongue claimants constituted nearly one in four of all claimants of non-English mother tongues in the United States; German was second in number of claimants followed by Italian and French; Polish and Yiddish also had more than 1 million claimants each. (1981, p. 491)

We can see how basic survey and census data does present interesting trends. It is only Spanish and French of the 'big six' minority languages in the USA which show any gain since 1940.

Census data does not of course tell us how many people actively use their languages in everyday life, and this is why surveys of actual patterns of language use are necessary. They can help to arrive at explanations for patterns of language shift or maintenance recorded in censuses. Repeated periodically, they can also investigate at least some of the many factors which speed up or slow down what is often believed to be an inevitable process of shift from bilingualism to monolingualism in the dominant language in immigrant countries. And in multilingual minorities, or new coalitions of previously distinct minorities, surveys can explore possible shifts from one minority language to another, alongside the use of the dominant language.

It has been argued that literacy is often an important factor in language maintenance and transmission from one generation to another (Zengel, 1962). The role of written varieties in the standardisation of language has been emphasised by Kloss (1968). And it is often a prestigious written variety which has provided the norms for the spoken standard in those linguistic minorities where there is now a close correspondence between spoken and literary forms. In those minority languages where there is a greater distance between spoken varieties and the standard written variety, deliberate codification or incidental factors may reinforce the standard form of the minority language: e.g. mother tongue teaching or video-tapes and films in the 'national' language (see Chapter 6 and p. 212 respectively).

Without longitudinal research we were of course unable to illustrate language shift over time, except in a limited way, by making careful comparisons between generations and age groups. We could only consider the factors which appear to facilitate the use, and therefore transmission from one generation to another, of the minority language. Simply by establishing particular empirical relationships we are not immediately able to account for those relationships.

Considering all the various factors we have mentioned so far, stable societal bilingualism among most linguistic minorities in England is highly unlikely. Unstable bilingualism, reflected in language shift and assimilation to the dominant language and culture, is much more likely. But these concepts of stable and unstable bilingualism (Fishman, 1967) are not in themselves very useful, because they do not help us to uncover the processes by which stability or instability may have arisen. As Gal reminds us in her book about the influence of industrialisation on Hungarian German bilinguals in a particular region of Austria:

> although it is possible to list the broad social circumstances in which various cases of language shift have occurred, it has proved considerably harder to isolate a specific set of factors whose presence allows one to predict a language shift. (Gal, 1979, p. 3)

The distinction between stable and unstable bilingualism may in fact depend upon differences in the duration of the process. A linguistic minority undergoing language shift may manifest the use of both languages for several generations. This was the case in Wales. As Lewis (1978) has pointed out, a situation of diglossia existed there for centuries, up until the nineteenth century. It was only with the massive industrialisation of South Wales and the advent of universal schooling through the medium of English that the process of shift to English began.

Both Gal and Lewis stress the fundamental economic factors underlying language shift. Other factors which we have not mentioned so far, but which are discussed by other authors in relation to non-indigenous minority languages, include periods of nationalism, pressure towards assimilation, education policies of the dominant group, and intermarriage (Clyne, 1976; Grosjean, 1982).

A number of other researchers who have worked in the very different settings of Austria, Belize, Belfast and East Africa (Gal, 1979; Le Page, 1978; Milroy, 1980; Parkin, 1974b) remind us that the study of the process of language shift needs to be set in a framework which can deal with linguistic variation in social interaction in specific localities.

This is where the use of network analysis can help elucidate certain theoretical problems beyond the reach of survey methods. The importance of the social networks of speakers was demonstrated in the early work of Blom and Gumperz (1972). They argued that we cannot explain the language use of different linguistic minorities simply by proving that they qualify as members of a speech community by virtue of being speakers of a particular language. It is only by looking at the informal networks in which speakers are enmeshed that we can begin to appreciate the pressures and inducements to conform to certain linguistic norms. So Gal, for example, to complement her sociolinguistic interviews did intensive obervational work, looking at the different types of social network of her subjects:

> Speakers' social networks affected the range of values and statuses they could symbolize in speech, and so differences between speakers in social networks were reflected in differences in language use. (Gal, 1979, p. 16)

> It is through their effects on the shape of social networks, on the statuses speakers want to claim and on cultural associations between linguistic varieties and social groups that macro-sociological factors can influence the language choices of speakers in everyday interaction. (Ibid., p. 17)

The work of Gal reinforces other studies, which stress that the identities of the participants in an interaction are the critical influences of language choice between languages or varieties known to all participants.

Le Page argues that each utterance a speaker makes is 'an act of identity'. And the important relationship between language use, network structures and ethnic identity is also demonstrated in Parkin's work on emergent and stabilised multilingualism in Nairobi. Parkin looked at polyethnic peer groups in one study and showed that the gangs and societies differed 'less in their actual use of their English or Swahili, but more in their claims regarding usage' (Parkin, 1974c, p. 203). Their perceptions of how they used language reflected their consciousness of their place in society and, as Parkin argues, their ideas about, and use of, language may reflect incipient changes in features of the social structure.

The changing association of some linguistic varieties with prestigious social categories, and others with stigmatised ones, is produced by social changes which influence the self-identification of speakers. In a situation of rapid social change such as that experienced in England, it is likely that the new generations of British-born bilinguals will have a wider and more complex linguistic repertoire than their migrant parents. Each new generation, then, reinterprets the relationship between linguistic forms and social groups, and consequently re-evaluates the prestige and meaning of different linguistic varieties.

Milroy's work has shown that there are strong pressures, in long-established neighbourhoods, especially among people with close-knit networks, for the maintenance of social and linguistic norms. If speech is used to symbolise specific social and ethnic identities in less stable social settings, then it is easier to understand Le Page's claim that speakers (in a multilingual society) use their resources of variability to express different aspects of a fluid social identity.

Domains, diglossia and code-switching

The two concepts of 'domain' and 'diglossia' have been particularly useful in the development of sociolinguistic studies of bilingual societies. Like the concepts of 'language status', 'ethnolinguistic vitality' and 'speech community', they have been important in helping sociolinguists to clarify and extend their investigation into potential social influences on language use and variation.

Fishman suggested in 1965 that the central question for sociolinguists was 'Who speaks what, to whom, and when?' In 1972 he argued that the analytic concept of 'domain' helped to link the analysis of patterns of language use at the level of face-to-face encounters, with widespread sociocultural norms and expectations (1972a). Fishman saw each domain – home, neighbourhood, school, church, workplace, official institutions, etc. – as differentiated into specific sets of distinct role relations. The assumption underlying this classification is that language use in a bilingual population will vary from domain to domain, each domain reflecting its particular kind of locality, with a particular kind of interaction, involving a particular kind of topic. Fishman developed the concept of domain as a means of illustrating (and, some critics would argue, of predicting) the very different linguistic outcomes likely in different types of bilingual settings.

Fishman also developed Ferguson's original 1959 definition of diglossia:

> a relatively stable language situation in which, in addition to the primary dialects of the language . . . there is a very divergent, highly codified, superimposed variety, the vehicle of a large and respected body of written literature either of an earlier period or in another speech community, which is learned largely by formal education and is used for most written and formal spoken purposes but is not used by any sector of the community for ordinary conversation. (Ferguson, in Dil (ed.), 1971a, p. 16)

While Ferguson argued that this superimposed or 'high' variety was not used by any sector of the community for ordinary conversation, unlike the dialectal or 'low' varieties, Fishman used the term 'diglossia' more generally, so that diglossia came to mean simply the functional distribution of two or more languages or language varieties within a speech community. In a diglossic situation in this broader sense the bilingual speaker may have greater choice of which language to use in spoken or written form: in Fishman's terms the 'domain' becomes a much less important predictor of language use.

For many researchers the term 'domain' has come to mean 'setting', but it is obvious that setting, however defined, is only one sociological constraint on an individual's language choice. The concept of domain is not rooted within any clear theoretical framework, although, as mentioned above, it was obviously an attempt to link discussion about language choice with wider social constraints on language use. Most fundamentally, the concept of domain cannot take into account the essentially conflictual nature of the relationship between a minority language and the language of a dominant society. Both concepts, domain and diglossia, assume a neatly defined choice between two discrete language systems, when in fact we are often dealing with variation within a more complex linguistic repertoire. A further problem with important methodological implications relates to who decides on the boundaries between domains, and on the basis of which criteria.

This latter point was particularly evident to us when we considered critically the wide range of social activities which might have been covered on our Adult Language Use Survey questionnaire. We partially rejected the assumptions underlying the notion of domain, especially when linked with diglossia, and aimed to explore for ourselves reported patterns of use. But we chose questions relating to particular spheres of social activity as well as to specific relationships. The attempt to develop one survey instrument which would be equally applicable to eleven different linguistic minorities brought to mind particular activities and relationships which were not appropriate for all linguistic minorities. During our analysis of the data we also had to remember that different institutions can have a different significance for one minority (or section of a minority) from that which it has for another – e.g. temple and mosque for Hindu and Muslim Gujerati speakers respectively.

One of the most serious criticisms of the concept of domain arises when it is linked with the notion of diglossia to imply that particular distributions of language functions and usage can explain language shift and maintenance (Pedraza and Attinasi, 1980). The concept of domain helps to identify and distinguish the diglossic characteristics of bilingual situations, and Fishman (1980) points to four possible combinations of bilingualism and diglossia. But any assumption, for example, that his combination of bilingualism without diglossia will lead to language loss and shift needs to be questioned:

> bilingualism without diglossia tends to be transitional both in terms of the linguistic repertoires of speech communities as well as in terms of the speech varieties involved per se. Without separate though complementary norms and values to establish and maintain functional separation of the speech varieties, that language or variety which is fortunate enough to be associated with the predominant drift of social forces tends to displace the other(s). (Fishman, 1971, p. 298)

At a very general level of analysis it is possible to say that, in England, there is a functional separation of majority and minority languages. Minority languages are rarely used in 'official' public interactions, institutions or the media, etc. This is a statement about overall societal bilingualism, with no explanation of why this should be the case. But this societal diglossia, in Fishman's sense, should not be – and indeed is not necessarily — reflected in some kind of individual diglossia, where an individual inevitably restricts the use of his or her languages or varieties to specific spheres of social activity. Most members of linguistic minorities in England are bilingual, and while one language or variety may be used predominantly in some places or with some people, no generalisation can be made for all sections of the population (old and young, male and female, the middle and working classes). As illustrated in Chapter 1, many members of linguistic minorities in England have repertoires including a range of different languages and varieties, and linguistic analysis which is 'biased towards the description of autonomous discrete systems' (Romaine, 1981, p. 123) hampers a dynamic appreciation of the fluid and complex variability of real language use.

Research on bilingualism has conventionally been concerned with instances of what Hymes (1974) has called 'bilingualism par excellence'; that is, with settings where alternate use of two discrete languages is the characteristic pattern within a particular community. There are, of course, many examples where there are no specifically linguistic criteria available for determining the 'boundaries' between different languages and varieties. One example is that of the Caribbean Creole-Standard British English continuum in Britain today, within which there are different varieties of English-based Creoles which originate in different islands in the West Indies, and there are new Black British Creole forms emerging (Edwards, 1979; Sutcliffe, 1982). The communicative repertoires of many of the new generation of Creole speakers in Britain include both these Creole forms and traditional urban varieties of English, making it impossible to characterise such elaborate multilectal repertoires solely in terms of the traditional models of bilingualism referred to earlier.

Sociolinguistic surveys are limited, then, in the exploration of internal patterns of variation in language use among different sections of a linguistic minority. But there are also more fundamental questions which cannot be answered by language surveys that depend upon self-report data. For example, we cannot find out by this research approach whether many bilinguals would use a language other than English more often if they were not prevented from doing so, or if they were positively encouraged to do so. Nor can we discover how we arrive at a situation where many British-born bilinguals do not have a real choice of languages to use, because language loss (during early adolescence in particular) means they no longer have the necessary skills in both languages.

One of the likely explanations of this lies in the power and pervasiveness of the dominant English language. It is the political, economic and social processes that encourage this situation, ensuring that English is used in some form or other in nearly all spheres of social activity, including the home, religion and even, increasingly, in community-run 'mother tongue' schooling. In addition, language-switching and borrowing are typical features of many bilingual settings, especially in minority language situations where inter-group barriers are breaking down. Changes in the structure of interpersonal relations lead also to the creation of new communicative conventions and discourse strategies (Gumperz, 1982b).

Code-switching from one language to another within the same conversation is a mode of communication which cannot be accounted for within the static structural-functional view of language use, represented by the domain-diglossia paradigm. The existence of this discourse strategy illustrates the actual and perceived non-separation of languages and varieties. However, in her analysis of the sociolinguistic situation that exists in Spanish-English bilingualism in New York, Poplack (1984) argues that code-switching does not necessarily result in language disintegration or loss. It may even sustain bilingual skills. Whether the code-switching is intra- or inter-sentential, it does not violate the grammar of either language. While only the most fluent bilinguals use the most complicated form of code-switching, most members make some use of it.

The phenomenon of code-switching reminds us that a minority language may come to have less communicative and more symbolic value over time. This is particularly evident in the case of adolescents who have almost lost their verbal skills in their first language, but who come to reassert their ethnic identity through distinctive patterns of language use or discourse strategies. We are now talking about language loss during the lifetime of an individual, and collective experiences of this process will of course influence patterns of language shift. There is, Gumperz suggests, code-switching among those who are most involved in, or most affected by, social change, e.g. the younger generation of speakers (Gumperz, 1982a). It is therefore interesting to hear of suggestions that when adolescents enter into young adult roles they appear to speak more of the minority language. As Pedraza and Attinasi remark, the increase in the use of Spanish in Puerto Rican Harlem 'may not be sufficient to reverse the shift to English preference evident from this segment of the community, but could be instrumental in maintaining bilingualism' (1980, p. 29). There is already a considerable body of literature on the expressive discourse functions of code-switching in bilingual settings (Gumperz, 1964; Gumperz, 1970; Blom and Gumperz, 1972; Luke and Richards, 1982). There are communicative settings in many bilingual communities where this mode of mixed discourse is an accepted convention, and constitutes a specialised form of verbal skill.

Much more research on the specifically linguistic aspects of bilingual discourse is needed before these phenomena can be better understood. Research of this kind usually involves the analysis of linguistic data from a tape-recorded corpus including different speech events. For example, Lavandera's analysis of recorded conversations among different speakers of Cocoliche, a variety of Spanish spoken by the minority community of Italian origin in Buenos Aires, concludes:

> For these speakers, Spanish and Italian are not independent codes, at least not more so than the different registers of a monolingual speaker. In fact, the dialect and Spanish are only labels assigned to different speech events where the circumstances of the interaction, the greater or lesser amount of attention paid to speech, the presence or absence of monolingual Spanish speakers, lead to a different apportioning of forms from the dialect and Spanish and to their distribution at different levels. (Lavandera, 1978, p. 403)

Speech community and emergent varieties

Another concept which is under some scrutiny among sociolinguists working with linguistic minorities in England is the concept of 'speech community'. As Romaine points out, 'The imbrication of social and linguistic structure in a given speech community is a matter for investigation and cannot be taken as given' (1982, p. 13). This point applies equally well to the concept of domain. Discussing sociolinguistic studies of indigenous 'communities' in Britain, Romaine concludes that 'even fairly homogeneous speech communities may display more than one direction of change and variation, and sub-groups within the community can be characterized by bimodal distributions with respect to the use of the same variable, i.e. they use it different ways' (ibid., p. 14). 'We scarcely know how heterogeneous some speech communities are' (ibid., p. 15).

It will be clear from the profiles of linguistic minorities in Chapter 2 that there is considerable social and linguistic heterogeneity among most linguistic minorities in England. Even if we focus on one city and discount younger children who are still learning their language or languages, members of the same family have different patterns of language use because of the different composition of their social networks. The type and place of economic activity are particularly significant in determining network structures in urban society.

Each speaker's linguistic repertoire will reflect just part of the totality of distinct language varieties, dialects and styles employed by members of the local linguistic minority. And their communicative repertoire may need to include knowledge of the sociolinguistic norms which allow the more fluently bi- or multilingual to communicate with the less fluent or even monolingual members of the linguistic minority.

This suggests that the concept of speech community, which implies a functionally integrated social system with shared norms of evaluation, cannot apply to the fluid social situations found among many bilingual minorities in England. Differences in values and social and ethnic identities will not be uncovered if we start from the common assumption of shared norms, and of an ethnic, religious or socio-economic homogeneity so often associated with the term 'community'. Gumperz has recently said the following about his earlier influential study with Blom in an apparently homogeneous, isolated Norwegian community:

> All residents spoke both the local dialect and a regional variant of Bokmal, one of the two accepted forms of standard Norwegian. However, all speakers differed with respect to where and for what communicative goals they chose among the two codes. What was normal usage for some in some situations counted as marked for others . . . Language usage in situations such as these is thus not simply a matter of conforming to norms of appropriateness but is a way of conveying information about values, beliefs and attitudes that must first be discovered through ethnographic investigation. (Gumperz, 1982a, p. 27)

Gumperz goes on to argue that traditional sociolinguistic paradigms which begin by isolating particular features of language use, and then seek to demonstrate that they correlate with extra-linguistically determined categories such as gender, age, social status or discourse context, are not enough. He argues that there is a need for a sociolinguistic theory which accounts for the communicative functions of linguistic variability and for its relation to speakers' goals without reference to 'untestable functionalist assumptions about conformity or nonconformity to closed systems of norms' (ibid., p. 29).

Dorian's research among bilingual Gaelic-English speaking people in

East Sutherland shows that there too there are no clear-cut boundaries between distinct speech communities – one of them bilingual, the other monolingual. She argues that the near-passive bilinguals and the low-proficiency 'semi-speakers' cannot be 'set off from the other aggregates by significant differences in language use', (Dorian, 1982), although on strictly linguistic criteria they would not qualify for full membership of the bilingual community. These 'marginal' members have outstanding receptive control of East Sutherland Gaelic and knowledge of the sociolinguistic norms which operate within the Gaelic-speaking community.

The parallel with non-indigenous multilingual minorities is striking:

> interaction networks which include both fully fluent Gaelic domi-nant bilinguals and low-proficiency semi-speakers or near-passive bilinguals, and even young English monolinguals are fairly common. (Ibid., p. 28)

Even when low-proficiency network members spoke rarely, or in a grammatically innovatory way, their verbal output was semantically well integrated with what preceded in the conversation.

Dorian's analysis leads her to accept two approaches to speech com-munities which do not define out members who have low productive capacity but high receptive capacity and who conform to sociolinguistic norms. However, her acceptance of Hymes's proposal that the social group rather than the language be taken as the starting point is not consistent with her statement that 'since all Gaelic-speaking fisherfolk descendants are bilingual they belong simultaneously to two speech communities' (ibid., p. 25).

As bilingual speakers develop their distinctive linguistic repertoires and discourse strategies out of two (or more) languages used in specific social contexts, it is sociologically very dubious to assume that separate membership of two 'speech communities' can be anything but a linguis-tic description. If she accepts the definition of a speech community as made up of people who regard themselves as speaking the same language, then the scope of the definition would need to be extended in the multilingual situations of England to include all those who regard them-selves as speaking the same minority language or all those who regard themselves as sharing a common collective (community) repertoire.

This is not a trivial debate about definitions! Hudson has provided a more elegant survey of the six main types of definition of a 'speech community' (and we cannot resist noting here his final comment that 'it is possible that speech communities do not really exist except as prototypes in the minds of people, in which case the search for the "true" definition of "speech community" is just a wild goose chase' (Hudson, 1980 p. 30). One of the definitions he cites which explicitly recognises the multilingual dimension is from one of Gumperz's earlier works:

> We will define [linguistic community] as a social group which may be either monolingual or multilingual, held together by frequency of social interaction patterns and set off from the surrounding areas by weaknesses in the lines of communication. (Gumperz, in Dil (ed.), 1971b, p. 101)

This definition in the form used here does not clarify who is to draw the boundaries between communities, nor does it make clear that weaknesses in the lines of communication may be assessed differently by insiders and outsiders. Le Page's approach, which avoids the term 'speech community' altogether, is based on the notion of groups which the individual speaker perceives to exist. Le Page's hypothesis is that each individual creates the systems for his verbal behaviour 'so that they shall resemble those of the groups with which from time to time he may wish to be identified' (Le Page et al., 1974).

Any suggestion that members of linguistic minorities belong to two or more 'speech communities' — that of the dominant English and that of the subordinate non-English language — is confusing and distorting. While it makes no contribution to a more dynamic sociolinguistic theory which recognises the relationship between language and ethnicity, it also reinforces the prevailing notion that members of ethnic minorities are 'between two cultures' — not full members of one or the other. Similarly, a recent questionnaire by some of those working on the concept of 'ethnolinguistic vitality' aimed at assessing 'how group members subjectively perceive their own group's position relative to salient outgroups on important "vitality" dimensions' falls into the same trap by imposing underlying dichotomies and limiting the options for self-definition (Bourhis, Giles and Rosenthal, 1981).

Many bilingual people are bicultural and have multiple ethnic identities (Pradelle de Latour, 1983). This is not necessarily the case, however; some people who use two languages on a regular basis are relatively monocultural, and a so-called monolingual person may be relatively bicultural.

In the United States where language shift takes place extremely quickly, one finds many English-speaking Native Americans and second or third generation immigrants who share two overlapping cultures. This is the case for many English-speaking Italian, Japanese and Polish Americans, for example, as well as for many American Jews. (Grosjean, 1982, p. 158)

The wide range of possible components in a Panjabi-English or Greek-English adolescent's linguistic and cultural repertoire reflects the complex relationship between patterns of language socialisation and networks of social relations, changing over time. They influence the youngster's perception of the competing or parallel pressures to social and linguistic conformity from the dominant majority and their own communities. Even within one local linguistic minority the norms about code-switching and notions about ethnic identity and about the relative autonomy of language varieties may differ.

Some bilingual adolescents have good communicative skills in their two languages but do not use one of them, or only do so in very restricted circumstances. Over time competence in this less-used language may therefore decrease. Other adolescents can skilfully demonstrate their knowledge of two distinct grammatical systems through the use of code-switching.

The only substantial sociolinguistic study of British-born Panjabi speakers in England emphasises these problems of sociolinguistic description, and of linguistic repertoires which cannot be separated out into discrete and autonomous systems. Agnihotri describes the emergence of a mixed code developing out of its speakers' selection of Panjabi and English according to place, person, topic and certain internal linguistic factors. This mixed code forms an integral part of the collective verbal repertoire of the 'community'.

Thus the Sikh children are being simultaneously exposed to Panjabi and English. The social pressures, the intensity of motivation and the opportunities available to learn are different in each case. The result of this complex interaction is the emergence of a mixed Panjabi-English code being increasingly influenced by English. The use of unadulterated Panjabi has nearly ceased to exist among the Sikh children in Leeds. It is the Mixed Code and not Panjabi which must be recognised as the medium of intra-group communication, as against English as the medium of inter-group contacts. (Agnihotri, 1979, p. 256)

This new emerging code, therefore, and the complex repertoire of which it is a part, are linguistic expressions of a social structural relationship. British Panjabi-speaking children are in the process of creating continually changing patterns of language use and social relations, which take on different characteristics in different social settings. While language use must be looked at, and can only be understood, as part of social activity, it is of course a crucial ingredient in making sense of experience. We have always to ask ourselves what the social meaning of the different languages and varieties is for the speakers themselves. Without this background knowledge it is difficult to devise appropriate questions about patterns of language use. The emerging cultures and linguistic repertoires of British-born adolescents of different linguistic minorities present a major challenge to many conventional forms of sociolinguistic description, and to sociological studies of inter-group relations in England.

4
Adult Language Use: preparing a survey

Research focus and fieldwork strategies

The main purpose of the Adult Language Use Survey (ALUS) under-taken by the Linguistic Minorities Project in 1980 and 1981 was to increase understanding of the patterns of language skills and use among adult members of linguistic minorities in a number of different urban settings in England. The information gathered was intended to help us analyse the current characteristics and likely future extent of bi-lingualism among post-World War Two migrants and their British-born descendants.

As well as helping in the task of formulating policy, ALUS was intended to provide an important contribution to the academic debate. It would, we hoped, contribute towards the kind of understanding of the wider social context which is essential for informed discussion about the educational implications of bilingualism. Besides giving an account of the development and administration of ALUS, this chapter shows how our decision to use survey methods raised crucial questions about the appropriate research strategy for working in urban multilingual situations. Although we faced particular difficulties in the sampling and fieldwork procedures, their resolution provided us with valuable insights into the social and economic position of different linguistic minorities.

Our interests in the issues outlined in Chapter 3 led us to design the ALUS survey instrument around the general themes of language use and language maintenance. We wanted to know about the patterns of language use, and the factors that seemed to support minority language use among linguistic minorities in England. With additional data on minority language teaching this would, we hoped, throw some light on the likelihood of language maintenance, or of shift away from the use of the minority language. We developed our research strategy and questionnaire around these themes.

The following factors seemed to us likely to be of importance in any given linguistic minority, although not all could be directly investigated by means of a survey:

(a) the range and level of spoken language skills of respondents (and to a limited extent of their interlocutors), and the relationship of skills to language use patterns;

(b) the extent and functions of literacy in both minority languages and English, and the role of literacy in the process of language maintenance;

(c) the patterns of language use and skills in the different generations, particularly in the context of the family;

(d) the position in the economy of a linguistic minority, and of individual respondents, and the effect this has on language use and maintenance;

(e) residential settlement patterns, size and concentration of linguistic minorities as a factor in language maintenance;

(f) the role in language maintenance of interpersonal network structures and participation in minority institutions;

(g) the relationship of attitudes to language maintenance, ethnic affiliation and language use patterns, with major social variables such as gender, age, education and occupation;

(h) the use of code-switching by bilingual speakers as a communicative strategy.

The range of linguistic minorities in England, the wide brief of the project, and the desirability of comparative work combined to suggest that ALUS should be designed to include as many different languages as possible, each in at least two out of three different cities. Coventry, Bradford and London were chosen in order to give a geographical spread, and to allow us to work with eleven of the nationally most numerous linguistic minorities which are represented in those cities. The languages chosen were Bengali, Cantonese/Chinese, Greek, Gujerati, Italian, Panjabi, Polish, Portuguese, Turkish, and Ukrainian. The Panjabi speakers were treated as two separate linguistic minorities: for ALUS these were designated 'Panjabi: Gurmukhi Script' and 'Panjabi: Urdu Script', abbreviated as Panjabi(G) and Panjabi(U) respectively. (See pp. 45f. for a fuller discussion.)

These eleven linguistic minorities represent a range of languages originating in different parts of Asia and Europe, with varied migration histories, from post-war Eastern European political refugees to more recent migrants who came to England in response to the demand for cheap labour in the expanding economy of post-war Britain (see p. 31). The resulting coverage is thus in a very broad sense representative of the range of linguistic minorities in the country as a whole.

For each of the linguistic minorities we attempted to select and interview a sample of speakers which was as representative as possible of that minority population within the city in question. The number of respondents in each sample was as large as we could manage, given the constraints of the number of linguistic minorities involved and the time and financial limits on our work. It was decided that a total sample for any local linguistic minority should, wherever possible, be at least 200, in order to give meaningful breakdowns between different kinds of respondents, for example males and females, younger and older. However, in the case of the smaller populations we were compelled to accept a lower target figure. In most although not all cases enough interviews were completed to come close to the targets we had set (see Table 4.1).

The local economic and political situations in which we were working led us to develop a specific set of strategies in the field. Most of the ALUS respondents lived in inner city areas, many of which are characterised by economic decline, and by a social and political context dominated by official majority institutions. In this kind of setting members of minorities often feel particularly powerless and insecure, and can be justifiably suspicious of the intentions of the local bureaucracy, especially in connection with their legal rights and with any

Table 4.1 ALUS actual (and target) sample sizes in Coventry, Bradford and London

	Coventry	Bradford	London
Bengali	79 (75)		185 (200)
Chinese	43 (50)	50 (50)	137 (150)
Greek			193 (200)
Gujerati	203 (200)		99 (100)
Italian	108 (100)		94 (100)
Panjabi(G)	200 (200)	98 (100)	
Panjabi(U)	86 (100)	177 (200)	
Polish	168 (200)	155 (200)	
Portuguese			197 (200)
Turkish			196 (200)
Ukrainian	48 (50)		
TOTAL	935 (975)	480 (550)	1101 (1150)

interest in sources of income or personal information. 1980 and 1981 were the years when the Nationality Bill was under discussion, and the threat and eventual passage of this legislation heightened the level of insecurity of all minorities who had any connection, however remote, with countries outside the UK. It was a period of recession and high levels of unemployment, which disproportionately affected members of ethnic minorities and inner city areas. During these years the relationships between inner city communities and the police reached a new low, culminating in the wave of 'riots' in the summer of 1981. More generally the rapid developments in information technology caused widespread concern about the confidentiality of personal data in a computerised society. All these factors and the resulting insecurities could have made our task impossible, and were in fact reflected in some of our contacts with minority language speakers.

It is very significant that one of the most frequent questions put to the interviewers by respondents was about where we had obtained their names. Many other respondents wanted assurances that their names would not be mentioned. Although interviewers explained the survey confidentiality rules before starting the interview, some respondents still needed assurances that their names would not be mentioned. Others found particular questions intrusive, or the large number of questions somewhat overwhelming. For example, several interviewers found that details of people's ages were not always readily forthcoming: sometimes because they were not precisely known, but in some cases, it seemed, because the respondent was aware of inaccuracies in records held by other official bodies. Other respondents expressed scepticism that the research would ever lead to action which would benefit the local people. However, on the whole we were able to overcome most of these difficulties by our awareness of potential sensitivities, or through the mediation of interviewers who themselves had been convinced of our goodwill.

It was essential, therefore, that a project which was based in a majority institution should earn and keep the confidence of the members of the linguistic minorities we were working with. This we felt to be important, first of all as part of our social responsibility to the people concerned, and secondly in order to ensure the success of the survey. Our approach therefore was positively to seek out and encourage the collaboration of individuals and organisations within the linguistic minorities, for a task which they might feel to be of benefit to themselves and their children. Our intention was that the findings of the project should eventually be made available in a form accessible to and usable by the minority organisations themselves, as well as by official bodies.

The use of the minority language as the main medium for interviewing was established as a principle of our work from a very early stage. ALUS can claim to be the first large-scale survey in England where major attention has been paid to the linguistic factors in interviewing, and where interviewing in English is the exception rather than the rule.

The need for our questionnaires and interviewers to be bilingual was only partly to ensure communication with the widest range of respondents. More importantly, it was to show that we recognised the legitimacy of languages other than English for serious public purposes, and in certain cases to show that we did not undervalue certain stigmatised dialects. Nor did we feel that we were likely to be given accurate answers to questions about use of particular language varieties if the questions were posed in a language which was itself distant from that most commonly used by the respondents. Thus the production of good translations and the recruitment of teams of bilingual interviewers from local linguistic minorities became crucial in the preparation of the survey. They were to work mainly in the minority languages, introducing themselves and the survey in these languages rather than in English. They were only to use English in those cases where the respondent asked them to do so, or initiated a language switch.

The interviewers were also instructed to record on the questionnaire any occurrences of code-switching in either direction. Since we thought it likely that the language use patterns during the interview would produce some secondary data of great interest to sociolinguists, we arranged to audio-record a sample of the interviews in most of the languages.

The remainder of the present chapter discusses in more detail how the survey instrument was designed, how the bilingual and collaborative strategies were implemented in the field, and how the samples were selected. The particular circumstances in which we were seeking to undertake survey work called for original approaches to each of these three tasks in the different linguistic minorities.

Many of our initial ideas on language surveys came from previous work in the tradition of the sociolinguistic surveys referred to in Chapter 3 (see also Ohanessian, Ferguson and Polomé 1975). We attempted to build on the existing strengths of this work, and to adapt it to a new set of local conditions. We introduced some new types of question based on our particular interests — for example, on functions of literacy, on the role of language in the ethnic economy, and on the importance of mother tongue schools and other minority institutions in the process of language maintenance.

A number of limitations are of course inherent in the survey approach to societal bilingualism. In the first place, the data is based on respondents' answers to questions about habitual practice, but which are given at a specific point of time and are therefore affected by the limitations of memory. Longer-term reflection on language use, for example by means of 'language diaries', might produce a different picture. Secondly, survey data is undoubtedly affected by the expectations of the respondent and the interviewer and by the nature of the interaction between them. For example, an interviewer from the same linguistic minority as the respondent, speaking in the minority language, might receive answers quite different to those given to a majority, English-speaking interviewer. Finally it must be stressed that survey data is essentially self-report data, and that observation or tape-recording over a longer period of time might reveal very different patterns of language use. This mismatch of self-report with actual behaviour was vividly illustrated in accounts of a number of the interviews. Some interviewers reported, for example, that respondents who had just said that they always spoke the minority language with their children, subsequently spoke in English to a child who had entered the room. (It must be acknowledged of course that the effect of the interviewer's presence here may have been the overriding factor in the situation.) Equally, other respondents who said they used only English were observed speaking in the minority language.

A further limitation of the survey approach is that researchers may wish to know the answers to questions about language use which respondents with no particular interest in language would not normally consider or articulate, or about facts which they are reluctant to talk about openly to a stranger. Therefore, in order to obtain the maximum amount of meaningful, relevant and accurate information, it was necessary to pay very great attention to the wording, position and manner of presentation of each question.

We decided to interview a single individual in each household, rather than whole families. It would have been possible to design a questionnaire in which every member of a household was interviewed separately, or even together, but this would have led to major complications in the gathering of the data and in data processing and analysis. This decision meant that most of the questions, and all the detailed ones about such topics as language learning history, were restricted to eliciting information about the individual respondents themselves. However, in order to establish the context in which respondents interacted with other speakers, it was essential to include certain questions about the language skills and use of other household members, and of workmates. Many interviews did in fact take place when other household members were present, and some interviewers reported cases where, for example, a husband or father attempted to answer questions on behalf of the wife or child, or where a lively discussion took place between family members. In other cases a woman suggested that the interviewer should put the question to her husband, or less frequently the reverse. And occasionally a respondent answered questions in the first person plural – 'We do this . . .' or 'We think that . . .' These examples illustrate the fact that survey methodology has developed from individualistic assumptions that are common in Western thought and culture, and may not be the ideal method for gathering detailed data on the sociology of language in different sociocultural settings.

Since the ALUS survey instrument was designed to be used for easy data-processing, most of the questions were precoded. Naturally, for the interviewers, this also proved much more convenient than having to write down extensive answers verbatim. After piloting had established the range of answers we could expect, only a small number of open-ended questions were retained, and these were mostly ones which could be answered in one or two words.

Routing instructions and the internal logic of the questionnaire were also a major design difficulty. Much time and effort was spent both before and after piloting on defining the possible paths through the questionnaire, and in clarifying the instructions to skip questions or sections in the case of respondents who fulfilled certain conditions. For example, in the case of a respondent who had not worked during the last two years, the interviewer would be directed to omit the questions on language in the workplace.

The recurring themes throughout the questionnaire were the language skills and language use patterns of the respondents, and of the people with whom they interacted. The questionnaire was structured in sections based on different social settings, such as the home, the workplace, and minority institutions. As well as the sections on language use, a literacy section and a section on attitudes to language maintenance were included. Questions about important demographic variables such as age, gender, occupation and religion were also posed.

However, since some respondents were likely to be very sensitive to questions about some of this demographic information, questions about migration history, contact with the country of origin, religion and home ownership were placed at the end of the interview, and worded with particular care. It became clear at the piloting stage that some potential questions, such as those on the details of the respondent's birthplace, birthdate and migration history, were likely to be threatening to respondents. Given the current climate of 'race relations' and the ongoing debate about immigration and citizenship policies, these were deliberately excluded from the interviews.

The questionnaire was designed to be generally applicable across a range of languages. This meant that all questions had to be relevant to as wide a variety of minority language speakers as possible. In order to facilitate analysis of the data, the questionnaire had to be constructed on the basis that for the majority of respondents only two languages – the main spoken minority language and English – were fundamentally significant on a day-to-day basis. We knew that this focus in the questionnaire on only two languages would not elicit a comprehensive account of the sociolinguistic situation of those linguistic minorities where multilingualism was common. This was the case for speakers of Chinese languages, or where a language of literacy distinct from the spoken language was used, for example Urdu for some Panjabi speakers, or where a non-standard variety was used in daily life, as among Italian speakers.

The most difficult question of all in this respect was the first one in the questionnaire, which indicated for the interviewer whether respondents saw themselves in fact to be users of the relevant minority language, and therefore whether or not the interviewer should proceed. This problem was closely bound up with our definitions of linguistic minorities (see p. 18), with the way we had defined the boundaries of the populations for sampling in ALUS, with our bilingual interviewing strategy, and with the instructions to interviewers about which potential respondents were to be regarded as within the scope of the survey. Even so, the interviewers occasionally found they had to deal with cases we had not anticipated. For example one Panjabi(G) interviewer in Coventry was surprised when the person who answered the door on one occasion was a man of European appearance. Undeterred, the interviewer asked him if he spoke Panjabi; since the answer was positive, the interviewer explained more and started to ask the questions in Panjabi, and to record the replies. The respondent turned out to be a man of Ukrainian origin who had learned some Panjabi from neighbours and customers in his shop. Eventually the interview switched to English and, since the level of Panjabi skills reported was rather low, it was decided in the end not to include the interview in the analysis of the data. A similar case involved an English person who, having heard about the survey, telephoned the project and asked to be interviewed. He wondered if he qualified as a 'speaker of Chinese' since he had spent time studying the language at home before going to live in East Asia. In the event we decided not to interview him, since he did not make regular use of a Chinese language at home.

In the pilot version of the questionnaire the wording of the first question was: 'Would you please list for me all the languages you know?' One of the languages listed, other than English, then provided the principal focus for subsequent questions. In cases where only one language, or one language plus English, was mentioned, everything ran smoothly. Usually this language was the one in which the interviewer had started to speak, in which the interview continued, and which had been anticipated in the selection of the household. However, in some cases, where more than two languages were mentioned, especially in linguistic minorities where different varieties are seen as uniquely appropriate for different functions, there was uncertainty for both interviewer and respondent about how to interpret and answer some of the questions. The general solution to this problem adopted after piloting was to rephrase the first question as: 'Which languages do you know besides (the named minority language) including regional languages and dialects?' thus defining from the start the language which was to be the focus of the interview.

However, there were five languages in the survey whose specific sociolinguistic characteristics forced us to special solutions, either in the wording of questions, or in instructions to interviewers and coders. In the case of Italian, Gujerati and Bengali, the problem with the first question arose because many of the respondents spoke a related language, or a non-standard variety, as a home language. In the Italian case, for example, while the focus of most of the questions was on standard Italian, the majority of respondents spoke one or more of a number of distinct regional 'dialetti'. For most of them the standard variety of Italian was first encountered at school, with the result that questions about early language learning tended to be answered with reference to the regional variety, and questions about literacy skills were often understood as referring to standard Italian. Respondents would have been uncertain what was meant if we had simply asked questions about 'your language', and might have denied or under-reported their language skills if they had thought all the questions were about the standard variety.

In order to simplify the handling of the data, the interviewers were instructed to elicit the names of particular local varieties in the first question, and in the questions about childhood language learning. In questions where the contrast with English was the main focus, however, they were told to ignore the distinction between non-standard and standard varieties. A very similar situation to the Italian one obtained in the case of the Sylheti speakers in the 'Bengali-speaking' samples, and of the Kutchi speakers among the 'Gujerati-speaking' ones, and the same solution was adopted.

There were related problems with Panjabi speakers for whom Urdu was the language of literacy. In addition to the functional division between Panjabi and Urdu and the oral use of both languages by some speakers, a further complication arose because of the many different spoken varieties of Panjabi. In particular, a large number of respondents used Mirpuri or another regional variety, but relatively rarely named it as their first or main language. Our solution to this problem was to frame literacy questions in terms of Urdu, and spoken language use questions in terms of Panjabi (with Urdu coded as 'other'). Then when regional varieties of Panjabi were mentioned the interviewers would treat them in the same way as they did relevant varieties in the Italian, Gujerati and Bengali questionnaires.

Finally, a large number of the Cantonese speakers in the sample were multilingual. Some had learned Hakka as their first language, and Cantonese as their language of schooling; some had grown up in families where one parent was a Cantonese speaker and the other a Hakka speaker; others were from a Vietnamese refugee background with a knowledge of Vietnamese gained at school, or from one parent, in addition to Cantonese. The language of literacy for almost all these speakers was the traditional common system of characters (overseas norm or Hong Kong 'quasi-norm' (Hsu, 1979)), which is intelligible to educated overseas speakers of all the Chinese languages. The sampling frame for these populations was designed to include all possible users of Cantonese, or written Chinese, not only those who had Cantonese as a mother tongue. Normally an interview would only be conducted when the interviewer and respondent could establish good communication through the medium of Cantonese, although in a few cases interviewers who knew Hakka or Vietnamese used their discretion to continue an interview with explanations in Hakka or Vietnamese where necessary. The solution adopted in terms of questionnaire design was to ask all questions about spoken language use with reference to Cantonese, even where it was not the 'mother tongue', and literacy questions about 'Chinese'. Hakka or Vietnamese would be mentioned in the list of languages known, and referred to as 'other' later in the questionnaire. In adopting such strategies for these five linguistic minorities, then, we were able in the end to maintain a reasonably consistent approach to the respondents across all eleven languages.

The questionnaire: section by section commentary

We now present examples of pages of the questionnaire in its different language versions with a brief commentary on each section. (See Appendix 3 for the full text of the English version of the questions.)

A. Language skills and learning history (Qs 4–44)

The primary emphasis in this section was on the history of language acquisition and learning, and on self-assessment of the current skills of individual respondents in the minority language. After the first questions listing all languages known and the currency of their use, questions focussed on language learning at home, at school and elsewhere. Information about the level of spoken and written language skills was elicited, and the information about the minority languages was complemented where relevant with matching questions about the acquisition of, and skills in, English. The respondent's history of schooling was also established, with particular reference to the number of years at school and the medium of education.

B. Literacy (Qs 45–70)

The questions here were designed to investigate a wide range of literacy functions in both the minority languages and English. There were four subsections, two dealing with reading and two with writing. Most of the questions about reading were split into two stages, since it became obvious in piloting that without this division there would be a confusion between a respondent's potential ability to read, e.g. signs and notices or newspapers, and the actual opportunity to exercise that skill in the British context. We were particularly interested to discover whether there was a functional complementarity of literacies in this respect; e.g. with personal letters and religious books most often associated with the minority languages, formal letters and textbooks in English. A general question about literacy in third languages (other than English and the minority language of literacy) was included, and interviewers were alerted to look out for scriptural languages such as Arabic in this context. The questions about library use were included in response to specific suggestions from librarians we had consulted. Further literacy questions were added to the later 'Language and Work' section in order to look at the economic value of literacy.

C. Language use in the household (Qs 72–80)

In this section we attempted to build a fairly detailed picture of the patterns of language use in the home. Because of the wide range of possible family and household structures, the easiest way to arrange this information was to list each household member in the order given by the respondent. When all the household members and their relationship to the respondent had been listed, the interviewers were asked to work down the columns in turn, asking a series of questions about each household member and the patterns of language use with the respondent. The inclusion of two questions about language use allowed for non-reciprocal as well as reciprocal language use.

D. Children and language (Qs 81–96)

This section was only relevant to households which included children or young people under the age of twenty-one, and for all other respondents interviewers were instructed to bypass it. Questions in this section attempted to uncover patterns of language use between parents (not necessarily the respondent) and children. There are questions about language use with infants and between children in the household. Secondly, it aimed to investigate the extent and nature of support which the adults in the household were giving in order to transmit the minority language to children. This last set of questions, which covered informal language socialisation in the home as well as more formal 'mother tongue' classes, was designed with a view to making comparisons with the results of our MTTD survey (see Chapter 6).

E. Language and work (Qs 97–113)

Given our understanding of the importance of economic factors in the

Figure 4.1 Sample page from ALUS questionnaire: Greek version

	VERY WELL	FAIRLY WELL	NOT VERY WELL	NOT AT ALL	
11. How well would you say you understand Greek when it is spoken to you?	1	2	3	4	42
12. How well would you say you speak Greek?	1	2	3	4	43
13. How well would you say you read Greek?	1	2	3	4	44

IF RESPONDENT CANNOT READ AT ALL, SKIP TO QUESTION 18

14. Did you learn to read Greek at home?	YES 1 NO 2	45
15. Did you learn to read Greek (also) at language classes outside ordinary school times?	YES 1 NO 2	46
16. Did you learn to read Greek at your ordinary school?	YES 1 NO 2	47
17. Roughly what age were you when you began learning to read Greek? WRITE IN NUMBER OF YEARS:		48–49
18. How well would you say you write in Greek?	VERY WELL 1 FAIRLY WELL 2 NOT VERY WELL 3 NOT AT ALL 4	50

IF RESPONDENT CANNOT READ AT ALL NOR WRITE AT ALL
SKIP TO QUESTION 24
Questions 19 to 22 have been dropped from this page

23. Which country were you in when you learned to read or write Greek? PLEASE WRITE IN:		51–52
24. How many years of full-time education have you had? PLEASE WRITE IN NUMBER OF YEARS:		53–54

Greek versions of the questions:

11. Πόσο καλά θά λέγατε ὅτι καταλαμβαίνετε τήν Ἑλληνικήν γλῶσσαν ὅταν τήν ἀκοῦτε;

12. Πόσο καλά θά λέγατε ὅτι μιλᾶτε τήν Ἑλληνική γλῶσσα;

13. Πόσο καλά θά λέγατε ὅτι διαβάζετε τήν Ἑλληνική γλῶσσα;

14. Μάθατε νά διαβάζετε Ἑλληνικά στό σπίτι σας;

15. Μήπως μάθατε νά διαβάζετε Ἑλληνικά σέ ἰδιαίτερα σχολεῖο, ἐκτός ἀπό τό καθημερινόν;

16. Μήπως μάθατε νά διαβάζετε τά Ἑλληνικά στό καθημερινό σας σχολεῖο;

17. Περίπου σέ ποιάν ἡλικία ἀρχίσατε νά διαβάζετε τά Ἑλληνικά;

18. Πόσο καλά θά λέγατε ὅτι γράφετε τά Ἑλληνικά;

23. Σέ ποιά χώρα ζούσατε ὅταν μάθατε νά γράφετε τά Ἑλληνικά;

24. Πόσα χρόνια ἔχετε πάει σχολεῖο;

Figure 4.2 Sample page from ALUS questionnaire: Panjabi(U) version

11-12

SECTION C: HOUSEHOLD LANGUAGE USE

ASK THE RESPONDENT QUESTIONS 72 TO 80 ABOUT EACH MEMBER OF THE HOUSEHOLD. WORK DOWN THE COLUMNS STARTING WITH THE RESPONDENT. WRITE IN EACH MARRIED COUPLE SIDE BY SIDE AND DRAW A LINKING LINE BETWEEN HUSBAND AND WIFE.

How many people live in this household including yourself? PLEASE WRITE IN NUMBER ____

I would like to ask you a number of questions about each person in the household in turn:

			1	2	3	4	5	6
			RESPON-DENT					
72.	Relationship to respondent, e.g. mother, husband, sister, friend, etc.							
73.	Sex of person	MALE FEMALE	1 2	1 2	1 2	1 2	1 2	1 2
74.	How old is this person?							
75.	Where was this person brought up (i.e. spent the first 16 years)?	OVERSEAS RURAL OVERSEAS URBAN OVERSEAS MIXED U.K. & OVERSEAS U.K. ONLY	1 2 3 4 5	1 2 3 4 5	1 2 3 4 5	1 2 3 4 5	1 2 3 4 5	1 2 3 4 5
76.	How is this person employed?	WORKS OUTSIDE HOME WORKS FOR PAY IN FAMILY BUSINESS ON PREMISES WORKS AT HOME FOR PAY FULLTIME HOUSEWIFE STUDENT/SCHOOLCHILD OTHER	1 2 3 4 5 6	1 2 3 4 5 6	1 2 3 4 5 6	1 2 3 4 5 6	1 2 3 4 5 6	1 2 3 4 5 6
77.	How well does this person know Panjabi?	VERY WELL FAIRLY WELL NOT VERY WELL NOT AT ALL	1 2 3 4	1 2 3 4	1 2 3 4	1 2 3 4	1 2 3 4	1 2 3 4
78.	How well does this person know English?	VERY WELL FAIRLY WELL NOT VERY WELL NOT AT ALL	1 2 3 4	1 2 3 4	1 2 3 4	1 2 3 4	1 2 3 4	1 2 3 4
79.	When the respondent & this person talk with each other, which language(s) or dialect(s) does the respondent speak in?	ONLY OR MOSTLY PANJABI PANJABI AND ENGLISH ONLY OR MOSTLY ENGLISH OTHER AND ENGLISH ONLY OR MOSTLY OTHER OTHER MIXTURE IF 'OTHER', PLEASE WRITE IN:	1 2 3 4 5 6	1 2 3 4 5 6	1 2 3 4 5 6	1 2 3 4 5 6	1 2 3 4 5 6	1 2 3 4 5 6
80.	When talking with respondent, which language(s) or dialect(s) does the other person speak?	ONLY OR MOSTLY PANJABI PANJABI AND ENGLISH ONLY OR MOSTLY ENGLISH OTHER AND ENGLISH ONLY OR MOSTLY OTHER OTHER MIXTURE IF 'OTHER', PLEASE WRITE IN:	1 2 3 4 5 6	1 2 3 4 5 6	1 2 3 4 5 6	1 2 3 4 5 6	1 2 3 4 5 6	1 2 3 4 5 6
			13-17	18-28	29-39	40-50	51-61	62-72

processes of language shift and maintenance, and the fact that a number of linguistic minorities are very strongly represented in 'ethnic' sectors or niches in the labour market, the section on language in the workplace was clearly of crucial importance. Interviewers were instructed to ask this set of questions, not only of all people currently working, but also of those who had been at work until a retirement or redundancy within the previous two years. This, we believed, was particularly necessary because of the current rapid rise in unemployment, especially among members of some linguistic minorities in Coventry and Bradford.

The first group of questions in this section attempted to locate the respondent within the local socio-economic structure. We had a number of reservations about the system of socio-economic groups adopted by the Office of Population Censuses and Surveys (OPCS), which is still widely used by social scientists, and in particular about its applicability to minorities. A series of questions was designed, therefore, to make possible our later use of alternative social and occupational categories, as well as the OPCS ones (see App. 3). For respondents in employment the questions were quite detailed, and respondents who were not working were asked about the occupation of other working members of the household.

Most of the questions about language use in the workplace were contained in a grid, somewhat similar to the household grid (Fig. 4.2). Respondents were asked to identify in their minds (but not to name) three workmates or colleagues with whom they were in close contact, their immediate supervisor or foreman, their employer or manager, and any 'subordinates', customers or clients. They were then asked a set of questions about the language skills of each of these individuals in the workplace and their own language use patterns with them. In order to check whether the three workmates mentioned in the grid were representative, linguistically speaking, of the whole workplace, two further questions were asked, about the total number of workers, and about the number who could speak the minority language.

F. Language outside home and work (Qs 115–32)

This section of the questionnaire was intended to investigate patterns of language use with some of the respondents' personal contacts. Questions about participation and language use in the context of minority institutions and other organisations were also included at this point, as were questions about language use in contact with various consumer services.

G. Attitudes to language teaching provisions (Qs 133-47)

We included a section of attitude statements (Likert scales) of limited scope, around the issues of language maintenance and educational policy. This section proved to be of great interest to many respondents, who welcomed the opportunity to express opinions rather than simply answer a battery of factual questions.

The pool of attitude statements in this section was constructed around the themes of the possibility of language maintenance, its desirability, and the educational policy which would foster it. The statements included both positive and negative wordings and were sufficient in number to combine into scales which would reduce the effect of random error in single items. Data from the pilot survey was analysed by a correlation matrix technique, and the items which were badly worded, or failed to distinguish between types of respondents, were discarded. In the final version of the questionnaire respondents were invited to express their level of agreement or disagreement with the set of fifteen attitude statements which were retained.

H. Personal information (Qs 148-56)

This section was intended to gather relevant personal information which had not been elicited earlier. Included in this final section were some sensitive questions which we thought might have prejudiced the continuation of the interview if placed earlier, for example about housing and visits to the country of origin. The opportunity was also offered for respondents to comment at greater length about any aspect of the survey.

Having completed the listed questions, the interviewer was asked to note down details of the time and date of the interview, together with any circumstances which might have affected the respondent, in particular the presence of other people during the interview.

Piloting and translation procedure

The ALUS questionnaire went through a number of versions before the final interview schedules were produced. The most crucial stage of this process was the piloting of a draft version, which took place in Coventry in the summer of 1980, about three months before the

Figure 4.3 Sample page from ALUS questionnaire: Polish version

SECTION G: ATTITUDES ABOUT PROVISION OF LANGUAGE TEACHING

READ THE INTRODUCTORY STATEMENT TO THE RESPONDENT AND THEN READ EACH STATEMENT SLOWLY AND CLEARLY
AND ASK IF S/HE AGREES OR DISAGREES WITH THE STATEMENT AND HOW STRONGLY

Wiele osób uważa, że utrzymanie języka ojczystego w następnym pokoleniu, może być, dla polskoję- zycznej społeczności, zadaniem bardzo trudnym. Niektórzy uważają, że rząd powinien pomagać w utrzymaniu języków mniejszości narodowych, poprzez popieranie programów nauczania, rozwijanych dotychczas przez te grupy społeczne. Chcieli- byśmy poznać Pana/-i zdanie w tej sprawie. Czy zechciał/-a by Pan/-i powiedzieć mi czy zgadza się Pan/-i, i w jakim stopniu, z następującymi stwierdzeniami:

Introduction. Many people think it will be difficult for the Polish speaking community in England to keep up its language over the next generation. Some people think that the government should help maintain such languages, perhaps by introducing the teaching of them in schools, perhaps by supporting the teaching programmes that the communities have set up already in many areas. We are interested to know your opinion on these matters, so can you please tell us whether you agree or disagree (and how strongly) with the following statements which I am going to read to you.

	strongly agree	agree	not sure	disagree	strongly disagree	
133. Nasza społeczność utrzyma swe obyczaje kulturalne i tożsamość nawet jeślibyśmy przestali używać naszego języka We can maintain the culture and identity of our communities even if we cease to use our languages	1	2	3	4	5	47.
134. Utrzymanie naszego języka w następnym pokoleniu jest możliwe, jeśli właściwe jego nauczanie będzie szeroko dostępne We can keep up the use of our languages over the next generation if there is proper teaching widely available	1	2	3	4	5	48
135. Powinniśmy zrobić wszystko, co możliwe, aby nasz język był wszechstronnie używany tu, w Wielkiej Brytanii We should make every possible effort to maintain the fullest use of our languages in Britain	1	2	3	4	5	49
136. Nauczanie naszego języka powinno być naszym dzieciom prawnie zapewnione przez rząd brytyjski The government should provide the teaching of our languages as a right for all our children in state schools	1	2	3	4	5	50

beginning of fieldwork proper. About seventy pilot interviews were conducted in six linguistic minorities: Cantonese, Gujerati, Italian, Panjabi(U), Panjabi(G) and Polish – with one or two interviewers recruited from each of these linguistic minorities.

The piloting gave us several different kinds of very useful information and experience. It gave an opportunity to test out our fieldwork procedures, including briefing and debriefing interviewers, logging-in and checking questionnaires; and it enabled us to assess the reception our survey was likely to have on the doorstep. In addition, interviewers were able to report back about instructions or questions which had been unclear, or which people had been reluctant to answer. For example, the problem discussed in the previous section, of the first question and the naming of languages, was only highlighted after the pilot interviews had taken place. As a result of piloting, the structure of the questionnaire was substantially revised and several questions were either modified or discarded. The literacy section was restructured to allow for the distinction between potential and actual reading of various items, since we became aware that there is no point in asking a question about whether the respondent can read business letters in, say, Urdu if in the course of everyday life in England such letters are always written in English.

Even after the revision of the survey instrument in Coventry, the questionnaire contained a few problems which only came to light after it had been used with over 800 respondents from six local linguistic minorities. As a result a final version was produced for use with Bengali and Ukrainian speakers in Coventry, and in the Bradford and London surveys. In it several questions were deleted, for example those about seeking professional advice (which respondents very rarely did), a few others were modified, and some of the routing instructions and coding categories were clarified.

The most important role of the piloting, however, was to test out our bilingual strategy, and to prepare the way for the written translations of the questionnaire. At the beginning we sought to obtain consistency in the wording used by different interviewers, and in different interviews by the same person. For this reason we felt it was essential to provide a standard written version of the questions in the eleven minority languages. In the case of the two Panjabi versions, we had hoped at first to produce a common translation differing only in its representation in two different scripts. Eventually, however, two slightly different versions were produced, with appropriate (mainly lexical) modifications for each linguistic minority.

In the pilot survey the inteviewers were given a monolingual English version of the questionnaire, and were asked to put the questions to the respondents in the minority language. Of course, they had been encouraged to study the questionnaire, and to try it out on friends or relatives before they conducted any interviews at the addresses we had supplied. Some of the interviewers in fact produced draft written versions of the questions at this stage for their own use, while others experimented with various oral translations of the English text. However, the final versions were not settled until our 'translation workshops'. At these three groups were represented: the researchers, who knew the intention of the questions in the English original; the pilot interviewers, who knew the problems of interpretation they had encountered in the field; and the language consultants, recruited because of their skills and experience in teaching and writing in the minority languages and/or in translation work. The workshops focussed on general strategies of translation, as well as on specific problems arising from individual questions. On the basis of the discussion there, the language consultants produced a draft written version which was circulated for comment to the pilot interviewers before being finalised. Thus, in the process of translation for the first six languages in Coventry, the pilot interviewers played a vital role. For later versions the translation workshops were replaced by a process of translation from English by a native speaker of the minority language, followed by an independent back-translation by a native speaker of English, leading, via the mediation of one of the LMP researchers at a meeting of all concerned, to an agreed final version which took account of any discrepancies revealed between the original and the back-translated English versions.

Many discussions took place at these 'translation workshops', which provided qualitative insights into the sociolinguistic situation of the different minority languages. One recurring point was the difficulty of translating such questions as 'How *well* do you understand/speak (the minority language)/English?' To some extent the problem derived from an ambiguity in the original English version. The aim had been to discover how *fluently* the respondent could speak or understand, but the wording could be construed as referring to the closeness to the standard language of the respondent's speech. Usually this type of ambiguity could be explained to the translators, and later to the interviewers, so that they could use the least ambiguous term. However, there was some evidence from interviewers that the answers to this type of question varied considerably between respondents from different linguistic minorities, according, for example, to the different criteria felt appropriate to the assessment of 'quality' in speech.

A second recurrent concern with the translators involved lexical items which referred to objects or concepts occurring exclusively in modern European urban society, and which would rarely have been used by people from a rural background before their arrival in England. For example, at the Panjabi translation workshop the two language consultants could not immediately agree on the most appropriate translation of the term 'novel'. The Panjabi(U) translator at first wanted to use an Urdu term, the Panjabi(G) one a Panjabi word, but finally both agreed with the pilot interviewers that neither of these terms was likely to be understood by many respondents in England and that it was better to use the English term 'novel' as a loan word in both versions.

Other general issues of translation arose in a number of languages. Firstly, there was the difficulty of accurately comprehending the intended meaning of the English version, which in some cases could only be fully grasped in the context of our overall intentions, and of the structure of the questionnaire as a whole. Secondly, there was the problem of finding the correct register or level of formality in the minority language. The English version had aimed at a simple, clear and straightforward style, deliberately avoiding both excessive formality, on the one hand, and colloquial idioms which might be particularly difficult to translate, on the other. We asked the translators to see that the written versions they produced were kept close to the spoken language, and we thought originally that the questions might be read out word for word without sounding unnatural.

However, in many of the linguistic minorities the gap between written and spoken forms is conventionally much greater than in English, and situations of diglossia are common. Thus some translators persisted in using a much more formal or literary style in their written versions than we had tried to signal in the English text. There was, it seemed to us, a greater danger of producing language which less-educated speakers of the minority languages would find stylistically very distant from their own, and which they might not even understand. We also became aware in some of the translators of negative attitudes towards common regional variants in their languages, or towards common borrowings of lexical items from English. We made great efforts to impress on the translators the importance of using a register which would be understood by and acceptable to the widest range of potential respondents, even at the cost of giving occasional offence to the purist.

In at least one local linguistic minority, some of the interviewers showed more than a little sympathy with the purists. The Bengali version of the questionnaire had been translated, back-translated and revised in the Midlands, and successfully used in Coventry early in 1981. Our aim had been to produce a version which would be easily understood by most people with Bangladeshi or Indian Bengali backgrounds living in England, including Sylheti speakers with little experience of formal schooling. Six months later some of the London Bengali-speaking interviewers forcefully expressed their disapproval that certain phrases had been translated into 'such poor Bengali'. It may have been the surprise at seeing colloquial and regional forms in print for the first time that produced this reaction. Indeed, most of the London interviewers were well aware that the spoken forms of language needed for communication with Sylheti-speaking familes of rural background living in Tower Hamlets would have to be quite different from the standard variety associated with middle-class town-dwellers from Calcutta or Dacca. A similar problem in questionnaire translation is reported by Elder in the case of another South Asian language, Tamil. His printer at first refused to allow his press to be 'polluted' by the production of 'low Tamil' in a questionnaire which had been painstakingly translated into the colloquial speech which would be used by twelve-year-old villagers in rural South India (Elder, 1973).

Specific languages raised their own problems. Panjabi(U) was the most difficult of all. Urdu is the high status national language for speakers of Panjabi of Pakistani background, and is the usual medium of literacy to the exclusion of Panjabi. We have already discussed some of the problems this produced in the design of the questionnaire. When it came to the translation stage, the normal practice for translators from this linguistic minority would have been to translate from written English into written Urdu. The main danger for us in such a procedure was that the use of Urdu would automatically have altered the formality of the situation, and the status and role relationship of interviewer and respondent, probably resulting in less reliable replies. In addition some of the respondents might not have had sufficient knowledge of Urdu to understand the questions when read aloud by an interviewer. In such cases the interviewer might have needed to give explanations in Panjabi, which would inevitably vary between interviews, thus risking a wide range of variation from the standardised form of questions.

Our solution to this problem was to stress that the translation had to be from English into everyday spoken Panjabi. We have already mentioned that our original intention was to produce a single spoken Panjabi version with two different written realisations, and that the translation workshop for Panjabi(U) was a joint one with the translators and interviewers for Panjabi(G). Together they tried to agree on a version in a variety of spoken Panjabi which would be acceptable and understood by the widest possible range of Panjabi speakers in Coventry. In the course of these discussions it became evident that we would need to produce separate written Panjabi versions, and the language consultants were asked to prepare these. The Panjabi(U) version, then, did in fact represent Panjabi, but was written in the Urdu script, resulting in the unusual situation for most adults of Pakistani origin living in England of readers producing Panjabi speech on the basis of a written representation of spoken Panjabi forms.

In both Panjabi-speaking teams in Coventry we discovered that some of the younger interviewers, who were excellently qualified in all other respects, possessed only limited reading skills in the Gurmukhi or Perso-Arabic scripts. In order to help them, special versions of the questionnaires were produced in which the Panjabi texts were transcribed in Roman script. In addition an oral version of the text was recorded on cassette to help these interviewers prepare themselves. This strategy worked well, and had the added advantage of making the texts of the two Panjabi versions more accessible to the researchers who were not literate in the South Asian scripts, but had some understanding of spoken Panjabi and Urdu-Hindi.

A similar problem over scripts arose in the Cantonese translations. The normal practice would have been to produce a written version in the largely common system of Chinese written characters. Since these could have been read aloud in any of the different Chinese languages, it was felt that an alternative strategy was necessary to preserve the agreed form of words. We therefore produced a Romanised version of the Cantonese translation, as well as an audio-cassette as a training aid. This approach had only a limited success, since our interviewers found the task of coping with the Romanisation very difficult. Many of them in fact preferred to make their own notes in Chinese characters as a guide to the Romanised version! For the London Chinese survey we provided a supplementary character version in standard form to all the interviewers. In any case by this stage of the fieldwork it had become clear that word-for-word consistency of spoken reproduction of the written texts on the part of the interviewer was less possible, and perhaps less important, than we had originally believed. Experience had shown that the most effective of the interviewers found it impossibly unnatural to read out the questions exactly as printed, and that a better rapport with respondents was achieved when discretion was used in varying details of the wording to suit the setting of the interaction. Nevertheless we continued to emphasise through our briefing and debriefing procedures the importance of some of the distinctions we had made in phrasing our questions, for example, between 'Can you speak?' and 'Do you speak?' and between 'Do you ever use?' and 'Do you know?'

The final stage in the preparation of the different written versions was the layout and photo-litho printing of the bilingual versions of the questionnaire (see p. 146). For the South Asian languages the master versions of the text were produced by calligraphers, while for the languages in European scripts appropriate typewriters were used. For each version we used the same format, with the minority language on the left of the page, the English text in the centre. The precoded alternative answers (written only in English), spaces for open-ended answers and coding were on the right of the page. The blank facing pages could be used for more extensive notes if necessary, and instructions were in English only. By and large this format worked well, although some interviewers had difficulty in switching from reading a question in the minority language to writing an answer in English. Several interviewers in various languages said it would have been easier if the instructions had been in both languages. There were also particular difficulties in the case of Panjabi(U) since Urdu is read from right to left, and in the layout of the grids.

Fieldwork procedures: preparation

Piloting and translating the questionnaire, and developing the bilingual interviewing strategy, were only two aspects of the preparation for ALUS. In this section we will discuss the difficulties we anticipated in fieldwork in the three cities, the steps we took to overcome them, and the ways in which we attempted to put into practice our principle of seeking the fullest possible involvement of local people in the research.

From our knowledge of the distribution of linguistic minorities it was evident that most, though not all, of the fieldwork for ALUS would have to take place in inner city areas. These districts are often regarded with some trepidation by organisers of social surveys, because they tend to produce special difficulties in fieldwork and generally low response rates. The rapid turnover of population, the large number of slum clearance and redevelopment projects, the higher proportion of hard-to-contact households, and the reluctance of some interviewers to travel in these areas, especially at night, have all been mentioned as factors hindering survey work (Wallman et al., 1980). Refusal rates tend to be higher than average in most such surveys, perhaps because of the lack of rapport between interviewers, who are often middle-class and from the majority, and respondents who tend to be working-class and/or from ethnic minorities. Such respondents may have justifiable suspicions of any person they see as a representative of the public authorities.

We expected to meet most of the difficulties mentioned above, and possibly additional ones related to the language factor and to the fact that our topic might reasonably be perceived as related to the politically sensitive 'race relations' situation.

Some of these problems are almost impossible to overcome. For example, the situation we encountered in one neighbourhood in Bradford illustrates the difficulty of rapid turnover of population and housing redevelopment. This area was known to be one of the focal areas of ethnic minority settlement, and our sampling strategy in this case used the electoral registers compiled in October 1980. On this basis, a number of sampling batches were assigned to polling districts in the area. However, by the late spring of 1981 when the ALUS fieldwork was taking place none of the dwellings selected in our sample for Panjabi(U) speakers in this neighbourhood remained standing! A similar situation arose in part of East London with the Bengali-speaking sample. In this case, fortunately, the local interviewers let us know of the demolition in progress before anyone was sent out on a fruitless mission.

Several strategies were developed to meet the challenge of the remaining problems. Many of these are developments of the methods used by De Lange and Kosmin (1979) in their work in Redbridge's Jewish community, and by the Ethnicity Programme of the Research Unit on Ethnic Relations in their work in Battersea (Wallman et al., 1980). Working with our conviction that the local minorities should be involved as closely as possible in the research process, we came to the conclusion that it was essential to devote several months to preparing the ground for the survey. Figure 4.4 shows the central position of local contacts in the research process at a number of different levels. The qualitative data derived from our fieldwork experience, and the low refusal rates, vindicated this decision to make a major investment of time and effort in establishing a good community base for ALUS.

Because of the work involved in staffing the fieldwork offices, and in the administrative tasks connected with fieldwork, we recruited extra temporary staff as fieldwork supervisors. In Coventry the LMP researchers were all involved in the day to day management of the survey as a whole, but each member took special responsibility for

Figure 4.4 Adult Language Use Survey: Sequence

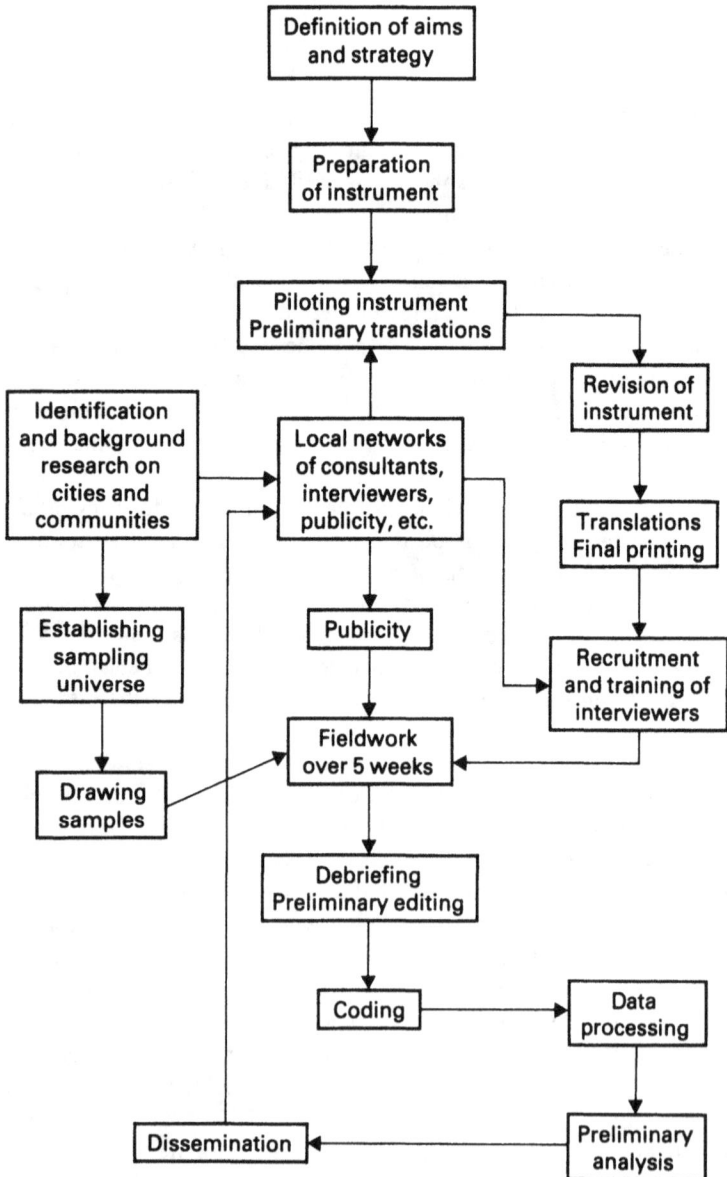

particular languages. They were assisted by a fieldwork co-ordinator who was later to join the staff of LINC. In Bradford a full-time fieldwork co-ordinator was also employed, together with a part-time language supervisor for the Polish-speaking team, while members of the research team acted as language supervisors for the other groups of interviewers. In London a similar situation obtained, with a fieldwork co-ordinator who also acted as language supervisor for the Gujerati speakers. There was also a part-time language supervisor for the Italian-speaking team, and three of the research team shared responsibility as language supervisors for the other five languages. In this way each interviewer was able to relate mainly to one person in the team, and each language supervisor had between ten and twenty interviewers to collaborate with.

The role of the language supervisor also involved a particular responsibility for making contacts within the local minority, and for organising the compilation of samples. In many cases it was interviewers or other people from the local linguistic minorities with a specialised knowledge of the local areas who undertook the large amount of paid clerical work that was also necessary, for example in preparing address lists.

In the very early stages of the project the LMP researchers had established or renewed contacts with a wide range of people working in the educational field in both statutory and voluntary sectors. These preliminary contacts covered several cities, including the three which were eventually chosen for ALUS. When the decision to work in three cities had been made, we asked our original contacts for more detailed advice, and people who had been mentioned by them also became part of LMP's expanding local networks.

Before we were ready to launch our main ALUS fieldwork in Coventry, the LMP research team spent about six months getting to know, and to be known in, a range of different linguistic minority as well as official networks of the city. Many people were contacted, even those with only a marginal interest in the organisation and results of our research. However, we were careful to avoid being identified exclusively with any particular institution or group, and in some cases we felt it best to avoid extensive contact with particular individuals or associations who might hinder rather than advance our progress. In some cases we were asking for help; in others the main purpose was to share information or to reassure people about our intentions. At the official level this meant meetings with staff of the education authority, the city planning department, the social services department and the library service, for example. We visited a wide range of voluntary organisations, including advice centres, the local community relations council and a number of churches. We also met with other researchers in related fields who were working in the locality, and made special arrangements to avoid overlap in terms of potential respondents.

Most important of all was our contact with the many minority organisations, especially those which were involved in the provision of 'mother tongue' teaching. We made numerous visits to such schools, often in the evenings or at weekends, and to temples, community centres and special functions. We also visited the homes or workplaces of some of the activists and officials of minority organisations. Some of the other activities enjoyed by the researchers included an evening of Gujerati dancing organised by a local temple on the occasion of the Navratri festival, an Urdu poetry reading and an invitation to participate in a meeting of the Ukrainian club on the subject of language maintenance. We were generally made very welcome, and great interest was shown in our work.

In Bradford and London we spent rather less time than in Coventry on this type of preparatory work. This was partly because we now had a more established set of fieldwork procedures, and partly because some members of the team had already established contacts in these cities, either from previous work or developed during the very early stages of LMP. Indeed, the presence of previous contacts was one important factor in the choice of these cities. Nonetheless we followed the same general principles of local involvement as we had done in Coventry, and once again found the effort involved very worthwhile.

In the two provincial cities our local offices were the base for all our work, since we felt it right not to emphasise constantly our connections with the University of London, although of course we did not conceal these to anyone who was interested. We presented ourselves therefore, for example on our headed notepaper, as members of the 'Coventry Languages Project' or 'Bradford Languages Project' respectively. In Coventry we were able to rent a vacant corner shop with a flat above it, situated in the heart of the neighbourhood where many people from the linguistic minorities we were working with had settled. It was within easy walking distance of many of the respondents' homes, and on a convenient bus route to the city centre. During the six weeks' fieldwork period the office was staffed by at least one person from 9 a.m. to 9 p.m. every day including weekends.

In Bradford we had the use of some rooms in a house belonging to Bradford College. It was conveniently situated for bus routes and for access to most of the addresses in the sample. However, the hours during which we could use this office were restricted to the period from noon to 7 p.m. on weekdays, and all day on Saturdays. The Bradford survey involved rather fewer people than the Coventry one, so the arrangements proved satisfactory. In Bradford we conducted the survey during the long days of the early summer: this was particularly fortunate since people had until a short time before been especially reluctant to travel on foot in the dark while a notorious local murderer remained at large.

Fieldwork strategy in London was somewhat different from that used in the provinces, in that we were working with linguistic minorities concentrated in a number of different areas of the metropolis. Since the office in the University was quite central and easily accessible, we made it the administrative centre for our fieldwork. However, we did also provide local drop-off points and a courier service for questionnaires from interviewers working in Haringey and Tower Hamlets, two of our major fieldwork areas at some distance from the centre. Even in London we would have preferred to use a local office if it had been possible to concentrate all the fieldwork in a small enough area.

Closely associated with our strategy of developing local contacts was our policy for publicity for the survey. We wanted as many potential respondents as possible to have a chance to hear details before they were visited. On the other hand we were concerned about possible negative coverage in the majority English language media. We decided therefore to concentrate our publicity in minority media and through local networks, and to produce most of it in the minority languages. Different linguistic minorities and different cities called for specific publicity strategies. Thus, as was most appropriate in each case, we asked minority organisations to display posters in the minority languages and to publicise our intentions at their meetings. Our outlets included mother tongue schools, temples, shops and majority institutions with good contacts with minorities, such as advice centres and clinics. Some local radio stations which produced programmes in the minority languages were willing to broadcast information about the survey, though the extent of coverage varied considerably in the different cities. Details of our work were also given to the minority language press, and the ALUS received wide coverage, with only one exception quite favourable. The exception was an article in a London-based Greek-medium paper which questioned the level of community involvement and the survey methodology we had adopted. In this case, together with one of the Greek-speaking consultants, we were able to arrange for publication of a second article in the same paper setting the record straight from our point of view.

Finally we produced our own information leaflet about the survey, printed in each of the different languages in parallel with the English version. (Urdu was used in the Panjabi(U) case since we felt this would be more widely acceptable than a Panjabi version in Urdu script to people who received it without explanation.) These leaflets were distributed fairly widely before the surveys, and then to all the respondents who completed an interview. This procedure helped us to ensure that respondents knew who we were, and could discuss our aims with other members of the family and with their friends, thus avoiding serious distortion. (See Figure 4.5.)

Sampling strategy

Obtaining representative samples for any social survey is clearly fundamental to the reliability of its findings. Achieving the required level of representativeness is particularly problematic when working with minorities within the general population. Such sub-populations are geographically distributed in a non-random way, and the conventional sampling frames are either inadequate or inefficient. The lack of language data in the national census for England means that census information is of very limited use for a language survey. Other surveys however, or electoral registers, can help in the construction of a sampling frame, and in some areas 'community' lists are available and may provide the most reliable basis for sampling. In our work on the ALUS we had to develop a number of strategies to tackle the problems presented by the different types of linguistic minorities (for fuller details of our sampling procedures see Smith, 1984).

The first stage for each local linguistic minority was to establish a sampling frame which included as many as possible (ideally all) of the households in which at least one member was likely to be a speaker of the minority language in question. We used three main sources, separately or combined, in order to create these sampling frames:

(1)   manual or computerised searches of electoral registers for distinctive ethnic names;
(2)   manual scanning of telephone directories for distinctive ethnic names;
(3)   'community' lists which were made available to us.

Each of these sources has a particular set of limitations. The use of sources such as electoral registers and telephone directories presents

Figure 4.5 Bilingual information leaflets about ALUS (collage)

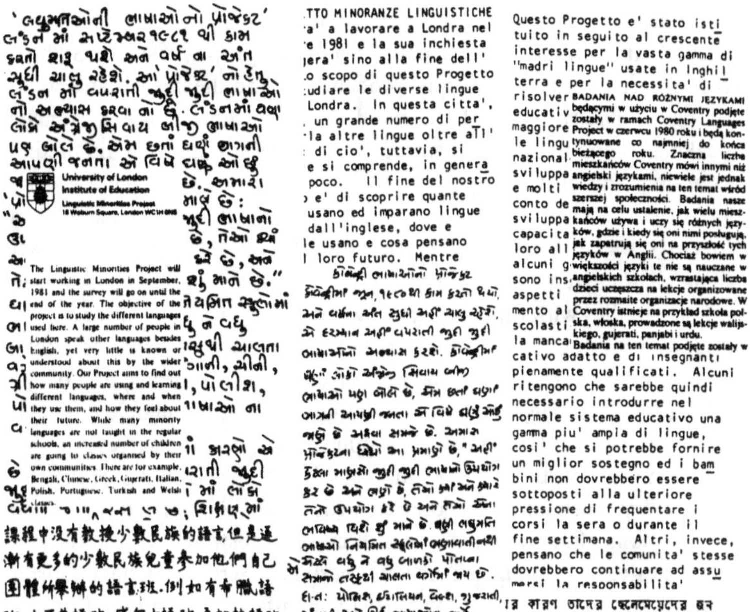

University of London
Institute of Education
Linguistic Minorities Project
18 Woburn Square, London WC1H 0NS

The Linguistic Minorities Project will start working in London in September, 1981 and the survey will go on until the end of the year. The objective of the project is to study the different languages used here. A large number of people in London speak other languages besides English, yet very little is known or understood about this by the wider community. Our Project aims to find out how many people are using and learning different languages, where and when they use them, and how they feel about their future. While many minority languages are not taught in the regular schools, an increased number of children are going to classes organised by their own communities. There are for example, Bengali, Chinese, Greek, Gujerati, Italian, Polish, Portuguese, Turkish and Welsh classes.

O PROJECTO DAS MINORIAS LINGUISTICAS teve início em Londres em setembro de 1981 e deverá prosseguir nesta cidade até pelo menos o fim do ano. Tem por objectivo o estudo das diferentes línguas em uso na cidade de Londres. Embora muitas outras línguas para além do inglês sejam utilizadas nesta área, a verdade é que a maior parte da população pouco conhecimento ou compreensão tem do facto. Este projecto tem por objectivo indagar qual é o número de pessoas que utilizam e aprendem as diferentes línguas, onde e quando as utilizam e quais os seus sentimentos à cerca do futuro dessas línguas. Se bem que muitas dessas línguas minoritárias não sejam ensinadas nas escolas inglesas é cada vez maior o número de crianças que frequentam aulas organizadas pelas próprias comunidades. Existem, por exemplo, aulas de bengali, chinês, grego, gujerati, italiano, polonês, português, turco e galês.

...TTO MINORANZE LINGUISTICHE ...a' a lavorare a Londra nel ...e 1981 e la sua inchiesta ...era' sino alla fine dell' ...o scopo di questo Progetto ...udiare le diverse lingue ... Londra. In questa citta', ... un grande numero di per... ...la altre lingue oltre all' ... di cio', tuttavia, si ...e si comprende, in genera... poco. Il fine del nostro ...e' di scoprire quante ... usano ed imparano lingue dall'inglese, dove e ...le usano e cosa pensano ...l loro futuro. Mentre

Questo Progetto e' stato istituito in seguito al crescente interesse per la vasta gamma di "madri lingue" usate in Inghilterra e per la necessita' di risolver... educativ... maggiore... le lingu... nazional... sviluppa... e molti... conto de... sviluppa... capacita... loro all... alcuni g... sono ins... aspetti... mento al... scolasti... la manca... cativo adatto e di insegnanti pienamente qualificati. Alcuni ritengono che sarebbe quindi necessario introdurre nel normale sistema educativo una gamma piu' ampia di lingue, cosi' che si potrebbe fornire un miglior sostegno ed i bambini non dovrebbero essere sottoposti alla ulteriore pressione di frequentare i corsi la sera o durante il fine settimana. Altri, invece, pensano che le comunita' stesse dovrebbero continuare ad assumersi la responsabilita'

BADANIA NAD RÓŻNYMI JĘZYKAMI będącymi w użyciu w Coventry podjęte zostały w ramach Coventry Languages Project w czerwcu 1980 roku i będą kontynuowane co najmniej do końca bieżącego roku. Znaczna liczba mieszkańców Coventry mówi innymi niż angielski językami, niewiele jest jednak wiedzy i zrozumienia na ten temat wśród szerszej społeczności. Badania nasze mają na celu ustalenie, jak wielu mieszkańców używa i uczy się różnych języków, gdzie i kiedy się oni nimi posługują, jak zapatrują się oni na przyszłość tych języków w Anglii. Chociaż bowiem w większości języki te nie są nauczane w angielskich szkołach, wzrastająca liczba dzieci uczęszcza na lekcje organizowane przez rozmaite organizacje narodowe. W Coventry istnieje na przykład szkoła polska, włoska, prowadzone są lekcje walijskiego, gujerati, panjabi i urdu.
Badania na ten temat podjęte zostały w

Collage by Judy Tasker

difficulties, arising from under-registration of minorities and bias towards social groups who are telephone subscribers. And the use of distinctive ethnic names is very much a blunt instrument. (For a fuller assessment of this see Smith, 1982a.) Firstly there are certain names which are common across different ethnic minorities. For example, we found that the name Mahers could belong to people of either Sikh or Irish ancestry with almost equal probability. And the name Mann could belong to Panjabi, English, German or even Chinese mother tongue speakers. Secondly, even where the distinctive ethnic name did predict accurately the ethnic origins of a potential respondent, there was no certainty that he or she could speak the language. For example, in Coventry we came across a person with a Polish name who was in fact a Canadian citizen and spoke no Polish, and in Haringey we discovered several families with Chinese names, whose families had lived for several generations in the Caribbean, who spoke only English and who described themselves as West Indians. Because of these complications, part of the task of our interviewers was to determine which of the people they met on the doorstep did in fact come within the scope of the survey.

Community lists too are only viable in the context of careful preparatory work and collaboration with local people. Even then there are questions of confidentiality which must be answered with sensitivity and honesty, and risks of bias towards certain subgroups of the minority population. These risks can be partially countered by the use of two or more complementary sources, but can never be totally eliminated.

Our collaboration with people in the local areas where we worked extended to the technicalities of drawing samples. In Coventry in the case of Panjabi and Gujerati the scanning of the electoral register was done by computer, in co-operation with the Planning Department of the local authority. In Bradford and Haringey we worked from information provided by the local Community Relations Councils on the basis of their manual scanning of the registers for South Asian and Greek and Turkish names respectively. In each case the distribution of distinctive ethnic names on the register had been broken down to polling district level, and the amount of time needed for devising the details of the sampling was substantially reduced.

The method we then adopted to select particular households depended mainly on the size of the local linguistic minority. For the very small minorities, such as the speakers of Chinese languages in Coventry and Bradford, an attempt was made to conduct an interview in every household we had identified. For others, where we had compiled a list containing up to 3,000 addresses of linguistic minority households, such as the Polish speakers in Coventry, we randomly chose one household in every n. In the case of very large linguistic minorities, such as the Panjabi speakers in Coventry or the Greek speakers in London (usually where the sampling frame was the set of households with distinctive ethnic names on the electoral register), a two-stage stratified sampling procedure was used. We first selected a limited number of polling districts in proportion to the number of linguistic minority households identified in each. The second stage was to select randomly the appropriate number of households within each polling district chosen.

The addresses in the samples were issued to our interviewers in batches of ten, wherever possible in close geographical proximity to each other. The interviewers were asked to attempt to obtain five completed interviews from each batch of ten addresses. They were to visit the households, and when they had confirmed that the relevant minority language was indeed spoken there, to negotiate an interview with a suitable adult member of the household. In order to maintain a balance of age and sex in the completed sample, we asked our interviewers as far as possible to attempt to obtain one younger (up to 35 years) and one older respondent of each sex within each batch of five interviews. In the course of our fieldwork we monitored this quota system and, where necessary, in the later stages of fieldwork gave revised instructions to the interviewers.

The range of sampling strategies used for ALUS, and the nature of some of them, mean that we are not in a position to measure the representativeness of our findings in a strict statistical sense. It is not possible, for instance, to generalise from our samples to the whole of a linguistic minority in a given city and to calculate confidence levels on our population estimates. For any of our variables it is also impossible to test statistically the significance of comparisons between local linguistic minorities. Such statistical precision, in fact, was never our aim. However, the efforts we have made to avoid bias, together with the size of our samples and the high response rates the ALUS methodology has ensured, mean that our findings are based on data which give, we believe, the best level of reliability and validity which could be achieved in the circumstances.

Fieldwork experience

The contacting and publicity work which was undertaken in each of the three cities was the main method by which interviewers were recruited. In some cases an advertisement for interviewers was placed, either in minority language media, or on notice boards in institutions where potential interviewers were likely to be found, e.g. local colleges or advice centres. However, many, if not most, of the interviewers were recruited by personal contact and recommendation. Informal interviews were held, where one or more members of the research team, together with a language consultant, assessed the applicant's suitability in terms of personality, fluency in English and in the minority language, and understanding of the survey's purpose.

Very few of the applicants were rejected at this stage, although a few others dropped out at the training stage or in the course of the survey, when it became clearer to them that considerable demands were involved in terms of time and personal commitment. The criteria for becoming an interviewer, besides the availability to work part-time (mainly evenings and weekends), had more to do with linguistic skills, personality and interest in the work than with academic qualifications or experience. Few of the interviewers had been involved in survey work before. All of them were fluent, and with a few exceptions literate, in both English and the minority language.

Although the interviewers were to be paid a fee for each interview, and expenses for travel and training time, no-one could expect to earn a very large sum. Those who completed twenty interviews received around £100 in fees and expenses. As a result of all these factors, the interviewing teams consisted of capable and committed people with a high level of bilingual skills, and a high level of interest in the work. One particularly rich source of interviewers was the mother tongue teachers and organisers who worked in the evening and weekend schools. The interviewers covered a wide age range from 17 to 60, and included both men and women. In some linguistic minorities, such as the Panjabi(U)- and Bengali-speaking ones, a special effort was made to recruit a team which would allow interviewers to be matched to their respondents in terms both of gender and of religious affiliation.

Towards the end of the fieldwork period the interviewers themselves were interviewed by the language supervisor using the ALUS question-naire, in order to enable us to take into account the possible effect of their own language skills and experience.

From these interviews we were able to build up a picture of the people we employed for comparison with the general population of respondents, although only some general data relating to the 125 interviewers will be presented now. Among the interviewers there were roughly equal numbers of men and women, although in Coventry the women outnumbered the men by about 60 per cent to 40 per cent. Approximately three-quarters of all the interviewers were in professional or non-manual occupations. Two-thirds of the interviewers were in employment and a further fifth were full-time students. Two-thirds of the interviewers were aged under 30. Nine out of ten said they had received twelve or more years of schooling. All of them reported high levels of skills in both the minority language and English, 92 per cent reporting 'very well' or 'fairly well' for all four questions about minority language skills, and 96 per cent for English skills. (The partial exceptions were mainly the younger members of the Panjabi teams in Coventry who had limited literacy in the minority language, and for whom we had devised the Romanised versions of the questionnaire.)

One characteristic which sharply distinguished the interviewers from the respondents was their high level of participation in local minority organisations. Nine out of ten of the interviewers took part in the activities of at least one organisation and, more significantly, nearly half either held, or had held, some office in an organisation to which they belonged. Most of these memberships were in minority institutions such as mother tongue schools, religious groups or minority social clubs. (For a comparison with the respondents see Table 5.12.)

The training of the interviewers was fundamental to the success of the survey. As soon as interviewers were appointed, they were given some background information and a copy of the questionnaire. They were asked to familiarise themselves with this in time for the training day session, which was usually held on a Saturday. The first half of the training day introduced the research team and the other interviewers, and a presentation was given of the overall purpose of the survey and the fieldwork procedures. The research team explained how the questionnaire had been designed, how the work related to the concerns of the minorities involved, how respondents had been selected and how liaison would be maintained during the survey.

Early on in the briefing sessions the interviewers were divided into pairs to practise putting some of the questions to each other in English. During the second part of the day the group met in the separate language teams, where there was an opportunity for discussion with their language supervisors about particular issues affecting the individual linguistic minorities, and a fuller explanation of the principles behind our trans-lations and bilingual strategy. The remaining time was devoted to further interviewing practice in pairs, this time in the minority languages.

Finally a wallet of documents was issued containing questionnaires, the interviewer's reference guide, the first batch of sample addresses (see Fig. 4.6), identity cards, assorted stationery, and information about such matters as local transport facilities.

The interviewers had to conduct their first two interviews over the following days, to deliver them to the office immediately, and to meet the language supervisor for an individual debriefing session within the week. The first interview was to be conducted with a friend as respondent, for practice only, and the second was to be with a respondent selected from the first batch of addresses. At the debriefing session the language supervisor discussed the experience with the interviewer, checked the responses in detail and, if necessary, edited the returned questionnaires with the interviewer's participation. Provided there were no major difficulties, the interviewer was then given another four questionnaires and asked to complete the first cluster of five interviews from the batch of ten addresses that had been issued on the training day.

After the first week we attempted to establish a weekly rhythm for each interviewer in which, for example, the interviews would be conducted at the weekend, delivered to the office, logged in and checked early in the week, and a regular debriefing arranged and conducted before the next cluster of addresses was issued. This pattern was not rigid, but it generally proved workable and ensured that liaison between interviewers and the language supervisor took place on a regular basis, and that checking and editing of completed questionnaires took place while the interviews were still relatively fresh in the interviewer's memory. These procedures enabled us to complete the fieldwork in each city with very little overrunning of our planned fieldwork schedule of five weeks in each place.

The close involvement of the interviewers with the local linguistic minority occasionally presented problems. For example one interviewer in one of the smaller populations studied was extremely reluctant to visit a particular address which appeared in the list he had been given. Eventually he explained that this was the home of his uncle, and that a family feud had been going on for a number of years. Evidently the parties involved were not on speaking terms (in any language)! This interviewer, who was one of the few to miss the briefing day, was even more surprised when he discovered that his cousin was also one of the interviewers. Eventually the interview at the uncle's address was carried out by a third, unrelated person.

At the end of the fieldwork the interviewers from each language team met together for a general debriefing session, where they were

Figure 4.6 ALUS: sample of address list and checklist for interviewers

CITY/WARD ~~TOWER HAMLET~~ SPITALFIELDS CLUSTER NO. ~~623~~ O(M

LANGUAGE BENGALI

Interviewer; Name _____

Address _____

_____

Tel. _____

Date issued 26/9/81   date returned 7/10/81

Completed S

RESPONDENT'S ADDRESS	VISITS MADE date time	INTERVIEW OBTAINED?	QUOTA
NAME ADDRESS	1) 27-9-81 10 A.M. in/out 2) _____ ____ in/out 3) _____ ____ in/out	1 yes 2 contact made & recall arranged (enter date in 2) 3 refusal comments _____ GONE TO BANGLADESH	m/f age ____
NAME ADDRESS	1) 2/10/81 11.a.m. in/out 2) 8/10/81 2PM in/out 3) _____ ____ in/out	1 (yes) 2 contact made & recall arranged (enter date in 2) 3 refusal Comments _____ _____	m/f age 23
NAME ADDRESS	1) 27.9.81 8 P.M. in/out 2) _____ ____ in/out 3) _____ ____ in/out	1) yes 2 contact made & recall arranged 3 refusal Comments _____ Moved to some other area	m/f age ____

able to exchange experiences with each other and with the researchers. These sessions produced an instructive range of qualitative insights and anecdotes, and were audio-recorded for future reference.

It was especially interesting for us to hear accounts of the experiences of the interviewers, who, after occasional initial suspicion, had for the most part met with a very warm welcome from respondents. Some had found a preliminary visit to make an appointment very useful, and had received great hospitality when they returned. Many were able to supply useful insights and interpretations, which the researchers or English monolingual interviewers would have missed. One Polish interviewer was told on several occasions, 'If you had started speaking in English I would have told you to go away.'

Some of the interviewers were received with great hospitality and were offered snacks or elaborate meals. A Portuguese respondent who worked as a cook had specially prepared a 'typically English' tea of cakes and Swiss roll for the Portuguese-speaking interviewer. One of the Chinese-speaking interviewers had visited three restaurants on three successive nights and been given a free meal in each. A Panjabi(U) interviewer in Bradford spent almost eight hours in two sessions, trying to complete an interview with an elderly lady who was serving in the family shop. In the course of the second session, amidst numerous interruptions from customers, the interviewer was called on to massage the aching limbs of the respondent. Other interviewers described how some elderly respondents who lived alone took full advantage of the chance to talk at length with anybody. On occasion, too, interviewers were able to supply important information and advice about welfare rights and resources, including the existence of local mother tongue classes. At the opposite extreme one Portuguese interviewer had to convince at least two different respondents that he was not a member of the CIA!

The regular weekly and final general debriefing sessions were one major source of information about the way the interviewers had carried out their task. In addition we encouraged them to make relevant notes upon the questionnaire itself, and in some cases these proved very informative. We felt it unnecessary to institute formal checking procedures to ensure that interviews had actually taken place. We were reassured by the high number of respondents who had given their names and addresses at the end of the interview, as people willing to help us if necessary with a further interview. These details were not recorded anywhere on the questionnaire. We also asked each interviewer to make audio recordings of a sample of their interviews, in the hope of gathering some linguistic texts for later analysis. The impression conveyed by most of these tapes was one of a high degree of interviewing skill, although detailed analysis of this valuable sociolinguistic data has yet to be carried out.

It was obvious to us that the teams of interviewers were a great resource for the future dissemination of our work, and offered potential for other local educational initiatives. Many of them were already active in the field of mother tongue teaching. At least one volunteered her services to a Saturday school as a result of her experiences with our survey; another one was subsequently employed by the LEA. Others were active in various community organisations, and were able to build on their experience with LMP for the furtherance of the work of these groups. Still other interviewers were willing to be referred to researchers in related fields, and have done further interviewing as a result. One interviewer embarked on a degree course, and wrote her dissertation on bilingualism. Above all, the interviewers provided a continuing network through which we could develop further understanding and disseminate the findings of LMP research. This is one of the most important and lasting benefits of undertaking a survey from a sound community base.

Response rates

Overall, we found the response rates in the ALUS satisfactory in each of the linguistic minorities and in all three cities. However, since there are several possible ways of measuring response rates, and because there were significant variations between cities and linguistic minorities, we set out the figures in some detail in Tables 4.2 to 4.5.

There are several outstanding features in Coventry:

(a) The very high response rate of the Italian speakers was largely the result of the high quality of the sampling frame which was employed, since it was based on a single relatively accurate 'community list' and personally cross-checked by one of the most knowledgeable people in the local Italian-speaking minority.

(b) The relatively high refusal rate amongst the Polish speakers (17 per cent) may have been influenced by a number of factors. In the first place the age structure of the population with its high number of over-50s and adult 'second generation', may have meant that a large proportion of people felt the survey was not relevant to them, since their children had grown up or had already ceased to use the minority language. However, the fact that a much lower refusal

Table 4.2 Response rates in Coventry

Language	Bengali	Chinese	Gujerati	Italian	Panjabi(G)	Panjabi(U)	Polish
(1) Total number of addresses selected in sample	186	82	463	136	404	217	283
(2) Total number of addresses visited by interviewers	133	77	368	124	309	184	279
(3) Number of interviews conducted	78	43	202	104	200	85	167
(4) 3 as % of 2	59	56	55	84	65	46	60
(5) Number of refusals	2	4	24	8	19	10	38
(6) 5 as % of (3 + 5)	3	9	11	7	9	11	17
(7) Wrong language as % of 2	20	6	21	1	9	22	9
(8) Non contacts as % of 2	12	8	7	2	12	11	6
(9) Removals as % of 2	8	25	11	6	8	15	12

Notes: (1) Ukrainian figures were not calculated
(2) Numbers in row 3 are not the same as numbers of interviews given in Chapter 5, because a small proportion were not accepted for analysis.

rate was obtained in the Italian sample (who have a similar age structure and apparently give less importance to minority language use and maintenance than do the Polish speakers), suggests the presence of an additional factor. Our guess is that the high refusal rate for Polish speakers reflects a high degree of isolation and mistrust of authority, and the difficulty we experienced in publicising ALUS in this minority, together with a lack of support on the part of the local priest.

(c) The high number of 'wrong languages' in the Gujerati (21 per cent), Panjabi(G) (9 per cent), Panjabi(U) (22 per cent), Polish (9 per cent) and Bengali (20 per cent) samples. These were the minorities in which we placed most reliance on analysis of distinctive ethnic names in drawing up our sampling universe. (A detailed account of the methods and limitations can be found in Smith, 1982a.) In the South Asian samples the majority of 'wrong languages' discovered by our interviewers were cases of Hindu names (in the Gujerati sample) and Muslim ones (in the Bengali and Panjabi(U) samples) which are less-than-certain predictors of language affiliation and use. The situation was more satisfactory in the Panjabi(G) sample because of the greater degree of correspondence between distinctive Sikh names and Panjabi speakers, and the higher chance of being right simply because of the high numbers of this linguistic minority in Coventry. Most of the 'wrong languages' in the Polish sample were Ukrainian speakers whose names were written in accordance with Polish spelling conventions.

(d) The high number of removals in the Chinese sample (25 per cent) is largely the result of the use of relatively dated sources, such as the telephone directory, in compiling the list of addresses. It is also possible that some of the Chinese names identified in the electoral register were students, and thus liable to move on very rapidly.

In Bradford the interesting features of the response patterns included the following:

(a) The high response rate in the Chinese sample (98 per cent) was achieved through the use of a very recent authoritative list of refugee families from Indo-China who had been resettled in the Bradford district. This was backed up by the work of a team of interviewers who were all intimately familiar with the population in question, since they had been involved with them in the resettlement programme. It is probably also due to the fact that almost all of the people interviewed were unemployed, and as one person put it, 'they've been interviewed so often since they arrived in the U.K. that they think surveys are a major feature of the British way of life'! As a result these respondents tended to be both readily available and particularly co-operative.

Adult Language Use: preparing a survey

Table 4.3 Response rates in Bradford

Language	Chinese	Panjabi(G)	Panjabi(U)	Polish
(1) Total number of addresses selected in sample	53	203	442	334
(2) Total number of addresses visited by interviewers	52	129	336	264
(3) Number of interviews conducted	51	99	172	156
(4) 3 as % of 2	98	77	51	59
(5) Number of refusals	0	5	15	44
(6) 5 as % of (3 + 5)	–	5	8	22
(7) Wrong language as % of 2	–	2	21	3
(8) Non contacts as % of 2	2	9	9	8
(9) Removals as % of 2	–	8	15	13

Note: Numbers in row 3 are not the same as numbers of interviews given in Chapter 5, because a small proportion were not accepted for analysis.

(b) The response rate of 77 per cent for the Panjabi(G) sample was especially good. This reflects the accuracy of the name analysis method, the relatively settled nature of these people in Bradford, and the good contacts and support for the survey in the institutions and media serving the Panjabi(G)-speaking minority.

(c) The high rate of refusal (22 per cent) in the Polish sample is probably similar in origin and effect to the situation in Coventry. The higher percentage or removals in Bradford is a result of our using an outdated 'community' list as one component in the sampling frame. In fact there was a notably higher proportion of removals amongst addresses taken from this community source, than among those discovered by name analysis of the electoral registers.

(d) The Panjabi(U) sample produced the lowest response rate in Bradford (51 per cent) with most of the loss in the form of 'wrong languages' or removals. Once again Muslim names proved less than perfectly accurate in predicting language use, since interviewers often discovered households where Bengali, Pushtu or Gujerati were spoken rather than Panjabi. The removals are accounted for by the rapid pace

Table 4.4 Response rates in London

Language	Bengali	Chinese	Greek	Gujerati	Italian	Portuguese	Turkish
(1) Total number of addresses selected in sample	447	329	399	237	217	446	402
(2) Total number of addresses visited by interviewers	323	295	317	213	167	339	343
(3) Number of interviews conducted	184	137	189	99	94	195	197
(4) 3 as % of 2	57	46	60	67	56	58	57
(5) Number of refusals	14	22	59	3	31	34	43
(6) 5 as % of (3 + 5)	7	14	24	3	25	15	18
(7) 'Wrong language' as % of 2	10	12	1	23	.6	.3	3
(8) Non contacts as % of 2	16	9	12	17	13	16	15
(9) Removals as % of 2	13	24	9	11	11	17	12

Note: Numbers in row 3 are not the same as numbers of interviews given in Chapter 5, because a small proportion were not accepted for analysis.

of slum clearance and redevelopment in inner city Bradford, especially in the focal zone for the people of Pakistani origin.

Generally speaking, response rates in London were lower than in the provincial cities, and the following features are worthy of note:

(a) The refusal rates in the four European samples were particularly high, with the Greek and Italian figures reaching over 20 per cent. It is possible that the pressures of life in London, or a general lack of interest in the language issue, prompted the refusals. The difficulty of building up good community liaison in the metropolis may also have played a part. In the Greek case for example the newspaper article about the survey already referred to (see p. 161) may have lessened confidence amongst potential respondents. In addition London as a whole, and Haringey in particular, following the piloting there of possible 'ethnic' questions for the 1981 Census, is an area which is highly sensitive in terms of the politics of 'race relations research'.

(b) 'Wrong Languages' were found to a significant extent only in the Gujerati, Bengali, and Chinese samples. The limited accuracy of Hindu and Muslim names as predictors of Gujerati and Bengali language affiliation replicates the situations in Coventry and Bradford. The Chinese 'wrong languages' in London were mostly English speakers, either third-generation descendants or widows of early Chinese settlers in Limehouse, 'ethnic Chinese' from the West Indies in Haringey, or Chinese-speaking students and professionals from Malaysia who use English and sometimes Hokkien rather than Cantonese.

(c) The level of removals and non-contacts was generally quite high in all the groups in London, reflecting the lifestyle of a highly mobile metropolis and in some cases the difficulty of maintaining up-to-date and accurate records for the electoral register and telephone directories. The rate of removals was particularly high for the Chinese sample, especially in Haringey where we had relied heavily on name analysis of the telephone directory, and where a number of the removals are likely to have been Chinese-speaking students, identified by their names from the electoral register. The high level of removals in the Portuguese sample reflects the status of these people as short-term migrant workers.

The degree of effort required to obtain the target number of interviews can be judged from Table 4.5, which shows the percentage of interviews completed with a single visit to the address in question. Overall fewer than 10 per cent of successful interviews required more than two visits to the address. The number of such repeated recalls was highest in the London survey, and with the Coventry Gujerati sample (perhaps in this case because the fieldwork took place in the middle of the Navratri festival).

*Table 4.5 Percentage of successful interviews achieved
on the first visit to the address*

City \ Language	Coventry	Bradford	London
Chinese	91	100	68
Gujerati	62		61
Italian	71		46
Panjabi (G)	78	69	
Panjabi (U)	66	69	
Polish	73	67	
Bengali	82		69
Greek			59
Turkish			62
Portuguese			51

Data-processing

The Adult Language Use Survey provides a far larger body of data than
any of the other surveys carried out by LMP. A questionnaire over
150 items long answered by nearly 2,500 respondents produced a set
of data with great potential and challenge for statistical analysis. The
constraints of space available in the present book mean that we can
only offer a thumbnail sketch of basic and preliminary findings. Second-
stage analysis of the ALUS data is being carried out in the course
of a two-year follow-up study by the Community Languages and
Education Project (funded by the ESRC at the Institute of Education,
employing several of the LMP team members). A series of publications
on more specialised topics arising from the data is envisaged, which will
eventually complement the data persented in the next chapter.

The task of data-processing was of necessity lengthy and complex.
The coding of the open-ended questions was undertaken by some of the
ALUS interviewers in each city, while the structure of the questionnaire
was fresh in their memories. Each coded questionnaire was then checked
by one of the research team or language supervisors. After punching
and transferring the data to computer, each data file was examined
by a checking program which pointed out range errors and major
inconsistencies. These were then corrected by reference to the original
questionnaires. This correcting sequence was repeated several times until
we were satisfied that the quality of the data could not be substantially
improved. Some data manipulation was carried out using FORTRAN

programs specially written by one of the researchers. The most important of these involved 'unpacking' data from the household grid and creating a separate data file for this section. In this each person mentioned by the respondent, including the respondent himself or herself, constituted a single case with a small number of demographic, language skill and language use variables for each. A further FORTRAN program was used on the data on knowledge of languages other than the language of the questionnaire (Qs. 4 and 5). Here twenty-five new variables were created, one for each language given by at least five speakers, each variable containing information about whether the language in question was known by the respondent and if so how recently it was last used. These variables were then added to the main data file, which generally matched the structure of the questionnaire as a whole and contained one case for each respondent, each case with a value for all the variables in the data.

From this point on the two sets of data were subjected to analyses which for the most part used the Statistical Package for the Social Sciences (SPSS). Some further data manipulation was carried out, and new composite variables were created where necessary. The cases in each file were sorted by town and language so that individual subfiles for each language in each city could be easily handled. The data presented in the following chapter is derived from our analysis of the two files. The response rates data was prepared and processed as a separate third SPSS file.

5

Patterns of language use

In this chapter our aim is to present basic findings for each of the local linguistic minorities surveyed by LMP in the three cities. We need to stress at the very beginning that the reader should be very cautious about making direct comparisons across local linguistic minorities, if they involve different languages spoken in one city, or even the same language spoken in different cities.

There are two reasons for this caution. Firstly, superficial comparisons between local linguistic minorities would take little account of the different periods of time the various minorities have been in England, or of their historical and political experience of migration and subsequent settlement. Different historical experience has resulted in wide variations in linguistic, social, structural and demographic characteristics. To account for this in any detail, and to relate such factors to the data presented here, it would have been essential to present the findings of related local social surveys, for example on housing, unemployment, social class. Even if information of this kind had been readily available, such a study would have been beyond the resources of LMP.

The second reason for caution about comparison is a more technical one. In Chapter 4 we discussed the variation in sampling strategies for the different local linguistic minorities, and our strategy of presenting the questionnaire in eleven different language versions. For the reasons mentioned there it is impossible to determine statistically the levels of confidence for our sampling procedures. Therefore it is not legitimate, even at a local level, to make statements on the basis of our data about for example the Polish-speaking population of Coventry, or the Gujerati-speaking population of Coventry. It is less legitimate still to compare two or more such populations. To extrapolate from these findings to the populations on a national level on the basis of data presented here would therefore be even more perilous.

Ideally the findings for each local linguistic minority would have been presented as the data from a series of separate surveys. However, in order to present the data economically, most tables and histograms are given with data about the nineteen different local linguistic minorities surveyed presented alongside each other, in alphabetical order of the languages. Our own comments and interpretations about differences between linguistic minorities are to highlight outstanding contrasts, which can only be explained when our sociolinguistic data is linked with the wider sociopolitical analysis outlined in Chapters 1 and 4. Some of these contrasts also raise interesting questions which need to be considered if we are to contribute to a more thorough appraisal of the position of particular linguistic minorities in England, and the development of specific educational policies.

The structure of this chapter follows to a great extent the structure of the questionnaire, in that we begin with questions on language skills and literacy, then discuss language use in the home and family. The data on language in the workplace, in free time and in minority institutions follows, and finally we present the data relating to participation in mother tongue teaching and attitudes towards it. For the most part the bases for tables and histograms are answers to questions in the interview, although in some cases simple composite variables or indices are presented.

The demographic pyramids of the respondents and their households presented in Chapter 2 enable us to fill out the description of our sets of respondents. Our aim of achieving balanced numbers of male and female respondents was broadly speaking achieved in all the linguistic minorities, with the exception of Polish and Ukrainian speakers in Coventry, and of Bengali speakers in London. In these three cases men outnumbered women. The age balance was also less than satisfactory in a few local linguistic minorities – notably again with more in the older age group among Polish and Ukrainian speakers, and to a lesser extent among Italian speakers. We believe that these imbalances largely reflect the demographic structure of the particular linguistic minorities, which result from their individual migration histories. Our main check – and it is a partially circular one – is to compare the demographic profile of respondents with that of the household members. This is illustrated in the population pyramids shown in Chapter 2. The fit between the age and sex profiles of respondents and those of household members seems to us a reasonably satisfactory one. However, because of the wide differences of demographic structure, comparisons between local linguistic minorities surveyed would be particularly misleading, if they were to take the form of statements about the inter-relationship of language use, or language skills, with sex or age. The variation attributable to these two independent variables is confounded by the variation attributable to demographic structure of the samples.

It is also important to remember the way in which linguistic minorities were defined for the purposes of the ALUS survey (see Chapter 4, pp. 162f.). The fact that sample addresses were selected according to various, mainly ethnic, criteria, and that individual respondents were chosen by the interviewers on the basis partly of availability, partly of the quota requirements, means that the category of 'speakers' of a particular minority language used in this chapter is merely a shorthand, which does not imply any sociolinguistic characteristics common to all respondents.

Similarly, in this chapter whenever we use the term 'minority languages', we are referring to the languages in which the different versions of the questionnaire were printed, for which the interviewing teams were recruited, and which formed the main focus of the questions. This point is particularly important in the case of Chinese, Bengali, Gujerati, Panjabi(U) and Italian. Our shorthand term 'Chinese speakers' grossly simplifies the sociolinguistic situation in which some speak Cantonese as a first or second language, some speak Hakka as a first language and some speak other Chinese languages. The common factor is that all would use the Chinese script for literacy. In the same way the term 'Panjabi(U) speaker' in this chapter does not imply that respondents can necessarily speak or read Urdu, merely that they all are members of the linguistic minority where speaking Panjabi and literacy in Urdu is the norm. The term 'Bengali speaker' is again a shorthand term, for it includes many respondents who speak Sylheti and who might consider Bengali as a second language. The same applies to the 'Italian speakers' in terms of the distinction between the non-standard varieties ('dialetti') and the standard variety of Italian ('la lingua italiana'), and to any respondents among the 'Gujerati speakers' whose language is actually Kutchi.

Language skills

We begin by presenting in Table 5.1 the remarkable range of the linguistic repertoires of the respondents. In almost all of the local linguistic minorities over 90 per cent of respondents reported some knowledge of at least two languages. Of course, the two languages most often reported were the language of the questionnaire and English: however, there were some respondents who mentioned more than one language, but not English. These cases were mostly among speakers of Chinese languages, where Cantonese and Hakka or Cantonese and Vietnamese were given; among Panjabi(U) speakers, where Panjabi and Urdu were the two languages involved; and among the London Bengali speakers, where Sylheti and Bengali but not English were mentioned.

Besides this widespread bilingualism among the respondents, very high proportions of respondents from several local linguistic minorities reported knowledge of three or more languages. The most notable cases are the Gujerati and Italian speakers in both Coventry and London and the Chinese speakers in Bradford, where over 80 per cent of respondents listed three or more languages. In fact in all cases, except the Greek-speaking linguistic minority in London, more than 40 per cent of the respondents mention more than two languages. There are, of course, very different reasons for this multilingualism among the different linguistic minorities: in the case of the Italian speakers, for example, it, is largely a question of use of non-standard varieties alongside the standard variety; among Gujerati speakers the knowledge of Swahili is strikingly high – originating from the strong East African connections; among the Polish speakers Russian and German were widely known, for obvious historical reasons; the mention of Greek by nearly half the Turkish-speaking respondents in London, and the absence of significant mention of Turkish by the Greek-speaking respondents reflects a power imbalance which existed between the two communities in Cyprus.

One important aspect of this knowledge of more than two languages from the point of view of educational planning is the position of Urdu and Hindi among the South Asian linguistic minorities we surveyed. It is clear that, although the three major spoken home languages are Panjabi, Gujerati and Bengali, nevertheless Urdu and Hindi, as two major national or official languages, are quite widely known and used. Their use as lingua franca may well increase among speakers of South Asian languages in Britain as time goes on. In view of their literary and symbolic value, support for them from schools and colleges is probably necessary beyond the level that the number of native speakers might otherwise justify.

In many cases these additional languages can be described as being in active use: that is to say, the respondents said they had used them within the previous four weeks. This was particularly so for Hindi and Urdu when given by respondents from the different South Asian linguistic minorities. For example, out of 152 Gujerati-speaking respondents in Coventry who listed Hindi as one of their languages, 143 had spoken it within the previous four weeks. In London the figure was 66 out of 75. Of the 44 Coventry Gujerati speakers who mentioned Panjabi, 43 said they had used it within the previous four weeks. For Panjabi(G) speakers in Coventry, 79 out of 103 who mentioned Hindi said they had used it in the previous four weeks. From these figures it seems probable that in Coventry a lot of communication takes place between Gujerati and Panjabi(G) 'mother tongue' speakers through the medium of Hindi, and some at least through Panjabi.

For Panjabi(U) speakers mentioning Urdu in Bradford, the figure for use in the previous four weeks was 125 out of 135, in Coventry 62 out of 65. Sometimes respondents made it clear that the variety they commonly used was not the language of the questionnaire, for example Sylheti for Bengali speakers, Italian dialects, or Hakka or Vietnamese for Cantonese-speaking respondents. In such cases this variety had been used by all or almost all of the respondents within the previous four weeks. Turkish speakers who mentioned Greek, Ukrainian speakers who mentioned Polish, and Portuguese speakers who mentioned Spanish, also usually claimed that they had used these languages recently. In contrast, among the Polish speakers who mentioned German or Russian, among the Italian speakers who mentioned French, and among the Gujerati speakers who mentioned Swahili, most had not used these languages in the previous four weeks.

From the commonly monolingual English perspective of the majority of people in Britain, this multilingualism constitutes a very impressive range of linguistic knowledge and use. Against this background we go on to look a little more closely at the patterns of language acquisition and self-rated skills of the respondents, in their main minority language and in English.

Nearly all respondents reported that both parents had spoken the language of the questionnaire to them when they were children (or in the case of Bengali and Italian speakers a related variety). The exceptions were, firstly, the Italian speakers in Coventry, 84 per cent of whom said their parents had spoken standard Italian or a non-standard variety of Italian to them and where many of the rest had used English; and secondly, the three samples of Chinese speakers: in Coventry only 14 per cent of them said their parents had used Cantonese, in London 72 per cent, in Bradford 86 per cent. In Coventry and London most of the remaining cases involved the use of Hakka, occasionally other Chinese languages, by one or both parents. Among the non-Cantonese-speaking respondents in Bradford, apart from two Hakka-speaking cases, the language used by one or both parents had been Vietnamese.

Table 5.1 Number of languages known by respondents

***** mentioning 3 or more languages   === mentioning 2 languages

All languages mentioned by more than 10% of respondents in a local linguistic minority appear in the histogram.

(1) A letter E is inserted in the histograms to mark the % mentioning English, A for Arabic, D for Italian dialects, F for French, H for Hindi, I for Italian, K for Hakka, M for Mandarin, R for Russian, U for Urdu, V for Vietnamese.

(2) G = German (Polish speakers); G = Greek (Turkish speakers).

(3) P = Polish (Italian and Ukrainian speakers); P = Panjabi (Gujerati speakers).

(4) S = Sylheti (Bengali speakers); S = Spanish (Portuguese speakers); S = Swahili (Gujerati speakers).

```
% of Respondents    10        20        30        40        50        60        70        80        90        100
                     :         :         :         :         :         :         :         :         :         :
                     :         :         :         :         :         :         :         :         :         :
Bengali
Coventry  N =  79   :***************H**********U***********************=============================E
London    N = 185   :**********A*********H*********U**********************************=S====E=========

Chinese
Coventry  N =  43   :*************M*********************************************====K=K=E============
Bradford  N =  50   :**********K*M************************************************************E=V==
London    N = 137   :**********V*KM***********================================E=====

Greek
London    N = 193   :***************============================================E

Gujerati
Coventry  N = 203   :************P*********S**********************************************H*******=============E=
London    N =  99   :**********U****S************************H*******************=============E=
```

Table 5.1 (continued)

% of Respondents	10	20	30	40	50	60	70	80	90	100
	:	:	:	:	:	:	:	:	:	:

Italian
Coventry N = 108 :***************F***********S**D********======E
London N = 94   :**************S=**F***D********======E

Panjabi (G)
Coventry N = 200 :************U**********************************H***********************===================E
Bradford N = 98 :***************U***********************H*****************==================E=

Panjabi (U)
Coventry N = 86 :***********A**U*****==========E===
Bradford N = 177 :***=U===E=========

Polish
Coventry N = 168 :***************F**I**********R****G*******************************===================E
Bradford N = 155 :**********I*G*R***===================E

Portuguese
London N = 196 :***********FI**********************************S*********************======================E

Turkish
London N = 197 :**G*******=====================E=

Ukrainian
Coventry N = 48 :**********I***********P*****************************==================E

In contrast, very few of the respondents in any of the local linguistic minorities said that home was where they had started to learn English. The highest proportion was among the Greek-speaking and Turkish-speaking respondents in London (18 per cent and 19 per cent respectively). In the case of respondents with origins in the British Commonwealth or Pakistan – the South Asian, Coventry and London Chinese-speaking, and the London Greek-speaking and Turkish-speaking linguistic minorities, over 50 per cent of respondents who could speak English said they had started to learn English at school. For the Ukrainian-, Polish-, Italian-, Portuguese- and (Bradford) Chinese-speaking respondents more than half said they had started to learn English elsewhere, often mentioning 'when I came to Britain'.

In order to compress the data on language skills into a smaller number of composite skills variables it was necessary to investigate first the relationship between the different types of skills (productive and receptive, oral and literacy) in the minority language and English. A series of Guttman scalogram analyses was performed on two sets of questions (11, 12, 13, 18 and 32, 33, 34, 35). This allowed us to check the distribution of scores for each variable, and to examine the correlations between the different skills and their implicational ranking. The conclusions from this procedure were that in almost all the local linguistic minorities –

(a)   the four different skills for each language were quite strongly correlated with each other; the correlation between oral and written skills was sometimes weaker;

(b)   the best point to dichotomise each item in order to reflect the distribution of item scores in any composite variables was the mid-point, i.e. to merge 'very well' with 'fairly well' and 'not very well' with 'not at all';

(c)   having taken the mid-point as the cut-off point the implicational ranking (order of difficulty) of the separate items for both languages was generally understanding – speaking – reading – writing. The only non-trivial exception was in the case of minority language skills for the Italian speakers in Coventry, where the order for skills was understanding – reading – speaking – writing. Probably this reflects the language experience of younger respondents who feel that their productive skills are less well developed than their receptive ones, especially if the questions were taken as referring to standard Italian rather than 'dialetti'.

On the basis of this analysis, in the presentation which follows in

Table 5.2, and in the interests of greater simplicity of presentation, we have reduced the eight original variables to four. So, for example, in column 1 of Table 5.2, only respondents who reported both understanding *and* speaking ability are included; in column 4 only those who reported both reading *and* writing ability. We have also simplified the four-point rating scale used in our interview schedule, and include here as positive answers only those reporting that they speak, read (etc.) 'very well' or 'fairly well'.

With only one or two exceptions, 90 per cent or more of the respondents in each linguistic minority reported at least a fair command of the minority language in question, so little comment seems necessary on the oral-aural skills in the minority languages. The exceptions are Italian speakers and the Coventry and Bradford speakers of Chinese languages, where there were sizeable numbers of respondents whose home language was Hakka or Vietnamese, rather than the Cantonese on which the questions were focussed. In this case it is possible that our questions about skills in the spoken language were taken to relate to the standard language, rather than to the dialects which many respondents used more commonly, though it is hard to say why this did not happen with Panjabi(U) speakers and Sylheti-Bengali speakers in London. The pattern of language use revealed in later questions by the Italian-speaking respondents, especially in Coventry, suggests the alternative hypothesis that language shift to English has advanced further with them than with other linguistic minorities.

Literacy in the minority language was never much less than 50 per cent, again with the exception of the Chinese-speaking respondents in Bradford, who were all refugees from Vietnam and in many cases were literate in Vietnamese. The literacy rates range from over 80 per cent of the Polish- and Ukrainian-speaking respondents, through notably high proportions of the Gujerati, Turkish and Bengali speakers, with the lowest rates among the Panjabi(G), Panjabi(U) and Chinese speakers in Coventry and Bradford.

In terms of skills in English the majority of respondents in almost all the local linguistic minorities reported understanding and speaking at least 'fairly well'. The predictable exception was amongst the recently-arrived Chinese speakers in Bradford. Although self-rated ability to understand and speak English among these adult respondents is lower than for the same skills in the minority languages, these figures indicate a very high level of competence in English. Polish speakers in particular, along with speakers of Turkish, Gujerati and Greek, reported the highest rates of oral-aural skills in English.

Table 5.2 Summary of language skills for ALUS respondents

% of respondents who —
(A) understand and speak the minority language 'fairly well' or 'very well';
(B) read and write the minority language 'fairly well' or 'very well';
(C) understand and speak English 'fairly well' or 'very well';
(D) read and write English 'fairly well' or 'very well'.

	Col A	Col B	Col C	Col D
Bengali				
Coventry N = 79	98	70	52	37
London N = 185	94	70	47	40
Chinese				
Coventry N = 43	79	51	44	30
Bradford N = 50	88	28	10	6
London N = 137	96	65	47	42
Greek				
London N = 193	94	66	72	57
Gujerati				
Coventry N = 203	98	84	74	64
London N = 99	98	79	76	72
Italian				
Coventry N = 108	73	63	83	39
London N = 94	81	69	65	34
Panjabi(G)				
Coventry N = 200	99	61	67	60
Bradford N = 96	99	54	54	45
Panjabi(U)				
Coventry N = 86	98	57	61	44
Bradford N = 177	99	47	36	28
Polish				
Coventry N = 168	92	82	91	64
Bradford N = 155	92	83	84	55
Portuguese				
London N = 196	88	74	50	27
Turkish				
London N = 197	98	80	75	46
Ukrainian				
Coventry N = 48	92	83	50	31

Levels of literacy in English are highest among Gujerati speakers in Coventry and London and among Polish and Panjabi(G) speakers in Coventry, at least as we have defined literacy for purposes of this presentation – an ability to read *and* write at least fairly well. In all local linguistic minorities English literacy skills are reported to be less high than literacy skills in the minority language. However, it is noticeable that in the case of the Panjabi(G) speakers in Coventry and the Gujerati speakers in London, the gap is quite small. It is not possible, of course, to tell from this data alone whether this distribution of skills in the different linguistic minorities relates to the differential levels of educational support available for developing literacy in English and the minority languages, whether in the country of origin or in England. It is possible, for example, that the high levels of biliteracy among the Gujerati speakers reflects their East African background, where English medium education went alongside positive efforts in Gujerati language maintenance.

In most of the local linguistic minorities surveyed fewer than half of the respondents said that they ever used other people to translate or interpret for them. Among the Italian speakers in London the figure was as low as 15 per cent. The exceptions were the Portuguese speakers in London (65 per cent), the Chinese-speaking respondents in London and Bradford (56 per cent in both cases) and the Panjabi(U) speakers in Bradford (53 per cent). The most frequently mentioned occasions where interpreters were used involved contact with official institutions, such as health services, schools, and local authority departments, or where paperwork was necessary. With the exception of the Chinese speakers in Bradford and London, official and professional interpreters were rarely mentioned, since bilingual family members or friends usually took the interpreter's role.

Differences in skills in both languages, across and within the various local linguistic minorities, seem to be related to length of schooling, place of upbringing, sex and age of respondents. These variables themselves are often interrelated, and are also closely related to the demographic structures and migration histories of the local linguistic minorities.

In order to assess the effects of schooling, upbringing, sex and age on language skills a series of statistical tests using the analysis of variance approach was applied to the four composite skills variables. The largest proportion of the variation in skills in almost all cases was found to be attributable to the place of upbringing and/or the length of schooling: respondents who had been brought up in the UK reported lower minority language and higher English skills, and respondents who had

Table 5.3 Language skills: significant (p <.05) effects of sex (G), upbringing (Up), age and length of schooling (Ed) on language skills composite variables

Composite skills variables	(1) Oral/aural minority language	(2) Literacy minority language	(3) Oral/aural English	(4) Literacy English
Bengali				
Coventry N = 79	Ed† Up	Ed Up Age	Ed G	Ed G
London N = 185		Ed Up	Ed G Up Age	Ed Up
Chinese				
Coventry N = 43	Ed* Age†	Ed*	Ed	Ed Up*
Bradford N = 50**	Ed†	Ed†	Ed	Ed G
London N = 137			Ed G	Ed G
Greek				
London N = 193	Up	Ed Up	Ed G Up†	Ed G Up
Gujerati				
Coventry N = 203	Ed† Up	Ed G* Age	Ed G Up† Age†	Ed G Age
London N = 99	Age†	Ed† Age	Ed G Age	Ed G Age
Italian				
Coventry N = 108	Ed Up	Ed Up	Ed Up	Ed Up
London N = 94		Up	Up†	Ed Up
Panjabi (G)				
Coventry N = 200	Ed* Up	Ed Up Age†	Ed† G Up	Ed† G
Bradford N = 96		Ed Up	Ed Up	Ed

Table 5.3 (continued)

Composite skills variables	(1) Oral/aural minority language	(2) Literacy minority language	(3) Oral/aural English	(4) Literacy English
Panjabi (U)				
Coventry N = 86	Up	Ed Up	Ed Up Age†	Ed Up
Bradford N = 177	G* Up	Ed G* Up	Ed G Up	Ed G Up
Polish				
Coventry N = 168	Ed Up	Ed G* Up Age†	Ed G	Ed G Up
Bradford N = 155	Ed G* Up†	Ed G* Up	Ed G	Ed G Up
Portuguese				
London N = 196	Ed Up Age†	Ed Age†	Ed Up	Ed Up
Turkish				
London N = 197	Up	Ed Up	Ed G Up Age†	Ed G Up
Ukrainian				
Coventry N = 48	Ed* Up	Up	Ed Up	Ed Up

* The effect was significant but was in an unexpected direction, e.g. in col (2) females reported higher skills than males.
† The effect was significant but was not a linear relationsip.
** Upbringing not included in analysis since all Bradford Chinese-speaking respondents were brought up overseas.

more than a few years of formal schooling tended to report higher levels of skills all round. Sex and age played a significant part only for respondents from some local linguistic minorities, for some skills. Usually females reported lower skills in English than males, while younger people reported lower levels of minority language skills, and older respondents lower levels of English skills. Exceptions are explicable only with reference to the sociolinguistic circumstances of particular local linguistic minorities. Table 5.3 summarises the significant effects of age, sex, place of upbringing and length of schooling. The effects listed are the ones which remained significant when other intervening variables were controlled for. For example, the sex effect was still significant when age and schooling differences across the sexes were held constant, and the age difference remained significant when the effect of place of upbringing was taken into account. Interaction terms, which were quite rarely significant in any case, are ignored.

In Table 5.4 we set out the proportions of the respondents from the various local linguistic minorities who have at least a minimal degree of literacy in both minority language and English, and those not reporting literacy in either of these languages. It will be evident that the latter category forms a very small percentage of all but the Panjabi(U) speakers, where many respondents have very few years of formal schooling, little knowledge of English, and where all would need to learn Urdu as a language of literacy. Overall, the 'biliterates' range from a minimum of 52 per cent for the Italian speakers in London, where very high numbers have literacy skills in at least one language, to a maximum of 90 per cent for the Polish speakers in Coventry.

Before going on to consider the findings concerned with patterns of language use between respondents and other members of their families, it is useful to give an account of the pattern of skills of all the members of respondents' households, including children and non-family members. This is presented in Table 5.5, which gives the proportions of respondents' household members from the different local linguistic minorities (including the respondents themselves and children below the age of 17) who were said by the respondent to know the two relevant languages either 'fairly well' or 'very well'.

The questions did not specify the particular language skills, but we assume from the context that respondents will have understood the enquiry to refer to spoken skills. At least half the household members and in most cases two-thirds or more, could speak in both English and in the minority language, with the obvious exception again of the Vietnamese Chinese respondents in Bradford.

Table 5.4 Literacy skills in English and in the main minority language

	Literacy* in two languages %	No literacy* in either language %
Bengali		
Coventry N = 79	70	10
London N = 185	68	9
Chinese		
Coventry N = 43	67	2
Bradford N = 50	58	6
London N = 137	69	2
Greek		
London N = 193	63	3
Gujerati		
Coventry N = 203	78	2
London N = 99	75	1
Italian		
Coventry N = 108	55	1
London N = 94	52	0
Panjabi (G)		
Coventry N = 200	65	8
Bradford N = 96	53	18
Panjabi (U)		
Coventry N = 86	59	27
Bradford N = 177	48	29
Polish		
Coventry N = 168	90	0
Bradford N = 155	78	0
Portuguese		
London N = 196	66	4
Turkish		
London N = 197	61	3
Ukrainian		
Coventry N − 48	88	0

Literacy in this table is defined as reporting ability to read and write at least 'not very well' in the relevant language.

The skills reported for household members were also tested by analysis of variance for the effect of sex, age and place of upbringing, there being no data available on length of schooling of household members. Age and upbringing produced significant effects in almost every local linguistic minority, with older people and those brought up overseas tending to have higher skills in the minority language, and

Table 5.5 Language skills of people living in respondents' households

% of people (including respondents) reported as knowing minority language or English 'very well' or 'fairly well', and % of bilinguals (i.e. knowing both languages 'very well' or 'fairly well').

	Minority language	English	Bilingual
Bengali			
Coventry N = 308	80	71	57
London N = 802	75	57	47
Chinese			
Coventry N = 213	49	55	26
Bradford N = 233	66	18	16
London N = 504	82	61	51
Greek			
London N = 673	82	79	63
Gujerati			
Coventry N = 973	87	79	69
London N = 383	85	80	68
Italian			
Coventry N = 387	58	89	50
London N = 339	76	86	65
Panjabi(G)			
Coventry N = 993	89	75	68
Bradford N = 471	87	75	67
Panjabi(U)			
Coventry N = 472	79	66	54
Bradford N = 941	86	67	62
Polish			
Coventry N = 465	71	93	65
Bradford N = 401	79	83	61
Portuguese			
London N = 592	78	69	50
Turkish			
London N = 761	87	80	70
Ukrainian			
Coventry N = 132	80	80	62

Base numbers include only those household members for whom respondents reported their language skills; those excluded are mainly small children.

lower skills in English, than the younger people and those who were brought up wholly or partly in the UK. Minority language skills were significantly related to sex only among the Coventry Gujerati and Polish speakers. In the former case females had significantly higher skills, although it is difficult to suggest why this should be so. In the latter case males had higher skills, probably as a result of marriages between Polish-speaking men and non-Polish-speaking women. Sex produced a significant effect in English skills in the Bengali (London), Gujerati (Coventry and London), Panjabi(U) and (G) (in both Coventry and Bradford), Italian (Coventry), Greek and Turkish local linguistic minorities: in each case males were reported as having higher levels of English skills than females. In these cases a combination of shorter formal schooling, and the fact that fewer women than men have had the opportunity to acquire English in the context of work outside the home, could explain the sex difference.

Language use

We examine now what were the actual patterns of language use in the respondents' homes. In the *Household Language Use* section of ALUS, after we had established how well the various household members were thought to know the minority language and English, we asked two questions about actual practice:

Q. 79: 'When the respondent and this person talk with each other, which language(s) or dialect(s) does the respondent speak in?'

Q. 80: 'When talking with respondent, which language(s) or dialect(s) does the other person speak?'

Table 5.6 lays out the patterns of language use between respondents and members of their households, without any reference to their level of skills in either of the languages concerned. It is important to stress that this data does not reflect the exercise of free choice by members of the household: in this context language use patterns are constrained because high proportions of particular linguistic minorities may have had little opportunity to develop skills in English, for example.

One of the main points of interest here is the question of how much the different languages are used overall in the different minorities. There are sharp contrasts, for example, between the Polish- and Italian-speaking households surveyed in Coventry on the one hand, where more than a third of the participants use English reciprocally, and the households of South Asian origin on the other, where no more than 5 per cent report using English reciprocally. It must be remembered too

that the figures in Table 5.6 will obviously reflect to a great extent the
level of language skills available to the speakers concerned.

In Table 5.7 we narrow the focus to those *family members* who
apparently do have a choice of which language they use, as suggested by
their reported skills. As it is respondents who are reporting their patterns
of language use in interaction, only the households where the respondent could speak both the minority language and English 'fairly well' or
'very well' are included in the table. Friends, lodgers, etc., are excluded
from consideration here, as are family members who were reported as
knowing either language 'not very well' or 'not at all'.

The proportions of this more narrowly defined set of interlocutor
pairs using the minority language reciprocally, vary from the surprisingly
high proportion of the Coventry Ukrainian speakers, through quite
high proportions of the speakers of South Asian languages in London
and Bradford (not so high in Coventry), to under a third of the Italian-
speaking bilinguals both in Coventry and in London. The general
impression is that across most of the local linguistic minorities, in those
family settings where bilingual language use is a realistic possibility, the
majority of interactions do take place in the minority language rather
than in English, and that it is very rarely that English is used to the
total exclusion of the minority language.

These patterns of language use by bilinguals were examined by
analysis of variance for the effects of sex, age and place of upbringing
of the interlocutor. The only factor which seemed to have a significant
effect on the language spoken to or by the persons involved in a large
number of the linguistic minorities surveyed was the place of upbringing.
People who were brought up overseas, even when they were bilingual,
were more likely to be spoken to and to speak in the minority language,
than people brought up in the UK.

The patterns of language use outlined in Tables 5.6 and 5.7 all involve
at least one adult, the respondent. The answers to our later question,
about the language used by the children in the household when talking
to each other, produces some interesting supplementary data. The
histogram in Table 5.8 shows the percentage of valid cases where the
respondents reported the children as speaking only or mostly English.
Such differences as there are between the local linguistic minorities
are broadly similar to patterns of adult language skills and language
use.

There are some interesting comparisons to be drawn here with the
data presented in Chapter 9 on the Secondary Pupils' Survey. The
pattern of widespread use of English among children with others of

Table 5.6 Languages used between respondents and all other household members

N = number of people in households (excluding respondents and missing cases).

(A) = % of interlocutors using only or mostly minority language** reciprocally* with respondents.

(B) = % of interlocutors using only or mostly English reciprocally* with respondents.

(C) = % of interlocutors using both English and minority language reciprocally* with respondents.

	Col A	Col B	Col C
Bengali			
Coventry N = 286	64	5	15
London N = 671	88	2	5
Chinese			
Coventry N = 157	57	10	19
Bradford N = 184	85	0	13
London N = 446	73	6	14
Greek			
London N = 548	51	16	18
Gujerati			
Coventry N = 760	67	2	22
London N = 340	66	3	27
Italian			
Coventry N = 284	21	37	19
London N = 269	34	16	20
Panjabi(G)			
Coventry N = 788	67	3	18
Bradford N = 404	76	2	14
Panjabi(U)			
Coventry N = 373	74	1	16
Bradford N = 809	82	1	10
Polish			
Coventry N = 302	36	35	15
Bradford N = 290	41	28	19
Portuguese			
London N = 420	67	12	10
Turkish			
London N = 607	60	7	16
Ukrainian			
Coventry N = 94	63	16	9

* 'Reciprocally' here indicates that the answers to the two questions (78, 79), were the same.

** 'Minority language' here includes 'other languages' such as Hakka and Italian dialects.

Table 5.7 Languages used between bilingual respondents and other
bilingual family members

(A) Number of pairs of interlocutors where both know both English and the
minority language fairly well or very well.
(B) % of A where minority language is used reciprocally all or most of the time.
(C) % of A where English is used reciprocally all or most of the time.

N = number of persons in households (including respondents)	Col A	Col B	Col C
Bengali			
Coventry N = 374	44	36	−
London N = 896	99	90	−
Chinese			
Coventry N = 213	14	2* (+ 3*)	−
Bradford N = 244	3	3*	−
London N = 597	58	60 (+ 12)	3
Greek			
London N = 758	167	59	6
Gujerati			
Coventry N = 992	371	58	1
London N = 457	80	73	3
Italian			
Coventry N = 394	80	31	16
London N = 367	95	17 (+ 20)	2
Panjabi(G)			
Coventry N =1025	346	51	4
Bradford N = 529	144	76	−
Panjabi(U)			
Coventry N = 482	101	62	2
Bradford N =1033	211	79	1
Polish			
Coventry N = 471	141	50	9
Bradford N = 449	83	54	2
Portuguese			
London N = 627	94	65	2
Turkish			
London N = 822	285	60	3
Ukrainian			
Coventry N = 144	18	16*	−

Figures in brackets are for Hakka (Chinese) and Italian Dialects used reciprocally.
*Starred figures are actual numbers (not percentages) given in cases where the
base figure is less than 20.

Table 5.8 Languages used between children – percentage reported
as using only or mostly English

		20	40	60	80	
Bengali						
Coventry	N = 59	:******************	•		•	37%
London	N = 119	:********	•	•	•	16%
Chinese						
Coventry	N = 30	:*****************************		•		60%
Bradford	N = 36	:	•	•	•	•	0%
London	N = 81	:**********	•	•	•	20%
Greek						
London	N = 99	:**				82%
Gujerati						
Coventry	N = 143	:******************* •		•	•	38%
London	N = 43	:***************** •		•	•	33%
Italian						
Coventry	N = 57	:***				86%
London	N = 59	:***				83%
Panjabi(G)						
Coventry	N = 154	:**********************		•	•	42%
Bradford	N = 73	:**************************		•	•	51%
Panjabi(U)						
Coventry	N = 68	:*********************		•	•	40%
Bradford	N = 146	:**************	•	•	•	25%
Polish						
Coventry	N = 53	:***				91%
Bradford	N = 35	:*********************************** •				69%
Portuguese						
London	N = 54	:************************************** •				74%
Turkish						
London	N = 120	:****************************** •				61%
Ukrainian						
Coventry	N = 18	:******************************** •				67%

their own generation is confirmed, as is our finding that children from Italian-speaking families tend to use more English than children from Panjabi-speaking families. Many of the differences seem to correspond to the length of time particular local linguistic minorities have been settled in England. However, it is not possible from this data to say whether a unidirectional process of language shift towards English is taking place, since longitudinal studies would be needed to determine whether the use of English is increasing over time, or whether childrens' extensive use of English is a particular feature of one period of their lives.

Language in the workplace

Economic relations between capital and labour play a fundamental role in the structuring of social relationships. Most members of linguistic minorities, as we have pointed out in Chapter 2, were led to settle in the UK in the context of work availability, sometimes involving a management's decision to employ cheap labour in various labour intensive, or declining, sectors of the economy. More recently the world recession, coupled with the growing trend in transnational enterprises towards the shifting of capital to Third World centres of production, has weakened the market position of labour, especially for the migrant and ethnic minority labour force. This has been reflected not only in high levels of unemployment, but in growing political pressures for the control and re-export of this labour force. The workplace is thus the main interface between these economic and political pressures and the members of linguistic minorities. Relations of production are a crucial factor in determining their social and sociolinguistic status in the eyes of the dominant majority. Conversely, the role of language in the workplace is a crucial factor in helping us to understand the relations of production in which members of linguistic minorities are involved.

The varied positions of local linguistic minorities in the local economies are products of the historical processes of industrialisation, colonialism, migration and institutionalised racism. Particular factories in a given locality employ disproportionate numbers of local linguistic minority members, while others employ mainly members of the majority working class. In certain situations minority members opt for self-employment, and are able to accumulate enough capital to establish small businesses. The resulting concentration of minority language speakers in particular workplaces or sectors of the economy may play a significant role in the maintenance of the language, because of the wider opportunities for minority language use. In areas like the East End of London, a particular sector of the local economy such as the garment trade may even produce a situation where minority language skills have a positive economic value within the local setting.

Although the data presented in this section does not allow us to test any formal hypotheses about the influence of the economic situation on language use or vice versa, it does offer some interesting insights into the importance of minority languages in the world of work.

Table 5.9 details the sectors of the economy in which our respondents were active. The first point of interest is the variation of male unemployment rates in the different local linguistic minorities. (Unfortunately this data is not available for five of the seven Coventry linguistic minorities, since the version of the questionnaire used in the first period of fieldwork did not record this with enough precision.) The male unemployment rate ranges from 71 per cent amongst the recently arrived Chinese-speaking refugees in Bradford through 31 per cent for the Panjabi(U) speakers in Bradford to a low of 2 per cent among the Portuguese speakers in London. By and large the Bradford and Coventry respondents show higher rates of unemployment than the London ones, and the European linguistic minorities lower rates than the South Asian ones. The particularly low rate for the Portuguese-speaking respondents reflects their status in Britain as migrant workers, with entry and residence being conditional on the possession of a work permit.

Employment opportunities appear to vary first and foremost according to the locality involved. In terms of sectors of the economy, most of the Coventry and Bradford respondents (with the exception of the Chinese speakers) were employed in manufacturing industry. The Chinese speakers in Coventry and London are concentrated almost exclusively in the catering and retail sector. In London the Italian- and Portuguese-speaking respondents reported that they were working mainly in catering and retailing or in the services sector. Of the London respondents only Bengali and Turkish speakers were employed predominantly in manufacturing. Greek and Gujerati speakers have the most widely diversified employment patterns, with up to a quarter of working respondents in the business and commercial sectors.

The work situation of respondents is shown in more detail in Table 5.10. In terms of employment status the Chinese speakers are most likely to be self-employed or in family businesses: over 50 per cent were employed in this way. Self-employment also appears to be common among the Greek and Turkish speakers in London, and among

Table 5.9 Type of industry in which respondents work as a
percentage of working respondents (n)

(When numbers are very small, only absolute numbers are given in brackets.)

(A) Manufacturing industry.
(B) Civil service or local authority.
(C) Business or commercial.
(D) Retailing or catering.
(E) Service and other industries (including transport).
(F) % of male respondents unemployed (here the base is the number of male respondents).
*   Data not available for these Coventry respondents.

	Col A	Col B	Col C	Col D	Col E	Col F
Bengali						
Coventry N = 38	53	11	(1)	24	11	27
London N = 87	62	9	8	13	7	16
Chinese						
Coventry N = 25	(1)	0	0	88	(1)	*
Bradford N = 6	....					71
London N = 67	3	3	13	69	12	18
Greek						
London N = 101	39	9	28	15	9	7
Gujerati						
Coventry N = 122	53	9	21	7	9	*
London N = 62	39	3	23	16	18	6
Italian						
Coventry N = 81	52	11	15	9	9	*
London N = 76	13	5	11	46	25	5
Panjabi(G)						
Coventry N = 126	64	6	3	10	15	*
Bradford N = 55	71	4	7	7	11	20
Panjabi(U)						
Coventry N = 44	55	2	18	11	14	*
Bradford N = 45	62	0	9	9	18	31
Polish						
Coventry N = 115	69	9	5	9	9	*
Bradford N = 94	46	13	11	23	7	9
Portuguese						
London N = 154	5	5	10	22	58	2
Turkish						
London N = 103	44	3	11	20	21	12
Ukrainian						
Coventry N = 32	66	9	(1)	9	9	9

Table 5.10 Employment situation of working respondents

(A) % of working respondents who are self-employed or in family business.
(B) % of working respondents who are responsible for employing or supervising at least one other worker.
(C) % of working respondents who work more than 40 hours a week.
(D) % of working respondents who have apprenticeship or professional qualifications.
(E) % of working respondents who are employed in non-manual occupations.

(When numbers are very small, only absolute numbers are given in brackets.)

	Col A	Col B	Col C	Col D	Col E
Bengali					
Coventry N = 38	(7)	24	34	16	32
London N = 87	17	23	24	20	23
Chinese					
Coventry N = 25	75	48	60	8	12
Bradford N = 6	••				
London N = 67	55	39	52	27	24
Greek					
London N = 101	36	30	38	33	38
Gujerati					
Coventry N = 122	14	30	25	27	38
London N = 62	23	27	31	23	47
Italian					
Coventry N = 81	11	17	21	31	19
London N = .76	22	32	41	25	24
Panjabi (G)					
Coventry N = 126	16	18	30	35	19
Bradford N = 55	13	9	38	20	11
Panjabi (U)					
Coventry N = 44	16	27	32	27	23
Bradford N = 45	29	16	56	25	18
Polish					
Coventry N = 115	5	22	13	43	24
Bradford N = 94	9	32	17	35	33
Portuguese					
London N = 154	1	14	29	16	12
Turkish					
London N = 103	27	30	37	30	20
Ukrainian					
Coventry N = 32	0	13	22	48	22

Panjabi(U) speakers in Bradford: in each case over 25 per cent of working respondents. Polish and Ukrainian speakers, on the other hand, are rarely self-employed.

Many of the respondents who reported that they were responsible for supervising or employing other workers are likely to be employers in small family businesses. This would certainly explain the fact that Chinese speakers were in such positions more frequently than other respondents. However, the relatively high proportion of Polish-speaking workers in both Coventry and Bradford, and of Gujerati and Panjabi(U) speakers in Coventry (over 20 per cent in each case), with supervisory or employer responsibilities, can hardly be explained in the same way, given the low rates of self-employment. It is more likely that these local linguistic minorities are well-represented in supervisory roles in manufacturing industry.

Many of the members of local linguistic minorities surveyed appear to work longer than average hours. Over half the Chinese- and Bradford Panjabi(U)-speaking working respondents reported working more than forty hours a week. On the other hand, the Polish-speaking respondents in both Coventry and Bradford did so in fewer than 20 per cent of cases. These patterns suggest that in many situations of self-employment and family businesses long hours are common. For example, some respondents working in small shops, restaurants and take-aways reported working eighty or more hours per week. Furthermore, in manufacturing industry in Bradford and Coventry in 1981 there were many situations where restricted overtime and short-time working had become the norm. A few years earlier many more people were working longer hours than was the case at the time of the survey. Finally, it should be pointed out that it is particularly difficult for a survey which was conducted in the home to provide an accurate picture of working hours, since those people who work longest are, by definition, the least likely to be at home when the interviewer calls, and will therefore be under-represented in the completed interviews.

Formal job training or professional qualifications were not often reported by the working respondents. In every local linguistic minority surveyed less than half of the working respondents said they had any training beyond the experience gained on the job. The Coventry and Bradford Polish- and Coventry Ukrainian-speaking respondents had the highest overall levels of formal training, with 35 per cent or more with qualifications, and the Bengali (London and Coventry), Portuguese (London) and Chinese (Coventry) speakers the lowest, with 20 per cent or less in each case.

The analysis of occupations is an even more complex process than usual, with the added problems of coding job-names and descriptions given (often imprecisely, e.g. 'engineering', 'textiles', 'business', 'factory work') by respondents speaking in the minority language. An attempt was made to relate this data to the socio-economic group categories used by OPCS (OPCS, 1980) and in Table 5.10 we have presented a simplified version of OPCS categories in which respondents' occupations are classified either as manual or non-manual. The non-manual category corresponds to the OPCS social classes I, II and IIIN, together with some imprecisely described occupations which were clearly non-manual, and the manual category to classes IIIM, IV and V together with imprecisely described, but obviously manual, jobs. This simplified system accounts for almost all the occupations mentioned in ALUS.

The Gujerati-speaking (Coventry and London) and Greek-speaking respondents had the highest proportions of non-manual workers. Nearly half the London Gujerati-speaking workers were in non-manual occupations. For all the other linguistic minorities surveyed, 70 per cent or more of the working respondents were in manual occupations.

Table 5.11 sets out some of the basic findings about language in the workplace. In every local linguistic minority surveyed, over 30 per cent of working respondents said they had at least one workmate who could speak their language. In the case of the Panjabi(U) and Panjabi(G) speakers in Bradford, the Bengali speakers in London, and the Chinese speakers in both London and Coventry, the proportion was over three-quarters. To some extent these figures are a straightforward reflection of the size and concentration of the local linguistic minorities. For example, there is obviously a greater chance of a Panjabi(U) speaker in Bradford having Panjabi-speaking workmates when there are approximately 37,000 such speakers in the city, than there is for a Ukrainian speaker in Coventry who is a member of a minority only a few hundred strong. However, numerical strength cannot account for the case of the Chinese speakers. Here we must also look at Column B in Table 5.11, which shows that roughly two-thirds of all Chinese-speaking workers in Coventry and London work in situations where *all* the fellow workers can speak the minority language (Hakka or Cantonese). This is not surprising given their concentration in small family businesses specialising in Chinese food.

For the London Bengali- and Bradford Panjabi(U) and (G)-speaking respondents, a third or more of the workers are in such 100 per cent minority language workplaces, while for Italian, Greek, Gujerati and Turkish speakers in London the figure is above 20 per cent. In all these

Table 5.11 Language use in the workplace

(A) % of working respondents where at least one fellow worker can speak the minority language.

(B) % of working respondents where all fellow workers can speak the minority language.

(C) % of working respondents (who work for someone else) where the boss can speak minority language*.

(D) % of working respondents who use only or mostly English to all the workmates listed in the grid.

(E) % of working respondents who said it was essential to read English for their job.

(F) % of working respondents who said it was essential to speak the minority language for their job.

	Col A	Col B	Col C	Col D	Col E	Col F
Bengali						
Coventry N = 38	34	18	20	53	63	11
London N = 87	79	39	32	18	37	38
Chinese						
Coventry N = 25	76	72	**	16	40	28
Bradford N = 6	....					
London N = 67	81	64	53	18	52	36
Greek						
London N = 101	66	26	51	37	60	28
Gujerati						
Coventry N = 122	39	9	2	57	81	4
London N = 62	69	21	2	32	75	7
Italian						
Coventry N = 81	43	6	3	61	63	3
London N = 76	65	28	31	42	51	16
Panjabi (G)						
Coventry N = 126	72	16	10	29	64	11
Bradford N = 55	80	33	8	24	47	13
Panjabi (U)						
Coventry N = 44	68	16	2	39	75	16
Bradford N = 45	84	42	11	9	40	13
Polish						
Coventry N = 115	47	2	1	62	69	2
Bradford N = 94	48	7	8	65	56	3
Portuguese						
London N = 154	56	12	5	32	50	7
Turkish						
London N = 103	58	22	31	40	58	19
Ukrainian						
Coventry N = 32	31	3	0	69	66	3

* The base for Col C is the number of respondents who gave the language spoken by their boss.

** Very few Chinese respondents in Coventry had a boss, since most were in small family businesses or self-employed.

cases we can see the importance of the 'cultural division of labour' and the existence and development of various local 'ethnic' economies (Hechter, 1975; Anthias, 1983).

The figures in Column C allow us to make a further important distinction, between those workplaces where 'the boss' can speak the minority language and those where he or she cannot. The former cases appear very infrequently outside London, but are common in the capital in the Greek-, Turkish-, Italian-, Bengali- and Chinese-speaking minorities. It is probable that most of these 'ethnic businesses' are relatively small. This is in contrast to the situation in the manufacturing industries of Coventry and Bradford, where larger firms controlled by managers from the English monolingual majority employed labour from many local sources, including the linguistic minorities. However, the fact that as many as 17 per cent of Panjabi(U) workers in Bradford work for Panjabi-speaking employers, coupled with anecdotal evidence about this minority's response to high levels of unemployment, may indicate that new sectors of the ethnic economy in Bradford are likely to grow quite rapidly in the next few years.

Actual language use in the workplace depends on many factors, including the language skills of the respondents and of the people they work with. Our way of assessing the pattern of language use was to ask respondents to list up to three workmates they were in most frequent contact with and to describe the patterns of language use with them. In Column D we present the percentage of working respondents who said they spoke only or mostly English to all the workmates they had listed. The figures range from 69 per cent for Ukrainian speakers in Coventry, to only 9 per cent for Panjabi(U) speakers in Bradford.

More interesting are the cases where there is a substantial difference between the figure in Column A, indicating the percentage of working respondents where at least one fellow worker can speak the minority language and the figure in Column D. In these cases (Bengali, Gujerati, Italian, Polish and Ukrainian in Coventry and Polish in Bradford), it appears that the option to use the minority language is not always exercised. This may be either because the workmates who can speak the language are not in close enough contact with the respondent to be included in the grid, or because a positive choice to use English is made. If the former is the case, it would merely be a reflection of the industrial structure of the Coventry factories with relatively large, ethnically mixed workforces. If it is a case of language choice, one possible conclusion is that the setting of the workplace is a constraint on the use of minority languages. However, more extensive analysis of the data will be needed to clarify the issue.

Working respondents were also asked specific questions about the value of spoken and reading skills in the minority language, and of reading skills in English, in direct relation to their jobs (Qs 106-8). Over 35 per cent of respondents in every linguistic minority surveyed thought that an ability to read English was essential for their job, often mentioning basic functions such as reading labels and instruction chits. The need for English literacy was most strongly felt by Gujerati speakers (who, as mentioned above, had the highest proportion of non-manual jobs of all the linguistic minorities). English literacy in the workplace was generally more valued in Coventry than in the other cities, perhaps because of the high proportion of respondents working in linguistically mixed factories, and in industries such as engineering where written job specifications are used.

Far fewer of the respondents felt that speaking the minority language was essential for their work. Only in the case of Chinese-speaking respondents in Coventry and London and of Bengali speakers in London did the figure reach 30 per cent. Once again this reflects the position of these local linguistic minorities in the 'ethnic' and wider economies. Reasons for needing to speak the minority language in the workplace usually centred around communication with workmates, or occasionally with customers or the 'boss'. Very few respondents said they needed literacy in the minority language for work.

Language use outside home and work and in institutional settings

The questions in section F of the questionnaire concentrated on patterns of language use in settings outside the home and workplace, for example with friends and in leisure time and in the settings of organisations of which the respondents might be members. Foremost in our minds in framing the questions had been the importance of personal contacts within the linguistic minority, and the role of organised 'ethnic' associations in the process of language maintenance.

Many interviewers pointed out to us that this section of the questionnaire contained assumptions about social life and organisation which derived from our own majority viewpoint. We learned from them of culturally specific patterns of interaction in the local linguistic minorities which could not be fitted into the framework of the ALUS questionnaire. For example, from the kind of questions we asked, we could not properly document the role of the extended family, the nature of social networks within local linguistic minorities, or the various sex-specific role relationships which a longer ethnographic study would have revealed. However, the surveys did reveal some interesting data about participation in formal organisations and self-reported language use outside home and work, which we now go on to present.

Many respondents did in fact report membership of clubs and organisations of various sorts, and many were associations where most of the members were speakers of the minority language. Religious groups were frequently mentioned, especially by Gujerati, Panjabi(G) and Ukrainian speakers in Coventry and by Polish speakers in Bradford (in each case over 50 per cent of respondents). Chinese, Greek and Turkish speakers mentioned religious groups much less often (fewer than 10 per cent). However, we need to be very cautious in interpretation here, for there are strong cultural differences in the organisation of religious activities by the various minorities. Therefore the respondents' patterns of attendance at religious groups, and their perception of the meaning of the question, may have varied immensely. For example, among Muslims, both male and female speakers of Bengali and Panjabi(U) usually said that their religion was very important to them, but only the men reported attendance at religious groups or mosques.

Also frequently reported was membership of social clubs: Polish (Bradford and Coventry), Gujerati (Coventry and London), Italian (Coventry), Ukrainian (Coventry), and Portuguese (London) speakers reported rates of participation of over 20 per cent of respondents. These figures reflect the importance of the social club in the community life of these particular local linguistic minorities. However, there may be a bias involved in some cases where the samples were drawn partly from lists provided by such organisations.

The other organisations sometimes mentioned were often 'ethnic' or 'cultural' associations. Those involving music and dance were quite popular among the Portuguese speakers in London (25 per cent of respondents), Gujerati speakers (in Coventry 19 per cent, in London 22 per cent) and among the Ukrainian speakers in Coventry (18 per cent). Between 10 per cent and 20 per cent of almost all the local linguistic minorities said they belonged to some sports club or group. In all cases fewer than 15 per cent of respondents said they played any part in political or union activities. Apart from the Chinese speakers in Bradford and London fewer than 10 per cent took part in courses of study.

Table 5.12 shows that most respondents in fact did mention participation in at least one organisation. The highest reported participation
rates are among the Ukrainian speakers in Coventry and the Gujerati
speakers in Coventry and London. The lowest rates appear among
Panjabi(U) speakers in Bradford. Column B shows that most of the
participation was in organisations where all or most members could
speak the minority language.

A smaller number of respondents said they were or had been office-
holders in at least one organisation. Most of these 'leaders' were male,
and were fluent speakers of English. Table 5.12 summarises the findings
in this section. It should be noted that the figures given here are actual
numbers of respondents in each category, not percentages. The figures
for our teams of interviewers in the three cities are also given, as these
provide a striking contrast. In fact it is probably in this characteristic
of their involvement in organisations, that the interviewers are most
different from the general population of their linguistic minorities.

Table 5.13 gives an indication of patterns of language use, or the
potential for using the minority language, in a range of settings outside
home and work. It highlights the importance of companions who speak
the minority language, the difference in neighbourhood language background for different languages and localities, the importance of film
and video for some languages, the striking popularity of 'ethnic' shops
in every group, and the preference for a minority-language-speaking
doctor where one is available.

Children and language maintenance

The next aspect of the ALUS findings which we have selected for
brief presentation and discussion here relates to questions in the survey
about how aware people were of mother tongue classes available in
their neighbourhood. We also include information on attendance at
classes, as reported by respondents with reference to young people in
the 5–18 age range in their households.

Most respondents in households where there were children, whether
they themselves were parents or not, said they were aware of classes
in which children could be taught the relevant minority languages.
As might be expected, there were some differences between the
respondents from the different local linguistic minorities as shown in
Table 5.14. These differences probably reflect the level of mother
tongue provision and the level of minority institutional organisation in

Table 5.12 Participation and office-holders in organisations

(A) % of respondents who said they took part in the activities of at least one organisation.
(B) % of (A) who said they took part in the activities of at least one organisation where all or most of the members could speak the minority language.
(C) Number of respondents who said they held, or had held, some office in a group they mentioned.
(D) Number of office-holders who were male.
(E) Number of office-holders who reported full skills in English.

	Col A	Col B	Col C	Col D	Col E
Bengali					
Coventry N = 79	52	34	4	4	4
London N = 185	35	88	9	9	6
Chinese					
Coventry N = 43	(19)	(8)	2	1	2
Bradford N = 50	(14)	(13)	0	–	–
London N = 137	41	63	10	10	7
Greek					
London N = 193	40	64	18	14	14
Gujerati					
Coventry N = 203	82	85	28	20	25
London N = 99	75	88	7	5	6
Italian					
Coventry N = 108	65	50	10	9	6
London N = 94	59	76	12	6	6
Panjabi (G)					
Coventry N = 200	79	87	15	13	15
Bradford N = 98	69	94	7	7	4
Panjabi (U)					
Coventry N = 86	52	87	12	12	11
Bradford N = 177	25	91	3	3	2
Polish					
Coventry N = 168	60	65	27	22	27
Bradford N = 155	74	82	23	23	14
Portuguese					
London N = 196	73	87	20	10	6
Turkish					
London N = 197	50	73	14	10	10
Ukrainian					
Coventry N = 48	100	90	29	23	8
INTERVIEWERS					
N = 125	89	65	58	32	56

Table 5.13   Language in a range of settings

(A) % of respondents who said they spoke only the minority language with the first person mentioned as someone they spent free time with (figures in brackets indicate those who spoke another Chinese language).

(B) % of respondents who said most or all of their neighbours could speak the minority language.

(C) % of respondents who said they had seen a film or video in the minority language within the last 4 weeks.

(D) % of respondents who said they sometimes visited a shop where the minority language was spoken by the shopkeeper or assistants.

(E) % of respondents who had a doctor who could speak the minority language.

	Col A	Col B	Col C	Col D	Col E
Bengali					
Coventry N = 79	57	5	35	82	17
London N = 185	80	49	74	86	50
Chinese					
Coventry N = 43	26 (+ 35)	2	37	95	5
Bradford N = 50	52 (+ 44)	14	24	96	0
London N = 137	73 (+ 16)	5	56	99	42
Greek					
London N = 193	54	15	35	90	35
Gujerati					
Coventry N = 203	70	13	64	98	32
London N = 99	74	6	66	97	51
Italian					
Coventry N = 108	25	3	9	75	18
London N = 94	35	16	6	93	64
Panjabi(G)					
Coventry N = 200	75	25	70	98	50
Bradford N = 98	78	32	67	91	43
Panjabi(U)					
Coventry N = 86	79	43	64	98	70
Bradford N = 177	79	70	57	96	69
Polish					
Coventry N = 168	39	1	4	89	12
Bradford N = 155	54	3	6	96	48
Portuguese					
London N = 196	71	17	25	73	42
Turkish					
London N = 197	73	45	64	96	45
Ukrainian					
Coventry N = 48	67	11	0	75	6

Table 5.14 Knowledge of 'mother tongue' classes

Data from Q93: Do you know of any classes where children can learn (your community language)?
% of respondents with children or young people under 21 in household only.

```
                          20        40        60        80

Bengali
Coventry  N =  67   :***        •        •        •        •        6%
London    N = 146   :********************************        •       66%

Chinese
Coventry  N =  33   :*******************************************      82%
Bradford  N =  47   :**         •        •        •        •        4%
London    N = 103   :**********************************       •       70%

Greek
London    N = 126   :*********************************************     87%

Gujerati
Coventry  N = 160   :**********************************************    91%
London    N =  70   :*****************    •        •        •       33%

Italian
Coventry  N =  78   :********************************       •       67%
London    N =  77   :*************************************************97%

Panjabi(G)
Coventry  N = 181   :****************************************       82%
Bradford  N =  89   :*********************************************     89%

Panjabi(U)
Coventry  N =  78   :**************************    •        •       56%
Bradford  N = 154   :*************************    •        •       53%

Polish
Coventry  N =  78   :*******************************************      90%
Bradford  N =  62   :*******************************************      92%

Portuguese
London    N = 121   :***************************************************97%

Turkish
London    N = 158   :*************************************     80%

Ukrainian
Coventry  N =  22   :*************************************************96%
```

the area. The exception is Panjabi(U), where the apparently low level of awareness may result from respondents and interviewers having perceived the question to be about Panjabi (or Urdu), when much of the teaching organised in the 'community-run' sector by this linguistic minority in fact involves Islamic studies and Qur'anic Arabic.

Table 5.15 shows the pattern of reported attendance at mother tongue classes for those households where there were children in the 5–18 age range. The non-attendance in the Coventry Bengali-speaking

Table 5.15 Attendance at 'mother tongue' classes

	(1) Number of households with children aged 5–18	(2) Number of households where at least one child attended in last 4 weeks	(3) 2 as % of 1
Bengali			
Coventry N = 79	62	0	0
London N = 185	119	39	33
Chinese			
Coventry N = 43	29	5	17
Bradford N = 50	33	2	6
London N = 137	86	25	29
Greek			
London N = 193	102	42	41
Gujerati			
Coventry N = 203	142	37	26
London N = 99	49	8	16
Italian			
Coventry N = 108	58	8	14
London N = 94	71	50	70
Panjabi (G)			
Coventry N = 200	148	33	22
Bradford N = 98	72	21	29
Panjabi (U)			
Coventry N = 86	65	23	35
Bradford N = 177	136	49	36
Polish			
Coventry N = 168	58	25	43
Bradford N = 155	41	10	24
Portuguese			
London N = 196	94	34	36
Turkish			
London N = 197	133	15	11
Ukrainian			
Coventry N = 48	19	6	32

families simply reflects the absence of available classes in the city at the time of the survey, and the extremely high rate of attendance (70 per cent) for the Italian speakers in London reflects our sampling strategy for this local linguistic minority which included the use of lists obtained from mother tongue classes. The figures for attendance are above the average for Greek speakers in London, Polish speakers in Coventry, and Panjabi(U) speakers in both Coventry and Bradford, and below average among the Turkish- (London), Italian- (Coventry), Gujerati- (London) and Chinese- (Bradford and Coventry) speaking households surveyed.

A wide range of reasons for non-attendance was given, and it is particularly interesting to look at the types of explanations given by the respondents from different local linguistic minorities. There were three most frequently mentioned reasons. First, there were situations where there were no classes locally available or where it was too far to travel. These reasons were especially common for the two sets of Panjabi-speaking respondents and the Bengali speakers in Coventry, for the Panjabi(U) speakers in Bradford and for the Chinese and Bengali speakers in London. Second, there were many respondents who said the children in their homes were too young, or occasionally too old or too proficient in the minority language, to make it worthwhile going to classes. Such reasons were frequently mentioned by the Ukrainian- and Polish-speaking respondents in Coventry, the Panjabi(G)-, Panjabi(U)- and Polish-speaking respondents in Bradford and by the Bengali-, Gujerati-, Italian-, Portuguese-, Greek- and Turkish-speaking respondents in London. Finally, a few respondents indicated that parents or children were too busy, or thought the classes were not very valuable given their other priorities. This type of reason was most frequent among the Chinese-, Italian- and Gujerati-speaking respondents in Coventry and London, the Panjabi(G) speakers in Bradford and the Greek-, Turkish- and Portuguese-speaking respondents in London. Occasionally specific problems with local classes were mentioned or respondents said the children were learning at home.

Attitudes to language maintenance

We move on now to attitudes among the members of the various linguistic minorities towards institutional support, from the LEAs or elsewhere, for their children's languages. This information comes from an analysis of the reactions to the fifteen statements on this topic with which respondents were invited to register their agreement or disagreement (see Chapter 4, p. 149). The attitudes section of the ALUS questionnaire is very different in concept and design from the other sections in that it seeks to elicit opinions, rather than to report on behaviour. It was also a difficult and unfamiliar exercise for many respondents, as they had to listen to a large number of sometimes quite complex statements and express their opinion of them in terms of a conventional five-point scale.

Before we piloted this section, we feared a number of things might go wrong. Firstly, some respondents might find the task too unfamiliar, too difficult or too disagreeable and fail to produce replies. In fact the amount of missing data in this section is minimal. Secondly, we felt that some respondents might exhibit generalised agreement or uncertainty tendencies across all the items. Again the statistical evidence suggests that this did not happen to any great extent. In fact we gathered from our interviewers that most respondents welcomed the opportunity offered by this section to express their views.

In order to simplify and reduce the amount of data to be presented, and to decrease the influence of random variation in individual attitude statements, factor analysis was carried out. Although there were minor differences in the factor structure revealed when separate analyses for respondents from each local linguistic minority were undertaken, the overall pattern was fairly clear and consistent across the languages. The best overall solution (which used an oblique rotation) suggested that there were two sets of items which were highly correlated to each other within the sets (but not to other items), and which produced systematic patterns of response in the different local linguistic minorities.

The first set of items constituted a fairly general factor concerned with the language rights and needs of minority communities. It reflected a high level of demand that the state should offer positive support to mother tongue maintenance and to the minority languages more generally. This factor is heavily weighted on the following items, which showed a high level of intercorrelation and tended to produce similar patterns of response across the different linguistic minorities. The overall mean scores on each item are given in brackets: a score of −2 would mean 100 per cent strong disagreement; a score of +2, 100 per cent strong agreement. (The numbers of the items are those used in the ALUS questionnaire.)

134 'We can keep up the use of our languages over the next generation if there is proper teaching widely available.' (+1.3)

135 'We should make every possible effort to maintain the fullest use of our languages in Britain.' (+1.4)

136 'The government should provide the teaching of our languages as a right for all our children in state schools.' (+1.3)

137 'The use of our languages in school lessons to teach other subjects would be a great help to our children.' (+0.6)

138 'Unless we make our children work very hard at learning our languages they won't be able to keep them alive in Britain.' (+1.0)

139 'The government should support our communities' efforts and give us money to organize classes for our children to learn our languages.' (+1.3)

140 'The authorities should produce versions of most official letters, notices, forms, and leaflets in our languages as well as in English.' (+1.0)

143 'The maintenance of our languages is the most important of all matters for our communities.' (+1.1)

144 'The government should employ far more doctors, teachers and social workers who can speak our languages.' (+1.1)

146 'More English people should be encouraged to learn our languages.' (+0.7)

There is an overwhelming agreement with these statements among the respondents from all the local linguistic minorities surveyed, confirming our observation that there is a widespead demand from linguistic minorities for public support for minority languages.

The ten items were combined by a simple linear transformation into a scale ranging from −100 for strong disagreement with all ten items to +100 for strong agreement with all ten items. There are some noticeable differences in the degree of agreement between the respondents from the various local linguistic minorities. However, it is on individual items that some of the most interesting and explicable differences occur. For example, on item 140 the demand for leaflets in the minority languages was greatest among the Panjabi(U)-speaking respondents in Coventry (mean = +1.6) and Bengali-speaking respondents in London (+1.5), and smallest among the Polish speakers in Coventry (+0.2). On item 136 the feeling that 'mother tongue' teaching should be provided as a right was strongest among the Bengali- (London) (+1.8), Ukrainian- (+1.8) and Panjabi(U)- (+1.7) and Panjabi(G)- (+1.6) speaking respondents in Coventry and weakest among the Polish speakers in Coventry (+0.8) and Chinese speakers in London (+0.8).

However, the variation within each local linguistic minority is minimal; when tested by analysis of variance for the effects of age, sex and length of schooling, the only significant effects were among the Ukrainian-, Greek-, Turkish-, Gujerati- (Coventry), Panjabi(G)-(Coventry), and Polish- (Coventry) speaking respondents, where the older respondents tended to score higher (i.e. agree more strongly) than the younger ones, and among the Polish- (Bradford), Chinese-(London), Italian- (London) and Greek-speaking respondents, where the ones who had fewer years of schooling had higher scores than those with longer schooling. The only significant sex difference was among the Bengali (London) speakers, where the males had higher scores.

The second factor revealed by the factor analysis was most heavily weighted on the following items (scores calculated as for factor 1):

133 'We can maintain the culture and identity of our communities even if we cease to use our languages.' (−0.6)

141 'Our communities are able to organise all the teaching of our languages that is needed without any help from the government.' (−0.4)

142 'There is no problem in maintaining our languages; they will not die out in Britain.' (−0.3)

147 'Our children will learn as much of our languages as they need to know from the family without special teaching.' (−0.8)

In many ways this factor appears to be the obverse of the first one, in that agreement with each of these statements would imply a lack of concern about the prospects of language maintenance and a laissez-faire attitude to language teaching provision. The overall level of disagreement, though weaker than the level of agreement on factor 1, suggests that on the whole our respondents were concerned about the prospects for their languages unless special provision was made.

These four items were also combined by a linear transformation into a scale ranging from +100 for strong agreement with all four items to −100 for strong disagreement to all four items. With the scores for the two sets of items now using the same scale, the mean scores for respondents from each local linguistic minority for both factors are shown in Table 5.16.

Table 5.16 Attitudes to language maintenance: factors one and two

| | Factor two +++ | | | Factor one *** | |
| | | Disagree | | Agree | |
	−100	−50	0	50	100
Bengali					
Coventry N = 79:	•	8.8 •	+	***********	• 55.0
London N = 185:	•	28.8 •	+++++	***********	• 55.5
Chinese					
Coventry N = 43:	•	16.3 •	+++	******* •	• 32.5
Bradford N = 50:	•	6.3 •	+	****** •	• 30.0
London N = 137:	•	17.5 •	+++	******* •	• 35.0
Greek					
London N = 193:	•	25.0 •	++++	********* •	• 46.0
Gujerati					
Coventry N = 203:	•	17.5 •	+++	********* •	• 45.5
London N = 99:	•	22.5 •	++++	******** •	• 37.5
Italian					
Coventry N = 108:	•	10.0 •	++	******* •	• 36.0
London N = 94:	•	10.3 •	++	********* •	• 43.5
Panjabi (G)					
Coventry N = 200:	•	30.0 •	+++++	**********	• 50.0
Bradford N = 98:	•	18.8 •	+++	******* •	• 36.0
Panjabi (U)					
Coventry N = 86:	•	23.8 •	++++	************	• 61.0
Bradford N = 177:	•	10.0 •	++	******** •	• 42.0
Polish					
Coventry N = 168:	•	3.8 •	+	****** •	• 32.5
Bradford N = 155:	•	8.8 •	+	********* •	• 44.0
Portuguese					
London N = 196:	•	26.3 •	++++	******** •	• 41.0
Turkish					
London N = 197:	•	7.5 •	+	**********	• 49.0
Ukrainian					
Coventry N = 48:	•	23.8 •	++++	************	• 61.0

The differences between respondents from different local linguistic minorities on the second factor scale appear to be very small. Individual item scores help to elucidate the patterns. For example on item 141 the Polish-speaking respondents in both Bradford and Coventry seem confident of the success of their own voluntary efforts (+0.2 and +0.3) in contrast with the Panjabi speakers in Coventry ((U) = −0.9, (G) = −1.1) (cf. Panjabi (U) in Bradford = 0.0). On item 142 it is the Panjabi(G)-speaking respondents in Coventry who appear most pessimistic about language maintenance (−0.9) while the Panjabi speakers in Bradford ((U) = +0.5, (G) = +0.2) and the Chinese speakers in Bradford (+0.5) and London (+0.4) and Portuguese speakers in London (+0.4) see least problem.

Variation within the linguistic minorities on this scale according to sex, age and length of schooling is negligible. Analysis of variance showed that the only significant factor was sex among the Coventry Bengali- and Bradford Panjabi(U)-speaking respondents, where the males scored higher, i.e. disagreed more strongly.

The two factors described above account for all of the statements in the pool except one:

145 'Our communities should completely abandon the use of our languages and should adopt the use of English everywhere.' (−1.5)

For respondents from almost all the minorities the mean score on this single item was in the range of −1.0 to −1.7, indicating a strong level of disagreement. The sole exception was the Chinese respondents in Bradford, where the score was +0.2. It is likely that as recent refugees they see learning English as their first priority. Furthermore, since most of them reported bilingualism in Cantonese and Vietnamese (with more Vietnamese used in the younger generation), it is possible that language shift away from Cantonese is felt, for the time being, to be irreversible.

This tends to confirm the overall picture, that in all the linguistic minorities surveyed there is a very high level of agreement with the idea that minority languages have an important role in England and should continue to have one. There is a greater degree of uncertainty as to the best strategy for language maintenance and about the urgency of the need for public support, but overall it is clear that language maintenance is seen to be desirable.

It must of course be admitted that the setting of the attitude statements in the context of the interview had raised the salience of the issue for the respondents. In addition, the values implicit in the questionnaire, and the presence of interviewers who were more likely than not to be enthusiastic supporters of the minority language, would tend to influence answers in this positive direction. It is clear, too, that sentiment does not always lead to action, in that although the vast majority say they support language maintenance, a smaller proportion of parents give it a high enough priority to make sure that their children attend classes (even where they know they are available). On the other hand the type of reason given for non-attendance suggests that it is practical problems rather than lack of interest that account for this. Our work on attitudes suggests clearly that there is considerable support among the adult population of the linguistic minorities for increased and improved mother tongue provision.

ALUS: some concluding comments

There are many factors which speed up or slow down what is often believed to be an inevitable process of shift from bilingualism to mono-lingualism in the dominant language of countries of immigration. 'Language shift', the habitual use of one language being replaced by the habitual use of another, is a reflection of power relations in a society producing a redistribution of social and linguistic resources from generation to generation.

The findings of ALUS serve, above all, to illustrate the complexity of the factors involved in the process of language shift. The different patterns of language skills, use and attitudes revealed in the different linguistic minorities might be expected, given the varied sociolinguistic relationships between the different minority languages and English, and the varied migration histories of their speakers. But we have also discovered major differences between members of the same linguistic minority in different cities, for example in the extent to which they use the minority language.

The major factors affecting language maintenance are likely, in fact, to be the fundamental external forces which influence the economic, political and social resources of a linguistic minority. There are also likely to be factors emerging from within the minority, and from within the situation of contact between cultures, this 'internal' response often being a reaction to outside pressure. Geographical concentration, time of migration, relationship to the local labour market, social mobility and degrees of social conflict and competition over scarce resources, all have to be taken into account in attempting to assess the key in-fluences on the process of language shift. Nor should we neglect the different kinds of majority and minority institutional support, such as radio and television programmes in minority languages, minority-owned press, community-run schools and churches. While we can describe some of the main social circumstances which encourage the maintenance of minority languages at local level, there is a need for much more comparative research before the parameters of language maintenance and shift can be isolated with confidence.

Given the wide range of factors influencing language maintenance and transmission from one generation to the next, it is not surprising that there are already very different situations within the same linguistic minorities in different cities. Language shift, and assimilation to the dominant language and culture, may be an overall national trend, but this does not preclude the possibility of a more 'stable' bilingualism for some.

6
Mother tongue teaching provision

This chapter discusses the preparation, administration and findings of the other community-based survey carried out by the Linguistic Minorities Project. The Mother Tongue Teaching Directory (MTTD) survey gathered information about all the mother tongue teaching provision in languages other than English in three areas where ALUS was also carried out: Coventry, Bradford and Haringey. In the context of this survey, the term 'mother tongue' is used to refer to all the languages used by the different linguistic minorities, including some of the national languages or languages of religion which are not necessarily used in the home. The term in fact appears in most contexts to be a shorthand for 'minority language': as such it is the product of historical developments in Britain, and reflects very much a majority view. The monolingual majority have tended to use the term 'mother tongue' without a very clear understanding of the distinctions set out in Figure 6.1.

The teaching provision considered includes classes where the languages themselves are not the main focus of teaching, but where pupils are learning other subjects through the medium of the language. It also covers classes where some of the students are from bilingual families and others are monolingual English, learning the minority language as a modern language. In our findings examples of the latter arrangement are few, and are mostly found in post-school classes, for example Italian in one of the Coventry Further Education colleges and Urdu at Bradford College. It appeared to us from the start — and this was confirmed by our MTTD surveys — that local linguistic minority organisations or overseas government agencies organised a very high proportion of these classes.

A community-based approach was adopted in all three cities, using as intermediaries bilingual interviewers from the various local populations. In the smaller number of cases where the teaching was part of the curriculum of an LEA school, the surveys were administered by

Figure 6.1 What 'mother tongue' refers to for the main minority languages in England

Often the users' 'FIRST LANGUAGE' (and considered as the 'HOME LANGUAGE')	a 'NATIONAL LANGUAGE'	a LANGUAGE OF RELIGIOUS AFFILIATION/ INSTRUCTION	a SCRIPTURAL LANGUAGE (Qur'anic Arabic = QA) (Sanskrit = S)
Spoken and written language			
Bengali	+for Hindus: Hindi,	also ....*	+for Muslims: QA +S
Cantonese, Hakka, Hokkien	Chinese		
Irish Gaelic	*		
Greek	*		
Gujerati	+for Hindus: Hindi,	+for Muslims: Urdu also ....*	+ QA + S +for Hindus: S
Hindi	+for Hindus: Hindi,		
Standard Italian	*		
Latvian	*		
Panjabi (Gurmukhi script)	for Sikhs * +for Hindus: Hindi,	also ...*	.....* + S
Polish	*		
Portuguese	*		
Serbo-Croat	*		
Spanish	*		
(Sylheti)	*		(+ QA)
Turkish	*		(+ QA)
Ukrainian	*		

Urdu (mainly for Muslims
  from cities in Pakistan · · · · · * · · · · · · · · · · · · · · · · · + QA
Vietnamese · · · · · · · · · · · · · *)
Welsh   (for some *)
African languages such as
Hausa, Ibo, Yoruba (West) · · · *
Swahili (East) · · · · · · · · · *
Bemba, Shona (South East) · · · *
Xhosa (South) · · · · · · · · · *

Spoken only (Vernacular)	RELATED	LANGUAGE(S)	OF	LITERACY
some African languages				
varieties of Arabic	Modern Arabic			+for Muslims: QA
English-based Creoles	Standard English			
& varieties of English	Southern British			
	Standard English			
Italian 'dialetti'	Standard Italian			
Cypriot Greek	Standard Greek			
Kutchi	Gujerati	+for Muslims: Urdu		+ QA
	+for Hindus: Hindi,	also . . . . *		+ S
	Urdu, also . . . . *			+ QA
Panjabi for Muslims from Pakistan:				+for Muslims: QA
Sylheti	Bengali			(+for Muslims: QA)
Cypriot Turkish	Standard Turkish			

for Jews: Hebrew

ALL COMMUNITY LANGUAGES'

post to the mother tongue teachers with copies sent in advance to the head teachers.

An assessment of the significance of mother tongue teaching provision must rely to a great extent on a basic understanding of the patterns of language use among adults, and of their attitudes towards this teaching provision: Chapter 5 dealt with these questions more fully. The importance for users of the language, for mother tongue teachers in 'voluntary' and LEA schools, and for our society as a whole, of establishing the scale of mother tongue provision, became increasingly evident in the course of our research. For example, the ALUS findings discussed earlier show that some parents did not know about existing mother tongue provision in their own area, that others did not send their children because of practical problems, and that others were constrained by cultural restrictions on, for example, girls not attending mixed classes after puberty.

At the time of our research we did not know how much parents knew about the issues in the mother tongue debate among educationalists, or whether knowledge of different options might have influenced the decisions they made for their children. Nor do we know from the ALUS or the MTTD survey findings the nature of the relationship between the parents and the teachers of the community-based classes. In some instances, of course, the parents and the teachers are the same people. It may be possible in the future to explore the connections within the ALUS data, for example between patterns of language use in the home and attendance at mother tongue classes. Such exploration may help to answer the question of whether there are significantly different proportions of children attending mother tongue classes from predominantly non-English-speaking monolingual homes, as compared with children from bilingual or predominantly English-speaking homes. The answer to a question like this has practical implications for the type of materials and teaching methods that will be needed, and the kind of admission policies appropriate for the classes. If the teaching in state schools develops in the form of modern language classes attended by, among others, pupils from monolingual English homes, it will become even more important to develop very flexible approaches.

Several researchers have discussed the range of objectives underlying the development of mother tongue teaching in the different linguistic minorities, objectives which may include cultural, linguistic, psychological and social factors (Elliot, 1981; Saifullah Khan, 1980a; Tosi, 1979). This mix of objectives is reflected in the range of languages taught, not all spoken at home, yet subsumed in the term 'mother tongue'. One of these factors may become more important at a particular point in time as a result of external circumstances, such as a planned visit to the homeland, or the marriage of a son or daughter. The ALUS findings have shown that the language use patterns of individual members of the same family often differ from one generation to the next. Personal experience of non-reciprocal patterns of language use, which sometimes occur as a result, can contribute towards parents' concern about mother tongue provision. This interest may of course be experienced differently by the parent, the young child and the teenager from the same family. Non-reciprocal patterns of language use in the family, where the children respond in English to the parents' use of the minority language, may suggest that the direction of language shift is primarily away from the minority language. However, the teaching of minority languages and their use in local minority organisations are important processes counteracting the apparently unidirectional shift, from minority language to English for all purposes.

Mother tongue schools and classes are likely to continue as important institutional bases for the maintenance and reproduction of minority language skills, as well as for ethnic or religious affiliation, but their detailed function and methods are likely to change over time. Some schools have already on their own initiative changed their objectives and the methods and content of teaching, for example in response to the changes in the linguistic experience of their pupils. The religious dimension in the teaching of many minority languages, for example Panjabi(G) or Hindi, tends to recede when the languages are integrated into the school curriculum. Other schools or classes may have changed in response to external events, such as the arrival of a new wave of migration from a different geographical area or political system, for example South Asians from East Africa in the early 1970s. Developments in local and national ethnic relations have also influenced the involvement of LEA schools in the 'mother tongue' issue (see p. 305), and the relationship between LEA and community-run provision, for example the increasing involvement by minority interests in local education policy-making in Bradford (see p. 307).

There is another important dimension that the ALUS and MTTD survey findings jointly throw some light on: the debate about the content of mother tongue teaching in the particular context of England. Although there are great differences in the aims and origins of mother tongue classes in the various languages, one of their main common functions is certainly the introduction of literacy. The relationship between oral skills and literacy varies in different minorities, and is especially complex in some multilingual populations for whom the language of literacy is not that spoken at home (see Figure 6.1). It is certainly important not to base all the arguments for supporting mother tongue teaching on an assumption that what is taught is identical to the child's home language, but rather to place mother tongue teaching in its sociolinguistic context. This wider context helps us appreciate the collective and symbolic value of those minority languages which are less languages of the home, and more community or national languages or languages used in literacy or for religious purposes. Affiliation to particular minority organisations, contact with people from urban backgrounds in the country of origin, access to libraries, newspapers and films are all likely to support the development of skills in the standard national language, rather than in the spoken vernaculars of most homes. It is only when we know more about their social circumstances that we can appreciate the relationship of pupils to their already acquired languages, and to the languages they are at present learning.

The ALUS findings, then, provide an important backdrop to an analysis of the role and development of the particular kind of schooling covered by the MTTD surveys. Once we have understood that mother tongue teaching is both a product of societal bilingualism and a means to reproduce it, we can begin to assess its likely influence on patterns of language use in the future. Only then can we appreciate its role as a parallel form of schooling.

Scope and aims of the surveys

Mother tongue classes are one of the main means of transmitting cultural skills from one generation to another. The MTTD survey findings therefore introduce a longer-term perspective than our other surveys, on the maintenance and development of minority languages in England. The actual efficacy of this formal language teaching for the younger generation has, however, to be assessed in relation to its social context, and in relation to how the teaching is integrated into the daily bilingual experience of its pupils. Some of the theoretical implications of these findings will be considered at the end of this chapter. Here we concentrate on the primary and immediate aim of the MTTD surveys: to provide a clear picture of what is actually happening. This information is needed in order to contribute towards the resolution of such policy issues as whether a child's first or community language should be taught at all; if it is to be taught who should be responsible for the teaching; where, when and with what methods it might be best undertaken.

The presentation and discussion of findings as basic as those arising from our MTTD surveys are still useful and necessary because, although mother tongue teaching has been going on in England for a long time, few people beyond those immediately involved have known much about its dimensions and sources of support until very recently. This has meant that not only have many minority organisations been ignorant of initiatives among other minorities in their own area, but that they have often also been unaware of developments among speakers of the same language in other cities. It was also the case that in 1976 many local education officers and local teachers too either had no knowledge at all of the existence of mother tongue provision, or did not recognise that it was fundamental to the general educational development of their pupils (Saifullah Khan, 1977a). When minority organisations asked for financial support, or minority teachers working in the LEA schools introduced mother tongue lessons in school breaks or after school, they were often perceived by the education authorities as isolated cases and not as reflecting a more general need. Many of the classes now supported by LEAs have in fact developed from the determined efforts of minority teachers on the staff of a school, who originally provided the tuition without much official support or recognition.

Since 1979 there has been much more public discussion about mother tongue teaching within the context of general educational development (see Chapter 7). The greatest impetus to the debate about mother tongue teaching has, however, been a result of the organised pressure and articulated demand coming from the linguistic minorities themselves. This was given a considerable boost in 1976 by the issuing of the Draft Directive of the European Communities on the Education of Migrant Workers' Children. The impact of initial almost total rejection by many educational authorities and teachers' unions of the principles it proposed, without constructive discussion based on sound information, produced a reaction from a wide range of minority organisations. In the period 1976 to 1978 the first formal links between the European and South Asian interests were forged, by the setting up of the Coordinating Committee for Mother-Tongue Teaching (now the National Council for Mother-Tongue Teaching, NCMTT), and through greater collaboration between mainstream educational, community relations, and minority organisations.

One way of briefly introducing the different relationships that mother tongue teaching organisations have with speakers of the relevant languages in their local areas, and with their LEA schools, is to describe some common forms of organisation for the main groups of languages. Firstly, for the Eastern European languages such as Polish and Ukrainian, the national languages of originally refugee populations which settled in Britain after the Second World War, schools were usually set up by parents' groups, often under the auspices of the local church. In most cases no help was received from the LEAs, although it is clear that in certain towns assistance was sought. These populations frequently provide well-organised locally-run provision, supported in some cases by central educational bodies such as the Polska Macierz Szkolna (Polish Educational Society Abroad), or by community organisations such as the Association of Ukrainians in Great Britain.

The second major group of languages includes Bengali, Gujerati, Hindi, Panjabi, and Urdu, the languages of those more recent South Asian migrants from the Indian subcontinent and from East Africa. After an initial period of settlement in Britain, most of these populations started teaching the regional or national language of the place of origin, together sometimes with languages needed for religious purposes. In many cases this provision was developed in conjunction with religious institutions. Sometimes the inability to keep up with the increasing demand for teaching resulted in assistance being sought from LEAs, and occasionally granted.

The third category of languages includes Greek, Italian, Portuguese, Spanish and Turkish, South European languages belonging, in some cases, to people who have a migrant worker status in British society. Whereas most of the previous populations mentioned have had little or no 'official' support from their countries of origin, most of the Southern European linguistic minorities have some kind of government support. This may take the form of provision of actual teachers or payment of their salaries, the supply of teaching materials, funds for accommodation, and other expenses. In some cases, there is also support from the churches or from local parents' associations. Some cases do not easily fit these major categories, such as the Chinese schools run under a variety of auspices including local parents' associations, student organisations, churches and missions, sometimes with help from the Hong Kong High Commission. A more systematic account of the distribution of these varied organisational structures is included later in this chapter.

The design of the MTTD surveys has to be understood within this context. Many of the problems we either foresaw or encountered were the product of the marginal and ambiguous status of so much of the existing mother tongue teaching in England. We had to choose research strategies that would reflect the full complexity of the situation, yet at the same time be useful to members of linguistic minorities and to the LEAs. We believed that a community-based approach would encourage confidence among those being interviewed and lead to great reliability of our data, as well as providing a great potential for returning and disseminating the findings among all those who gave us information. We needed also to develop an instrument that would document equally satisfactorily the provision outside and inside the mainstream LEA school system. We aimed to provide data in a standardised form which would allow comparison between mother tongue teaching provision organised by local populations and by LEA schools. Finally, while we wanted to assemble at least basic data on all mother tongue schools and classes in each area we studied, we felt that those mother tongue teachers who so wished should have the opportunity to provide a more discursive account of the circumstances of their work and their attitudes to it.

This suggested a two-stage approach, using two questionnaires. One would elicit essentially quantitative data, which could be coded for computer processing and for circulation in tabular form, for example to minority organisations and LEAs. The other would collect more detailed and more qualitative information, of particular interest to other local minority organisations and to mainstream teachers' organisations.

Since we could conduct this survey in only three areas, we thought it important to ensure that the MTTD survey instruments could be taken over and used after the end of our project. This was also LMP's aim for the two school-based surveys discussed in Chapters 8 and 9, but it was particularly important for the project to build up the community-based support for the MTTD surveys, to ensure that it would be used effectively by minority teachers' organisations, as well as by those working in the LEA school system.

To this end we sought the advice and collaboration of the National Council for Mother Tongue Teaching (NCMTT). From January 1981, LMP and LINC researchers worked closely with NCMTT's representatives to revise the questionnaires and prepare the Manual of Use. While LMP-LINC piloted the questionnaires, this joint LMP-LINC-NCMTT group revised them and prepared the Manual of Use. At the time of writing, NCMTT is planning the promotion of the Directory, so that survey data from further areas might be fed into a national data bank at the Centre for Information on Language Teaching and Research in London.

The development of the two questionnaires

During the preparation of the MTTD survey the initial discussions focussed on the distribution of our questions between two questionnaires, Stages 1 and 2, and on a consideration of the most feasible ways of administering each of them.

The plan was to draft one survey instrument which would cover the mother tongue teaching organised and run by both the linguistic minorities and by LEA schools. The agreement to aim at this reflected our recognition that there was often no obvious distinction in classroom practice between teaching in LEA schools and teaching supported by 'voluntary' agencies. It was only at the analysis stage that we became fully aware of the many organisational structures somewhere in between what we had originally thought of as two distinct sectors, 'LEA' on the one hand, 'voluntary' on the other. It could have been argued that each type of administrative arrangement needed a different questionnaire. However, the logistics of the situation demanded simplicity wherever possible – simplicity in format, in language and in interviewing strategy. So it was agreed that the distinction between the two stages would be in terms of their different aims, rather than the different organisational structures within which they would be used.

In Stage 1 many responses were to be made in the form of a choice of a limited number of briefly described options or single words. In Stage 2, on the other hand, many of the questions were open-ended, encouraging the teachers to answer in their own terms and at as great a length as they wanted. It was also agreed that both questionnaires would be used with all the respondents, always encouraging the teachers to give more than the minimal information. The answers were to be completed by the teachers themselves in both the LEA and community-run classes, and in addition sometimes by the organisers of the community-run classes. Teachers working in LEA schools were to receive their questionnaires by post, but in the case of the community-run classes bilingual interviewers from the local area would assist the mother tongue teacher to complete the questionnaires.

The first major difficulties arose when we drafted the two questionnaires. The first version was piloted in Coventry and Bradford, and a revised version was used in Haringey; the latest version to date was arrived at after our pilot experiences. We shall refer to these as Version 1, Version 2, and Version 3 respectively. On several occasions problems of choosing and phrasing a question, so that it had the same meaning and relevance for the teachers in LEA and community-run schools, led us to consider again the desirability of aiming to collect the information in a standardised form. (For example, Question 9 and Question 10 in Version 1 were subsequently dropped.) But this problem arose also within what we were still at that stage calling the 'voluntary' sector, because of the wide range of types of provision among the different local linguistic minorities. For example, in Question 8 of Stage 1, Version 1, we asked for the number of pupils sub-divided by age, but some schools grouped all ages in the same class, or groupings were formed across ages according to the level of skills. Another major task involved balancing the value of the information we wanted, against the possibly damaging misunderstandings which might be involved in asking for it. In Version 1 of the Stage 1 questionnaire we did not ask any question about teachers' salaries, but in Version 2 of the Stage 1 of the questionnaire(s) used in Haringey we did ask questions on this topic requiring a yes-no answer, and we also asked for financial details in Stage 2.

Some questions seemed simple to formulate, but the answers to them did not prove easy to interpret. For example, in the Version 1, Stage 1 questionnaire used in Coventry and Bradford, Question 4 asked for a list of languages taught: but in those cases where more than one language was actually taught – 11 out of 44 questionnaires in Coventry and 18 out of 46 questionnaires in Bradford – we were not able to extract from the completed questionnaires the specific number of pupils studying each language. This means that for the MTTD survey as a whole, it was not possible to arrive at the number of pupils learning each language in the city until we had done some follow-up questioning in several schools. In the Version 2 questionnaire, the equivalent question asked for numbers of pupils in different age groups or classes for each language taught or used.

We were constantly faced with the need to choose between what could be asked simply and without ambiguity in the Stage 1 questionnaire, and what could not, and therefore had to be assigned to the Stage 2 questionnaire. The agreed administrative procedure for this Stage 2 allowed for elaboration of the basic details in the Stage 1 questionnaires. At the same time, we had to keep in mind the reasons for attempting these surveys, and the scope of what we could realistically aim to achieve. We had to consider the related questions of audience, methods of contacting respondents, interview settings and alternative methods.

It had always been our aim that the teachers themselves should complete the questionnaires. We thought this would be straightforward in the LEA schools where the teachers received the questionnaires by post, and we treated each class as the basic unit. We did not know as yet of the range of different situations we would encounter, for example single teachers teaching different languages to different classes in one or more than one school; peripatetic teachers teaching one language in different schools; pairs of teachers teaching the same pupils; single teachers teaching more than one language in the same classroom at the same time. On the other hand it became evident that in some of the teaching that was not LEA-supported the apparently standard terms of 'school' and 'class' were being used to designate quite different situations. The word 'school' usually refers both to the pupils, gathered together on single premises and distributed by age among different classes, and to the premises themselves. This may be the case among certain community-run schools, for example a Gujerati school in Coventry which brings together 300 pupils every weekend on LEA school premises, or in many churches, gurdwaras, mosques or temples which run large-scale schools on their own premises. But more often than not a voluntary school is an organisation operating on different premises, each of which may accommodate one or several classes. On the other hand, one 'school' which operates on single premises may actually consist of one group of ten to twenty pupils aged from 6 to 15. Or again, the same LEA premises may be used at the same time by different organisations ('schools'), each of which may consist of one or more than one class.

In view of this variation we had to decide in each case, very often with the help of the interviewers, on the number of questionnaires to be filled in, and on the person or persons to be interviewed. The interviewers had the task of completing the Stage 1 questionnaire with the teacher or organiser most closely involved, and leaving the Stage 2 questionnaire for completion later. In the large schools the headteacher or organiser was not necessarily in close touch with the teaching, and the teachers were not always able to give details of total numbers of pupils on the roll, for example. Foreseeing these and other difficulties, we developed a careful administrative procedure which was based on the local survey administrators' preliminary compilation of a very detailed contact index. The postal procedures for surveying the LEA classes were reassessed, as were the procedures involved in briefing and debriefing the local bilingual interviewers. Some of the resulting changes in the procedures and alterations in the questionnaire are discussed in the following sections. As in the ALUS, we asked the MTTD interviewers to work with a language policy where the initial approaches were always made in the respondent's first language, and any switch to English as the medium for the interview was made only on the respondent's initiative.

(a) The Coventry Survey

The Coventry MTTD Survey was carried out in the spring of 1981, using Version 1 of Stage 1 and a draft of Stage 2. The survey was administered by LMP-LINC, who had already completed the Adult Language Use Survey in the city at the end of 1980. The local knowledge built up from ALUS helped to locate and make contact with schools and with potential interviewers. LINC, the LMP dissemination project, established the 'contact index', using as a starting point information from a research study completed by a local mother tongue teacher (Nagra, 1979), information from the LEA's Minority Groups Support Service, and the fieldnotes of the LMP researchers. We also wrote to the LEA, asking them to confirm the accuracy of their most recent list of mother tongue classes in LEA schools.

The recruitment of bilingual interviewers for the community-run schools was on the basis of criteria such as familiarity with the local scene, understanding of language teaching, and acceptability to potential respondents especially with reference to religious affiliation. We also looked for good listening ability, and tried to avoid domineering personalities. In some cases we were in fact able to work with ALUS interviewers again.

The first problem raised during the preparation of the contact index was over the exact limits of the area to be covered by the survey. It was decided that the boundary would be the city itself, but where pupils living in Coventry attended classes in the relevant languages located outside Coventry these classes would also be included. The only case of this kind was the Italian teaching in Nuneaton.

When we circulated the questionnaires to mother tongue teachers in LEA schools, at first we simply let the headteacher know what was happening, but after one or two criticisms from headteachers, we adapted the procedure so that heads too were sent copies of the questionnaires a week before the mother tongue teachers received theirs. At the briefings, we discussed the content of the questionnaire, the aims and objectives of the work and our proposed three-step interviewing procedure. Interviewers were to contact the most appropriate persons and pay them a first visit. At an arranged time, they would complete Stage 1, explain Stage 2 and leave it with the interviewees for them to complete. The third visit was intended to allow interviewers and interviewees time to read the completed form together, and to fill in the gaps before finalising the answers. Notes of guidance on these procedures were given to the interviewers at the end of the briefing session for reference. We encouraged open discussion of foreseeable problems and of anxieties on the part of the interviewers. They were then given the list of schools or classes to be contacted, and asked to ensure that they interviewed the most appropriate person.

A major difficulty with our interviewing procedure only became apparent later. Although the preparation of the contact index had taken a lot of time, and had involved many local contacts by phone and in person, it was still not detailed enough in terms of suggesting exactly who was the best person to interview. At their debriefing session many interviewers, while in the main speaking of a warm reception, mentioned the difficulty of this choice, and of finding a good time and place for the interview. In some cases one person at the school insisted that they had all the information, but it later became clear that they had only a partial picture; in others enthusiastic teachers would start to answer the questions in the middle of a busy class, and have to break off when their attention was required by students.

To give effective guidance to the interviewers, we concluded that it was necessary to include much more information in the contact index, including the time and place of classes, the most appropriate respondents, and their home telephone numbers. The interviewers also taught us that the first two steps of the three-stage procedure mentioned above could be merged into one: that is, if the correct contact was made by phone or in person, respondents were usually willing to complete Stage 1 on the spot. In fact the interviewer had to complete it together with the respondents, so it was advisable to proceed immediately.

The MTTD interviewers also helped us appreciate several other points. They would have benefited more from the briefing session if they had received the guidelines and questionnaires in advance, with their letter of appointment. The most appropriate respondent for Stage 1 was not necessarily the best respondent for Stage 2: often the organiser was best for 1, the teacher for 2. Some questions were felt to be sensitive, and the respondents might be anxious about the use to which the answers would be put — most obviously questions about salaries and premises. Our original categorisation into the 'voluntary' and the 'maintained' sectors was far from clear-cut. Our practices of giving one form for each language class in LEA schools meant that some teachers, particularly peripatetic teachers, had to complete several forms with almost identical information. Our practice of giving one form for each organisation in the voluntary sector was inadequate where the organisation held different classes on different premises, and occasionally of different languages.

The main Coventry survey was carried out over a period of three weeks, but during this period we failed to secure interviews from several 'voluntary' classes or schools. In no cases were there refusals, but we had problems in tracing teachers who were away on holiday or who did not live locally. For example, one interviewee filled in the Stage 1 form but never sent Stage 2, having arranged to marry in the meantime and having left the country. Four sets of Stages 1 and 2 questionnaires were lost in the post between Coventry and London, and the interviews had to be repeated. One interviewer emigrated to Australia with a set of complete questionnaires, and these interviews too had to be repeated!

The delays in completing the data in these cases, and the clarification of some incomplete or ambiguous answers in other questionnaires meant that a longer time than we had planned elapsed before the full set of questionnaires was ready for coding. And during the data-coding stage, the categorisation system for the classes had to be adapted to account for the cases which did not fit neatly into our initial division between 'voluntary' and 'maintained' sectors.

(b) The Bradford Survey

The Bradford MTTD Survey produced similar problems, and some new difficulties reflecting the different situation of mother tongue teaching in Bradford. For this survey we wanted to collaborate with a local institution, to see how feasible our procedures were when administered by another team, and to encourage greater local involvement in the research and in the follow-up to the survey. We chose inner Bradford as the area to be covered (i.e. not including those areas like Keighley and Bingley only incorporated into Bradford Metropolitan District in 1974). Two staff members of the Centre for Multicultural Studies at Bradford College supervised the administration of the survey. They elaborated the contact index procedure, after we had stressed the need for its thorough preparation before the actual administration period for the survey itself. The organisers at Bradford College developed a very efficient means of cataloguing all the incoming information from their circular letter and telephone calls. Before the interviewers were briefed, the college had a full list of schools and classes, and in most cases the name of the individuals to be interviewed along with their telephone numbers.

Head teachers of LEA schools received the details of the survey before the mother tongue teachers completed the questionnaire and, as there were at that time few LEA schools with mother tongue teaching and no peripatetic teachers in Bradford, this aspect of the survey proved relatively simple. In the 'voluntary' classes and schools, the main initial difficulty that we foresaw was a higher percentage of schools which were likely to be suspicious of the motives of the survey. There were many mosque schools in Bradford with a greater number of respondents with minimal English, a greater amount of provision focussing on the language of religion, and a population who either felt under a threat from the underlying secularising tendencies of western schooling or were aware of the often prejudiced criticism of their language teaching efforts. Some of the mosques fulfilled the needs of several local linguistic minorities teaching together for example speakers of Pushtu and Panjabi, or speakers of Gujerati and Panjabi. In these cases we had to be particularly careful in appointing sensitive interviewers from the different local populations.

The biggest problem that emerged after the Bradford survey, and while we were also coding the Coventry responses, was over the definitions we used of what we were still calling the 'voluntary' and 'maintained' classes, and of the way this division related to the different forms of administration for the survey. In Coventry teachers of classes organised by the LEA, and peripatetic teachers from the LEA support service, received their questionnaires by post. But in both Coventry and Bradford there were also 'voluntary' community-run schools and classes using LEA school premises, and their teachers were interviewed in person along with teachers in the 'voluntary' sector operating outside LEA school premises. Moreover, some bilingual LEA teachers also taught mother tongue classes at lunch breaks or after school-time, in addition to their other teaching commitment in the school. A few of them perceived this teaching also to be 'voluntary', as they received no extra pay for the extra hours of work. There were also a few classes in Bradford that were organised within the LEA schools' timetables, but where foreign governments paid the teachers' salaries and supplied the teaching materials used. It was this complexity which finally led us to abandon the criterion of ownership of premises for determining 'maintained' or 'voluntary' status (see p. 250). It also made us realize that the procedures used for deciding whether to administer the questionnaire by post or in person would not always fit the categories into which the school or class had originally been put.

Another difficulty raised by the survey of the 'voluntary' sector in Bradford led to a major alteration of the Stage 1 form. We found that we were unable to obtain overall totals for Bradford of pupils of mother tongue classes in each linguistic minority, because there were some schools which taught the same children two or more languages, and we had not asked for a language breakdown. In the few cases that occurred in Coventry the interviewers or local advisers had provided the breakdown, and it was clear that different sets of children were usually involved. In many Bradford mosques, however, the teaching of the national and of the religious language to the same groups of children alternated on different days of the week. We therefore had to introduce a more specific question where appropriate, asking about the languages taught and the number of pupils studying each. There remained one problem for which no solution could be found within the resources of the survey: probably a small number of children were counted twice, because they attended different classes at different times in the same or in different languages. For example, they may have had two to four hours mother tongue teaching in their LEA school, and in addition attended evening or weekend classes at their local gurdwara, mosque, temple or other voluntary school.

(c) The Haringey Survey

The experience of administering the survey and processing the information from Coventry and Bradford led to the revision of the Stage 1 questionnaire. The resulting Version 2 was then used in the Borough of Haringey in North London. While this new questionnaire proved more satisfactory for the coding of the data, particular features of the situation in London led to a new set of problems for the administration and analysis of the survey.

Working in a London Borough emphasised in particular the arbitrary nature of local government boundaries, in terms of the spread of mother tongue teaching provision. Haringey contains only a small part of the large multilingual population of the whole metropolis. Keeping to the LEA boundary often meant only partial coverage of the classes organised by the larger, longer-established community organisations.

For example, the Greek Parents' Association had nearly one hundred classes at the time of the survey, spread right across North London. There were also classes in various languages organised in premises outside the borough, but where students were recruited in large numbers from within Haringey. We decided to include only those mother tongue schools or classes outside Haringey attended by a substantial number of pupils living in Haringey, and when there appeared to be no classes in the particular language within the borough boundaries. Our focus could then remain on the young people living in Haringey, and we could point not just to existing local provision but also to potential local need. When the MTTD survey is used in other conurbations, it may be useful in presenting the data to distinguish even more clearly than we did between provision within the LEA boundaries, and provision for pupils living in the area but situated in premises located outside the LEA (which may be covered in another local MTTD survey).

The process of developing a contact index had been carefully refined by the time we worked in Haringey, but this survey showed up new difficulties which could not be easily overcome if we followed the established practice of using two different administration procedures. We had arranged to collaborate with the local Community Relations Council, to gain experience of a different type of base for the administration of the survey. The two bilingual community workers most directly involved had excellent contacts with the Greek Cypriot and Turkish Cypriot populations, and with a few other linguistic minorities. But the nature of their own job restricted the time they could spend on following up contacts, potential interviewers and classes in the smaller minorities. Their experience reminded us that the local administrative group needs to cover the full range of languages and needs to be in a position to allocate a great deal of working time and resources to the compilation of the contact index.

Also, to our surprise, we found it difficult to obtain from a single source an up-to-date account of publicly supported mother tongue teaching provision. A few classes we found in the public domain were not known to the LEA and some others were supported by bodies like social services or libraries rather than by the LEA. It was also difficult in some cases to determine where the premises of classes actually were. As in Coventry some local community organisations, for example, did not have a 'school' on one set of premises, but a series of classes at different addresses. We needed to find out about the provision at each address, which meant in some cases contacting several times the same teacher, who taught on two or three different sites. There was a greater number of teachers in Haringey teaching the mother tongue in LEA schools who were also teaching in the 'voluntary' classes, sometimes on the same site. Such teachers would receive a postal questionnaire and then later be approached also for an interview in person! There were also a few cases of mother tongue classes which were clearly LEA-supported but jointly organised with the local communities. Haringey reflected an organisational structure that may become increasingly common in the future: this is a situation where the LEA has started to pay the salaries of a few teachers belonging to a minority organisation who now also teach classes provided within the LEA school curriculum.

The scope of mother tongue teaching

This section of the chapter presents details of the 'mother tongue' classes and schools which we found in Coventry and Bradford in 1981 and in Haringey in 1982. Our data here covers the classes initiated and run by the LEA or by individual LEA schools, as well as those provided by individuals and minority community organisations. We included classes, in other words, both inside and outside LEA school premises, during and after regular school hours – at lunch hours, in the evenings, at weekends.

The Version 1 questionnaire used for Stage 1 of the Coventry and Bradford Surveys is reproduced in Figure 6.2. (The layout and the wording of several of the questions used in the Coventry and Bradford Stage 1 surveys were changed before the Haringey Survey was conducted, as explained earlier in this chapter.)

The Stage 2 questions, which were the same in all three surveys, are included as Appendix 2. With very few exceptions all the schools and classes approached also answered these more detailed questions. Some data from Stage 2 is discussed later in this chapter (see p. 257).

Languages taught as 'mother tongues'

In Table 6.1 we set out the languages taught in the three areas at the time of the surveys which fell within our definition of mother tongue teaching (see Fig. 6.1). By 'class' we mean a single group of pupils learning a single language.

In Coventry, the languages in which we found mother tongue classes represented all but one of the languages reported in our 1981 Schools

Figure 6.2 The MTTD survey questionnaire – Stage 1: 4 pages

PLEASE RETURN TO:	Date sent:	LEAVE THIS COLUMN BLANK
	Date returned:	Serial No.
		Month Year

MOTHER-TONGUE TEACHING DIRECTORY

STAGE 1

This form is being sent to people involved in organising mother-tongue schools and mother-tongue classes.

PLEASE FILL IN OR TICK AS APPROPRIATE.

1. Main address where classes are held:
   (If there are other addresses please write them on the back page of this form.)

2. Write here the number of classes which your answers below refer to:

3. When was the mother-tongue school or class started? 19 ____

4. List the languages taught:

5. What is the total number of pupils on the roll?

6. How many of these pupils attend regularly?

7. How many mother-tongue teachers are there in your school?

SPECIMEN VERSION OF 1981

PLEASE <u>DO NOT</u> WRITE IN THESE (— —) CODING SPACES.

8. Please write in the approximate **number** of pupils in each of the following age groups:

	under 5	5 – 7	8 – 10	11 – 13	14 – 16	over 16	
number of pupils							35 – 46
number of hours spent attending classes each week							47 – 58

9. What is the minimum number of hours per week that a pupil attends? _____ 59 60

10. What is the maximum number of hours per week that a pupil attends? _____ 61 62

11. Who supports your teaching in the following ways? PLEASE TICK WHERE APPROPRIATE.

	(1) no funds	(2) your organisation's resources	(3) fees and contributions from parents	(4) embassy or High Commission	(5) Local Education Authority	
(a) teachers' salaries						63 – 67
(b) teachers' travel expenses						68 – 72
(c) exercise books and paper						73 – 77
(d) textbooks and teaching aids						3 – 39 / 7 – 8
(e) rent of rooms						9 – 13
(f) exam entrance fees						14 – 18

Cols. 1 – 5 as Card 1
Col. 6 : 2

SPECIMEN VERSION

12. If you have any other expenses in running the school please write down what they are: _____ 19 20

and who pays for them: _____ 21 22

13. Name of organisation (or authority) responsible for running your class or school: _____ 23 24

PLEASE <u>DO NOT</u> WRITE IN THESE (— —) CODING SPACES.

14. When do the classes take place? TICK MORE THAN ONE IF NECESSARY.

		After school or evening:—
(1) before school begins ☐		(6) one weekday ☐
(2) during school lesson time ☐		(7) two weekdays ☐
(3) during lunch or other breaks ☐		(8) three weekdays ☐
(4) one day at the weekend ☐		(9) four weekdays ☐
(5) two days at the weekend ☐		(10) five weekdays ☐

15. Please specify if you have any other arrangement: _____

_____

16. If you entered pupils for public examination last year, please write the language(s) offered at the top.
Then fill in the **numbers** of pupils in the appropriate boxes.

LANGUAGE(S)	took	passed	took	passed	took	passed	took	passed	took	passed
C.S.E.										
G.C.E. 'O' LEVEL										
G.C.E. 'A' LEVEL										
INSTITUTE OF LINGUISTS										
ANY OTHER										

17. Please name any other exams which you use: _____

18. Are you planning to enter pupils for examinations this year or next year? _____

If there are any other addresses (for Question 1) or comments that you would like to make, please write them here:

SPECIMEN VERSION OF 1981

SIGNATURE:

DATE:

Stage II of this questionnaire will soon be available from:

Linguistic Minorities Project
University of London
Institute of Education
18 Woburn Square, London WC1H 0NS

Name of person who has completed this form (in block capitals):

_____

Address for future correspondence:

_____

_____

_____

Telephone: _____

77 78
Month

79 80
Year

THANK YOU FOR COMPLETING THIS FORM! PLEASE RETURN IT AS SOON AS POSSIBLE

Table 6.1 'Mother tongue' teaching in Coventry, Bradford and Haringey: origin and numbers of classes

Languages	Coventry 1981		Bradford 1981		Haringey 1982	
	Year in which first surviving classes began	Number of classes in 1981	Year in which first surviving classes began	Number of classes in 1981	Year in which first surviving classes began	Number of classes in 1982
Arabic	–	–	1974	12	1976	1
Bengali	1979	–	1981	2	1980	3
Chinese	1963	3	1979	5	1972	11
Greek	1974	3	1979	3	1955	90
Gujerati	–	20	1957	9	1981	1
Hebrew	1974	–	–	–	1904	7
Hindi	–	6	1976	3	1981	2
Irish Gaelic	1956	–	–	–	1980	1
Italian	–	9	1971	18	1975	12
Latvian	1973	–	1949	2	–	–
Panjabi	1953	30	1970	29	–	–
Polish	1978	10	1954	10	–	–
Serbo–Croat	1975	1	1978	1	–	–
Spanish	–	1	–	–	1979	6
Turkish	–	–	–	–	1959	5
Ukrainian	1955	2	1948	15	–	–
Urdu	1973	8	1974	16	–	–
Urdu/Arabic	1973	13	1957	58	1980	4
ALL LANGUAGES TOGETHER		106		183		143

'Urdu/Arabic' classes are classes where Urdu is taught as a subject within the context of the teaching of Islam and where the same pupils are also taught to read the Qur'an in Arabic. Spoken Panjabi seems to be used largely as a medium of instruction in these classes. The Chinese classes attended by Haringey children are held in premises just outside the borough, but about a quarter of the pupils are from Haringey.

Language Survey as having more than eighty speakers in LEA schools, and some languages with fewer than eighty, viz. Spanish, Ukrainian and Serbo-Croat (LMP/LINC, 1983). For Bengali, where there had been some provision before 1981, difficulties in finding a teacher had led to the discontinuation of the classes, although there were 137 Bengali-speaking pupils recorded in the schools.

In Bradford too the languages in which we found classes covered all but one of the languages reported by more than eighty pupils in our 1981 Schools Language Survey there, and again included some languages with fewer speakers, in this case Arabic, Greek, Latvian and Serbo-Croat. There did not seem, however, to be classes in Pushtu, although 415 pupils reported using the language at home (LMP/LINC, 1983). Most of these pupils would be from Pathan families, and some would be learning Urdu, the national language of Pakistan, as well as Arabic for religious purposes.

In Haringey the languages in which we found classes in 1982 represented nearly all the languages reported in our 1981 Schools Language Survey as having more than sixty speakers in LEA schools. We were not, however, able to discover in Haringey itself classes in Panjabi or Portuguese, nor does there seem to be any mother tongue type provision for speakers of French-based Creoles, who have settled in this area of London in considerable numbers. There were, on the other hand, classes in Irish Gaelic and in Hebrew, which both had fewer than sixty speakers recorded in the Haringey Schools Language Survey (LMP/LINC, 1983).

Table 6.1 also shows that the classes in the different languages were founded in different periods, relating of course to the settlements of the various populations. After the earliest class we have reference to — the Hebrew one started in 1904 — the next group of classes is from Eastern Europe, with foundation dates ranging from 1948 to 1955. The South European classes begin to appear also in the mid to late 1950s, but most of them date from the 1970s, as do all the Chinese classes. Again, although two of the classes for South Asian languages began in 1957, and one in 1970, all the rest had been founded in the previous ten years. Nevertheless, in Coventry and Bradford it was these classes, teaching different South Asian languages, which accounted for more than 80 per cent of the pupils currently attending mother tongue classes. A similar figure applied to the Southern European languages in Haringey, with Greek alone representing some 70 per cent of the mother tongue learners.

Table 6.2 gives some notion of the extent of mother tongue teaching

Table 6.2 'Mother tongue' teaching in Coventry, Bradford and Haringey: rolls and attendance

Town	Coventry 1981			Bradford 1981			Haringey 1982		
Languages	(a) Pupils on roll	(b) Pupils attending regularly	(c) (b) as % of (a)	(a) Pupils on roll	(b) Pupils attending regularly	(c) (b) as % of (a)	(a) Pupils on roll	(b) Pupils attending regularly	(c) (b) as % of (a)
Arabic	–	–	–	161	130	71	15	14	93
Bengali	–	–	–	44	40	91	42	39	93
Chinese	20	17	85	75	70	93	194	170	88
Greek	35	32	91	33	33	100	2073	2003	97
Gujerati	343	258	75	213	197	92	82	82	100
Hebrew	–	–	–	–	–	–	80	67	84
Hindi	25	25	100	40	28	70	20	12	60
Irish Gaelic	–	–	–	–	–	–	20	20	100
Italian	117	88	75	141	136	96	174	156	90
Latvian	–	–	–	6	6	100	–	–	–
Panjabi	763	669	88	555	427	77	–	–	–
Polish	104	100	96	130	109	84	–	–	–
Serbo-Croat	13	9	69	14	10	71	–	–	–
Spanish	33	20	61	–	–	–	128	113	88
Turkish	–	–	–	–	–	–	139	108	78
Ukrainian	19	16	84	87	87	100	–	–	–
Urdu	66	54	82	249	202	81	–	–	–
Urdu/Arabic	356	345	97	1838	1773	96	75	65	87
ALL LANGUAGES TOTAL	1894	1633	86	3586	3248	91	3042	2849	94

in the three areas surveyed. Alongside the languages taught are the number of pupils and students reported for each of these languages on the questionnaires returned to us. We report both 'pupils on roll' and those 'regularly attending': the percentages in column C for each area do not support the sometimes heard suggestion that the nominal rolls of such classes were very much higher than the actual numbers attending. However, it should be noted that teachers and organisers of classes did not always have very exact records to consult when completing their returns. They may have interpreted the term 'regularly' differently, and we know there were some pupils who were probably counted twice, since they attended more than one set of classes.

We set out to include any language classes which contained at least some pupils or students for whom the language being studied was a language used in the home by members of their families, or in the locality for religious or ethnic minority community purposes. Most of the classes consisted entirely of such students. However, a few of the classes also included students for whom there was no particular family or community connection, but who had some other reason to want to learn the language. This is likely to be increasingly the pattern for a number of languages at both school and further and higher education level, as educational institutions incorporate local ethnic minority languages into their mainstream provision. It also illustrates clearly why the term 'mother tongue' teaching will less and less satisfactorily cover new developments in the teaching of the languages concerned, and already therefore has only a limited usefulness.

Age of pupils

Table 6.3 shows the age distribution of the pupils and students attending the mother tongue classes in Coventry, Bradford and Haringey.

It is noticeable that the number of 11- to 13-year-olds attending mother tongue classes was slightly larger than the numbers of 8- to 10-year-olds in two of the three areas, and only slightly smaller in the third, although it is often believed that there is a sharp drop-off in attendance in the early teens. The proportions of very young pupils were not strikingly high either, contrary to another of the popular stereotypes about such classes. Taking account also of the comparatively small number of students over 16 (not detailed in Table 6.3), it is clear that mother tongue teaching in the three areas surveyed was an activity above all involving the 5- to 16-year-olds.

Material support from the Local Education Authorities for mother tongue classes

As mentioned earlier, when we undertook the surveys we expected to be able to make a simple division of the mother tongue classes in the three areas into two categories: those which were staffed and paid for entirely by the LEA, and those which relied entirely on human and material resources provided by the various communities concerned. In fact the situation turned out to be much less clearcut than that: although there were examples of classes clearly in each of these categories, a substantial number fell somewhere in between, into a mixed category. That is to say, they drew on some resources provided by the LEA, mainly free or subsidised use of school premises outside usual school hours, and some from elsewhere, for example from community associations, religious organisations, high commissions or embassies. The main support from embassies or high commissions is in the form of teachers recruited on short-term contracts from the countries of origin – almost entirely the Southern European countries. Some of their teaching is done in premises rented by them, some on LEA premises, some even in mainstream curricular time – for example Italian in some Bradford high schools. However, the existence of such input should not be seen as absolving the LEAs from their own responsibilities towards mother tongue teaching, and it is on that aspect that we concentrate in what follows.

In analysing the material support available for the classes from the education authorities we identified the key factors as follows:

(1) **Whether the LEA paid the teachers to undertake this teaching,**
    i.e. was the teacher employed by the LEA, with the classes in question as a part of the weekly teaching load expected of that teacher, and *not* as extra work assumed voluntarily?

(2) **Whether the LEA provided the teaching accommodation free of charge.**

This is the data represented in categories A, B and C of Table 6.4 under the general heading of 'Material Support for Classes from LEA'.

Even the term 'class' in this context is less straightforward than we first expected! As indicated earlier we use it to mean a single group of pupils learning a single language. A few cases were reported to us of the same teacher supervising the learning of more than one language by different pupils in one classroom: to give a clearer overall picture we

Table 6.3 *Age groups of pupils in 'mother tongue' classes in Coventry, Bradford and Haringey*

Town	Coventry 1981				Bradford 1981				Haringey 1982			
Languages	age under 8	age 8–10	age 11–13	age over 13	age under 8	age 8–10	age 11–13	age over 13	age under 8	age 8–10	age 11–13	age over 13
Arabic	–	–	–	–	60	10	30	60	5	6	4	0
Bengali	1	11	–	–	0	12	28	4	12	10	7	13
Chinese	7	13	3	5	35	28	6	6	74	74	25	17
Greek	30	62	13	2	14	9	4	1	379	533	514	462
Gujerati	–	–	72	154	20	40	95	57	15	25	35	7
Hebrew	0	2	–	–	–	–	–	–	18	37	25	0
Hindi	–	–	2	8	5	10	10	15	5	5	5	8
Irish Gaelic	4	–	–	–	–	–	–	–	0	3	2	15
Italian	–	29	9	35	2	12	34	105	10	47	78	39
Latvian	9	–	–	–	4	1	0	14	–	–	–	–
Panjabi	16	142	219	100	94	109	180	159	–	–	–	–
Polish	3	20	39	29	28	26	24	52	–	–	–	–
Serbo-Croat	4	5	5	0	3	4	3	0	–	–	–	–
Spanish	–	3	17	9	–	–	–	–	24	47	33	24
Turkish	0	–	–	–	–	–	–	–	26	46	27	33
Ukrainian	0	9	2	5	24	12	14	32	–	–	–	–
Urdu	–	31	11	12	0	18	40	169	–	–	–	–
Urdu/Arabic	60	133	126	42	485	487	542	323	16	30	13	16
All Languages Total	134	460	518	401	774	778	1010	997	584	860	768	634
Age Groups as % of Total for All Languages	8.9	30.4	34.2	26.5	21.7	21.9	28.4	28.0	20.5	30.2	27.0	22.3

The total of the separate age groups does not always correspond either to the total numbers on the rolls or to the total attending regularly: cases where the information on age groups was not supplied were omitted from this table.

Table 6.4 Material support from LEAs for 'mother tongue' classes

(A) Number of classes for which the LEA provides *both* teachers' salaries and accommodation.

(B) Number of classes for which the LEA provides *either* teachers' salaries *or* accommodation.

(C) Number of classes for which the LEA provides *neither* teachers' salaries *nor* accommodation.

Town / Languages	Coventry 1981			Bradford 1981			Haringey 1982		
	A	B	C	A	B	C	A	B	C
Arabic	–	–	–	1	1	10	0	0	1
Bengali	–	–	–	0	2	0	0	3	0
Chinese	0	0	3	0	0	5	0	0	11
Greek	0	3	0	0	0	3	12	4	74
Gujerati	4	14	2	1	0	8	0	0	1
Hebrew	–	–	–	–	–	–	0	0	7
Hindi	5	0	1	0	1	2	0	0	2
Irish Gaelic	–	–	–	–	–	–	1	0	0
Italian	2	0	7	0	18	0	0	0	12
Latvian	–	–	–	0	0	2	–	–	–
Panjabi	13	11	6	6	0	23	–	–	–
Polish	0	10	0	1	0	9	–	–	–
Serbo-Croat	0	0	1	0	0	1	–	–	–
Spanish	0	0	1	–	–	–	0	0	6
Turkish	–	–	–	–	–	–	0	1	4
Ukrainian	0	2	0	0	0	15	–	–	–
Urdu	6	2	0	13	3	0	–	–	–
Urdu/Arabic	0	0	13	0	0	58	0	2	2
ALL LANGUAGES TOGETHER	30	42	34	22	25	136	13	10	120

broke down such cases into 'classes' in the sense defined in the previous sentence.

We did not seek to identify individual teachers in our surveys, and this has the consequence that we cannot always be sure when the same person appears, for example, as a teacher of an LEA class at one time in the week, and again at some other time, as a teacher of a community-run class. Any overall total of teachers involved in mother tongue teaching in our three areas would have been misleading, and would not have done justice to the input of expertise by many mainstream bilingual teachers in LEA schools and community-run provision. They are an important group of teachers who are increasingly being asked to help bridge the gap between the official and the unofficial school systems.

In understanding the problems faced by mother tongue teachers as compared with their colleagues in other fields of language teaching, it is clearly important to have some notion of what material resources they are able to draw on to supplement the human resources which they often have in abundance. The major expenditure headings involved in mother tongue teaching are certainly payment to teachers, although many teach on a voluntary basis, and also payment for premises. Of course, in some of the non-LEA classes the teacher may be unpaid, and premises may be provided without charge by some public or private institution or private individual. Information for some classes in this connection was fuller than for others, so there are some inevitable gaps in this data.

Other material support sometimes provided by LEAs includes textbooks and teaching aids, exercise books and paper, and examination fees. Details of these were included in the Appendices to our First Reports on the MTTD Surveys for each area. Parents, teachers or community resources were drawn on for such additional expenses as administration, stationary, trips, prizes and building expenditure.

Attendance at mother tongue classes

Table 6.5, setting out our data on hours of attendance at mother tongue classes, demonstrates that for most children in most linguistic minorities the weekly commitment in terms of time was not very large — averaging around two to four hours. There is a particular exception for some of the embassy-supported classes, in Italian and Spanish for example, and a clear exception as far as some of the classes in Arabic, Bengali and 'Urdu-Arabic' are concerned. These last are often devoted at least as much to Islamic instruction as to narrowly defined language teaching, and some children attend classes for two hours or so daily during most of the week.

The experience of mother tongue teachers

The data presented in the last section is derived from an analysis of the Stage 1 questionnaires. Despite the problems of devising and administering the surveys in Coventry, Bradford and Haringey, these findings provide a good indication of the scope of mother tongue schools and classes in the three cities where we worked, as far as the number of

*Table 6.5 Weekly hours of attendance by pupils at 'mother tongue'
classes*

Town	Coventry 1981		Bradford 1981		Haringey 1981	
Languages	Average	Range	Average	Range	Average	Range
Arabic	–	–	d	1–10	2	–
Bengali	–	–	4	–	e	3–10
Chinese	2	–	2	–	3	–
Greek	4	–	3	–	3	1–4
Gujerati	2.5	1.5–3.5	3	1.5–4	2	–
Hebrew	–	–	–	–	4.5	3–5
Hindi	2.5	1–3.5	2	1–2	2	–
Irish Gaelic	–	–	–	–	1	–
Italian	b	1.5–6	3	2.5–3.5	4	3–4
Latvian	–	–	4	–	–	–
Panjabi	2	1–4	2.5	1–4	–	–
Polish	3	–	3	2–3.5	–	–
Serbo-Croat	4	–	4	–	–	–
Spanish	6.5	–	–	–	no information	
Turkish	–	–	–	–	3	1–4
Ukrainian	2	–	3	2–4	–	–
Urdu	2	1.5–3.5	2	1–3.5	–	–
Urdu/Arabic	ci	2–10	12 cii	5–14	ciii	2–23
Urdu/Panjabi/ Arabic f	–	–	21	–	–	–

Notes to Table 6.5
(a) *'Average'* figures for weekly attendance were arrived at by adding the numbers
    of hours reported for each separate age group (see Table 4.3 for breakdown
    of age groups) on each questionnaire, dividing that total by the number of
    age groups for which information was given, then rounding up to the nearest
    half-hour.
(b) *Age group differences*: There were only very small differences between hours
    attended by pupils of different age groups within each language, with the
    exception of the Italian classes in Coventry, where those under the age of 14
    averaged five and a half hours and those 14 or over averaged two and a half
    hours.
(c) *Urdu/Arabic classes:*
    (i)   In Coventry the range within each age group was considerable: two to
          ten hours for the 5- to 13-year-olds, and two to seven and a half for the
          14- to 16-year-olds, for example, so no average is included.
    (ii) In Bradford, with the exception of one entry for the over-16s, the range
          was nine to fourteen hours, so an average is included.
    (iii) In Haringey the range is so large in nearly all age groups that an average
          is again not included.
(d) *Arabic in Bradford*: For the age groups between 11 and 16, we have an
    entry of ten hours and another of one hour, so no average is included.
(e) *Bengali in Haringey*: For the age groups between 5 and 13, we have one
    entry of ten hours so no average is included.
(f) *Urdu/Panjabi/Arabic*: These are classes where Urdu is taught as a subject
    within the context of the teachings of Islam and where the same pupils are
    taught to read the Qur'an in Arabic. Spoken Panjabi seems to be used largely
    as a medium of instruction in these classes. Some Gujerati-speaking children
    study Urdu and/or Arabic, or Hindi, in addition to, or rather than Gujerati.

linguistic minorities involved, the number and age of pupils, the organisational and financial arrangements are concerned.

Several important points emerge from the comparison of basic figures from the three cities. First the findings from each city cover a wide range of minority languages. As we stressed in Chapter 1, it is important to remember that the mother tongue teaching issue is not solely a question for the South Asian minorities, although they are often the largest and sometimes the most vocal in their demands. Second, organisational and financial arrangements differ greatly not only between, but also sometimes within, linguistic minorities. As mother tongue teaching is increasingly recognised by LEAs, there will be an increasing overlap between the LEA and community-run provision. But, important as these general conclusions are, great care needs to be taken in the interpretation of Stage 1 findings. This is another role of the data from Stage 2, which helps to fill out the details of what is actually happening within any one linguistic minority in specific LEA or community-run schools.

One of the reasons we were able to gather this information in such a complex situation, covering both LEA and community-run provision, was our community-based research strategy and the involvement of bilingual interviewers. The interviewers could often build on existing relationships of trust and the series of visits for the completion of both questionnaires allowed respondents to share their experience at some length. The interviewers were also important at the beginning of each survey in uncovering new provision, advising about unforeseen difficulties, and in contacting respondents. The Coventry and Bradford interviewers also played a major part in our revision of the questionnaires, as we have described in an earlier section of this chapter (see p. 234).

A few mother tongue teachers who had received no outside support, and were aware of criticism of their efforts, were naturally quite suspicious of the motives of the survey. The majority, however, were eager to participate, hopeful of its use in publicising their problems, and could have been frustrated by the exclusive use of the Stage 1 questionnaire, which gave them little opportunity to express their views. So one of the main roles of the Stage 2 questionnaire was to complement the basic data in Stage 1 by encouraging respondents to 'open up' on important preoccupations. While the standardised findings of Stage 1 could provide a quick overview, and comparison of data between linguistic minorities and between cities, it did not cover some of the most important questions, for example about teachers' qualifications and pay, methods used and problems faced by teachers. Responses on such questions were not easy to categorise into a very limited set of options, because of the great range of situations involved. Interviewers in Stage 2 were therefore asked to encourage respondents to record whatever they felt relevant, and in those cases where the respondent was not fluent in or at ease with English the interviewer completed the questionnaire with him or her.

One of the findings most clearly illustrated in the previous section of this chapter is that the majority of the mother tongue classes in the three areas taken as a whole (83 per cent in Haringey, 74 per cent in Bradford and 32 per cent in Coventry) had no support from the LEA for teachers' salaries or accommodation at the time of the survey. That is to say, they were in our category C – see Table 6.4. Even when schools or classes were receiving partial support (category B), usually it was only in the form of free or subsidised accommodation, and they were still often run by local community organisations or overseas government agencies. And many of the classes within the curriculum of LEA schools, and with teachers paid by the LEA (category A), were set up through the initiative and perseverance of a bilingual teacher on the staff of those schools. The following extracts from answers to Question 1 of the Stage 2 questionnaire are illustrations of this process:

'The class was started in 1979 because of the interest shown by the children, head teacher and myself. The class attracted many children in the beginning but the number dropped afterwards due to the changes made in lunch hours. Another reason for the drop in numbers was because many other interesting activities were going on at the same time in school during lunch hours.

'The class consisted of Panjabi-speaking children in the beginning. Soon after Urdu-speaking children asked if they could be helped to learn Urdu. So a group for Panjabi language and a group for Urdu language were taken at the same time.' (Primary school teacher working in lunch hours for no extra pay)

'The first initiative was from me as a mother and teacher. I approached the head teacher and discussed with him the possibility of extra-curricular or integrated lessons for Greek speakers in the school. Contacts were made with the parents by letter and then by phone. The next step was bringing the parents into the school for discussion about the organisation and running of the classes. There is full

co-operation and the classes run twice a week from 3.30 to 5. p.m.'
(LEA primary school teacher)

Without qualifying the distinctions established in our categories A,
B and C, it would be easy for outsiders to overestimate the amount of
financial and organisational support given by LEAs to mother tongue
teaching. Some are quite anxious to appear to be doing more in this
direction than they actually are.

Any explanation of what is actually happening, and why the pattern
of provision is as it is, depends upon an understanding of the socio-
economic position of the minority in question, its relationship to the
wider majority society, and to the school system in particular. We
were already familiar with the three cities and some of the linguistic
minorities through our Adult Language Use Survey, and the data from
our Schools Language Survey gave us an indication of the number of
bilingual pupils who were potential beneficiaries of mother tongue
provision (see Chapter 8). But to understand the nature of the existing
contact between mother tongue classes and the LEA, it is also necessary
to know about the history of local language politics over the past few
decades (see pp. 86 and 93 in Chapter 2). It is only within this wider
social and educational context that we can begin to interpret appropriately the findings of both Stage 1 and Stage 2 of the MTTD surveys.

Answers to the questions in Stage 2 on the history and aims of the
classes often gave an indication of how provision had developed in
response to internal changes in the population, and as a reaction to
external factors such as the lack of support from the LEA and feelings
of threat from the dominant English language and culture. Here are
two comments of this kind:

'This association started the school in February 1955. The reason
was for our Ukrainian children to learn their mother language.
They have to learn to read and write it for the maintenance of our
identity and culture. The main subjects have always been: language
(spoken, reading, writing), geography, history and literature. The
English schools used to cripple our identity . . . we want our children
to be taught their culture from the point of view of our group, not
from their point of view. We know who we are.' (Ukrainian teacher,
community-run school)

'The original aims of the temple were to teach children to write,
read and in some cases speak Panjabi. Most parents just wanted their

children to learn to read and write letters. Later, however, as the school became more organised and larger, a few children began to sit for 'O' level examination.' (Panjabi teacher in Sikh gurdwara)

Answers to questions about the development of the school or class also help to counter the kind of simplistic assumptions sometimes made by outside observers, who often suggest one unchanging aim for mother tongue teaching. In their minds it is often not that of language teaching, but preservation of the culture, or religious instruction. In many cases there is in fact a mixture of objectives, reflecting the close interdependence of linguistic and cultural maintenance:

'The present aims are basically the same as the original aims. Children are taught to read and write in Panjabi and also encouraged to speak more Panjabi rather than English. Also we aim to teach the children about the Sikh religion and of course the reading books used also teach a lot about religion and about our customs and traditions.' (Panjabi teacher in Sikh gurdwara)

Answers to some of the questions in Stage 2 give details of the varieties of the languages taught in the classes and spoken by the pupils at home, and of other subjects taught in the classes. These answers confirm that mother tongue classes in some linguistic minorities in particular aim to teach related cultural traditions as well as the standard language.

'The reason for which Spanish classes were established is mainly the teaching of the language, culture and history of Spain for the children of Spanish immigrant workers.' (Spanish teacher of evening class funded by Spanish Embassy held in LEA junior school premises)

(The aim of the school is) 'to inculcate an understanding of, and commitment to, the principles of the orthodox Jewish religion, i.e. ethical conduct, religious practice and ritual Jewish history and the Hebrew language.' (Hebrew teacher in synagogue)

'Our main aim is to teach the mother tongue to the Turkish children. We also teach folk dances, music and religion once a month. We are trying to teach the Turkish culture and some general subjects such as history, maths, geography, etc.' (Turkish teacher of community-run, embassy-aided school)

Some sceptical outsiders use the difference between the vernacular used at home and the literary standard taught in classes to counter the linguistic and cognitive arguments supporting 'mother tongue' teaching. They forget two important factors: the linguistic distance between spoken vernacular and written standard is equally marked for many indigenous English-speaking pupils at LEA schools, so that questions of transference from one variety to another are not new to language teachers. Secondly, the successful learning of any language is inevitably related to the social (and not solely to the narrowly linguistic) experience of the pupil, and the perceived interest and usefulness of the language. The national or regional languages, or languages for religious purposes, are well integrated into the social experience of the pupils. As other answers clearly show, the language-learning itself is in most cases separated from other subjects taught in these languages, for example music and dance, history and traditions, religion, crafts. But the existence of teaching about these other subjects provides an opportunity for more extensive use of the spoken or literary varieties. Among minorities with an increasing number of pupils with minimal skills in their mother tongue, they can provide crucial support for a living language. This is another reason why the introduction of mother tongue teaching in LEA schools may be seen to complement, rather than compete with, existing community-based initiatives.

Questions about teachers' pay and qualifications were deliberately left for the Stage 2 questionnaire of the MTTD survey because of their potential sensitivity. It was appropriate that they should be linked together in the questionnaire. Another frequent 'outsider's' criticism of existing provision is over the lack of formal qualifications of many teachers. However, the low rates, or complete absence, of pay for mother tongue teachers in many community-run schools (categories B and C), the lack of openings and options for promotion for teachers in LEA schools, and the lack of training facilities for 'voluntary' mother tongue teachers, make it hardly surprising that many of the teachers do not have qualified teacher status in England. A sizeable number of mother tongue teachers in each city do nevertheless have degrees in the language taught, in another language, or in a non-language subject, or have a teaching qualification. A recurring theme among the answers to the Stage 2 questionnaire is that of the need for initial and in-service training of teachers:

'We have difficulties to find available competent teachers. Now it is not too bad. In other parts of the country the older pupils have become teachers of Ukrainian for the new generation.' (Ukrainian teacher, community-run school)

'We face a lack of experienced teachers.' (Urdu teacher, mosque school)

It is not possible to estimate the total numbers of mother tongue teachers in each linguistic minority or city from these surveys, for reasons we explained in a previous section. Part of the difficulty too is over the very varied statuses of the teachers: there are part-time and full-time teachers, and a range of temporary helpers. In some schools there is high teacher turnover.

The answers to questions about pupils' attendance, teaching materials and methods, examinations, administration and funding must not be interpreted at face value either. For example, the number of pupils on the rolls and the details of the duration, timing and age ranges of classes deriving from Stage 1 answers must not be taken as a straight-forward representation of need. It simply indicates how many pupils attend a set of existing classes at a particular time. Attendance patterns have to be assessed with an appreciation of all the constraints on the development of more provision or of greater demand. Questions in Stage 2 often provide information about the difficulties faced in the organisation and teaching of the mother tongue. As Wilding reports on the situation in Leicester in 1981:

> The only classes available are organised on a voluntary basis with little or no assistance from central or local government. The majority of parents expressed an interest in sending their children to these classes if they were available locally. However, they were also concerned about over-burdening their children with too much study and about the quality of the provision. (Wilding, 1981)

Some of our ALUS findings (see Tables 5.14 and 5.15) also indicated that some parents did not know about available provision or found time or place inconvenient. On the other hand, there are comments in some of the answers to the Stage 2 questionnaire casting doubt on the school's ability to deal with the demand or with waiting lists.

Similarly, since the numbers of pupils entered by schools for language examinations may reflect overall priorities in the curriculum of the school or class, no conclusions should be drawn about level of demand without knowledge of the availability of appropriately trained teachers, and the existence or suitability of the examinations offered.

The answers to questions about materials and methods also show that mother tongue teachers themselves often raise questions about the appropriateness of their methods, and their lack of resources or of training opportunities:

'Originally (1963) the books were imported from Greece free of charge. These books were also used in the Greek schools in the mainland of Greece. In 1969 when I took over I imported textbooks from America especially written for Greek American children. These books were most suitable.' (Greek teacher, local community-run school in LEA premises)

'I think the books must address the students who are born here and we would like to use some of the teaching materials of the state schools where we are teaching at, e.g. video, charts, audio-visual aids, notebooks, etc.' (Turkish teacher, community-run, embassy-supported classes)

'We could improve our teaching if we were offered financial aid by the local authority.' (Urdu teacher in local mosque)

'I would like the University of London to bring the Greek language used in the examination paper up to date, in particular with spelling.' (Greek teacher, local community-run school in LEA premises)

Where respondents have simply described their teaching methods, these are sometimes quite traditional, but this does not necessarily mean that they are satisfied. The implications for teacher training and materials' development need to be considered at local as well as at national levels, and within the perspectives of the mother tongue teachers. The separation of voluntary and LEA-based provision inevitably restricts both parents and teachers in their ability to assess potential options. Experience with the LEA has deterred some from expecting any substantial support from LEAs, or trusting their motives in more recent initiatives. But it is particularly important to note that among some of the classes with the most traditional methods and attitudes, a number of mother tongue teachers expressed the wish for the LEA schools to take over or also to offer mother tongue classes:

'I believe that the teaching of the mother tongue is more effective when this teaching will be introduced in the mainstream schools of this country.' (Greek LEA teacher, paid for lessons after school)

'We are doing a job which is the local authority's responsibility, to provide facilities to teach these languages.' (Urdu teacher, mosque school)

When we had completed the drafts of the first written reports on each of the MTTD Surveys, we sent copies to all the respondents for comment and correction. We include here some extracts from the responses to this initial feedback. The first is from the principal of a community-run Ukrainian school:

'The Report . . . gave rise to an unexpected reaction. It renewed the importance of an objective that was formulated by the Ukrainian community well over 30 years ago, and that was to retain its national identity by passing on its knowledge of Ukraine to a generation of children born outside its borders. This renewal of an important objective was due to the fact that:

(a) the report showed that the Ukrainian community was not working in isolation in retaining its identity and that over time more and more ethnic groups were making every effort to attain the same objective; and that

(b) an organisation such as yours which was outside the ethnic boundaries of any one particular group had shown an interest in the projects run by ethnic groups themselves. Consequently the feeling was that your findings will help all ethnic minority groups gain some profitable support.'

The second extract is from a full-time teacher of Greek in an LEA comprehensive school:

'I believe that the introduction of mother tongue teaching in the multiracial school curriculum is very important for the complete improvement of the communities' members. It gives more help to the children who come from the minority groups to learn English also more effectively. From my long experience teaching mother tongue (modern Greek) in the country I found that the mother tongue is very helpful for my pupils to learn more and better English. We use translation from one language to another and vice versa. The children enrich their vocabulary in both languages and they can express themselves in a better way. A lot of my pupils passed the GCE 'O' level and 'A' level with very good results.

The presence of a teacher of a mother tongue at a school is very essential. He is the link between school and home and he can offer his services to both teachers and parents. He can understand the pupils' problems and he can help to the solution of them.

. . . better scales [ought] to be given by the Authorities to the full-time teachers of the mother tongues because they teach from beginners to GCE 'O' and 'A' levels, they offer very great help to both school and parents and I cannot see the reason why the qualified full-time teachers of the mother tongues do not have the same rights and promotions than teachers of the other subjects.'

The role of mother tongue schools

This last section of the chapter will comment on some of the sociological and sociolinguistic implications of mother tongue teaching. Put simply, what is the role of mother tongue schools and classes in the process of language maintenance or shift?

Earlier in this chapter we argued that there are two institutions which have a particularly important role in the transmission of minority language skills over time: the family and the minority organisation. The ALUS data in Chapter 5 reminded us of the role of both these institutions as well as the more diffuse role of local social networks, including contacts with friends, relatives and workmates. However, ALUS did not look in any detail at other institutions which also play some part in minority language maintenance and shift, especially the press and videos.

As we have stressed before, the main drawback with ALUS is that it cannot help us draw firm or detailed conclusions about language shift since it referred only to a single point in time. Even a superficial comparison between the patterns of language use among users of the same language in different cities reminds us that the historical, economic, demographic and political features of the local situation are primary influences on patterns of language use.

So before we move on to look at bilingualism and education in the following chapter, it is important that we recognise that mother tongue classes provide an institutional focus not just for the maintenance of language skills but also for their transmission from one generation to the next. More generally but crucially, we should also remember that the existence of community-based language teaching influences the ethnic and religious affiliations of bilinguals and the potential for mobilising these affiliations. Emphasising some of these issues is also important because discussion about mother tongue teaching has until now often tended to focus simply on its relationship with the LEA school system, without much consideration of its role within an existing context of inter-group relations.

The other major contribution of such a discussion is the introduction of a longer-term perspective. While we have details of the development of individual schools in the Stage 2 questionnaire, and these are very instructive in their own right, we also know that the schools or classes of each linguistic minority (or sub-sections within) have different organisational relationships with the LEA school system and other state institutions. We need to look at what is happening to hinder or encourage collective organisation or reproduction of cultural and linguistic skills.

A sociological appraisal of the role of mother tongue teaching involves enquiring into who is organising the provision for whom, and how providers and consumers are related to each other and to other institutions in the wider society. We cannot assess the function and consequences of mother tongue schooling unless we explore the structural relationship of the classes to the local population, to local minority institutions and to majority institutions. There are some linguistic minorities with relatively few members who have access to, or participate in, local minority institutions. Where such families have few local contacts of similar language background, language support in the home alone is unlikely to be enough to counter the process of language shift towards English. But even where bilingual families depend upon mother tongue teaching to maintain fluency, the frequent emphasis on the learning of literacy is unlikely to compensate for the limited opportunities to use the mother tongue orally.

Whatever the success of mother tongue classes in teaching oral skills or literacy to younger members of a local linguistic minority, the provision itself is a form of collective activity often encouraging the continuing use of the language other than English among the adults involved in organising it, as well as the pupils themselves. And whatever the objective of the provision, it demonstrates a need that is not being met by the LEA school system. Even in those LEAs that are appointing bilingual teachers or supporting existing community-run provision, their coverage will in most cases be very partial, supplementing rather than substituting for existing provision. There is no immediate likelihood therefore of LEA intervention undermining community-run initiatives.

The existence of support for mother tongue provision is one of several ways in which linguistic minorities may be perceived by members of the majority to be a threat to the objectives of the state school system specifically, and to the society more generally. This 'potential' for alternative development or separation can be used as a powerful resource in negotiation with the dominant majority. And it is the specific reaction of the dominant monolingual majority in terms of cultural assimilation, and in terms of language education, which is likely to influence the way linguistic minorities will react against the neglect of their languages or the denial of their existence.

Whatever its 'official' objectives, the actual power of minority language provision to foster and develop the use of the mother tongue, or in an increasing number of cases to reawaken a latent skill, will depend more on the youngsters' opportunities to withstand the pressures of English, and on their opportunities to use their 'mother tongue' in a range of role-relationships. When the local spoken variety of the minority language is supported by literacy in the standard form, or when the spoken standard takes over from the local variety, the several varieties of the minority language used in social interaction are likely to be integrated into the speaker's cultural and linguistic repertoire. Language is not just a means of communication, or a rallying point for collective mobilisation, it may also become an identity resource (see p. 26).

The existence of support for mother tongue teaching therefore leaves open the possibility for young people to extend their oral and literacy skills in their mother tongue or in the related national or religious language. For some teenagers in particular, the nature of the body which sponsors the teaching, and the way in which the classes are run, will influence their take-up and their commitment to it. School or classes may be closely integrated into existing social networks and traditional hierarchies of social relations. Some organisers and teachers may resist, and others may accept the social and linguistic changes being created by subsequent generations. At present there are some classes which clearly reinforce the status quo within the linguistic minority by supporting existing patterns of social control. Despite, or even because of, this traditionalism, these initiatives may contribute to a more effective resistance against the cultural assimilation of dominant institutions. But purist attitudes towards the languages being learned are unlikely to encourage participation of British-born teenagers whose linguistic repertoires reflect their complex and changing patterns of ethnic affiliation. It is important for us to be aware of the changes in organisation and objectives of the organisers of mother tongue provision in subsequent generations, and in different settings where minority associational life may differ considerably.

It is useful to introduce here a more sociolinguistic perspective on the institutional role of mother tongue schools or classes. Even where it is possible to find similar patterns of language use in different linguistic minorities in the same city, or in the same linguistic minority in different cities, the impact of mother tongue teaching provision on language retention will depend on a range of other factors supporting the use of the mother tongue. One of these factors involves the subjective and objective relationship between the language of the home and the language taught.

Although the language of literacy or the spoken standard may be linguistically quite distant from the local spoken variety, if it has an important social value or utility for the learners it will be incorporated in their linguistic repertoires. Where learners have the opportunity to use the standard variety, oral skills in that variety may then develop, and where they have access to written texts or materials, literacy skills may develop in support of rather than in conflict with the oral vernacular. Sometimes the linguistic distance between the spoken and standard varieties is also legitimized socially by official institutions — with, for example, the taught variety acquiring higher status in the school system. However, some researchers suggest that the learners' subjective assessment of the relative worth of these varieties in such circumstances is bound to influence the objective steps faced by teacher and learner in transferring from one to the other.

Some commentators have made a point of distinguishing the vernacular and the taught mother tongue, even when they are linguistically similar, to express the dangers of parents or teachers adopting 'a teaching mode'. The vernacular, they argue, can only spread by practical use:

> It is learned from people who mean what they say and say what they mean to the person they address in the context of everyday life. This is not so in taught language. (Illich, 1981, p. 36)

> Language exempt from rational tutorship is a different kind of social phenomenon from language that is purposefully taught. Where untutored language is the predominant marker of a shared world, a sense of power within the group exists, and this sense cannot be duplicated by language that is delivered. (Illich, 1981, p. 33)

Language contact in multilingual England does not only involve contact between English and the other languages of England. The experience of migration forces the reorganisation of social networks, and the experience of the bilingual children of migrants involves social networks crossing subcultural or class boundaries within and between linguistic minorities. A heightened awareness of cultural and linguistic boundaries and of their role in signalling social distance may stimulate such attempts by organisers and teachers in mother tongue schools and by parents in the home to develop informal language policies.

This perspective reinforces the view not only that mother tongue teaching may have little impact, but that vernacular speech may lose its essential power if there is an attempt formally to teach it. This point introduces the key distinction which will be elaborated in the next chapter, between informal acquisition of the spoken vernacular, and formal acquisition of the standard language of literacy.

Many mother tongue schools are consciously or unconsciously aiming to impose a standard spoken variety through the teaching of literacy. Where the vernacular is well established, or English is the medium of instruction, success is likely to be limited. Among pupils with restricted opportunities to use their vernacular, and possibly greater opportunity to use another variety, or among pupils whose families are upwardly aspiring, teaching of or through the standard variety may have greater success. A speaker's attitude towards the different languages or varieties in his or her potential repertoire is a major factor influencing the languages learned, used and preferred. These attitudes of bilinguals are of course influenced by how they perceive other people's attitudes towards their own languages, as well as the different meanings their language varieties come to have in daily interaction. So, to understand the likely impact of the teaching of any particular mother tongue, it is necessary to understand the symbolic value of the activities related to the teaching, and the symbolic value of the language variety taught.

7
Bilingualism and education

Language and adults

The previous chapters have presented details of the varied patterns of language use and mother tongue teaching in a range of linguistic minorities in three cities in England. They provide the necessary context for the following chapters of the book, which present and discuss the findings of two surveys of linguistic diversity among pupils in LEA schools. The findings of these school-based surveys complement the data presented in Chapter 6 on pupils attending mother tongue classes organised mainly by minority organisations. Without an understanding of the ways in which social and economic factors influence patterns of language use within the different linguistic minorities, of the kind laid out in the first part of the book, it would be more difficult to draw out the educational implications of the data collected within the school context.

The aim of this chapter is to initiate discussion of the educational implications of societal bilingualism. It focusses partly on the findings already presented, in an effort to provide the basis for an assessment of the data which is presented in Chapters 8 and 9. Moving on from the issues of adult language use and the teaching of the mother tongue, the chapter discusses some aspects of language education for adults, and the issues raised by the language socialisation of their children. Then, from the perspective of pupils' experience in the home and in the local community, we consider the role of the LEA school system, especially the implicit and explicit language education policies which affect both bilingual and monolingual pupils.

Throughout this book we use the term 'education' in its broadest sense, and distinguish it from the narrower concept of 'schooling'. We have already drawn attention in Chapter 6 to the existence of two parallel school systems: the 'official' LEA school system and the 'unofficial' school system run by linguistic minority organisations. The processes of learning which go on throughout life, and the data from the Adult Language Use Survey presented in Chapters 2 and 5, point to the importance of the relationship between the informal language acquisition process of the home and the more formal or guided language learning offered in LEA and community-run schools.

Many adult migrants found their formal language learning in their country of origin of little immediate help in coping with daily activities or finding employment on arrival in England. For some, however, schooling in the country of origin had provided access to literacy in their first language, and therefore access to information and literature obtainable in that language in England. For some, schooling overseas had also provided certain experience of learning English. Most fundamental of all, however, their general experience of education in the country of origin influenced many adults' attitudes to formal education. Their notion of a formal school system for children is likely to have affected their own belief in their ability to learn another language whether informally or formally, and also their perceptions of the role of the school system in England. Speaking of the particular contribution of the bilingual teacher, Majid writes:

> The bilingual teacher can use her/his understanding of the students' culture to minimise the difficulties of this transition, specifically to reassure and encourage students who because of their age, family situation, perhaps lack of formal education, feel little confidence in their ability to gain a new language. Take, for example, the case of a middle-aged Bangladeshi woman with three or four children who comes from a small village and speaks a dialect of Bengali. She does not see the importance of going out or of learning English 'at my age'. (Majid, 1984, p. 32)

Many newly-arrived migrants had little opportunity to learn another language in supportive, friendly surroundings. Many were preoccupied with earning a living, and some worked almost exclusively with their own co-lingual countrymen or countrywomen, using the minority language at work as well as at home. Among those who could have found the time to attend classes, there were many who did not have the confidence, or did not consider that formal English language classes were appropriate for adults. Both of these feelings were particularly likely among those members of linguistic minorities who had become aware of the low status of their vernacular, or of their lack of literacy (Majid, 1983). It was many of these parents who were particularly concerned to concentrate their children's language learning efforts on English only, perhaps not realising how learning English exclusively would be likely to decrease the children's interest in their family's mother tongue. This partly explains why many parents became interested in formal mother tongue teaching for their children only after a period of some years in England, except in the cases where mother tongue teaching was closely associated with religious instruction, as for example among Muslim Panjabi or Gujerati speakers, or with the preservation of a 'true' history and culture of a lost homeland, for example among Polish and Ukrainian speakers (Saifullah Khan, 1977a; Elliot, 1981).

For some parents the main motivation for their interest in mother tongue teaching was to ensure that they or their relatives back home could communicate with their children. For others it was often anxiety that their children would lose their culture and religion, an opportunity for social mobility, or wider economic opportunities in the future. But the organisation and development of mother tongue classes and schools by migrant adults should not be interpreted solely as an expression of the value of maintaining the language, culture and, at times, religion of the country of origin. Community-run schooling often also reflects a disillusionment developing from a perceived rejection by the majority, and a dissatisfaction with the values and attitudes promoted in the LEA school system. In this respect the mother tongue classes come closer in function to the 'black' supplementary schools set up by Afro-Caribbean minority organisations in England.

This last point reminds us of the reactive dimension of social and linguistic change among linguistic minorities. In England these minorities now include a large number of speakers educated fully in England, with only a small, and probably decreasing, proportion of monolingual speakers of languages other than English, for example, older women not working outside the home. The size and the detailed composition of the bilingual population in England is certain to change considerably, the main factors likely to affect the development of bilingualism being general economic and social processes. For example, economic exclusion and severe unemployment encourage the development of ethnic niches in local economies. The Chinese restaurant trade may prosper or decline in the longer term, but while the service exists it offers an economic opportunity to children with the appropriate linguistic skills, for example to serve customers, or deal with wholesalers. Similarly the increase in self-employment and small retail businesses in some cities of England may encourage the young to use or learn their mother tongue; while helping in the shop they will hear or use the language with many of the customers. Bradford is an example of such a place: the decline of the textile industry there has led to increasing unemployment among older migrants, and increasing activity in the ethnic economy among the younger bilingual men. In addition in certain local economies unemployment among men may lead to the increased employment of women, who thereby alter the traditional role relations in the family, and the traditional assumptions about which members of the family should learn languages of wider communication.

The impact of a changing economy is closely related to another feature of contemporary social change: the extent of institutional racism and the increase in overt social discrimination and physical assaults. The contemporary 'race' relations situation leads to considerable psychological and economic insecurity for large numbers of bilingual adults. This is especially the case for those labelled by the dominant society as 'black', who are subject to the increasingly restrictive immigration and nationality legislation, and are the object of economic and cultural exclusion by majority institutions. So far, however, language use has not played a prominent part in public discussion of the ethnic conflicts emerging in England. The use of particular languages in particular situations may express personal allegiance to a particular ethnic category, but in everyday life bilingual and bidialectal speakers perceive that the use of their mother tongue is acceptable only with specific interlocutors or in specific settings. In other words, there is an accommodation to the prevailing norms of social interaction in many public and official situations.

For members of minorities or indigenous subcultures, linguistic and cultural allegiance is influenced by the perceived reaction of the dominant majority group to one's own personal and collective definition of self. Membership of a group at any one time may be as much a product of the feeling or experience of common imposed disadvantage, as a product of personal socialisation. Degree of allegiance to a particular class, ethnic or linguistic category may not correlate very closely with the level of the relevant social or linguistic skills. For example, many of the older migrant generation had little choice: even if they had access to dominant institutions and English speakers, they did not have the opportunities to learn the language and the social skills necessary for participation in certain spheres of activity. However, their offspring, some of whom may have apparently 'chosen' to lose their mother tongue in the late primary or early secondary school years, often begin to revalue it for new reasons. Among some South Asian youth there are also signs of the development of Hindi-Urdu as a lingua franca instead of, or in addition to, a home language like Panjabi or Gujerati. For some this may have been stimulated by the video revolution which has brought Indian Hindi-Urdu medium films into the home. For others it is a skill specifically cultivated for communication with other South Asian youth of different language backgrounds. Although all the peer group may also speak English, at certain times and in certain settings there may be a felt need to express affiliation with certain categories of people or their interests.

The very different needs of individual bilingual adults in England mean that it is hard to draw out from our data specific implications for social and educational policies. The ALUS findings in Chapter 5 remind us that it is hazardous to generalise even within one linguistic minority, as there are important differences between the sexes and between the various socio-economic categories, as well as between co-linguals in different cities. The previous comments, however, suggest a possible range of options for adult education and training in the future. As the number of adults needing basic training in English decreases, the number needing more advanced and specialised English will increase. Similarly, now that the need for translators and interpreters is beginning to be recognised, there is a greater appreciation of the professional training needed for those with appropriate linguistic skills.

It is possible to develop strategies for community interpreting within an advanced ESL group, which would prepare interested students for the kind of work that is involved in interpreting . . . In this way skills can be developed which could lead to the trainee joining a community interpreters training course and obtaining work in a demanding and vital job area. (Baynham, 1984, p. 15)

In both cases, however, language training can all too easily be expected to solve broader social, communicative or institutional inequalities. Monolingual English-speaking people in daily contact with the learner of English do not always recognise that it is often their English cultural assumptions and expectations which cause problems in communication (UNESCO, 1982). In industrial language training there has been a gradual realisation of the need for management as well as workforce training. Cross-cultural communication training has been applied to 'gate-keeper' situations, with the intention of reducing or eliminating institutional and often unintentional racism (Gumperz, 1983).

Our initial aim was to provide communication skills for people who spoke little English. But once we participated in the environment, we immediately recognised that a basic mastery of linguistic forms in English is not sufficient to make communication effective. We also realised that native speakers of English need training as well . . . Training, we argue, can help members of the majority group to examine the differences in their evaluation of what happened in an interaction, to monitor their own language behaviour, to become aware of how the differences occur and consider alternative strategies. (Furnborough, Jupp, Munns, Roberts, 1982, p. 248)

There are now signs that training schemes for community interpretation services too will include training for those in the majority population, like police, magistrates or doctors, who may make use of such services.

It is surprising that there has so far been very little discussion about teaching English to adults through their mother tongue. Attention has focussed almost exclusively on the acquisition of skills in English as a second language, perhaps because teaching methods were developed almost entirely by monolingual English speakers. They had rarely themselves experienced or understood how the development of oral and literacy skills in the learner's mother tongue could help acquisition of the equivalent English language skills. Bilingual methods of teaching have not been used mainly for two reasons: first, so-called direct methods of language teaching do not require that teachers should be fluent in their pupils' first language. Secondly, when English as a second language methods developed in Britain in the 1960s there was no major recruitment of bilingual teachers, partly because the methods were best suited to monolingual English-speaking teachers and partly because of underlying assimilationist and monolingual perspectives on language learning (Saifullah Khan, 1983). There are clearly both pedagogic and political reasons for recruiting more bilingual teachers into ESL for adults (Sayer and Bajpai, 1984) and in Industrial Language Training. Dittmar has suggested that the conditions that must be fulfilled if 'language instruction of immigrant workers is to be effective' are socio-political and linguistic:

socio-political in that the successful teaching of a language depends on a social and a political framework that juridically fosters the learning of a foreign language and positively influences approaches to learning; linguistic in that the subject's unguided linguistic level must be amply known in order for judicious and effective instruction to be formulated. (Dittmar, 1982, p. 151)

While there exist very few classes for the formal teaching of the mother tongue to adults, one important development is in the teaching of occupational skills through the medium of the mother tongue, with parallel support in English.

> It is not only in teaching language that the bilingual teacher has advantages. For adults learning in this country one of the main hindrances of speaking English as a second language is that by and large you are forced to learn English before you can learn anything else. Linked skills (teaching English alongside skills teaching) has challenged this, and bilingual teachers of subjects other than English are ideally placed to overcome this problem. (Henry, 1984, p. 22)

And classes set up primarily for younger learners sometimes also attract adults – in some cases from monolingual English backgrounds as well as from bilingual backgrounds.

These classes for adult English monolinguals tend to be in the higher-status European languages, but there is also an increasing number attracted to Hindi-Urdu or Panjabi classes. They are often professionals such as social workers, youth workers, teachers or police who work with people from one of the South Asian linguistic minorities (Russell (ed.), 1982).

The language skills of adults and their opportunities to use or learn other languages are likely to influence not only their own views about language learning, but also their expectations of language use among younger family members. Other factors also affect their adoption of 'language policies' in the home. Some refugee populations, and others who settled in comparatively small numbers in different parts of the country, understood from their early days in England that keeping their culture and language alive involved a deliberate effort to use the language at home, and the teaching of the language in community-run schools. Many migrants from bilingual backgrounds coming into larger settlements may have assumed that their children would become bilingual without special effort on their part. It was only after many parents experienced a decrease in their children's skills or interest in using the mother tongue that they made systematic arrangements for the teaching of the language to their offspring.

An increasing awareness of the overwhelming dominance of English in England has often been accompanied by an increasing personal insecurity. For some South Asian and Chinese families, for example the loss of the child's mother tongue may reinforce parental fears that the wider society is undermining their traditional values and culture. For most South European migrants there are more possibilities for regular travel to and from the country of origin, which may help to strengthen their cultural and linguistic resources. Whatever the actual material options available to members of linguistic minorities, it is their perception of their situation that will influence their sense of belonging. Their assessment of the value of retaining and developing their mother tongue and cultural skills is often constrained by the limited information available to them (see p. 306) and the negative treatment they have often experienced in British society. While some migrants were ready in their early years of settlement to accept often severe social and psychological costs for the sake of economic security and of schooling for their children, few of their British-born offspring will have the same reactions. It is in fact among the children and grandchildren (and even great-grandchildren, if the American experience teaches us anything) that we are likely to see language become a more salient marker of ethnic identity and a focus for collective organisation.

Bilingualism and socialisation

Patterns of language use are not only products of the economic and social stratification in our society, but also help to reproduce them. At the end of Chapter 6 we discussed the role of language in the transmission of culture, and several useful perspectives for an assessment of the long-term impact of mother tongue teaching organised by linguistic minorities.

The role of language in the perpetuation of social inequality between different social classes has been a major focus of educational debate over the last few decades in England. The effects of class-related dialects or modes of communication have been compared (Trudgill, 1975; Bernstein, 1971). Some writers have focussed on the way in which the schools operated traditionally almost entirely through a middle-class standard dialect. This imposed a disadvantage on those pupils who were not already conversant with this variety, related underlying values and discourse strategies (Trudgill, 1975; Lawton, 1968). Others have focussed on the power of the earlier socialisation of children, and the effects on their subsequent experience of transition to new modes of communication and social relations (Bernstein, 1971; Wells, 1982).

Both perspectives are important in our attempt to understand the educational experience of bilingual children in English society. Research into the language education of minority pupils in England needs to be placed firmly in this tradition of enquiry, given the socio-economically and politically subordinate status of the newer minorities in Britain. However, before we can begin to make the necessary connections, we have to ask a series of questions about the similarities and differences between the experience of monolingual English-speaking working-class pupils and that of pupils of linguistic minorities in England. We need to consider the detailed mechanisms which control the distribution of cultural and linguistic resources. We also need a clearer understanding of children's differential experiences of schooling and of its relationship with other processes of socialisation. In particular we need to know if there are differences according to whether children are middle- or working-class, monolingual or bilingual.

The dominance of Southern British Standard English is maintained through a range of institutions, such as the media and the school system. The school is the prime example of an environment where the dominant English subculture works against the interests of both bidialectal and bilingual pupils. Within school and in the wider society, however, the assimilationist and racist perspective intervenes to separate the 'white' indigenous working class from their bilingual peers, especially those defined as 'black'.

The position of 'white' bilingual pupils may throw some light on the process, and also focus our attention on the fundamental issues at stake. Even though their 'invisibility' (in terms of 'race' as defined by colour) may shield them from the negative attitudes and stereotyping accorded to pupils of Afro-Caribbean or South Asian origin by some of their teachers, it seems that sometimes they have to conceal their bilingualism. This is evidence of another, equally insidious, kind of racism.

The next section will deal with the past and present impact of the school, and of school language policies, on pupils from linguistic minority backgrounds. But the primary socialisation of the child in the home and the locality will first be considered, to help us understand the patterns of language use already established before formal schooling begins. The linguistic minorities studied in our research covered a great range of family structures, with many non-culturally specific differences deriving from such considerations as whether migrant families were reunited or not. An understanding of the influence of different family structures on the language socialisation of the child is of fundamental importance, but it must be remembered that different family composition may be as much a reflection of economic and housing problems as of immigration laws and patterns of migration.

More detailed research is necessary to understand the various situations in which informal language learning takes place, and its impact on the overall socialisation of the child. However, basic knowledge about traditional processes of socialisation, and an appreciation of the perceived threat felt by many minority parents, would suggest that the primary linguistic socialisation of the home is a powerful force and needs to be assigned even more importance by educationalists. Different patterns of language socialisation have a great influence on how children 'succeed in school'. Speaking of one of the three communities she studied in Piedmont, South Carolina, Brice Heath, for example, explains:

> parents believe that when their children go to school, they will continue to learn the same way they know how – by watching, listening and trying. The school for the children, however, is a sudden flood of discontinuities in the ways people talk, the values they hold, and the consistency with which the rewards go to some and not to others. (Brice Heath, 1983, p. 348)

Possibly one of the most important factors influencing the transition from home to school is not simply how much English is known, but how it is integrated into existing patterns of social relations, in terms of meanings associated with literacy:

> The different types of uses of reading and writing of Roadville and Trackton have prepared the children in different ways for negotiating the meaning of the printed word and the production of a written text. (Brice Heath, 1983, p. 348)

Like many English working-class children, many bilingual children do not begin to integrate the English middle-class culture of the school into their cultural and linguistic repertoire before they start school. But unlike many English working-class children, bilingual children may have already mastered the communicative skills associated with switching languages or language varieties according to context and audience (Wiles, 1984; Miller, 1983).

So it is not enough just to say that bilingual children learn different languages. We must also realise that they come to perceive and use the languages in different ways, and that this gives their languages different meanings in their eyes. And the way children come to use them is not just a product of the linguistic skills of family members or the norms set by their elders, but of how their local network of social relationships is structured. The networks within which children interact need to be better known before we can understand fully their patterns of use – why they use a language or variety and the appropriate way of doing so.

In his work on the early language development of children from monolingual English families Wells argues against the existence of a simple relationship between oral language development, social class and subsequent attainment. He found that the quality of a child's conversational experience was more important than social class in accounting for differential success in language development. In addition, among the children he studied (who were all monolingual) literacy was an important predictor of educational attainment at the age of seven (Wells, 1982).

In most minority families, as in indigenous English families, every member of the family has at least a slightly different language history, linked to an individual history and pattern of social interaction. But in the case of many minority families, especially those who still have parents of the migrant generation, differences in language use between members of the same family may be particularly dramatic. This explains the wide range of variations and the non-reciprocal pattern of language use referred to in Chapter 5. The ALUS questionnaire looked at literacy-related activities between adults and children in the first language, but more detailed exploration of these interactive contributions to language learning among bilingual children would be useful.

The influence of variations in children's social networks will be better understood if we realise that they entail potential communication problems between the different members of the family, within and between generations, and that these problems may in turn exacerbate other structural tensions produced by the migration process. For example, some monolingual wives who have joined their now English-speaking husbands after several years of separation may have had little opportunity to learn English, especially if they have never taken up employment (Wilson, 1978). This is also the case when, having taken up employment, they work alongside their own countrywomen (Anthias, 1983; Merdol, 1982). These wives may be mothers who know little English, and who feel increasingly isolated from their own children, unable to understand their talk or their interests, and afraid that they cannot fulfil their maternal role successfully.

More generally, adult migrants often face a reorganisation in the traditional hierarchy of power relations within their family or kin groupings. At a time when they are coping with the economic and social adjustments to life in Britain, they may need to utilise their children as English-speaking intermediaries when dealing with the medical, social and employment services. This may involve the undermining of the traditional hierarchy within the family, which itself is likely to influence patterns of language use. This may also be the case when wives take up employment outside the home, especially in an English-speaking environment which alters the economic relationship with the husband (Saifullah Khan, 1979a). We need to remember that often adults' employment history influences their knowledge of the English language, so that differential access to economic activity often produces an unequal distribution among family members of linguistic resources, and of knowledge about the wider society.

If these tensions correspond to an existing association of English with a competitive or threatening 'outside', the use of English can develop negative associations. Then both parents and children alike may develop an unconscious resistance to acquiring the language. However, for many children the impact of the mass media and the importance of local peers become increasingly powerful, and they learn more or less successfully to deal with the conflicting messages received from the socialisation of the home, of the media and of majority as well as minority peers. Of course, in those families where English is integrated into their own conceptual system – as a desired language for communication outside the family, or an acceptable language for use with certain family members and friends in certain circumstances and for certain topics – the use of English is likely to have a different and more positive meaning.

Both working-class English monolingual children and bilingual children may therefore face a disjunction between the value attributed to a language variety at home and the value it is given at school. The transition from the culture of the home to the culture of the school is not just an enforced shift in patterns of language use, it involves adjusting to a new set of social relations and values. Those values deemed until then by the child to be natural and legitimate are questioned and, with the other mechanisms also supporting the dominant language beyond the school, the home language may come to be devalued in the mind of the pupil.

> What is central to the transition is a change in patterns of social interaction, and since this interaction is quite largely mediated through language, particularly in the school setting, the ease with which the transition is made will depend to a large extent on the child's ability to communicate effectively through language. (Wells, 1981, p. 143)

Few monolingual working-class English children or their bilingual peers acquire the cultural capital needed for 'success' as defined by the school system. This is true even for many who would perceive themselves as 'middle-class'. The cultural and linguistic rift between school and home restricts the teachers' and the schools' ability to utilise or foster the social and linguistic skills often already acquired by bilingual and bidialectal children.

Later sections of this chapter will outline the arguments for a language education policy in schools which would take account of both languages, arguments which rest upon contemporary views about language education and education for a multicultural society. Many of these ideas are based on the knowledge of the linguistic and sociopsychological processes relating to the individual's experience of growing up with two or more languages.

It is hoped that our concentration on language use and mother tongue teaching in local populations in the first half of this book will have impressed upon the reader the force of wider social processes in the language acquisition of bilingual pupils. It is only when we appreciate the cumulative effect of the individual experiences (of bilingual pupils, of monolingual teachers, of parents, professionals and policy-makers) that we can begin to recognise the power of institutions to influence different futures for different sections of the population. When we try to conceptualise the language experience of children in the context of their patterns of social relations with adults, peers and institutions, then we realise that it is not just the differential impact of different processes of socialisation and education which have to be accounted for. We need to analyse the structural relationships between these processes and how children subjectively experience them. Halliday and Bernstein express this same point in different ways:

> Although each child's language learning environment is unique, he also shares certain common features with other children of a common social background; not merely in the superficial sense that the material environments may well be alike — in fact they may not — but in the deeper sense that the forms of social relations and the role systems surrounding him have their effect on the kind of choices in meaning which will be highlighted and given prominence in different types of situations. (Halliday, 1978, p. 25)

> the different focussing of experience . . . creates a major problem of educability only where the school produces discontinuity between its symbolic orders and those of the child. (Bernstein, 1971, p. 183)

Language and education policies for schools

In attempting to describe the English Local Education Authority response to the linguistic needs of pupils with languages other than English, it is important to remember the high degree of organisational and curricular autonomy enjoyed by individual LEAs, schools and classroom teachers, and the relatively limited role of the central government and its agencies in this field. There are Her Majesty's Inspectorate (HMI) reports and DES circulars from time to time, describing trends and recommending broad lines of action. But, as in other areas of the curriculum, there is little actual direction from central to local government, even about appropriate patterns of institutional arrangement. The major exception to this was the guidance given by the DES (DES, 1965) over 'dispersal' of immigrant children, so that no school would have more than about a third of non-English-speaking pupils. This policy was evolved rather hurriedly in response to the stated anxieties of some majority parents in England about their own children's general educational progress in schools where there were many 'immigrant children', as they were called at that time. However, the DES guidance was expressed in terms of what was considered desirable for effective English language learning, and it resulted in the 'busing' policies adopted by Ealing and various other LEAs, which always involved the minority children being transported out of their home areas, rather than other children being brought into the inner city schools.

> In order to maintain the standards of education in schools attended by large numbers of immigrant children with language difficulties, special arrangements must be made to teach them English. . . . This will often mean special classes . . . for at least part of the day, although from the beginning they should join as far as possible in the normal social life of the school. . . . Such arrangements can more easily be made, and the integration of the immigrants more easily achieved, if the proportion of the immigrant children in a school is not allowed to rise too high. The Circular 7/65 suggests that about one third of immigrant children is the maximum that is normally acceptable in a school if social strains are to be avoided and educational standards maintained. Local Education Authorities are advised to arrange for the dispersal of immigrant children over a greater number of schools in order to avoid undue concentration in any particular school. (DES, 1965)

It should be noted that many authorities, including Inner London and Birmingham, firmly resisted the suggested dispersal policies, and continued with alternative arrangements of their own, based on reception centres and classes, and on peripatetic teaching services.

As far as materials and methodology were concerned, the Schools Council was the main agency involved in the development and dissemination of 'good practice' in the language education of 'immigrant children'. The Council was a body set up in 1964 financed mostly by the LEAs, and controlled mainly by them and by teachers' union representatives until its dissolution twenty years later.

This pattern means that, although it is possible to detect broad lines of development, and even 'phases', in the policies in operation in different areas over a period of twenty years or so, it has to be remembered that in each period the arrangements and practices of these different phases as set out below are likely to have existed at the same time in different areas. The three broad stages, however, can be characterised as follows.

The first stage lasted through the 1960s in most parts of the country. The emphasis was on 'Teaching English to Immigrants', seen as an activity basically separate from other educational activities, involving the creation of separate institutional arrangements in the form of 'induction' or 'language' centres, or in some cases 'reception' or 'withdrawal' classes within ordinary schools, where at least the initial stages of learning English were undertaken. The teaching was done in groups which were as far as possible homogeneous in terms of their level of English, and which consisted only of 'non-English-speakers'. The children in the withdrawal classes were able to spend part of their time in ordinary classes, interacting with English speakers inside and outside the classroom.

Associations of Teachers of English to Pupils from Overseas (ATEPOs) were founded in various parts of the country from the early 1960s onwards, and in 1967 came together in a National Federation of ATEPOs – the acronym then reinterpreted to stand for 'Association for the Education of Pupils from Overseas', but publishing a journal from 1967 to 1971 still under the title 'English for Immigrants' – the same title as the earlier government pamphlet (Ministry of Education, 1963). The influential book *Teaching English to Immigrants* (Derrick, 1966) was published in 1966, and formed the basis for the Schools Council Project in 'English for Immigrant Children' – based at the University of Leeds from 1966 to 1971. The SCOPE project developed its Stage 1 materials for use above all in language centres and in withdrawal classes. These materials were adapted to the British urban 'multi-racial' context, and to the relatively child-centred British primary tradition, but were essentially based on the dominant English as a Foreign Language model of the time – an audio-lingual, structuralist, 'direct method' approach. At best this simply did not take account of the mother tongues of the learners, and in its crudest manifestations involved the active discouragement of languages other than English, certainly in the classroom, probably in the school as a whole, and possibly even in the home.

The use of English as both medium and target language is explicable in terms of the background and training of most of the teachers re-cruited to teach English as a Second Language (TESL) in England. Although dedicated to the interests as they perceived them of the pupils in their charge, and in some cases coming to this work from a background in teaching overseas, the vast majority of TESL teachers were themselves monolingual in English, with little or no knowledge of their pupils' home languages. They therefore had little choice but to operate entirely through English. In addition, they found backing for such an approach in the writings of language teaching theorists who emphasised the overriding importance of using the target language to the maximum extent possible in the classroom, preferably exclusively. The predominantly assimilationist attitudes which still governed the special arrangements made at this time for 'the education of immigrant children' reinforced these attitudes.

The second stage in the evolution of language education policies dates from the late 1960s and early 1970s, by which time the children were beginning to be referred to as 'ethnic minority' pupils, rather than 'immigrants', since more and more were in fact British-born. The Schools Council's SCOPE Stage 2 materials, piloted about this time and published in 1972, were very different in form and in their pedagogical basis from the Stage 1 materials. Most importantly, they were topically based and designed for use in linguistically heterogeneous groups, in fact for use in ordinary mainstream classes not exclusively made up of children from homes where languages other than English were spoken. It was assumed now that such children would be learning alongside children from families of Afro-Caribbean origin and from English working-class backgrounds. Both of these groups of children also spoke varieties of English which differed from the Standard English which was still the only approved language for 'serious' educational purposes. Minority pupils then were increasingly to be found in the mainstream of language education as it was conceived in those days. This makes it appropriate, after a brief diversion into the question of the special response to Afro-

Caribbean children's linguistic needs, to say something about the position at this period of children who had English as a mother tongue.

A separate Schools Council Project on 'English for West Indian Children' had been set up in Birmingham in 1967, first of all to look into the specific linguistic characteristics of such children, and then to provide appropriate learning materials. This project concluded at a fairly early stage of its work that there was very little evidence that the formal linguistic differences between the West Indian English used at that time by West Indian children in Britain, and the English of their local peers, had very much effect on the learning processes of the children concerned. Apart from a few lexical and semantic differences, the obvious contrasts seemed to be essentially in a small set of morphological markers occurring quite frequently in spoken English and less frequently in written English (Schools Council, 1970).

The materials which the Project produced, under the title 'Concept 7-9: a course in Language and Reasoning', included a 'Dialect Kit' specifically for children of West Indian origin. This kit was designed to help pupils relate their West Indian English to written Standard English, without devaluing the spoken varieties. However, most of the materials were intended to stimulate the development of effective communication strategies, based around such functions as 'classification' and 'similarity and difference'. In the pilot versions, and in the illustrative content of the published materials, it was made clear that such materials were as appropriate for speakers of other languages, and for native English speakers, as they were for children of West Indian origin. In spite of the explicit denial of such a position, there was a suggestion of an underlying 'language deficit' model in some of the Concept 7-9 materials, with echoes of the Bereiter and Engelmann approach to the linguistic education of 'disadvantaged' black children in the USA (Bereiter and Engelmann, 1966).

Around the same time the sociologist Basil Bernstein and his associates were investigating the inter-relationship of social class and language. Contrary to the intention, certainly of Bernstein himself, some of this work was being interpreted with reference to working-class English-speaking children as suggesting that many children were arriving at school with inadequate linguistic resources for learning purposes, and thus were failing in school because of these 'deficits'. Bernstein's work was in fact developed from the premise that educational failure – or 'underachievement', as it has come to be referred to in relation to children of West Indian origin in Britain (Rampton Committee, 1981) – is a social problem rather than a linguistic one. His sociological approach focussed on an important linguistic aspect, referred to by Halliday in the following terms:

> the subcultural environment as this is embodied in and transmitted through the language. In other words, the 'language difference' may be significant, but if so it is a difference of function rather than of form. (Halliday, 1978, p. 24)

The explanation for socially related variation in language in terms of 'difference' rather than 'deficit', associated in the USA with the work of Labov in particular (1966 and 1972), and in Britain with that of Trudgill (1974 and 1975) and of Rosen (1973), was beginning to gain ground by the early 1970s.

The curricular implications of a 'difference' as compared with a 'deficit' model of sociolinguistic variation involved a shift to recognition of the languages and varieties which children brought with them from home to school, rather than the more traditional insistence on Standard English as the only medium appropriate for formal educational purposes. Trudgill's *Accent, Dialect and the School* (1975) sets out this position with reference to children who speak English dialects. Rosen and Burgess's *Languages and Dialects of London School Children* (1980) extends the arguments to stress the common elements in the position of speakers of indigenous and non-indigenous dialects, and of speakers of other languages. It also illustrates persuasively the liberating implications of adopting such a position for the secondary school English curriculum in particular.

In contrast to the USA, in Britain the debate on the role of language in education was conducted almost entirely in terms of class-based 'deprivation' and 'disadvantage' rather than of colour. The particular situation of children of South Asian and other non-English-speaking backgrounds in Britain was still generally seen as a special case, fortunately not considered in the context of linguistic deprivation at all.

The Bullock Report, published in 1975 and deriving from a commission of enquiry whose original terms of reference related to a supposed decline in standards of literacy attained by school pupils, encouraged the movement towards schools developing their own explicit policies on 'language across the curriculum'. These policies were designed to cover issues to do with the medium of learning, rather than the content, and were intended to be the concern not only of English language and reading specialists, but also of teachers of all other subjects. Bullock also had a special chapter on the needs of

'Children From Families of Overseas Origin', which included the now much-quoted assertion that

> No child should be expected to cast off the language and culture of the home as he crosses the school threshold, nor to live and act as though school and home represent two totally separate and different cultures which have to be kept firmly apart. (DES, 1975, p. 286)

This kind of statement also reflected the evolving attitudes to 'multicultural education' in general. In these there was an increasing realisation that it was necessary for the schools to make some adaptations towards their new intakes, rather than expecting the changes to come entirely from the pupils. In the first place, changes in this direction tended to affect such areas of the curriculum as social studies, religious education, history and literature, but they were eventually to begin to permeate the language curriculum too.

The Bullock Report's recommendations, along with the EC 'Mother Tongue' Directive (eventually adopted in 1977, but circulating in draft form by 1976), probably provided the major 'external' stimulus for the transition to the third stage in the evolution of language policy. But of course the pressures from minority parents and organisations beginning to question the more or less exclusive concentration on English were also of vital importance.

A realisation by parents that non-English mother tongues could not simply be expected to develop without some institutional support had led to the growth of mother tongue classes and schools, meeting at first almost entirely outside LEA school hours and on a voluntary basis (Saifullah Khan, 1977a; see also Chapter 6 of this book). Classes in, for example, mosques and gurdwaras, the earlier established Polish Saturday schools, and Welsh language Sunday schools, often associated language teaching quite closely with religious instruction. As indicated in Chapter 6, the growth of mother tongue teaching was related in part to parents' wishes to keep open the verbal channels of communication between the generations, partly to their wish to combat some of the Western European secular values promoted by LEA schools, as well as to other factors.

Organisations such as the Commission for Racial Equality (CRE) saw LEA educational support for mother tongue teaching as a necessary part of the full recognition for the rights of minorities which they existed to promote. They therefore supported the adoption of the EC Directive (EC, 1977) whose Article 3 requires member states to 'promote the teaching of the mother tongue and culture of the children of migrant workers'. It was only at a later stage that the DES and the National Union of Teachers gave public recognition to the importance of the mother tongue in the educational process (DES, 1981; NUT, 1982). Institutions of the state system at last began to discuss the desirability of the use of minority languages in certain circumstances alongside English as a medium for learning. There was also initial discussion of their being offered as a target language in which to establish literacy in a second language. They began too to become more widely available as exam subjects at secondary school level, although rarely beyond 'O' level, and some practical experience of curriculum development in this area was beginning to accumulate (NCLE , 1982).

A final strand in the arguments coming together by the early 1980s in favour of greater support for the languages of linguistic minorities from the mainstream education system derives from developments in thinking about modern language teaching. There are at least two elements at work here. First is the continuing belief that diversification of languages offered, away from the existing overwhelming dominance of French in British schools, is desirable simply in terms of any reasonable definition of the country's specific language needs in the modern world (BOTB, 1979). Second is a growing understanding that modern language teaching in schools may do better to focus on the development of a general language learning capacity, and of a positive interest in language and languages among all pupils, than in trying to achieve during the school years anything approaching full native speaker mastery of a single language (Hawkins, 1981).

In this context, the particular languages studied in school become much less important. The existence in the school and in the locality of speakers of a range of different languages becomes an excellent reason for including these languages as part of the basic language curriculum which is put before the pupils, to be built on in later life when specific linguistic needs become more apparent. Of course, these linguistic goals may be shared by pupils with English as a mother tongue as well as by those with other mother tongues (Garson, 1982). The Graded Objectives in Modern Language movement, which aims to make possible public certification of much more limited achievements in modern languages than is represented by GCE 'O' levels, should help to make easier the introduction of some of the minority languages into the mainstream linguistic curriculum (Reid (ed.), 1984). And the draft criteria for the proposed new 16+ exams in modern languages, which put much more emphasis on oral-aural than on written skills, should also assist (Moys, (ed.), 1984).

To sum up, looking over the twenty-year period from the early 1960s to the early 1980s, we can see a three-stage progression. In the first stage the linguistic consequences of post-war migration were seen purely in terms of special separate arrangements to teach English to 'immigrant pupils'. In the intermediate stage the learning of English by such pupils was integrated into the English learning of all pupils, and the teaching of the languages of linguistic minorities was seen in terms of separate 'mother tongue teaching' provided only for those with family connections with the languages. In the present stage the languages brought to school from the homes of minority language pupils are beginning to be made use of alongside English for learning purposes, and are beginning themselves to be made more widely available as targets for learning by all pupils who have been made aware of their potential interest.

Multicultural education and language

Some of the developments in language education policies described in the last section show that interest in the wider implications of bilingualism has developed in England comparatively recently. The exclusive concentration on the acquisition of English in part reflected attitudes in the society relating to 'visible' ethnic minorities in general, and to bilingual minorities in particular. It also represented a short-term pragmatic response to the immediate needs of non-English speakers, rather than a longer-term assessment of the overall implications of bilingualism for both bilingual and monolingual individuals and for the country as a whole. As indicated in the last section, the first positive recognition of the importance in school of the home language of children of ethnic minorities arose in fact among teachers of children from families of Afro-Caribbean origin.

This section attempts to link these developments in language education with multicultural education as it developed from the late 1960s onwards. Since then the wide variety of activities and rationales underlying multicultural pedagogy have expanded into a complex mesh which has become the centre of intense debate. The role of mother tongue teaching and the use of minority languages in mainstream schools are clearly central to this debate for those who are genuinely committed to developing education for life, not just in a multicultural, but also in a multilingual society. However, there are a range of different reasons why there have at times been uneasy relations between individuals and associations concerned with these issues.

Although in one sense language is where the multicultural education debate began in the 1960s, the question of mother tongue teaching was not an issue of public debate until the mid-1970s. The initial focus was rather on English as a second language, as the previous section has described. The first notable recognition of the importance of this issue was in the Bullock Report, published in 1975, which asserted the need to adopt 'a positive attitude towards the languages and varieties of "immigrant" pupils':

> Their bilingualism is of great importance to the children and their families. In a linguistically conscious nation in the modern world, we should see it as an asset, as something to be nurtured, and one of the agencies that should nurture it is the school. Certainly the school should adopt a positive attitude to its pupils' bilingualism and wherever possible should help maintain and deepen their knowledge of their mother-tongues. (DES, 1975, p. 294)

Although there was no indication of how this was to be done, this report contributed to the developing debate about education in a multicultural society. When Bullock stressed the importance of home-school continuity in linguistic terms, there were clear parallels with the situation of indigenous working-class dialect speakers and their bilingual peers. Both suffered from the negative attitudes to non-Standard English and to languages other than English which reflected general values in the wider society, for example, in the media and in job recruitment agencies. Similar attitudes were expressed overtly by some teachers, institutionalised in school policies, and perpetuated by parts of the teacher training system.

By the early 1970s the multicultural debate had been focussed on ways of reassessing the policy and practices of the school to reflect the multicultural nature of society. Discussions about curriculum content, racist books, black or Asian studies were central. The discussion about linguistic diversity in the classroom had its origin in the obvious fact that, if the different cultural backgrounds represented in the school were to be equally respected, then this policy must include recognition of the pupils' different languages. For some schools and teachers this was a matter of developing linguistic awareness systematically within the classroom curriculum for all pupils, monolingual and bilingual. In other schools a more superficial recognition of the existence of different languages was all that was attempted, for example in the form of displays of charts and posters. At this early stage in the debate about 'mother tongue' teaching, there was very little knowledge about the substantial amount of existing language teaching organised by the different linguistic minorities in England, and few teachers of geography, history, sciences, maths, or even of 'modern languages' felt that it concerned them. Multicultural education was still seen by most as a matter of specific curriculum content, rather than an 'approach' which should permeate the whole curriculum and life of the school, very much like 'language across the curriculum'. Most of the limited discussion that took place on linguistic aspects of the multicultural curriculum centred around whether teaching minority languages in the secondary school might be divisive, rather than positively supporting cultural and linguistic pluralism.

It is appropriate at this stage to summarise the range of approaches which come under the general umbrella of 'multicultural education'. For convenience they are broken down here into four overlapping levels of commitment to multicultural education which reflect different views about the role of the school system and about the meaning of the term 'education'.

First, multicultural education may simply mean *a minimal recognition of the multicultural and multilingual nature of society and of the school*. Such a position represented a genuine and substantial shift for some from an unrelentingly assimilationist perspective; for others, it was merely an indication of their general liberalism. A second position on multicultural education involves a more fundamental *reassessment of curriculum content and teaching methods*, most often initiated by individual teachers, but sometimes by, for example, NAME (National Association for Multiracial Education) groups or by the staff of an LEA. Some of these attempts did not result in very thoroughgoing changes, since they met considerable resistance or suffered from lack of resources in terms of time and materials. The effect in the end was that many attempts slipped back into something very like the first approach.

A third position involves *incorporating specific provision for minority pupils*, either in association with the kind of activities mentioned in the first position, which meant that multicultural education was perceived to be essentially for pupils of ethnic minority families; or in association with the kind of activities mentioned in the second position, which meant that multicultural education had important contributions for both ethnic majority and ethnic minority pupils. The fourth position involved *supporting initiatives taken outside school*. This was either associated with the first position outlined above, which often meant that there was little commitment to fundamental change within the school system, or a recognition that 'help' could be given to existing initiatives. Sometimes, however, it was associated with the second or third positions, reflecting minimal confidence in the ability of the school alone to make any substantial contribution to improving social relations between pupils and parents of different ethnic and linguistic backgrounds.

The debate about multicultural education has gradually become more emotive and conflict-ridden. This is partly because of the different interpretation based on unclear concepts, unstated assumptions, different philosophies and priorities, and reflecting existing tensions in educational policy-making in England. The term 'multicultural education' refers sometimes to a strategy aimed at an ideal, leading to change in the status quo. This necessarily involves all pupils and all aspects of schooling, so that it should be called schooling for a multicultural society. And sometimes it seems to refer to the kind of teaching which can be implemented to face specific 'problems', supposedly only found in schools in multicultural localities. The distinction is between a stress on the need for fundamental social change, and a limited acknowledgement of the need for adjustment only where there is a multicultural population.

Much of the heat within the debate has arisen from attempts to expose the real motives, or political philosophies, for example assimilationist or liberal or pluralist, underlying so-called multicultural practices. Participants in the debate include teachers who are looking for solutions to immediate classroom problems, as well as researchers who can afford to take a longer-term perspective. Among both categories there is of course the whole range of attitudes, from conservative to radical, and members of ethnic or linguistic minorities themselves also span the full political spectrum. The most damning critique of 'multiculturalism', from two black researchers, argues that multicultural education has helped to foster rather than counter racism (Mullard, 1980; Stone, 1981). Emerging from a racist society, multiculturalism merely legitimises racism, while containing black resistance.

There are also critics and supporters of education for a multicultural society who have very different views of the role of schooling in society. For example, Bullivant sees the school system 'as an institutionalised way of formally transmitting the culture of a society', allowing 'knowledge managers' to control the life-chances of children from particular ethnic groups:

> Multiculturalism, in all its confusion, may be a subtle way of appearing to give members of ethno-cultural groups what they want in

education, while in reality giving them little that will enhance their life chances, because a great deal of multicultural education emphasizes only life styles in a safe, bland and politically neutral panacea. (Bullivant, 1981, p. ix)

Earlier in this chapter we stressed that schooling is only one part of the education process, and that its impact depends as much on power relationships between the school and the local populations as it does on the content of the curriculum and the teaching methods. There are many teachers who believe that schooling is one of the most effective ways of providing equal opportunities for all pupils. There are others who see schooling as a vehicle of social control, reproducing the class structure and the stratification of the labour force for a capitalist economy. Those sharing the latter perspective are primarily concentrating on decreasing inequalities between socio-economic groups, and are suspicious of the individualistic child-centred pedagogies which aim to build upon the cultural and linguistic skills of individual pupils, without reassessing the underlying distribution of power and principles of control underpinning the form and content of pedagogic relationships. There are protagonists of both views who believe in the involvement of the local community in the school. For those with a more political interpretation of schooling, policies go beyond parental involvement in teaching or decision-making to look at ways in which they can help young pupils combat racism. Such strategies include establishing school anti-racist policies and pedagogies which acknowledge and involve interaction with the local community.

Understandably in the English context, anti-racist education has developed from and remained associated with racism on the basis of colour. Considering anti-racist education as a much more effective strategy for education for a multicultural society, many of its proponents forget that racialist beliefs may also focus around language as well as other phenotypical differences.

The mother tongue debate

The mother tongue debate, as it is called in England, has focussed predominantly on questions of how best to support the existing mother tongue teaching organised by linguistic minorities, and on the most appropriate ways to introduce mother tongue teaching into the state school system. In the early days of the debate these two questions were often presented in discussions as a matter of 'either/or'. However, subsequent developments in both community-run provision and in LEA schooling suggest that both contributions will remain relevant for a long time.

The main questions about provision would perhaps be more usefully discussed in terms of the long-term objectives on the one hand, and short-term priorities on the other. Even those who see the eventual objective to be the incorporation of mother tongue teaching in LEA schools — a goal strongly supported by teachers and educationalists actively involved in the debate — are still aware of the present contribution of community-run schools and classes. They accept the likelihood that in some areas and in the smaller, more scattered linguistic minorities this type of provision will remain the only kind of formal teaching. Among the most radical, and also among the most traditional teachers involved in this debate, there are small numbers who argue for no contact at all with the mainstream system. There are, however, probably sizeable numbers of mother tongue teachers and organisers who would like LEA financial support, without ceding control over the content or organisation of their teaching.

The general positions just outlined in fact represent a much wider range of opinions which are formed within a context of restricted options, information and often of suspicion or uncertainty. The schemes set up by many LEAs have involved either a relatively small number of pupils, or relatively few hours per week. Tackling just a tiny part of the potential need, as perceived by organisers of community-run provision, these LEA initiatives are rarely seen by community-run mother tongue organisers as a major threat. However, existing tensions between the school authorities and minority organisations are often exacerbated by LEA-supported development which takes little account of existing expertise in the local populations, or does not involve the participation of experienced community teachers.

There are some other fundamental questions which need to be considered before the very real problems of implementation divert attention away from the wider educational issues involved. What are the educational needs of monolingual children growing up in a multilingual neighbourhood, a multilingual society and a world of increasing international contact? And what is the responsibility of the state towards the educational rights of bilingual children (Skutnabb-Kangas, 1984)?

In the early days of the mother tongue debate in England, the recognition of the educational value of bilingualism for bilinguals focussed on suggestions for teaching the languages as exam subjects at

secondary school, for those pupils who had learned the appropriate
language outside school. It also encompassed support for existing
community initiatives by, for example, reducing rent for teaching
accomodation, or giving small grants for books and materials: but only
very rarely were teachers' salaries paid (see p. 250). Such policies were
grounded on principles developing in multicultural education for recognising and improving the status of the cultures of ethnic minorities
within the school. They were also based on discussions about equal
opportunity, in education to develop the pupils' full range of cultural
and linguistic resources, and in society to recognise the right of minorities to develop their own initiatives.

But as the educational proposals were gradually extended to incorporate linguistic diversity, language across the curriculum and
language awareness for all pupils, the debate also spread to consider
the contribution of linguistic and cultural diversity in a range of other
subjects, such as mathematics and geography. There was a clearer
articulation of the role of language in education, and a greater interest
in the way the acquisition of more than one language might influence
cognitive development and educational achievement as assessed by the
'official' school system. Coupled with the child-centred pedagogy which
prevailed at least in the early years of schooling, it was therefore
natural that the mother tongue debate should extend its focus towards
appropriate provision for primary school children. This focus was concerned with the socio-psychological and linguistic processes experienced
by bilingual children, and valued the potential resources they brought
to a multilingual classroom. By this time, more participants in the
debate argued that the teaching of the languages of linguistic minorities
in secondary schools should be a part of the modern languages curriculum and be open in principle to all pupils – monolingual or bilingual.

The latter half of the 1970s and the early 1980s was a time of
increasing financial cutbacks in education, and of increasingly overt
racism at the national and official level, as well as at the local, and
unofficial level. The strength of educational arguments supporting
societal and individual bilingualism was increasingly acknowledged
among educationalists, and deeply felt by many bilinguals themselves.
Yet no substantial effort was initiated to deal with two of the most
basic underlying requirements for a realistic development of mother
tongue teaching, whether in LEA or community-run schools: teacher
training (Craft and Atkins, 1983) and materials development (Tosi,
1984b). Despite the setting up of the Schools Council Mother Tongue
Project in 1981, and of the RSA pilot scheme for an in-service teacher

training scheme in 1983, these questions are still unresolved. The related problem of examinations has also only begun to be tackled systematically (Broadbent et al., 1983). Had this work been further developed, the organisational and resource implications might not have proved so inhibiting to those already convinced of the case for mother tongue teaching. The non-availability of appropriately trained staff, and the timetabling and financial problems, certainly became the main arguments put forward by some administrators and teachers against the introduction of minority languages into schools. Those whose reactions were influenced by assimilationist and, at times, racist views also saw the mother tongue debate as yet another issue concerned with the special needs of ethnic minority (normally perceived of as 'black') children. A monolingual perspective reinforced the view that 'they' should assimilate, and that the only practicable way to teach English was to ignore skills in the first language.

There were also other potential conflicts among teachers from both minority and majority backgrounds, who supported the view that questions of minority language teaching should be placed firmly within the framework of education for a multicultural society. Restricted finanical resources and lack of political support for multicultural education policies brought into sharp relief different priorities. On the one hand were those of many ethnic minority or mother tongue teachers, impatient with vague commitments and inadequate or no material support for bilingual pupils wishing to retain their first language. On the other hand were those of many other teachers or teacher trainers who were primarily concerned to help monolingual teachers respond to linguistic diversity in the classroom (Saifullah Khan, 1980b). A more recent tension within the teaching profession is also exacerbated by the economic situation and its undermining of job security. The appointment of mother tongue teachers in LEA schools at a time when there are cutbacks of staff, and in some cases particular pressures on modern language departments, has led to resentment among some modern language teachers in secondary schools. Those already having difficulty in defending their own 'minority languages' — Spanish, Italian, Russian, even German — against the further encroachments of French sometimes see the claims of these new 'minority languages' as particularly threatening.

For many educationalists actively campaigning in the mother tongue debate the EC Directive (EC, 1977) on the education of migrant workers' children was considered marginal, if not positively unhelpful. It was significant in that it demonstrated official recognition of the importance of mother tongue provision, although the actual right of an individual child to receive such provision was taken out of the original draft proposal at the insistence of Britain and West Germany. But some foresaw that such a statement from the European Communities was likely simply to exacerbate the existing governmental hostility to interference in the development of national 'policy' or in the functioning of a decentralised system. Others were suspicious of the apparently economic motives underlying the ideal of a free-movement of labour, linked in many European countries with policies on migrant labour and insecure legal status for ethnic minorities (Brook, 1980).

Any assessment of the impact of the Directive needs to consider who it was addressed to, and how it was publicised. The Department of Education and Science and Her Majesty's Inspectorate often stressed the inappropriateness of the Directive for the decentralised education system in England and the settled, no longer migrant workforce, many of whom are British nationals. However, despite the very real legal and institutional differences, the social and educational experience of migrant or refugee families throughout Western Europe has some basic similarities (Castles, 1980).

In the period between promulgation and implementation, the DES held several conferences to discuss the implications of the Directive. And in July 1981 they issued Circular 5/81 to all LEAs giving information about the Directive and about related research, but hardly making any clearer which policy response from LEAs they considered appropriate. They did, however, back up an earlier oral commitment that the terms of the Directive were to apply equally to children of workers from other member states of the EC and from non-EC countries.

Some LEA officers shared resentment at EC involvement, and thought it better to avoid reference to the Directive in their local discussions. But the text or spirit of the Directive was used positively in some situations, to impress upon the audience the level of international backing for educational policies supportive of bilingualism.

This is an appropriate place to stress that, in comparison with other European countries, the mother tongue debate in England was increasingly situated within the discussion about schooling for all children living in a multicultural society. It is our view, however, that this general area of educational debate and the more specific question of developing the skills of bilingual children should also be firmly grounded in its social context, which involves an analysis of factors beyond the school which affect cultural processes in general and language learning in particular. Yet the European Directive talks also about the teaching of the 'culture of the country of origin'. While some of the EC-sponsored pilot projects have done much to foster the notion of intercultural education (CEFISEM-CEFREM, 1982), many other initiatives by the member states have been restricted by the recruitment of mother tongue teachers from the countries of origin. Many of these teachers not only have very prescriptive attitudes to the new varieties of the mother tongue developing among children of migrants, but may also be out of touch with the social reality of their pupils' lives in their parents' country of immigration, and, at times, have almost no contact with the other staff in their schools (Enschede, 1983).

The above outline has shown indirectly that the European discussions about the education of bilingual children of migrant, immigrant or refugee origin is not a discussion about bilingual education as it is understood in many other parts of the world, especially in relation to indigenous minorities. This is all the more remarkable when we remember that some European countries are officially bilingual, for example Belgium and Switzerland, or have sizeable national minorities within or straddling their borders, for example Italy and Sweden. It is not so remarkable, however, if an historical perspective is adopted, which recognises the processes of cultural domination and predominant monolingualism of the state school systems in most member states, for example France and Wales.

In those settings where there is no minority language with large numbers of speakers in a small locality, there are genuine financial and practical problems hindering any kind of bilingual scheme. And when the minority language and its speakers are perceived to have a low status, there are problems of involving monolinguals from the dominant group. However, it is still significant that in many countries of Europe there has been relatively little discussion about the many alternative types of bilingual schemes used in various parts of the world, or about the well-established teacher training and teaching methods which could be adapted to the varied local situations in Europe. In some more centralised education systems the development of standard national principles and practices mitigates against flexible response to local needs. This is one great advantage which England derives from its de-centralised system. But wherever the mother tongue issue is, as its name suggests, linked with minority needs rather than with majority benefits, local initiatives will remain relatively powerless and marginal, without strong support from local authorities and the central government.

The mother tongue debate in England so far has focussed on provision of language teaching in the later stage of secondary school, or on the development of oracy skills in the early primary school. There has been little serious discussion about the use of two languages as mediums of instruction, beyond the very earliest stages of schooling. This, of course, would involve the introduction and development of literacy in both languages throughout the school. A partial exception is found in the development of ILEA's 'World in a City' bilingual materials, designed for optional use in social studies classes by pupils already literate in one of a small range of languages other than English (Wright, 1982). It is only relatively recently that the problem of continuity, linking primary and secondary provision, has been discussed.

This is an important point, because in the earlier days of the debate many researchers looked for parallel situations in other countries to seek 'evidence' of the positive advantages of supporting rather than ignoring a bilingual child's full linguistic repertoire. The cases most often referred to were very instructive, so long as the very different social contexts were recognised. There were only a few projects set up in England which helped to assess different approaches to mother tongue provision or bilingual instruction. The EC Bedfordshire project from 1976 to 1980 produced teaching materials in Italian and Panjabi for children aged 5 to 8, along with strategies for co-operation between teachers of these languages and teachers in mainstream schools (Simons, 1979). The DES MOTET Project in Bradford was a full-scale, unfortunately rather short-term, experimental programme to investigate the linguistic and more general educational effects of teaching carefully selected groups of children in their first year of compulsory schooling the usual infant curriculum, but half through the medium of Panjabi, half through English (MOTET, 1981). The EC/ILEA/Schools Council Mother Tongue Project began work in May 1981 to produce materials, in the first place in Bengali and in Modern Greek, to develop literacy in these languages for primary school children alongside English, and also to develop strategies whereby monolingual English teachers could encourage their bilingual pupils to make use of both languages for learning purposes (Houlton and Willey, 1983). Interestingly, another Schools Council project, set up in 1981 under the title Language in the Multicultural Primary Classroom, while concentrating on developing with teachers strategies for improving the English learning opportunities of pupils in linguistically mixed classes, nevertheless also encourages more use of mother tongue in the classroom.

Prior to the MOTET Project in Bradford, researchers and education-alists in England had turned to research in several other countries to provide an understanding of the most appropriate provision which might be adapted to the English context. Work carried out among Finnish speakers in Sweden related to a migrant language situation in which the minority from a neighbouring country was socially and economically subordinate (Skutnabb-Kangas and Toukomaa, 1977). This research stressed the need to consolidate the mother tongue before acquiring the second language. But the 'language shelter' programmes proposed seemed to many English readers either to be inappropriate (because of the extent of existing bilingualism among pupils in England), impractical (because it proposed programmes extending over a considerable number of years), or divisive (because of the reinforcement of existing social segregation).

The other country which played some part in the discussion in England was the Canadian French-English situation (Official Languages Act of 1969). However, although French was the lower-status language, especially before the 'Francisation' programme in Quebec in the 1970s, both French and English are major world languages. This fact, and the higher socio-economic and motivational resources of the parents of pupils involved in the well-researched immersion programmes, were believed to have contributed toward the excellent results of different types of bilingual programmes (Lambert, 1972). It is surprising, however, that the programmes which immersed pupils from the same home language into full-time schooling in the other target language did not receive more attention in England. Their main aims, besides the learning of a second language, were to change pupils' attitudes towards the target language and its speakers, and to help monolinguals to demystify the phenomenon of bilingualism (Lambert, 1983).

In both the Swedish and the Canadian cases the situation of the non-indigenous 'migrant' or 'non-official' languages did not receive the same attention from education policy-makers. While in Sweden all bilingual children have the right to some home language support within the state school system, it is usually only for a few hours a week, and this provision is not part of a wider school programme promoting societal bilingualism. In 1977 the Ontario government started the 'Heritage Language Programme', providing funds for the teaching of languages of mostly post World War Two immigrants outside regular school hours. In 1979–80 there were approximately 76,000 students enrolled in this programme (Cummins, 1983a). This latter example and the case of Australia are the two with perhaps the closest parallels to the situation in England. The main issues of teacher training, materials development, control and responsibility for the teaching and its content are very similar. Indeed, there are now increasing links between teachers and researchers in these countries. Several of the teacher training schemes in Australia, and the materials and curriculum initiatives, have much to teach practitioners in England. A recent survey of Australian 'ethnic' (= mother tongue) schools has provided a good indication of the minority interest in language retention, and of the institutional constraints against recognising it (Norst, 1982a and b). Australia also has a range of bilingual education schemes (Tosi, 1982b) and teacher training schemes for bilingual teachers working in the state schools (Garner, 1981).

Bilingual education in the USA has quite a different ethos. Whereas many of the European and Australian initiatives are building up from small beginnings, often through overt conflict between minorities and the local or national school system, the American experience has been one of massive financial and legal support from State or even Federal level (once some test cases were won in San Francisco). Despite the development of bilingual schemes, in some cases involving English monolinguals, and covering many areas and languages (Cummins, 1983b), most of the schemes were transitional and assimilationist in concept or outcome. The underlying rationales for the schemes were also established within a compensatory framework, focussing on the acquisition of English, and not giving equal importance to the maintenance of the first language.

These brief references to the situation in other countries, where the different linguistic minorities also have very varied sociolinguistic and socio-economic positions, remind us of the complexity of the issues involved. Not least there are the political and institutional responses of governments and local education authorities which are critical for any appreciation of patterns of language use and learning, both informal and formal. The focus of the debate, and the priorities established by political, legal and financial bodies, greatly influence the commitment to, and content of, schemes set up to support mother tongue acquisition.

An earlier section in this chapter has stressed, however, that certain developments are bound to fail or have minimal effect when there is no central government financing or support for materials and curriculum development or teacher training. In England the first major initiative looking at the development of materials for use by bilingual teachers and support for monolingual teachers working in multilingual classes was only established in 1981 (see p. 299). There is high expectation and some impatience from different minorities for the Schools Council

Project materials. In the meantime, many local groups from different linguistic minorities have continued, or started up new working groups (Russell (ed.), 1982).

The other notable need for the development of mother tongue teaching and implementation of mother tongue schemes is in the field of teacher training. The DES regulations on recognition of overseas teacher qualifications have hindered the appointment of more bilingual teachers. Bilingual teachers teaching other subjects and other professionals interested in mother tongue teaching have had few opportunities open to them, and understandably worry about the status and promotion prospects of this very new area of professional development. There have been a few local initiatives encouraging mother tongue teachers in community-run schools to participate in local in-service training, but no clear route has yet been established to give them access to appropriate initial courses and accreditation (Craft and Atkins, 1983).

The diversity of situations both regionally and internationally suggests that no one model should or could be established at a national level, although support at that level is needed. Besides the question of the relative institutional importance of LEA and community-run provision and the interrelationship between them, each locality manifests its own sociolinguistic situation which will make the alternative types of scheme more or less feasible for specific populations. But it should be remembered that probably somewhere between 375,000 and 500,000 pupils in England and Wales come from homes where English is not the first language, and that 'more than half of these children live in just 12 English LEAs' (DES, 1982).

Where a linguistic minority is concentrated locally, the introduction of a few hours of mother tongue teaching each day in LEA schools may be sufficient for the introduction and development of literacy. Where there is not much support for speakers in daily activities in the locality, the few hours of formal mother tongue teaching would need to be supplemented with other language use with parents, in mother tongue schools or classes, or through bilingual teaching programmes in LEA schools.

Information on bilingualism

One of the main characteristics of the debate about bilingualism and education in England has been the lack of information on which the different parties in the discussion could rely. For many readers the main contribution of this book will be the gathering together of a range of rather basic, but hitherto unfamiliar, data. However, as we write this book in 1983, we are acutely aware of the amount of data and discussion we have had to omit, and the likelihood that by the time the book is published some of the data may be out of date. Our assessments and interpretations too may be less useful in the light of new developments, some of which took place after we had completed the main Linguistic Minorities Project surveys in 1980-81.

The LINC project has been involved in some LEA policy initiatives, in part catalysed by the conduct of the two LMP school-based surveys discussed in Chapters 8 and 9. For example in Bradford, the LEA decided in 1983 to 'draw together (on a regular basis) information about pupils' bilingualism and ESL proficiency . . . to ensure that the Authority takes full account of the cultural and linguistic backgrounds of pupils and that it can identify and make provision for their educational needs' (Bradford LEA, 1983). Examples of the impact of the active dissemination of our community-based survey findings could not be included in the previous chapters in this book, because the LINC project's work with local networks of organisers of mother tongue provision, teachers and parents in different linguistic minorities was just beginning to develop at the time of our writing.

Previous sections have provided examples of decisions taken on the basis of minimal information, which have affected the development of the mother tongue debate. Two obvious examples come to mind. The EC Mother Tongue Project in Bedford had a false start because the local educationalists proposed to work with Hindi mother tongue pupils, as well as with Panjabi and Italian mother tongue pupils. Since hardly any of the potential pupils turned out in fact to be Hindi mother tongue speakers, Hindi had to be dropped at the very beginning (Simons, 1979). The other example of a lack of informed understanding about the significance of bilingualism in education was shown clearly in the content of discussions in Parliament on the draft Mother Tongue Directive, and in the arguments put forward by a range of individuals and institutions in their criticism of the Directive. Much has changed since 1976, but there remain many areas where the lack of basic data is delaying implementation of new schemes, or is being used as a reason to delay them.

Two aspects which should be of crucial concern to all researchers go beyond this basic first step of becoming aware of the need for useful or interesting data, and actually gathering it. First there are the different uses the data may be put to. Once the data has been interpreted and the findings qualified by the researchers, how will these findings be used, by whom, and for what purpose? Because of the power relationships between the many different categories of people involved in the issue, for example parents from the majority and the various linguistic minorities, organisers of mother tongue teaching, mainstream education policy-makers, administrators and teachers – the availability and use of the findings may become a contested issue. As we felt strongly about the social responsibility of researchers, one of the objectives of LINC was to ensure that all interested parties had access to the results of the research instead of it being appropriated by, for example, the most powerful among them in their own interests. Because the various audiences had different and often conflicting expectations and interests, we knew we had to foresee and counter potential misuses of the findings by each of the parties concerned. Our experience is that the findings, the research methods and the interpretation of data are of potentially equal interest to the wide range of people who have helped us complete our research. The test is in which form our findings are most useful, to whom we should direct them, and how best we can accomplish their dissemination in such a way that they can be taken over and used by the different target audiences.

The second aspect is related to the kind of surveys we have developed and administered, but not dependent on it. However much description or analysis of the patterns of bilingualism or minority language teaching we can provide, none of this will by itself necessarily convince the sceptical of the potential of bilingualism for personal enrichment and creativity, or for opening up new channels of knowledge and economic exchange. There is a limit to what research publications can transmit: even when they use the more immediate approach of case studies, or personal accounts or quotations, books and reports reach a limited audience (Grosjean, 1982). Some people do not want to read them, others have no access. There are some who have access but cannot 'decode' the data or its presentation, so as to make sense of it and relate it to their own interests or needs.

This leads us to the issue of what people perceive to be not just useful information but relevant knowledge. The example of the development of specialist ESL provision for children of linguistic minorities in England is a case in point. Those who perceived the situation through assimilationist and monolingual perspectives quite understandably did not see why and how a serious lack in their knowledge of bilingual pupils' linguistic and cultural backgrounds might affect these pupils' educational development. As late as the mid-1970s many education and community relations officers, for example, did not express surprise or embarrassment when they reported they had minimal information, or no information at all, about local mother tongue schools or classes (Saifullah Khan, 1977a).

The response of the local school systems in the 1960s to the arrival of a substantial number of pupils from diverse cultural and linguistic backgrounds presented a challenge to many accepted values and practices. Despite an official commitment to ensure that all children should have equal opportunities, change was and still is relatively slow, reflecting resistance to the questioning of traditional assumptions about education, institutional arrangements and teacher training and practice.

The systems' response to the new educational challenges depended particularly on the definition of the situation on the part of the most influential decision-makers, especially education officers, advisers and head teachers. This definition was influenced by the political context at national and local levels and, taken together with what was considered to be the relevant information, provided a framework within which the relevant action was proposed. Many of these factors have (as indicated in previous sections) developed over time on the basis of assimilationist attitudes. For example, the desirability of cultural and linguistic integration for the sake of national cohesion was perceived in terms of uniformity, and its achievement encouraged by policies stressing assimilation to the dominant majority. The argument was put in terms like these: 'We are all equal, therefore we are all the same, so why should pupils be treated differently?' A process of integration within the framework of cultural and linguistic pluralism, whereby national unity and democracy would be built upon diversity and equal partnership was not envisaged.

The orientation of what was happening in ESL and mother tongue teaching provision was, of course, continually modified and altered in the light of experience, especially at the local level, through the activities of teachers and increasingly of minority parents and organisations. The essentially assimilationist perspective of the dominant 'host' society did not need to justify its position on the basis of a detailed knowledge of its clientele. The initial language policies developed in response to the perceived needs of bilingual children did not stimulate an interest in their full linguistic repertoires, nor did they encourage exploration of various bilingual methods of language teaching such as, for example, teaching ESL through the medium of both English and the pupil's mother tongue.

Requests for support from community-run schools or classes might be received by school caretakers, lettings departments or urban aid committees in social services or planning departments. But few authorities were moved into enquiring about exactly what were the needs, what was being taught, or where and how the teaching was taking place in their area. It was not relevant: there was no consciousness of a lack of knowledge, or of the value of an informed understanding. This is particularly surprising when we remember that during the 1960s and 1970s there was increasing concern about home-school liaison and the development of schools which would be open to the wider local community.

One of the main reasons that some LEAs began to acknowledge their lack of information and understanding of the sociolinguistic situation in their areas was the increased demand for support expressly addressed to them by different minorities. Some local groups and teachers' associations began to campaign for mother tongue teaching to be introduced into LEA schools. Another reason for increased recognition that this was an issue which would not go away came from the principles and practices emerging in the parallel discussions about language across the curriculum, and education for a multicultural society. All of these developments helped towards an acknowledgement of the contribution of the unofficial community-run schooling, and of the rights of all children to develop their full potential.

Even then there was a period when some local groups or education authorities thought the most relevant information was about the 'demand' for mother tongue teaching, usually from parents but sometimes also from bilingual pupils. Most of those who carried out local surveys to assess this demand expected to use the raw results as a means to judge the likely take-up of an as yet unspecified type of provision. While there was recognition of the problems of using survey techniques to establish people's attitudes, there was no initial assessment of the information base from which the answers would emerge. Many bilingual parents did not know what the issue was about, or indeed that there was one. They needed information about the school system, including what it aimed to do and what it offered. Others were worried about the motives for this recent interest. Like many monolingual English parents, many parents of bilingual families have not been given the opportunity to consider the relevance of the use of more than one language in the home and at school to general educational development and to consider how skills in the two languages may reinforce one another. Another major consideration relates to the difficulty of imagining the possible options that the LEA might actually offer. There was sometimes an equal difficulty for parents in envisaging how the community-run school could be altered, even when parents were less than pleased with it. As the discussion at the end of Chapter 6 suggests, the number of children attending mother tongue classes should not be assumed to be an accurate indication of the magnitude of the need, nor a statement of satisfaction with what is offered.

To understand the existing relations between members (especially 'representatives') of linguistic minorities and their local LEA, it is necessary to understand the information base from which initial decisions were taken by LEAs, and how the available information and patterns of communication reflected and restricted the way linguistic minorities presented their case. But it is not, of course, just a question of the lack of understanding of each other's resources, objectives and potential contribution. Tension was often introduced by miscommunication at an early stage, and this fed back into future relations, for example when there were new approaches to the LEA for assistance, or when the LEA recruited specialist staff to meet specific 'needs'. The mutual assessment of need was itself often conflicting. Often community-run mother tongue teaching was negatively criticised (directly or indirectly) by 'progressive' and secular-minded teachers, on the grounds that it was based on 'traditional' values and obsolete teaching methods. It was and still remains difficult for the dominant majority, judging from the outside and within its own framework, to understand the intricate relationship between religion, culture, ethnic identity and language (particularly written language) for many members of linguistic minorities. This outsider's assessment, and the new problems of principle which it raised, were reasons which often contributed to refusals of grant applications. Initial rejections shaped subsequent relations with LEAs, either in the form of more persistent demands, or in an increased determination to be self-supporting. Both of these kinds of responses have led to either resentment of LEAs, or suspicion of what is seen to be their belated interest in the issue.

The widely publicised demands by Muslims in Bradford at the beginning of 1983, for a more effective way of influencing the ethos of the schools in which their children were being educated, is the culmination of a long process of rejection over the last few decades. This is a case which vividly illustrates how present circumstances cannot be abstracted out of their socio-historical context, and how language education issues will always remain closely tied to questions of religious or national sentiment.

In the light of the haphazard and sometimes contradictory information which many bilingual parents receive then, there is a need to
consider the most appropriate ways to raise the issues of bilingualism.
These include the parents' role in supporting their children's language
acquisition, the alternative provision that could be offered, and the
rationale behind different methods. Some parents are not clear about
the likely impact of the different policies that could be adopted.

Similarly there are many mother tongue teachers who, while aware
of the main questions in the mother tongue debate, have had very
little time to work out how they could alter their practice or organisational arrangements, and often they have very little means to improve
them. The gradual development of a network of mother tongue teachers,
nationally through the National Council for Mother Tongue Teaching
and locally through local materials development or teachers' groups,
has done much, not only to support people who were otherwise working
in isolation, but also to open up channels of information within and
between different linguistic minorities.

The structural gap between the LEA school system and community-
run initiatives, whether organised by embassies or local groups, has done
much to prevent and then to distort communication between monolingual and bilingual teachers who are interested in the overall language
education of their pupils. Some of the implications of these parallel
forms of schooling, and of the linguistic minorities' bilingual perspective as compared with the majority's monolingual one, need to be
remembered when reading the following chapters. Some monolingual
teachers' and monolingual pupils' lack of knowledge about the bilingualism of the pupils they teach or study with is striking. The raw data
from the SLS contained sizeable numbers of 'wrong' or 'incorrect'
language labels. For example, in the four LEAs with a high proportion
of children from families originating in both parts of the Panjab, many
instances of the language labels 'Indian', 'Pakistani' or 'Pakistan' with
no further information were recorded ('Indian' 120 times in four LEAs,
'Pakistani' 110 times in Bradford and Waltham Forest and 'Pakistan' 80
times in Bradford, Peterborough and Waltham Forest). And labels like
these were not confined to a small number of schools (LMP/LINC,
1983).

There are several possible explanations for this phenomenon, and
only detailed case studies could establish which is most accurate. Either
the teachers never questioned the pupils, but entered on the form those
pupils they thought were bilingual, using the labels they are accustomed
to using in daily life when referring to the languages, cultures or national

origin of the pupils' parents; or the teachers did question the pupils and were actually given the answers recorded. In these cases, it may be that the very young pupils only knew the name of their language under the label used by the surrounding dominant majority, which they have 'accepted' as appropriate in the school context. It may also be that the pupils did know the name or names of their languages, but either they thought their teacher would not understand (and they reported the label they thought the teacher could 'take in'), or they had internalised the view that bilingualism is a problem, and they gave a vague answer to hide a reality perceived as problematic. Some may have made a more conscious decision that they were not going to reveal something so intimately valued to a teacher who had never acknowledged their language before, or possibly had even denigrated it. In any case, the question remains of why it is that some teachers did not feel the necessity for further enquiry.

Some LEAs and some teachers may, without great conviction of their potential, have accepted the different surveys as one-off exercises rather than as initial and necessary steps in a continuing process. But our experience has shown that it is their reactions to these kinds of experiences which make a great and lasting impression. It is the revelation of their own or of others' ignorance, of their pupils' unwillingness to participate or their tendency to volunteer 'dominant' and vague labels of classification, which stays with those who are involved in the research process, as much as, and perhaps more than, the circulation of facts and figures from the survey findings.

Although we are beginning to assess the short-term impact of our information-gathering and dissemination exercises, we have no means of assessing the long-term impact. Our own impression is that a slow and, at the beginning, a less committed approach, but one founded solidly on the basis of interest from a range of advisers, language specialists and a teacher-support team, can have a more profound impact in the long term than an 'efficient' and prompt start supported only by the authority's adviser for multicultural education, and maybe by the Chief Education Officer.

It is perhaps appropriate to end this chapter with a comment on the focus and uses of educational research. Although we were ambitious in the number of LEAs we covered in the Schools Language Surveys, we were also aware that technically the most smooth administration of a survey can actually jeopardise the impact and follow-up of the research by those who participated in it. The feedback from respondents and administrators is invaluable for the researchers' assessment of the wider context and of the ways in which information is selected and used. This feedback provides insight into the different strategies that can be used to ensure that the findings of the research return to those who are active participants in the situation. Only a small part of this situation can be described and analysed in research findings.

8
The Schools Language Surveys

The context for the Schools Language Surveys

When the Linguistic Minorities Project began its work in the autumn of 1979 there were no publicly available and comprehensive data about the languages known and used by school pupils in England from the different linguistic minorities. By contrast in Sweden, for example, figures on the home languages of pupils throughout the country are collected and are made freely available on a national basis. A number of British education authorities, schools and teachers had informal and partial knowledge of the linguistic background of their pupils. But this was usually derived in rather unsatisfactory ways from information about the ethnic or national origin of the pupils or their parents, or about the level of fluency in English and the need for provision in teaching English as a second language (ESL). In a number of areas schools had continued through the 1970s to collect statistics on the basis of the officially abandoned DES definition of 'immigrant pupils', which did not cover all of the British-born children of families of immigrant origin (DES, 1970).

It was becoming increasingly obvious, however, that more and more British-born children came from homes where English was only one of the languages used. This made it clear that linguistic data, rather than data related to birthplace or nationality status, was needed for planning policies encompassing support for languages other than English used at home, as well as ESL.

The Inner London Education Authority (ILEA) was the only English education authority which had accepted this need, and conducted a full Language Census in all its schools. This type of enquiry was first undertaken by them in autumn 1978, and repeated in January 1981 and January 1983 (ILEA, 1979, 1981, 1983). In fact the origins of the 1978 Census lay in ILEA's decision 'to investigate the adequacy of its

311

policy on special assistance to pupils whose educational progress was regarded as being retarded by communication difficulties arising from lack of fluency in, or unfamiliarity with, the English language' (ILEA, 1979, Section 2). The questionnaire distributed for completion by schools was headed 'Statistics of Pupils for Whom English is Not a First Language', and the reason given in the Education Officer's covering letter for asking schools to include information on the first language of the pupils 'needing additional English help' was simply 'so that we can organise specific help'.

In other words, the invaluable information which this first ILEA enquiry produced about knowledge of languages other than English among its pupils was essentially a by-product of an enquiry into ESL needs. More than 10 per cent of all ILEA pupils in 1978 were recorded as having such knowledge, with Greek, Turkish and Bengali as the most widely spoken languages then. However, the close association of the question about first language with that about possible difficulties with English may have confirmed negative connotations of bilingualism in some teachers' minds — and probably led to an underestimation of the extent of bilingualism among the Authority's pupils at that time.

Some confirmation of these reservations about the design of the 1978 Enquiry are found in the results of ILEA's second enquiry in this field in early 1981 — this time clearly labelled *Language Census*, but with a significantly different subtitle for the questionnaire to teachers — 'Statistics of Pupils with a Home Language other than or in addition to English'. One of the categories explicitly offered this time for reporting the 'Stage of English Learning of these Pupils' was 'Full Competence', perhaps helping to reduce the negative associations. The overall percentage of ILEA's pupils recorded in this connection was now nearly 14 per cent, with a particularly sharp rise in the numbers of reported Bengali speakers. Bengali took the place of Greek as the most frequently occurring language other than English, almost certainly because of the wives and children rejoining husbands and fathers who had first come to Britain without their families.

Another weakness in ILEA's pioneering approach to the gathering of information about the linguistic resources of its pupils is the absence of enquiry into literacy skills. If the function of such language censuses is to make possible the planning of more systematic support from schools and education authorities for home language maintenance, then some data on the extent of literacy would seem essential. Certainly much of the existing effort that goes into mother tongue teaching is directed to establishing some basic competence in reading and writing in the various languages. And one of the major focuses of the Schools Council/ ILEA Mother Tongue Teaching Project is the question of how children who are not literate in their mother tongue can best be helped to achieve literacy, and then to extend it.

The contribution which ILEA's Research and Statistics Branch has made to knowledge in this field, however, has stimulated much discussion on bilingualism within the Authority, and led to the production of a positive policy statement on 'Bilingualism in the ILEA: the Educational Implications of the 1981 Language Census' (ILEA, 1982).

The other recent experience which LMP was able to draw on was Rosen and Burgess's 'Survey of Linguistic Diversity in London Schools', which led to the publication of *Languages and Dialects of London School Children* (Rosen and Burgess, 1980). Their survey was based on interviews and discussion with 4½ thousand first-year secondary pupils in twenty-eight schools in Inner London and Haringey. It involved teachers in recording the answers to thirty-four questions put to these children in a group setting designed to make possible relaxed enquiry and discussion. The detailed attention paid in this study to the context of questioning, and to the need for careful preparation with teachers, were features of this survey which the LMP researchers benefited from. They strongly influenced our approach to the design both of the Schools Language Surveys, and perhaps even more directly, of the complementary Secondary Pupils' Surveys (see Chapter 9).

Rosen and Burgess had focussed their enquiries on the full range of linguistic diversity in London schools, including, for example, indigenous non-standard dialects and Caribbean varieties, partly perhaps because they were involved in training teachers of English who had to deal with all the children in a class. Speakers of English-based Creoles share many socio-historical characteristics with speakers of languages other than English, and can be considered also as members of linguistic minorities, particularly in terms of the power relationships that exist between them and speakers of Southern British Standard English (see Chapter 7). Similarly, speakers of indigenous regional and low-status social dialects of English share some of the educational experience of speakers of languages other than English, in that schools very frequently undervalue those dimensions of their linguistic repertoires that most often find expression outside school (see p. 285). However, the scale of our task meant that in our Schools Language Surveys, at least, a different approach from that of Rosen and Burgess had to be used. Above all we knew that, if we were to receive the co-operation of the very large number of teachers necessarily involved in a comprehensive enquiry across all the schools and the whole age range in an authority, we would have to confine ourselves to a much smaller number of questions, rather simply worded.

It was this need to involve a large proportion of the teaching force in the conduct of our surveys which made the process of negotiation with LEAs elaborate, and occasionally unsuccessful. The degree of autonomy enjoyed by individual LEAs and schools, in matters relating to the collection of data on their pupils, meant that in each new area the different groups of people involved in the conduct of the survey had to be persuaded of the benefits to be gained from such an enterprise. It was clear in some areas that, although the education officers were convinced of the case for a language survey, they anticipated that objections were likely to be raised by local teachers' unions, or by their political masters – the councillors on the local education committee. In most cases, sometimes after the investment of substantial time and effort in consultation and discussion, objections were overcome. But in others they were not, for a mixture of reasons which were rarely made totally explicit to the LMP team.

The factors at work, however, seemed to come down to these. Firstly, the authorities sometimes realised they might have to spend more money to meet needs revealed by such a survey. Indeed, some of the LEAs foresaw the implications of SLS almost exclusively in material terms, and little or not at all in qualitative terms involving changes in teachers' attitudes. Secondly, we encountered a reluctance in schools to undertake what was sometimes seen as yet more pointless form-filling, imposed to some extent by an outside agency concerned with educational research – believed by some teachers to have no practical or immediate outcome. Finally there was a not unreasonable fear on the part of teachers and head teachers about possible misuse of statistics which would be seen as in some way 'ethnic', or related to the countries of origin of the pupils' families. Some ways of overcoming these sorts of objection are discussed in the final section of this chapter.

Although the above reservations were on the surface different in origin, expressing a range of local sectional concerns and vested interests at the time of negotiation, they seem to us on reflection often to have been covertly rooted in deeper societal attitudes – for example, in racism towards minorities in general, or in a monocultural and parochial attitude towards bilingualism and linguistic pluralism in particular. Such attitudes among the dominant culture may rarely be made explicit, but were in some cases the unspoken basis for resistance to the survey. Another indication of this association may be found in the sources of support for the conduct of a Schools Language Survey — often those most heavily committed to multicultural or to anti-racist education. Such people took it for granted that bilingualism was a resource rather than a handicap, and that accurate and comprehensive information was a necessary basis for reform in language policy.

The overt objections were of course related to the national and local political situation at the time of the surveys. This was characterised in the first place by severe and continuing cutbacks in public expenditure, only partly accounted for in the field of education by falling schools rolls. In the second place, as already mentioned, the new nationality and immigration legislation affected in particular some of the largest ethnic minorities which our survey was likely to be concerned with. In this setting teachers faced with the proposal to conduct such a language survey occasionally reacted negatively, if they thought that expenditure might be 'diverted' from other areas which they felt to be more important. But they were equally likely to object if they thought that pupils or parents already feeling threatened by the direction of change in immigration and nationality legislation might be put at more specific risk through identification as somehow 'different' in terms of their linguistic background.

We had some evidence too of blatant discriminatory and racist reactions to the possibility or the actuality of the research. This reaction developed from the position that the LEA was once again proposing to give special attention, and possibly to allocate extra expenditure, to certain categories of 'black' or 'immigrant' pupils who had already, these objectors believed, had excessive attention. People taking this position saw the only special need to be for assistance in learning the English language, in order that children should become as 'English' as possible as quickly as possible. This then was the context within which we had to design our Schools Language Survey.

The scope of the Surveys

The function of the collection of data on linguistic diversity among school pupils was intended in part at least to be for the use of the DES and LEAs in developing policy. In addition, certain obligations had been imposed on the UK Government by the EC Directive of 1977 on the education of Migrant Workers' Children, whose Article 3 refers directly to the need to 'take appropriate measures to promote, in co-ordination with normal education, teaching of the mother tongue and culture of the country of origin' (EC, 1977). It was clear then that the data collected by the Schools Language Surveys should be such as to assist not only the DES at national level, but also LEAs and individual schools at local level. Administrators, teachers, and minority parents were beginning to consider what sort of systematic arrangements might be made to support the maintenance and development of skills in languages other than English, for pupils who already had some of these skills. Some were also asking why these newer minority languages could not be made available more generally throughout the school system.

The overall intention behind our design, therefore, was to elicit basic information on:

(a)   the full range of languages spoken at home by pupils in the LEA schools,

(b)   the numbers of pupils speaking each of the languages,

(c)   the proportions these pupils represented of the totals surveyed,

(d)   age and gender-related differences in the incidence of speaking, reading and writing skills, and

(e)   the distribution of the bilingual pupils and of the different languages across schools and classes.

We were also determined from the beginning to design and conduct the surveys in such a way that schools, teachers and pupils could benefit in the short term, as well as in the long term.

With this in mind the survey questions were formulated and piloted. We needed firstly a 'screening question', which would identify those pupils who did make some use of languages other than English, and who could then each be asked a small number of further questions. The first question of our Schools Language Surveys (see Figure 8.1 for the full layout) asks therefore: (Q1) 'Do you yourself ever speak any language at home apart from English?' It was intended to be put by the teacher individually to every child in the class, and only pupils who answered this question positively were to be asked the further questions in the survey and to have their answers recorded.

Clearly this is not the only possible formulation that might have been used. We might, for example, have asked 'Do you ever *use* . . . or . . . *know* any language apart from English?' which would in principle have picked up receptive as well as productive skills. In the end we rejected this, on the grounds firstly that 'use' or 'know' in this context were more ambiguous than 'speak', and secondly that speaking would probably be taken to represent in the respondents' minds a more tangible and substantial level of skill than the other terms. As it was,

Figure 8.1 SLS questionnaire: 4 pages

Linguistic Minorities Project

Schools Language Survey

HEAD TEACHERS PLEASE COMPLETE

SCHOOLS USE THIS COLUMN

Please leave this Column Blank

Name of Local Education Authority:		*6—7*
Name, Address and Telephone No. of School: *Please use rubber stamp if possible*		*8—10*
Type of School:		
Age range of Pupils in school in years Youngest pupils: Oldest pupils:		*11*

[diagonal watermark text: SPECIMEN VERSION OF 1981]

CLASS TEACHER PLEASE COMPLETE

TEACHERS USE THIS COLUMN

Please leave this Column Blank

Name of Class/Form/Group for which information is recorded here:		*12—13*
Number of pupils in Class/Form/Group:		*14—15*
Number of pupils absent at the time of this Survey:		*16—17*
Age range of pupils in this class/form/group to nearest full year Youngest:		*18—19*
Oldest:		*20—21*
Date of completion of this Survey:		*22—27*
Name of teacher completing this form: *Please print*		

Please put this first question individually to *all* pupils in your class:–

Question 1. 'DO YOU YOURSELF EVER SPEAK ANY LANGUAGE AT HOME APART FROM ENGLISH?'

Do not enter on this form pupils who answer 'no' to this first question. But for each pupil who answers 'yes', ask, and record answers to the following questions. (Where even a modest skill is claimed, treat this as a positive answer.)

Question 2. 'WHAT IS THE NAME OF THAT LANGUAGE?'

Question 3 'CAN YOU READ THAT LANGUAGE?'

Question 4 'CAN YOU WRITE THAT LANGUAGE?'

TO RECORD ANSWERS, PLEASE PUT A CIRCLE AROUND FIGURE 1 or 2 AS APPROPRIATE

Pupils Answering 'yes' to Question 1		Question 2 Name of Language Spoken	Question 3 Can Pupil Read it?	Question 4 Can Pupil Write it?	Notes on Dialect, Language of Literacy, Country, etc.	LEAVE THIS COLUMN BLANK PLEASE					
28-29	30		31	32		X 33	A 34-36	B 37-39	C 40-42	D 43-45	E 46-48
01	boy – 1 / girl – 2		yes – 1 / no – 2	yes – 1 / no – 2							
02	boy – 1 / girl – 2		yes – 1 / no – 2	yes – 1 / no – 2							
03	boy – 1 / girl – 2		yes – 1 / no – 2	yes – 1 / no – 2							
04	boy – 1 / girl – 2		yes – 1 / no – 2	yes – 1 / no – 2							
05	boy – 1 / girl – 2		yes – 1 / no – 2	yes – 1 / no – 2							
06	boy – 1 / girl – 2		yes – 1 / no – 2	yes – 1 / no – 2							
07	boy – 1 / girl – 2		yes – 1 / no – 2	yes – 1 / no – 2							
08	boy – 1 / girl – 2		yes – 1 / no – 2	yes – 1 / no – 2							
09	boy – 1 / girl – 2		yes – 1 / no – 2	yes – 1 / no – 2							
10	boy – 1 / girl – 2		yes – 1 / no – 2	yes – 1 / no – 2							
11	boy – 1 / girl – 2		yes – 1 / no – 2	yes – 1 / no – 2							
12	boy – 1 / girl – 2		yes – 1 / no – 2	yes –.1 / no – 2							
13	boy – 1 / girl – 2		yes – 1 / no – 2	yes – 1 / no – 2							
14	boy – 1 / girl – 2		yes – 1 / no – 2	yes – 1 / no – 2							
15	boy – 1 / girl – 2		yes – 1 / no – 2	yes – 1 / no – 2							
16	boy – 1 / girl – 2		yes – 1 / no – 2	yes – 1 / no – 2							
17	boy – 1 / girl – 2		yes – 1 / no – 2	yes – 1 / no – 2							
18	boy – 1 / girl – 2		yes – 1 / no – 2	yes – 1 / no – 2							
19	boy – 1 / girl – 2		yes – 1 / no – 2	yes – 1 / no – 2							
20	boy – 1 / girl – 2		yes – 1 / no – 2	yes – 1 / no – 2							

IF YOU NEED TO ENTER MORE PUPILS, CONTINUE OVERLEAF

For continuation from overleaf only: <u>PLEASE DO NOT BEGIN HERE.</u>

Please put this first question individually to *all* pupils in your class:—

Question 1. 'DO YOU YOURSELF EVER SPEAK ANY LANGUAGE AT HOME APART FROM ENGLISH?'

Do not enter on this form pupils who answer 'no' to this first question. But for each pupil who answers 'yes', ask, and record answers to the following questions. (Where even a modest skill is claimed, treat this as a positive answer.)

Question 2. 'WHAT IS THE NAME OF THAT LANGUAGE?'

Question 3 'CAN YOU READ THAT LANGUAGE?'

Question 4 'CAN YOU WRITE THAT LANGUAGE?'

> TO RECORD ANSWERS, PLEASE PUT A CIRCLE AROUND FIGURE 1 or 2 AS APPROPRIATE

Pupils Answering 'yes' to Question 1		Question 2 Name of Language Spoken	Question 3 Can Pupil Read It?	Question 4 Can Pupil Write It?	Notes on Dialect, Language of Literacy, Country, etc.	LEAVE THIS COLUMN BLANK PLEASE					
28-29	30		31	32		X 33	A 34-36	B 37-39	C 40-42	D 43-48	E 46-48
21	boy — 1 girl —2		yes — 1 no — 2	yes — 1 no — 2							
22	boy — 1 girl — 2		yes — 1 no — 2	yes — 1 no — 2							
23	boy — 1 girl — 2		yes — 1 no — 2	yes — 1 no — 2							
24	boy — 1 girl — 2		yes — 1 no — 2	yes — 1 no — 2							
25	boy — 1 girl — 2		yes — 1 no — 2	yes — 1 no — 2							
26	boy — 1 girl — 2		yes — 1 no — 2	yes — 1 no — 2							
27	boy — 1 girl — 2		yes — 1 no — 2	yes — 1 no — 2							
28	boy — 1 girl — 2		yes — 1 no — 2	yes — 1 no — 2							
29	boy — 1 girl — 2		yes — 1 no — 2	yes — 1 no — 2							
30	boy — 1 girl — 2		yes — 1 no — 2	yes — 1 no — 1							
31	boy — 1 girl — 2		yes — 1 no — 2	yes — 1 no — 1							
32	boy — 1 girl — 2		yes — 1 no — 2	yes — 1 no — 2							
33	boy — 1 girl — 2		yes — 1 no — 2	yes — 1 no — 2							
34	boy — 1 girl — 2		yes — 1 no — 2	yes — 1 no — 2							
35	boy — 1 girl — 2		yes — 1 no — 2	yes — 1 no — 2							

2/81

Purpose

This survey is being done to find out how many of the pupils in your school use languages at home other than English or in addition to English. Information of this kind is useful in working out language policies to meet the varied needs of pupils in schools.

Putting the Questions

We suggest that you put the questions to the pupils *individually*, if possible not in front of the class as a whole, since some pupils will certainly be shy about referring to what they may regard as an 'odd' linguistic background. We ask you to put the first question to *all* the pupils in your class, even when you think it very unlikely that the pupil concerned ever uses a language other than English, because experience shows that teachers are occasionally unaware of a pupil's linguistic background.

Form of Words

Since even quite small differences in the wording of a question can produce significant differences in response, *please use the form of the question indicated*. But, whenever you judge that it is absolutely necessary to put a question in a different way, please try to convey the essence of the question as accurately as possible.

Language Practice and Language Use

Occasionally pupils may quite reasonably, in answer to your first two questions, give the name of a language like French which they are learning at school and *practising* at home, rather than using for communication. Please do *not* include such answers on this form but include, for example, Arabic or Hebrew being learned for religious purposes, if the pupils tell you about them.

Naming of Languages

Try to find out the actual name of the language. Pupils may first give answers to Question 2 which refer to a country or region where more than one language is spoken — for example, 'Malaysia', 'Belgium', 'Indian', 'Pakistani', 'Swiss', 'Chinese'. In such cases you may have to put further questions to the pupils or perhaps to parents, if they are accessible, to obtain the particular language name. (Indicate the source of the information recorded if it is not the pupils themselves.)

If you are still not able to establish the language name, try to find out the name of the country or region where the language originated and write that in the *Notes* column.

We list below examples of the languages most commonly spoken in England at the moment. In brackets after these language names we have included examples of terms which pupils may give in answer to Question 2: these terms often refer to related spoken or written forms of the languages, regional varieties or names of countries.

ARABIC (Yemeni)	HINDI	SERBO-CROAT ('Yugoslavian')
BENGALI (Sylhetti)	ITALIAN (Sicilian)	SPANISH
CANTONESE (Chinese)	POLISH	TURKISH (Cypriot)
GREEK (Cypriot)	PORTUGUESE	UKRAINIAN
GUJERATI (Kutchi)	PANJABI ('Gurmukhi')	URDU
HAKKA (Chinese)	PANJABI (Mirpuri)	YORUBA

It is the names of the major spoken languages, like those printed on our list in capital letters, that we would like you to write in the column headed 'Question 2'. (There will be many pupils who speak languages not on our list of examples, and these of course should also be recorded whenever appropriate.) Any information given to you on dialects, additional languages, etc., like the terms we give in brackets, should be written in the *Notes* column.

Caribbean and other Creole Languages

If the pupil says he or she speaks 'Jamaican', 'West Indian' or 'patois', or names another Caribbean country or island, please enter 'Creole' in the *Language* column and write the exact term used by the pupil within quotation marks in the *Notes* column. Do the same for English-based Creole languages from other parts of the world such as the Pacific or Indian Ocean, and for non-English Creoles such as those from Mauritius or Dominica.

Pupils with Several Languages

If, in answer to your Question 2, pupils mention more than one language, please try to establish which is the most used, insert this in the *Language* column, and put the other languages in the *Notes* column.

Language of Literacy

Some pupils may report a written language which is different from the spoken language: for example, many pupils speak Panjabi but write Urdu. In cases like this, enter the spoken language in the *Language* column and the written language in the *Notes* column with an 'L' after it. (L=Literacy).

Thank you for helping with the Survey! We would be interested in hearing about your experience in using this form. If you would like to know about the work of our Project in general, or some particular aspect of it, please attach a note to this form or write to:

Linguistic Minorities Project,
University of London Institute of Education,
18 Woburn Square, London WC1H 0NS.

we were criticised by one head teacher, for example, for including the word 'ever' in this question, on the grounds that it would only encourage pupils to exaggerate the extent of their use of the languages in question. Our intention in including the 'ever' was to avoid the implications of habitual use which would have been there without the adverb, habitual use which would in turn have been extremely difficult to define consistently. The third word, 'yourself', was included because we became aware in the course of the earliest pilots of the ambiguity of the English 'you'. It might be taken as referring to 'all of you at home', whereas we wished to ask specifically about the individual pupil. As far as 'at home' was concerned, that particular setting was chosen for our enquiry simply because it was likely to be the most important one apart from school in terms of language socialisation (see p. 278). Finally, the inclusion of the phrase 'apart from English' was a necessary explicit acknowledgment of the fact that we, and the teachers putting the questions, understood that even where pupils did sometimes speak other languages, it was quite common for these to be used alongside English, not necessarily to the total exclusion of English. There was in this last phrase, however, an ambiguity for speakers of English-based creoles: the survey may have picked up only those pupils who consider such varieties as distinct from English.

The wording of the question was cumbersome, but we were aware that sensitive teachers were quite likely to vary the wording, and we wanted to make sure that the essence of the question was clearly conveyed. In the end, we amended our original note for teachers about the importance of using consistently the exact words of the question which we had devised. We accepted explicitly that teachers might need to use a different form of words particularly with younger children, but urged that the substance of the question as embodied in the wording we had arrived at should be conveyed.

This first question is the only one which is designed to be put to all pupils in a class. We have no way of knowing how many teachers did in fact put this question to all the pupils, even collectively. Some will certainly have asked it only of those pupils whom they believed likely to speak another language. The information on our survey forms is therefore only about those pupils who were recorded by their teachers as responding positively to that first screening question. In other words, if anything, we think our totals may understate the actual numbers of speakers of languages other than English. Pupils who did respond positively were then asked the question: 'What is the name of that language?' and we discuss in the next section of this chapter how we approached the data which this question produced.

Naming of languages

The problem of interpreting the raw data is particularly difficult with reference to the naming of languages by pupils, to the ways in which these names were recorded by teachers, and to how they were coded and then regrouped under conventional language labels in the process of analysis.

There was a wide variation in the amount, kind and quality of information in respect of language names in the questionnaires as we received them from the schools. Most cases were straightforward, with a single, well-known language name entered on the form. A small number of the difficult cases can be put down to a failure to follow the instructions carefully enough, but many problems were the result of the intrinsic complexities involved in naming languages and varieties, or of the design of the survey instrument itself.

Sometimes it appeared that the child could not give the language name. In others it seemed that the teacher could not discover a recognisable language name, but had made a note about the country of origin, or even about the ethnic or religious identity of the child. Although these responses were not ideal, they could at least be coded and some kind of interpretation attempted.

Some problems arose from the language labels themselves. These were of four distinct types:

(a)   There were unfamiliar or non-standardised spellings of less common language names. Some of these could be reconstructed with a fair degree of confidence by reference to books such as Voegelin and Voegelin (1977); others were deciphered with less certainty.

(b)   Pupils might name their languages, or a teacher might record the name given, with reference to an ethnic, national or religious group (e.g. 'Pathan', 'Indian', 'Cypriot', 'Hindu') rather than to a particular language.

(c)   Our experience in a number of LEAs suggests that the term used to refer to a language or dialect varied according to the pupil's or teacher's perception of the status of this language or dialect in the wider society, either in the country of origin (e.g. 'Urdu' given for Panjabi), or in England ('Pakistani, given for Panjabi, 'Italian' for Sicilian, 'Indian' for Hindi, Gujerati, or for Indian languages less commonly spoken in Britain such as Malayalam, Marathi, or Telugu).

(d)   The level of detail in a pupil's answer or in a teacher's reporting of it might be affected by very local factors, such as the kind of relationship already built up between teacher and pupil, or even what other pupils in the class had just said. Some teachers in classes where there was a large number of pupils of one linguistic minority gave detailed information about dialects and places of origin, while others in classes with fewer pupils answering 'yes' to the first question, or where a wide range of languages was reported, gave little more than the language name.

Coding languages: from language labels to language groupings

In view of the complexities outlined above it was important to devise a consistent coding framework for the languages reported, especially the South Asian languages. In transferring the data to the computer a scheme was used which attempted to preserve the maximum amount of detail, and yet made it possible eventually to group together the many different language labels given by pupils and teachers into broader categories. The presentation later in this chapter of the data for the languages given in answer to Question 2 is based largely on these groupings. In this chapter we use the term 'language groupings' which only broadly corresponds to 'linguistic minorities' used elsewhere in the book. Insofar as we have local linguistic minorities here, the boundaries are set by researchers' post-hoc classification of teachers' labels.

South Asian languages

The North Indian language situation was discussed more fully in Chapter 2, with particular reference to the inter-relationship of national, regional, religious and linguistic categories. It was pointed out there that, for example, it would be desirable from the point of view of planning support for mother tongue teaching to be able to sub-divide the wider category of 'Panjabi speakers' on the basis of religious affiliation which is closely related to potential language of literacy. Unfortunately, the data obtained in SLS does not allow us to make these distinctions in an immediate and straightforward way. This is partly a reflection of the method by which pupils and teachers were asked to record answers to a single question. Since neither of them may have a detailed knowledge of the linguistic background, some answers offered and recorded refer to the local spoken dialect used at home, some to the regional standard spoken language, and others to the language of community loyalty or to the language of literacy.

Thus a number of pupils from families of Pakistani origin reported speaking Urdu, when it is likely that their first spoken language is one of the regional varieties of Panjabi, and that Urdu for them is essentially a language of literacy which may also be a second spoken language. In answer to Question 2 other children of similar language background reported speaking Panjabi.

When the language label 'Panjabi' occurs without further information about dialects, region of origin of the pupil's family, or other languages known, it is not possible to deduce which written language – i.e. Panjabi or Urdu – an individual Panjabi-speaking child is likely to learn. However, in order to simplify the interpretation of data the different language labels given for these Panjabi speakers were grouped into four categories. The grouping was done on the basis of the coding of the answers to Question 2 about the pupils' first-mentioned spoken language, and is as follows:

(1) Those cases where the word 'Panjabi' appears with no further specification, we refer to as 'Panjabi unspecified'.

(2) Those cases where 'Panjabi' is given with further detail which links it with the Sikh minority, where the Gurmukhi script is generally used, are referred to as 'Panjabi(G)' (= Panjabi-Gurmukhi script).

(3) Those cases where 'Panjabi' is given and is further specified in a way which indicates some connection with the predominantly Muslim population of Pakistan, where Urdu is generally the language of literacy, are referred to as 'Panjabi(U)' (= Panjabi-Urdu). Dialect names such as 'Mirpuri' and 'Hin(d)ko' are included in this grouping.

(4) Those cases where the word 'Urdu' is given with or without a further geographical or dialectal specification, although in many of these cases we are pretty sure that the spoken variety is some dialect of Panjabi, are referred to simply as 'Urdu'.

There are also pupils who were recorded as giving a geographical term such as 'Pakistan' or 'India' rather than a language name. It is likely that some of these, although we cannot tell how many, are speakers of Panjabi.

Creoles

This is a large group of diverse languages, whose common characteristic is that they arose in a colonial situation out of contact between a European language and some other language or languages. These were reported in quite large numbers in several of the surveys. In analysing the data we have divided them into two main categories:

(a) 'French-based Creoles' include all cases where the word 'French' appeared on the form or where some geographical term was mentioned which made it highly probable that the Creole in question was French, e.g. 'Mauritius'.

(b) 'English-based and all other Creoles' (abbreviated in Table 8.2 to 'Creoles') include all other cases where the word 'creole' appeared, together with such terms as 'Jamaican', 'patois'. It is possible that some of the unspecified Creoles are in fact French-based, but where there was no clear evidence available, we included them in this second sub-grouping.

'Chinese' and other groupings

'Chinese' refers to a group including all language labels referring to one of the regional Chinese languages, e.g. Cantonese, Hakka, as well as the general label 'Chinese'. In other language groupings simple language labels, and those which give more detailed geographical or dialect specifications, were all grouped together under the name of the national or regional official language, e.g. 'Kutchi' is subsumed in 'Gujerati' and 'Sicilian' in 'Italian'.

Most of the findings presented in this chapter are based on the groupings set out above.

Consultation and preparation for the Survey

We had decided at an early stage to involve as many teachers as possible in the survey process, rather than to rely on, for example, specialist teachers of English as a second language who might be expected to be familiar with the linguistic background of the pupils concerned. This decision was related to five main factors. Firstly, we believed that many teachers other than those teaching ESL might know a great deal about their pupils' languages, and be interested in learning more. Secondly, we did not want to reinforce the view that bilingualism is a narrowly linguistic matter, only related to language learning and teaching and only of concern to language teachers. Nor did we want bilingualism to be seen as a handicap for learning English, to be treated within the framework of 'remedial' ESL courses. We wanted rather to support a view of bilingualism as related to the overall conceptual development and social experiences of all pupils, therefore the concern of all teachers. Thirdly, we felt that carrying out SLS might be a valuable consciousness-raising exercise, and therefore in this respect the more teachers involved the better. Fourthly, we were aware that the findings of SLS might have an impact on policy makers, leading to a change of attitudes and to decisions involving all teachers. So, the more teachers could be involved in the carrying out of the survey, the more they would be able to respond to the practical implications of the findings. Finally, the sheer scale of the task made it essential that most teachers should in any case assist in the data collection. Given this decision to use most of the teaching force in connection with the survey, it was necessary to invest considerable effort in the briefing of the teachers and administrators concerned.

The Notes of Guidance, printed on the survey form, contained the inescapable minimum advice to teachers. These notes cover the purpose of the survey; the explanation of why the questions should be put individually to pupils; comment on the importance of staying close to the wording of the questions; advice on dealing with pupils with several languages; and those with languages of literacy different from their spoken languages; and comment on what turned out to be the major problem for the teachers who administered the survey and for the researchers who processed and interpreted the data – the naming of languages, including Caribbean and other Creole languages.

We arranged for the distribution of survey forms some time in advance of the week designated for the actual administration of the survey. They went firstly to the education officers, local inspectors, advisers and specialist staff who would be involved in responding to queries from the schools at a later stage. Then small sets were sent to the head teachers so that they could discuss the implications and procedures with their staffs. Finally the full numbers needed by schools for completion were dispatched a short time before the survey week began.

Open meetings were arranged by four of the LEAs participating just before the survey week, or at the very beginning of that week. There representatives from any school could put questions and comments to education office and research team staff about the administrative procedure proposed, and about the purpose of the survey. During the designated survey week a special telephone enquiry service was available, to answer questions that arose in the process of carrying out the survey. It was usually provided by local specialist staff.

Survey administration and response

With the help of local education office staff who followed up the usually rather small number of reluctant schools, data was obtained on virtually all the pupils in the five areas which we surveyed comprehensively in 1980-81 – the Peterborough division of Cambridgeshire, Coventry, Bradford, the London boroughs of Haringey and Waltham Forest.

There were slight variations in the age ranges covered. These related partly to the different times of year when the surveys were carried out, partly to different views about the desirability or feasibility of including the youngest pupils, and partly to the varying transfer ages between school stages. The summer term was the least satisfactory for the older pupils, many of whom were involved in public examinations and therefore less likely to be available in school. For this reason Haringey, for example, included pupils only up to the fourth form, i.e. aged about fifteen, in the survey. At the other end of the age range Coventry excluded nursery and reception class children in the infant schools, on the grounds that it would not be possible to convey to them meaningfully the substance of the questions, and that schools in any case already had similar information on their pupils. Bradford on the other hand included children down to the age of four, relying very heavily of course on the mediation of parents, siblings and speakers of the various languages involved to obtain answers from these younger children.

We have no detailed evidence about how the survey was in fact conducted in different schools, and to what extent our suggested procedures were adopted. However, through the dissemination process in Coventry and Bradford, we have begun to form an impression of this. Not all schools and teachers followed our guidelines to the letter of course, or even indeed in spirit. We must presume that some teachers did not feel able to give the survey a very high priority within their overall workload, and may even have allowed feelings of hostility to the children most immediately concerned, to senior school staff, to their immediate

The Schools Language Surveys

Figure 8.2 Proportions of bilingual pupils and main languages reported as SPOKEN in five LEAs

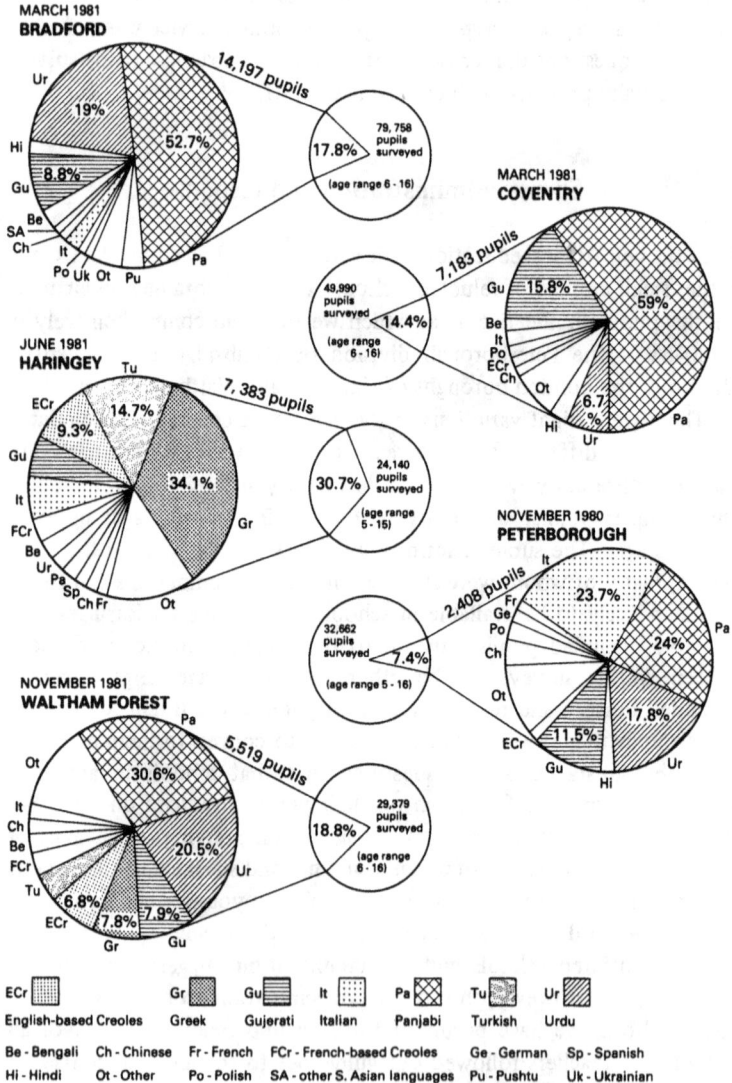

superiors, or to academic researchers, to influence what they recorded. However, it is equally clear from the amount of detail included in some of the notes which teachers added to the basic data, that many went to enormous trouble to record relevant information as fully and accurately as they could. It would be a valuable follow-up to the Schools Language Survey research to undertake some case studies of the different procedures adopted in different schools.

Overall it seems that in addition to the data generated by the survey, the process of putting the questions to the children, and the effort of interpreting their answers, was a highly educative one for many teachers. For some of them it may well have been the first occasion on which they had had to wrestle with the problems of, for example, naming the languages or varieties apart from English used by their pupils, and trying to work out how these related to religious or overall cultural background. In other words mounting such a language survey can have a secondary function as a large-scale in-service training exercise in language awareness.

Findings of the surveys

Bilingual pupils in five areas

In the five areas where LMP conducted Schools Language Surveys in 1980 and 1981, the numbers of pupils recorded by their teachers as speaking at least one language at home other than English are shown in Figure 8.2. We use the shorthand expression 'bilingual pupils' and Figure 8.2 also shows the proportions that such pupils represented of the total numbers surveyed.

Most frequently mentioned languages

The languages represented in the different LEAs which we surveyed varied considerably, both in terms of the number of different languages reported, and in terms of the particular languages which were most frequently mentioned. The basic picture as presented in Figure 8.2 is elaborated in Table 8.1.

It will be seen from the data presented in Figure 8.2 and Table 8.1 that, although in each of the areas we surveyed there are quite wide ranges of languages used at home, the ten or twelve most frequently

Table 8.1 Main languages reported in five LEAs

(A) Total number of pupils recorded as using a language at home other than English.
(B) Total number of identifiably distinct languages reported.
(C) The most frequently reported spoken languages or language groupings as % of (A), to the nearest whole number.
(D) Total of (C) as cumulative % of (A).

	Bradford		Coventry		Haringey		Peterborough		Waltham Forest	
(A)	14,201		7,189		7,407		2,408		5,521	
(B)	64		50		87		42		65	
(C)	Panjabi	53	Panjabi	59	Greek	34	Panjabi	24	Panjabi	31
	Urdu	19	Gujerati	16	Turkish	15	Italian	24	Urdu	21
	Gujerati	9	Urdu	7	Creoles*	9	Urdu	18	Gujerati	8
	Bengali	3	Hindi	3	Gujerati	6	Gujerati	12	Greek	8
	Pushtu	3	Italian	2	Italian	6	Chinese	4	Creoles*	7
	Italian	3	Bengali	2	French -based Creoles	4	Polish	2	Turkish	4
					Bengali	3				
	Polish	1	Polish	2			German	2	French-based Creoles	3
					Urdu	2			Bengali	3
	Hindi	1	Chinese	1	Panjabi	2	Hindi	2	Chinese	2
	Chinese	1	Creoles*	1	Spanish	2	Creoles*	1	Italian	2
	Creoles*	1			Chinese	2	French	1	Hindi	1
	Ukrainian	1			French	1			French	1
(D)	95%		93%		86%		90%		91%	

* 'Creoles' here means English-based and other non-French-based Creole languages

occurring groupings of these languages in each area account for at least 85 per cent or 90 per cent of the children concerned. From the point of view of potential educational support for minority languages this suggests that the kind of objection which is based on the logistic problems arising from extremely large numbers of different languages in particular areas has only limited force. Some LEAs are already showing how a considerable impact can be made by beginning with support for the most widespread three or four languages in an area, before going on to tackle, probably on a more centralised basis, the languages with fewer or more scattered speakers. Table 8.1 also points to the dominance, outside London at least, of the South Asian languages among linguistic minorities in England. Panjabi, Urdu and Gujerati in particular, Bengali and Hindi to a lesser extent, are spoken by substantial numbers of children in virtually all the areas we looked at. Only Italian and, in North London, Greek, Turkish, and English-based and French-based Creoles are otherwise prominent in this numerical sense. Speakers of Chinese languages are found in smaller numbers in each area surveyed, as are speakers of Polish outside the London boroughs where we worked.

Literacy in languages other than English

Questions 3 and 4 in the SLS were intended to elicit information about the general incidence of literacy in languages other than English. The resulting data is again of course mediated through teachers, and says nothing about the degrees of skill represented by the responses. We gave only 'yes' and 'no' options for answering the two questions 'Can you read that language?' and 'Can you write that language?' and our note to teachers on this point asked that 'even a modest skill should be treated in this context as a positive answer'. However, although the data set out in the following section related to the different languages, it should be interpreted with this in mind. We believe that it indicates how even very simple questions can provide interesting and consistent patterns of response.

In some of the most frequently occurring languages or language groupings in the Schools Language Surveys, the questions about reading and writing were complicated by the fact that the written language concerned was not always the same as the spoken language used at home. We use the term 'language of literacy' in such cases, but this covers two rather different kinds of linguistic skills. The first is where the language of literacy is a national language fairly closely related to

Table 8.2 Literacy of bilingual pupils in five LEAs: all languages together

	Bradford (n = 14,201)	Coventry (n = 7,189)	Haringey (n = 7,407)	Peterborough (n = 2,408)	Waltham Forest (n = 5,521)
(1) % of bilingual pupils reporting some degree of literacy in any of the languages other than English referred to by them	52.3	41.4	50.5	50.5	49.0
(2) % of the bilingual pupils reporting ability to read the spoken language given in answer to Qs 1 and 2 of SLS	36.7	37.5	48.6	45.0	41.0
(3) % of the bilingual pupils reporting ability to write the spoken language given in Qs 1 and 2 of SLS	28.8	31.3	40.9	37.1	31.5

Notes

(1) 'Bilingual pupils' here is used as a shorthand for pupils reporting one or more languages in addition to English.

(2) For SLS Questions 1 and 2 see reproduction of survey form.

(3) The percentages in lines 2 and 3 are slightly different from their equivalents given in our Reports to LEAs (and in our *Summary of Findings from Five LEAs*) because of the different base used.

(4) For a breakdown of the figures by language grouping see Table 8.4.

the spoken language and used in the family's country of origin as the major medium of education and official communication. The most notable examples in this category are Urdu for speakers of Panjabi whose families originated in Pakistan, pre-partition India and East Africa; and standard Italian for speakers of regional dialects. The second category of languages of literacy includes those languages being learned for religious purposes, and in these cases in particular there may be a quite limited knowledge of the equivalent spoken language. The most frequently found example in this category was Arabic, learned by Muslims from a variety of different language backgrounds (see Figure 6.1, p. 225). For a small proportion of pupils in each place we surveyed, knowledge of both kinds of languages of literacy was reported. Table 8.3 sets out the incidence of such languages in our five areas.

Table 8.3 Languages of literacy

	Bradford	Coventry	Haringey	Peterborough	Waltham Forest
(1) Total no. of pupils reporting any literacy in a language other than English	7,427	2,979	3,739	1,217	2,704
(2) Total no. of pupils reporting separate languages of literacy	3,146	272	61	146	674
(3) Numbers of pupils reporting two separate languages of literacy	597	35	2	2	83

The overall differences in the literacy rates for each area may well relate to the different proportions of each language group in the locality, since the specific rates of literacy vary considerably between languages. Table 8.4 sets out the position for some of the languages most frequently reported in the areas we examined.

To take only the most obvious contrasts pointed up by Table 8.4, we may note that, whereas around two thirds or more of those speaking Polish, Italian and Chinese languages report some degree of literacy in a language other than English, around one third of those in the Hindi,

Gujerati or Panjabi(G) groupings do so. We can only speculate on the reasons for this contrast, which may relate, for example, to a longer settlement history giving a greater opportunity to organise effective mother tongue teaching, or to rather different attitudes to linguistic and cultural assimilation among these different linguistic minorities. The higher rates of reported literacy among girls than among boys in several of the groupings correspond to the widespread evidence of such differences in the educational literature on language-achievement in general, and literacy in particular.

Language skills and age

It is sometimes asserted that, given the almost total lack of encouragement by the LEA school system in most places for the maintenance of languages other than English, early language skills may be lost after only a few years in school.

We have no data bearing directly on this question, since there was no longitudinal element in our design. However, we set out in Table 8.5 the proportions of each age group replying positively to Question 1 of the SLS, which gives some indication of the inter-relationship of age and use of more than one language. This age distribution, of course, is intimately related to the size of the age cohorts in the bilingual population as a whole, and of the different linguistic minorities of which it is composed. Broadly speaking, all LEAs seem to show greater proportions of bilinguals in the primary age groups. This has to be set in the context of overall falling rolls (except in Bradford). In all authorities we can expect the bilingual population to increase both in absolute numbers and in percentage terms as the years go on. (The evidence from ALUS tends to confirm this: see Chapter 5.) The possibility of language shift to English, or that language skills in minority languages have already been lost or under-reported by older children, make such predictions very difficult.

There were age differences in literacy rates too. In most languages the lowest literacy rates were of course reported by the youngest children. In some there was a straightforward increase in reported literacy with increasing age (Italian in all five LEAs, for example, Greek in two of them). However, there was a tendency for the oldest (14+) age groups in some languages to report lower literacy rates than those in the age groups beneath them (Gujerati in two LEAs, Panjabi-unspecified in three).

Table 8.4 Literacy rates in the main language groupings

Pupils reporting literacy**	Bradford %	Coventry %	Haringey %	Peterborough %	Waltham Forest %	All five LEAs %
Panjabi						
(a) unspecified	54	34	37	46	39	46
(b) Urdu script	52	56	–	66	55	53
(c) Gurmukhi script	39	35	–	–	39	37
Urdu	59	55	52	54	55	58
Gujerati	34	37*	25*	23*	33	33
Bengali	56	51	50	–	48	52
Hindi	29	36	23	–	28	31
Chinese	56	61	69	69	57	64
Italian	72	63	59	63*	68	65
Greek	–	–	60*	–	55*	60
Turkish	–	–	49*	–	46	50
Polish	66	79	–	–	–	71

– Indicates that there are fewer than 80 speakers in this LEA.

* Indicates that there are statistically significant sex differences in the literacy rates, with in all cases smaller proportions of boys than of girls reporting literacy.

** 'Literacy' here means that pupils reported that they can read or write at least one of the spoken languages given, or have reported a separate language of literacy.
Percentages are of the total number of pupils reporting spoken skills in the relevant language.
For Panjabi see explanation on p. 324.

The Schools Language Surveys

It is not possible to say from our data alone whether this latter phenomenon is the result of adolescents forgetting, or under-reporting, their literacy skills, whether it is simply a feature of the current 14+ age cohorts, or whether it relates to some combination of these and a range of other factors. Some languages vary in this respect in the different LEAs, with Urdu literacy for example being reported in increasing proportions with age in Haringey and Peterborough, but falling in the other three areas. Literacy in Bengali similarly increases

Table 8.5 Percentage of each age group* reporting use of a language other than English at home

Age-group*	LEA Bradford	Coventry	Haringey	Peterborough	Waltham Forest
5	14.9	11.5	30.6	6.4	20.6
6	22.4	15.6	30.8	7.1	21.2
7	19.7	14.8	34.2	5.2	19.8
8	22.6	15.3	34.3	8.4	20.5
9	16.5	16.1	29.5	5.9	22.3
10	18.2	12.4	33.0	8.3	20.4
11	17.7	15.2	30.6	5.4	19.8
12	15.3	14.5	29.0	8.9	18.0
13	16.2	15.2	29.1	8.4	19.0
14	14.3	12.8	31.1	8.5	16.7
15	11.5	12	28.9	7.4	15.2
16	9.5	11.3	28.8	7.7	13.9

* *Note on 'age-group'*: More than 90% of the pupils surveyed were entered on survey-forms with age ranges of no more than two years, e.g. 11- to 13-year-olds. Only these pupils are included in Table 8.5. The mid-point of the interval between oldest and youngest in each group is used as an indication of the average age in the groups.

with age in Coventry, but decreases in Haringey and Waltham Forest. Clearly, the degree of support which schools can offer to pupils wishing to establish literacy in the minority language is likely to be a major factor in influencing future trends in these rates.

Table 8.6.1 Panjabi* speakers in Coventry schools

Primary schools		Secondary schools	
Number of pupils	Number of schools	Number of pupils	Number of schools
1–10	41	1–50	9
11–20	7	51–100	2
21–30	8	101–200	4
31–40	4	201–389	3
41–100	12		
101–86	6		

* Figures are for 'Panjabi unspecified' + 'Panjabi (G)'; as defined on p. 324.

Table 8.6.2 Gujerati speakers in Coventry schools

Primary Schools		Secondary schools	
Number of pupils	Number of schools	Number of pupils	Number of schools
1–10	41	1–50	11
11–20	10	51–100	3
21–79	4	196	1

Table 8.6.3 Greek speakers in Haringey schools

Primary schools		Secondary schools	
Number of pupils	Number of schools	Number of pupils	Number of schools
1–10	29	1–50	4
11–20	22	51–100	6
21–30	8	101–72	3
31–40	9		
41–76	9		

Distribution of bilingual children over schools

An important consideration for LEAs and schools convinced of the need to maintain and develop pupils' skills in other languages alongside English, is the way in which the speakers of the various languages are distributed among different schools in an area. For the less frequently occurring languages in an LEA some kind of centralised provision would obviously have to be made – possibly even extending to co-operation between neighbouring authorities.

To illustrate the situation with reference to some of the more widespread languages, we take the examples of Panjabi and Gujerati in Coventry and of Greek in Haringey. We have not presented these figures here broken down by age group, but a few further simple calculations will show that there are in principle possibilities within at least some LEA schools for offering support to the larger linguistic minorities.

Dissemination and follow-up to the Schools Language Surveys

The SLS work closely involved teachers, and the reliability of the findings depended in the end on their attitudes towards the survey, and their ways of carrying it out. Their approach revealed whether or not they understood the research aims and objectives, and this determined the starting point for the active dissemination which followed.

Throughout the survey work, we endeavoured to monitor and assess what was revealed about the teachers' attitudes and sociolinguistic knowledge. Although from a commonsense point of view some would say that disseminating information comes after research has been completed, we became more and more convinced that active dissemination starts with and develops alongside the research process, and requires special attention at every stage of it. So we begin here with a discussion of the teachers' meetings which preceded the surveys themselves.

In three out of four LEAs, the general pattern of attendance at these meetings was low, in spite of the fact that in each case each school had been invited to send at least one representative. In three authorities the meeting was held after school hours; in one of them, where more than 280 schools were to be surveyed, 90 teachers attended, and about 25 teachers in each of the other two authorities for respectively 98 and 160 schools to be surveyed. In one authority the meeting took place during school hours, and around 40 teachers attended out of the 98 schools to be surveyed.

The questions asked during the meeting showed that nearly all the teachers attending were at least partly aware of the difficulties, and thinking beyond the merely technical aspects. The survey had also forced them to consider the relevance of such an exercise, and their attitudes to the pupils concerned. Most seemed keen to do the job as well as possible.

We were unable to work out whether the numbers of those attending reflected the proportion of teachers in each authority already conscious of and committed to the object of the research, or whether their presence and reactions were more a reflection of the education officers' and advisers' commitment, or of the value placed on linguistic and cultural diversity by the LEAs as a whole. It did not seem possible to answer these questions at that early stage.

During the survey week the questions and comments received by the telephone advice services threw more light on how much teachers knew. 'How should we record the age of the group surveyed?'; 'How should we question so as to get a reliable answer from younger pupils?'; 'What about the West Indian kids?'. There were also many questions on language names and labels, particularly with reference to pupils whose families came from Pakistani or Indian Panjab. The overall impression was that teachers were discovering a sphere of their pupils' daily lives little known or previously ignored by them. But we had no way to assess the reactions and attitudes of those teachers who did not ring the advice service, who were of course the majority. The analysis of the findings confirmed the impression of a need to develop a greater sociolinguistic and sociocultural awareness among teachers who were not themselves from linguistic minorities.

The active involvement of teachers in this kind of survey is not only essential for the reliability of the findings: at a later stage it influences the impact of the dissemination of findings. Only when teachers are thoroughly briefed beforehand and actively involved in the survey work, do they become aware of the importance of the issue, not only for children from linguistic minorities but for the whole school system. And only then can the findings be made use of in an active and constructive way, with a greater chance of fostering changes in attitudes and teaching practices.

To return to our discussion on the reliability of the findings, it became clear that the preparation for active dissemination had to be tackled at three levels — administrative, psychological or pedagogical, and sociolinguistic.

At the administrative level the preparatory work, briefing sessions and the survey itself had to be organised in such a way that heads and teachers were given time to understand how vital it is to define clearly and consistently the groups to be entered on a single survey form, preferably with age ranges of no more than two years. It was also vital to record accurately the name of the school, the number of pupils on the rolls of the group surveyed, the number of absentees and the age range of the group. In the recording of the basic information, the most obvious cases of 'missing information' in the five authorities surveyed were where the sex of the pupil was not recorded, or where it had not been indicated whether the pupil read or wrote the language reported.

At the psychological or pedagogical level, unless further case studies are conducted, it will remain impossible to assess the impact on the reliability of findings of the way the survey was actually conducted. But it became clear that there was a great need to make teachers aware of what it means for children in Britain to be asked the questions in the survey: they had to understand how important it is to find out the most appropriate time, place and circumstances and devise the most effective ways of making it easy for the children to answer the questions fully and openly. And they had to think about the errors which needed to be avoided as far as possible in setting the context for the questions beforehand. Part of this awareness was to understand why all the children in the class must be asked the first question of the survey: 'Do you yourself ever speak any language at home apart from English?'

At the sociolinguistic level teachers had to be helped to identify clearly the languages and dialects reported by children, and to be encouraged to consult advisers for difficult cases. They also had to learn to distinguish between religious, national or geographical labels such as 'Hindu', 'Yugoslavian', 'Nigerian' and actual linguistic labels. They also had to be ready to put the necessary supplementary questions which would lead to a full and accurate recording of the pupils' linguistic skills.

Thus active dissemination has to consist of two stages. Preparing teachers before the survey (i.e. dissemination of the objectives and methodology of the survey) is just as important as reporting on the findings (i.e. dissemination of the outcome of the research). The evidence of this appeared at every stage of our work and has been reinforced by LINC's subsequent work on the dissemination of findings.

The process of active dissemination after the survey involves assessing several strategies, based on the following assumptions:

(a)   Research findings which are not made available to all those concerned are not fully utilised. It is also possible for findings to be manipulated by people or institutions in positions of power retaining them for their own purposes.

(b)   Research findings which are made available to a wide public are in danger of being misunderstood, and intentionally or unintentionally misused.

(c)   Active dissemination means strategies to reach those educationalists who will not by themselves look for findings in academic reports, or even in booklets displayed on staff-room shelves. It also means reaching those sections of the population that have little or no access to all kinds of 'official' reports. The impact of the findings also depends on the exchanges they give rise to between a variety of target publics who are all involved in the issue, but who may rarely meet together.

(d)   Active dissemination also means the monitoring of the interpretation and use of findings once they are made available.

LINC has used several different strategies for the first stage of active dissemination of SLS findings in Bradford and Coventry, and in the London boroughs of Haringey and Waltham Forest.

In this stage a small circle of recipients — LEA officers and administrators, Advisors and Heads of Unit at authority level — were sent a first report on SLS findings, giving an overall view of linguistic diversity in the LEA. Then a second report — a breakdown of findings for each school — was sent out. This involved around 90 per cent of the schools surveyed in each authority receiving a report on linguistic diversity among the pupils in that school, together with a summary of the findings for the whole authority (96 schools in Haringey, 98 in Waltham Forest, 150 in Coventry and 267 in Bradford).

Schools with a high percentage of bilingual children received several copies of the report for distribution amongst the teachers. A sample copy of the full first report was also sent to each school. Thus all schools, including those with no bilingual pupils, had access to the detailed information on the LEA. Central offices (e.g. Education Office, Language Resource Centre, Multicultural Education Service) in every LEA also received a copy of each of the reports sent to individual schools.

The following aspects proved to be of particular importance in the dissemination process. First, the content of the report had to be assessed in relation to the target publics. The kind of information to be obtained from the data was defined so as to meet the expectations and also the likely needs of potential users. These expectations and needs had been previously assessed and were constantly reassessed in the course of the dissemination process.

Second, qualifications on the interpretation and use of the data had to be carefully thought through and then spelt out, so as to diminish the risk of misinterpretation and misuse. The range of foreseeable distortions had to be assessed as realistically as possible. This implies an understanding of the educational and social context in the country and in the local authority, over a period and at the particular time of dissemination.

Third, the amount of information to be offered, and the number of qualifications attached to it, had to be decided upon so as to avoid two extremes: it should not be so simplistic as to mislead, nor should it be so complicated as to overwhelm. In the latter case the indifferent or hostile reader can easily find an excuse to dismiss 'complicated' data, and the well-meaning may get lost or discouraged.

Fourth, the layout was important. A way had to be found to make sure that the qualifications would be read, and yet the core of the statistical data would be clearly set out. Both needed to catch the reader's attention.

Achieving these exacting goals proved to be a time-consuming exercise, but a rewarding one. The hypothesis that a constructive relationship between research and dissemination processes is possible was worked out in the day-to-day collaboration of LINC and LMP.

The attempt to write the first report for Coventry raised a number of questions which led LMP to refine their analysis of the data. After the reports were sent to Coventry and Haringey education officers, LINC organised a series of meetings with groups of administrators and groups of teachers to present and discuss the findings. These discussions led us to prepare summaries of the findings. Through the feedback from different levels in these two authorities, LINC gained a better understanding of what the target audiences needed, and of how best to present research findings of this kind.

After productive meetings with education advisory staff in Bradford, LINC/LMP improved the qualifications and presentation of the data for the Bradford report, and for the later Waltham Forest survey we were able to produce a first report which was of practical use to a variety of people. Its shape and content were used for revised versions of the first report which were sent to Peterborough, Coventry, Bradford and Haringey LEAs.

The circulation of the first report and the first meetings with administrators, advisers and teachers provoked feedback from many angles. It unveiled tensions, channels of communication and non-communication, and stimulated different categories of people to various kinds of follow-up. Active dissemination meant being ready to acknowledge and respond to a variety of these 'ripple' effects. It meant watching, analysing and making sure the information was progressively taken up by a variety of intermediary individuals and institutions who contribute to the process of change in the education field.

The second, school-based, reports on the Schools Language Surveys aimed to help Education Officers see how the bilingual pupils in their Authority were distributed through different schools, to relate this distribution to other factors, and to assess the educational implications. Since a better knowledge of the patterns of linguistic diversity may lead to special measures in the field of language and intercultural education, these reports may help policy-makers decide upon the appropriate distribution of resources to individual schools. Another aim of the second report was to help teachers and pupils relate their own school situation to the overall picture of linguistic diversity in the area presented in the first report.

9
Sharing languages in the classroom

Aims and scope

In the early stages of the design and implementation of the Schools Language Survey (SLS) discussed in the previous chapter, LMP also began work on an alternative approach to the investigation of linguistic diversity in schools. This eventually took the form of the Secondary Pupils Survey (SPS). From the outset, our intention was for these two surveys to have different but complementary functions. The aim of the SLS was to provide a comprehensive sketch of the distribution of spoken language and literacy skills over the school population as a whole in a number of different local authorities. This emphasis on comprehensiveness necessarily implied that only a few rather simple questions could be asked, and that the questions had to be asked and answers recorded by teachers.

We also wanted to look more directly and in detail at children's use of language, and at their experience of language learning both inside and outside school. For those children who were not bilingual, we also wanted to see how much they knew about the languages around them, in school and in their locality. We felt that a small-scale survey, involving pupils themselves in answering questions about their own past and present language learning, use and experience, would allow more detailed insights into the significance of different languages in children's lives in England. We also wanted to see if we could provide some indication as to whether bilingual children would be more (or less) willing to disclose what they might regard as rather intimate information, in the form of written answers on a questionnaire (SPS) as compared with talking to their teacher (SLS).

The SPS was designed to involve all the pupils in a class, so that there was no question of any preliminary dividing up of the pupils by their teachers. This, of course, would have defeated a major object of the survey: to elicit pupils' own perceptions of parts of their linguistic repertoires. We shared with other researchers such as Rosen and Burgess (1980) the view that bilingualism has to be seen within the wider context of linguistic and cultural diversity in England, and can only be sensitively investigated in the school setting by recognising the inter-ethnic dynamics of the classroom. Using this questionnaire exclusively with the children assumed by their teachers to be bilingual might easily have damaged the sometimes fragile climate of relationships which exists among pupils and teachers.

We therefore designed our questionnaire with two main routes through it. One route was for those who from the beginning mentioned that they had earlier in their lives used more than one language – the so-called 'bilingual route' (pages 2-5 of the questionnaire). The other was for pupils who at least in the first place defined themselves as having started life with only one language – the 'monolingual route' (pages 6-9). Interestingly, we found that some pupils who initially chose the monolingual route showed, when answering later questions, that they knew more about other languages than they had at first volunteered.

In any case, most apparently monolingual English children have quite varied verbal repertoires, which may include indigenous social and regional dialects of English, as well as context-related stylistic varieties. The repertoires of some may also include, for example, Afro-Caribbean creoles or patois, or British varieties deriving from these. For some children the variety of English which they speak may be so different from Standard English, either in form or in symbolic value, that they will want to define it as a separate language. Since in this survey we were trying to elicit the pupils' own accounts of parts of their linguistic repertoires, we tried to include questions which would be relevant to these so-called monolingual pupils, would give recognition to their special linguistic experience, and would encourage their interest in the different linguistic experience of their classmates.

But the focus was not only on the range of languages that pupils say they speak, read or write now. We tried also to establish what degree of skill they had, by asking pupils for their own assessment of their current language skills – receptive and productive skills in both oral-aural and written modes (see SPS questionnaire page 2). The survey also explored, in cases where children have current experience of more than one language or variety, their patterns of language use with different interlocutors – what language or language variety they chose when speaking with different members of their family or with friends (questionnaire page 3). The other major area of interest in the SPS was in pupils' formal and informal language learning experience, inside and outside school (questionnaire pages 4-5, 6-7), and in the perception by monolingual children of languages spoken at school or in their neighbourhood (questionnaire pages 8-9).

Design and administration of the Survey

The questionnaire design

The fact that, in contrast to SLS, the SPS was designed for completion directly by the pupils themselves imposed certain constraints and requirements both on the terminology that could be used, and on the layout of the questionnaire. We believed originally that a task of this nature could only be set for older secondary school students, since this age group would find it easier to reflect on their language experience, and to cope with the task of filling in what was necessarily a fairly complex questionnaire. In fact we found that pupils as young as 11 were able to complete the questionnaires, with varying degrees of help from their teachers.

The opening question focussed on early linguistic experience, and it was the pupil's answer to this which should have determined the initial choice of route through the questionnaire, broadly speaking the 'bilingual' route through green pages 2-5, or the 'monolingual' route through orange pages 6-9. We anticipated that most pupils would answer this first question in one of four ways: (i) by saying they only ever used English at home, (ii) by indicating that they grew up speaking only a language other than English, (iii) by naming two different languages such as Greek and English, Gujerati and English or Panjabi and Urdu, or (iv) by listing, perhaps alongside English, an English-based creole or a regional variety of English.

Each of the two colour-coded routes comprised a different set of questions. The green route on pages 2 to 5 was devised for those who reported that, whether or not they also knew any English, they used a language other than English with their family before they first went to school. The orange route on pages 6 to 9 was for those who reported that they used only English at home with their family in their early years. It is important to realise that this second route was in fact selected by a number of pupils whose parents had probably grown up speaking another language, and in whose homes this language was still

Figure 9.1 SPS questionnaire: 11 pages

This is a project about languages. We are trying to find out how people learn and use different languages and we hope you may be able to help us by answering our questions.

1 Talking about languages

**This is NOT a test or an exam.
There are NO right or wrong answers.
We just want YOU to tell us about YOUR language or languages.**

Please answer our questions by filling in

the boxes   or bubbles

on every page unless we ask you to skip further on.

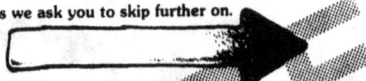

1 Thinking back to the time before you ever went to school, which language or languages did you first use with your family?

I used...   and ...   and...

2 Write in the name of the country the language or languages came from.

from ...   from...   from...

If you only put English in the bubble above, go to the <u>orange</u> pages, page **6**

If you put something else, go to the <u>green</u> pages, page **2**

2 Speaking, reading and writing

3 Think back again to the language or languages you used before you ever went to school and fill in either the top bubble or the bottom two bubbles.

Before I went to school

I only used ...

I mostly used...

I also used...

TICK ONE BOX FOR EACH QUESTION FOR EACH LANGUAGE

4 Can you **understand** this language if it is spoken to you now?

yes, quite well
only a little
no, not now

5 Can you **speak** this language now?

yes, quite well
only a little
no, not now

6 Can you **read** this language now?

yes, quite well
only a little
no, not now
never could

7 Can you **write** this language now?

yes, quite well
only a little
no, not now
never could

8 Do you understand only English now?

yes ☐ no ☐

If you ticked **YES**, go to the orange pages, page **6**

If you ticked **NO**, turn over the page, to page **3**

3 Talking to your family and friends

9 Which two languages do you mainly use now with your family and friends?

I use... and...

FINISH EACH OF THE SENTENCES BELOW BY PUTTING A TICK IN ONE OF THE BOXES.

IF, FOR ANY REASON, THE SENTENCE DOESN'T APPLY TO YOU, TICK THE FOURTH BOX IN THE ROW.

When I'm talking...

	I use	and	BOTH LANGUAGES USUALLY	DOESN'T APPLY
10 to my father I usually speak				
11 to my mother I usually speak				
12 to my brother(s) I usually speak				
13 to my sister(s) I usually speak				
14 to my grandfather(s) I usually speak				
15 to my grandmother(s) I usually speak				

When I'm spoken to...

16 my father usually speaks to me in				
17 my mother usually speaks to me in				
18 my grandfather(s) usually speak(s) to me in				
19 my grandmother(s) usually speak(s) to me in				

20 In school breaks, my friends and I usually speak in

21 Please write in the names of any other languages spoken in your family.

4 Learning languages

22 Apart from the two languages you mainly use, write the names of any other languages you understand at all.

23 Do you go to any language classes besides English, French, German or Latin (inside or outside school)?

yes ☐ no ☐

If you ticked NO, go to page 5

If you ticked YES, carry on with this page

24 Which language or languages are you learning at these classes?

I am learning...

25 About how many hours a week do you spend at these classes?

Each week I spend about ☐ hours

26 When do you go to these classes?

in school lesson time

in lunch hours or breaks

after school or in weekday evenings

at weekends

27 Where do you go to these classes?

in your own school

in another school

in a mosque, gurdwara, temple or church

somewhere else (say where)

28 How long does it take to get to these classes? about ☐ minutes

Go now please to question 33 on page 5

5 Learning Languages continued ...

29 When you were younger, did you ever go to classes, inside or outside school, to learn any languages besides English, French, German or Latin?

yes ☐ no ☐

If you ticked **NO**. go to the last page, page **10**

If you ticked **YES**. carry on with this page

30 Which language or languages did you learn at these classes?

I learnt ...

31 How old were you when you **started** going to these classes?

about ☐ years old

32 How old were you when you **stopped** going to these classes?

about ☐ years old

33 In your language classes did you learn about any of these things at the same time?

religion ☐
dance ☐
history ☐
music ☐
culture and traditions ☐
only language ☐
anything else (say what) ☐

Skip the **orange** pages. Now go to the last page, page **10**

6 Languages in your family

34 Is there anyone in your family who grew up speaking a language besides English?

yes ☐
no ☐

If you ticked NO, go to question 38 on page 7

If you ticked YES, carry on with this page

35

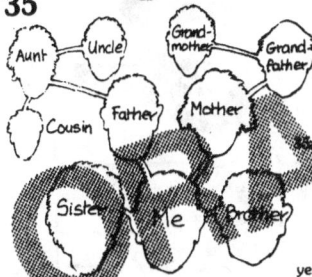

FILL IN ONE BOX BELOW FOR EACH RELATIVE WHO GREW UP SPEAKING A LANGUAGE BESIDES ENGLISH. THEN WRITE THE NAME OF THE LANGUAGE THEY SPOKE IN THE BUBBLE.

Aunt — Uncle — Grandmother — Grandfather
Cousin — Father — Mother
Sister — Me — Brother

My ___ grew up speaking
My ___ grew up speaking
My ___ grew up speaking
My ___ grew up speaking

36 Do they still speak this language?

yes ☐ ☐ ☐ ☐
no ☐ ☐ ☐ ☐

If you ticked NO in all the boxes you filled in, go to page 7

If you ticked YES in any of the boxes carry on with this page

37 How well can you understand this language when your relative speaks it now?

TICK ONE BOX FOR EACH RELATIVE WHO STILL SPEAKS A LANGUAGE BESIDES ENGLISH

I understand most of what they say
I understand some of what they say
I understand a few words
I understand nothing at all

7 Languages out of school

38 Out of school, have you ever learned to speak any language apart from English?

yes ☐   no ☐

If you ticked NO, go to question 43 on page 8

If you ticked YES, carry on with this page

39 Which language did you learn; and if you learnt another language what was it?

I learnt ___ and then I learnt ___

TICK ONE BOX FOR EACH QUESTION FOR EACH LANGUAGE

40 Can you speak this language now?

- yes, quite well
- only a little
- not now

41 Can you write this language now?

- yes, quite well
- only a little
- not now

42 Where did you learn this language?

- from someone in the family here in England
- during a visit to another country
- when my family lived in another country
- at classes out of school
- somewhere else (say where)

8 Languages at school

43 Is there anyone in your class who speaks a language besides English?　yes ☐　no ☐　don't know ☐

44 If you ticked YES, please write the names of the language or languages in the bubbles below.

☐　☐　☐　☐

45 Have you studied any languages at school?　yes　no

If you ticked *NO*, go to question 49 on page 9

If you ticked *YES*, carry on with this page

46 Fill in one or more of the bubbles below.

I've studied...　and ...　and ...

47 How well do you think you **speak** these languages?

TICK ONE BOX FOR EACH LANGUAGE YOU HAVE STUDIED

very well			
fairly well			
not very well			
not at all			

48 How well do you think you **write** these languages?

TICK ONE BOX FOR EACH LANGUAGE YOU HAVE STUDIED

very well			
fairly well			
not very well			
not at all			

9 Languages in your district

49 Near where you live, does anyone speak any language(s) besides English?

yes [ ]   no [ ]   don't know [ ]

50 Are there any signs and notices in languages apart from English near where you live?

yes [ ]   no [ ]   don't know [ ]

51 If you ticked YES to either question 49 or 50 above write the names of the languages in the box.

[ ]

Now please go to the last page, page **10**

10 Almost finished!

52 Apart from the languages you are already studying at school, there may be others you would like to learn. If so, please fill in the bubble.

I would like to study ...

53 Are you a boy or a girl?   boy   girl

54 Which year were you born in?   19

55 How long have you lived in Britain?   about   years

56 What religion are you?

57 Which country were you born in?

58 What is the name of your school?

59 Which class are you in?

60 What is today's date?   day   month   year

Please write over the page anything else you would like to say about the questions we asked or didn't ask. For example if you speak different languages with different grandparents or with elder or younger brothers or sisters we would like to know.

Thank you!

sometimes spoken, but who did not speak it themselves, or at least no longer did so. Such pupils could be expected to make an initial choice of the green 'bilingual' route, but would find questions from page 3 onwards not relevant to their situation. Therefore an additional routing instruction was given, telling them to pass on to the orange 'monolingual' pages. Such pupils were treated, for the purposes of analysis, as a separate 'mixed' category. Their choice of a mixed route in itself said something important about the children's linguistic background.

Pages 3 and 4 of the questionnaire were aimed specifically at assessing the extent to which those pupils who currently used a language other than English drew on their bilingual repertoire in daily interactions with their family, or with friends at school. Pages 4 and 5 investigated present or previous involvement in language classes (other than those in the main conventional school languages), and whether they were organised outside or inside ordinary school time.

In the orange pages of the questionnaire, intended for those who identify themselves as monolingual English speakers, the focus was on sociolinguistic awareness, and on contact with languages other than English. This contact might be inside or outside the home, in the form of language learning experience both formal and informal. The questions on page 6 were designed in particular to give some indication of the extent of language shift between generations. In the SLS, it will be remembered, the wording of the key question was designed to locate only those pupils who currently had a productive oral skill in a language other than English. Those teachers who followed the SLS instructions to the letter would not have recorded pupils who had once spoken, but no longer spoke, other languages; nor would they have noted pupils who claimed only to be able to understand, but not to speak, another language. Questions 34 to 37 in the SPS were designed to investigate these dimensions of language experience.

The questions on page 7 had two different purposes. Firstly, they were intended to establish the extent of exposure to out-of-school language learning for those pupils who had not used a language other than English in their infancy. Secondly, they were designed to see whether many children, even where they came from an essentially monolingual family background, had learned languages outside school, for example through living in another country.

Finally, in the 'monolingual' section, pages 8 and 9 were in part about the observation of languages other than English in use by fellow-pupils in school or in the general area around the school, and in part about the pupils' experience of school language learning.

The last page of the questionnaire was designed for all the pupils to complete, whichever route they have followed. It asked among other things about religious affiliation, which is closely connected to literacy traditions for some languages at least. It should be noted that the names of those completing the questionnaire were not requested and indeed in the Teachers' Guidelines it was made clear that anonymity was expected.

Piloting and redrafting the questionnaire

In the first few months of 1980 the SPS questionnaire went through a number of drafts, with the aim of producing a design that would provide a straightforward yet engaging exercise for the pupils to be involved in. The first pilot for the SPS was carried out during the months of May and June 1980 in a small number of secondary schools in the outer London boroughs of Harrow, Enfield and Croydon. Over 300 boys and girls aged 11 to 16 were involved at this stage.

LMP researchers observed several of the piloting sessions, and were struck by the degree of interest many pupils showed in completing the SPS questionnaire, although it was at that stage still without illustrations. In some classes the activity generated spontaneous discussion between pupils and teachers, and between pupils of different linguistic backgrounds. It was this that first suggested to us the potential curricular value of SPS – an extension of its original purpose as a survey instrument.

The experience of the pilot survey led to further simplification of the questionnaire, to improvements in both wording and layout, and to the drafting of a set of guidelines for teachers who might be conducting the survey elsewhere. These incorporated some of the ideas and suggestions brought up by the teachers in the schools where the pilot surveys were carried out. They stressed, for example, the need for careful introduction and placing of the questionnaire in an appropriate context of interest in linguistic diversity, and they discussed the degree of help which might be necessary for pupils of different ages and ability. This aspect of the use of the questionnaire is developed more fully at the end of this chapter, but first we present details of the administration and findings of surveys themselves.

The Surveys in Peterborough and in Bradford

In late 1980 a revised but still unillustrated version of the SPS was administered to all first-year pupils in the eleven secondary schools in the city of Peterborough, a total of some 1,700 11-year-old pupils who had already completed the SLS some weeks previously. This was the first large-scale use of SPS, and the age group and sample size in Peterborough were those requested by the education advisory staff there, who hoped to build on the findings from this age cohort of pupils at later stages in their secondary careers.

A meeting for all the teachers involved was held after the administration of SLS and before that of SPS in Peterborough, and the discussion there provided useful input for the teachers' guidelines. The seeds of the idea for an illustrated version of the SPS questionnaire, whose design and production was co-ordinated soon after by LMP's sister project LINC, and first used in Bradford, were probably also planted at the time of the Peterborough survey.

Our intention in using SPS in Bradford in early 1981 was to obtain data from a fairly large sample of secondary pupils in the 14-15 age range. The maximum size of survey adminstratively feasible would have been about 1,500. In practice we decided in collaboration with LEA advisers to survey around 1,100 children, and to conduct the research in schools concentrated in the city of Bradford itself, rather than including the outlying parts of Bradford Metropolitan District.

The selection of schools in which the survey took place was intended to be broadly representative of the range of upper schools in the city. Therefore the survey included single-sex and mixed schools, inner city schools with a high proportion of pupils from South Asian linguistic minorities, and Roman Catholic secondary schools with children from Eastern and Southern European linguistic minorities on their rolls.

Although we had chosen this wide range of schools in an attempt to make the sample broadly representative of the city, we became aware that, if a whole year-group in all the schools was surveyed, it would not contain enough bilingual children to make detailed analysis of that subgroup worthwhile. Therefore we arranged for schools with more than 10 per cent of bilingual pupils to survey larger numbers of children than schools where the proportion of bilingual pupils was less than 10 per cent. In this way we hoped that somewhere between 30 and 50 per cent of the pupils completing SPS in Bradford would be bilingual, as compared with the approximately 18 per cent for Bradford Metropolitan District as a whole.

The selection of particular groups or classes in Bradford within the agreed year-group was under the individual school's control, and we have no way of determining whether the classes chosen were representative of the whole year-group. We simply accepted the co-operation of these schools, and offered them advice as to the best criteria for selecting pupils within the school. The SPS in Bradford was in the end completed by a total of just over 1,000 pupils in eleven different schools – the first to use the illustrated version of the questionnaire.

Findings of the Peterborough and Bradford Surveys

Before going on to present the findings of SPS in Bradford and Peterborough, a few comments are necessary about the quality of the data that was collected. It is obvious that the very varied atmospheres in different classrooms, and the differing amounts of interaction between pupils, must be borne in mind when interpreting the results. Inevitably the task of filling in such a complex questionnaire proved difficult for some of the 11-year-olds in Peterborough, and even for the 14-year-olds in Bradford, despite the use of the illustrated version there. This meant that the preparation of the data for computer analysis showed up a higher proportion of 'inconsistent' data than in any of our other surveys.

In preparing the data for analysis therefore, we identified a number of distinct types of difficulty, and edited the data accordingly. Firstly, there was a small number of questionnaires which we had to exclude altogether because they had been filled in so inconsistently or incompletely: the loss rate here was no more than 1 per cent. The biggest problem in the design of the questionnaire in both cities proved in fact to be the routing instructions. Most of the dozen or so difficulties in this group concerned the choice of the mixed route, and some editing was necessary. However, where the routing was consistent with most or all of the answers, the decision of the pupil was respected: we did not reclassify any pupil from the monolingual to the bilingual groups solely on the basis of skills and use of a minority language reported on the orange pages. The major remaining problem was the large but varying amount of missing data for each question. With a few exceptions, this information was irretrievable, and the result is that every variable on the questionnaire had to be analysed with different numbers of valid cases as the base.

Despite all these problems, and some inevitable inaccuracies introduced at the stage when the data was coded and punched, we believe we have a body of data which is broadly representative of the age-groups in the two cities, and as accurate as can be expected from a self-completion questionnaire conducted in a classroom setting.

Bilinguals and monolinguals

The primary indication as to whether a child can be classed as monolingual or bilingual in SPS was the number of languages listed in answer to the opening question about languages first used in the family. In Bradford 74 per cent out of the 1,011 cases which were analysed listed English and no other language. In Peterborough 90 per cent of the 1,768 cases analysed gave only English. These children were classified as 'monolingual'. Included in this group were fifteen cases in Peterborough where pupils had specified a dialect of English instead of or in addition to 'English', and had then consistently followed the orange monolingual route in the questionnaire. Such pupils, for example, reported 'Australian', 'Canadian' or 'American English'. 'Scottish', 'Jamaican', 'Welsh' and 'Irish' were also given, and for the most part it was clear that such cases reflected the fuzziness of the boundaries between language and dialect and between ethnic, national and linguistic criteria. At least some of the Irish and Welsh cases, however, evidently represented real cases of bilingualism in two distinct languages and were therefore assigned to the 'bilingual' or 'mixed' categories.

The remaining 259 pupils in Bradford and 168 in Peterborough mentioned at least one language which was not English as the language first used in the family. Among these, nearly 40 per cent in Bradford and nearly 30 per cent in Peterborough mentioned English as one of their first languages. A smaller proportion mentioned at least two languages other than English as first languages.

Of these early bilinguals, about 90 per cent in both Bradford and Peterborough followed the green route, indicating that they were currently bilingual or multilingual. The remaining pupils followed the mixed route, indicating that they now considered themselves monolingual English speakers.

Table 9.1 sets out the languages given in answer to the SPS's first question by all the pupils in the two LEAs who answered this question, and who did not give only 'English'.

Table 9.1 Language or languages first used with families (Q.1), excluding 'English only' answers

Languages and language groupings	Peterborough (10% of pupils surveyed)			Bradford (26% of pupils surveyed)		
	Only one language given	English and the other language given	Two languages other than English given	Only one language given	English and the other language given	Two languages other than English given
Panjabi	18	7	8(Urdu)	74	41	23(Urdu) 1('Indian')
Urdu/'Pakistani'	18	3	4(Panjabi)	29	13	4(Panjabi)
Gujerati	14	5	–	12	2	–
Bengali	–	1	–	3	2	–
Hindi/'Indian'	3	–	1(Panjabi)	1	3	–
Pushtu	–	–	–	4	1	–
Italian	22	16	–	1	7	–
Chinese	3	2	–	1	–	–
Irish/Welsh/'Scottish'	3	5	–	1	8	–
Other	13	16	2	2	15	2

Note: Not included in this table are 4 pupils in Peterborough and 9 pupils in Bradford, who mentioned 3 different languages used in the family.

The bilingual pupils

In this section we shall set out in more detail the patterns of language skills, use and learning reported by the currently bilingual pupils who had followed the green route. In Bradford Panjabi(U), Panjabi(G) and Urdu speakers (see Chapter 2, pp. 45 f, for a discussion of these categories) account for more than three-quarters of these pupils, and in all but a very few cases the current second language was reported as English. The religious affiliation given by these speakers enables us to estimate with a fair degree of confidence which pupils would use, or seek to learn, Urdu or the Gurmukhi script. More than 80 per cent of the Panjabi or Urdu speakers who gave their religion were Muslims; the remainder, with a few exceptions, were Sikhs. In Peterborough the main languages in our bilingual category were Panjabi, Urdu and Italian, which together accounted for 61 per cent of the green route respondents. Only very few pupils gave two languages other than English.

Table 9.2 shows the level of skills in the minority languages reported in the two cities by the bilingual pupils of all language groups together: the percentages given are of all the pupils choosing the green route.

Table 9.2 Minority language skills reported (Qs 4-7)

(A) Bradford: 'Green route' pupils (N = 230)

Skill	Quite well	Only a little	Not now or never could
Understanding	93	7	–
Speaking	86	11	2
Reading	36	31	34
Writing	29	33	38

(B) Peterborough: 'Green route' pupils (N = 153)

Skill	Quite well	Only a little	Not now or never could
Understanding	91	9	–
Speaking	85	15	–
Reading	39	30	31
Writing	31	31	38

Language use with family and schoolfriends

The patterns of language use for the bilingual pupils were only analysed for the cases where English was one of the two main languages used currently with family and friends.

Table 9.3 sets out the data from the answers to the questions on page 3 of the questionnaire.

There was a clear pattern among bilingual pupils, which suggested that English was used most of the time with the younger generation, while the mother tongues were used more often with parents and grandparents. There were also some indications, at least in Bradford, that the minority languages were used more when speaking to females, e.g. to mothers and sisters, than to males.

The girls in the sample showed no statistically significant differences in terms of language use from the boys, although in Bradford more girls than boys reported using only English with most of their relatives. The differences between the patterns for Peterborough and Bradford probably relate to the different linguistic composition of the sample. There were more Italian speakers in Peterborough, and a comparison of them with the Panjabi- and Urdu-speaking respondents in the same city suggests, for example, that while nearly two-thirds of the Panjabi or Urdu speakers use only the minority language when speaking to their fathers, less than a quarter of the Italian speakers used only Italian. When talking to their brothers, about three-quarters of the Italian speakers used only English, and a single speaker reported using only Italian. This compares, among the Panjabi and Urdu speakers, with over 40 per cent using only Panjabi or Urdu to their brothers, under a quarter only English, and the rest a mixture.

The apparent tendency among these younger bilingual adolescents to use more English, or both their languages, with their siblings should not be interpreted as an indication of their language loss, nor indeed of a general pattern of language shift among all British-born members of all linguistic minorities. As children from linguistic minorities grow up, and particularly during their school years, the pressures from the predominantly monolingual monocultural majority, in terms of both language use and more general patterns of behaviour, are very difficult to resist. These pressures can take many different forms: absence of reference to, or even covert or overt opposition to, their 'home' language and culture in and around the school; the all-pervading and compelling influence of the English-medium media and music of the subcultures of British youth, within as well as outside their home, and of course among

Table 9.3 *Language used by bilingual pupils with family members and schoolfriends (Qs 10–20)*

	Peterborough				Bradford			
	N	% minority language	% English	% both equally	N	% minority language	% English	% both equally
To my father I usually speak:	129	51	17	32	203	71	16	13
To my mother I usually speak:	32	62	13	25	209	78	11	11
To my brother(s) I usually speak:	112	16	50	34	200	19	60	21
To my sister(s) I usually speak:	107	17	49	34	189	25	54	21
To my grandfather(s) I usually speak:	83	74	16	10	127	87	6	6
To my grandmother(s) I usually speak:	95	78	13	9	130	78	6	16
My father usually speaks to me in:	128	62	16	22	203	76	14	9
My mother usually speaks to me in:	133	70	14	16	206	87	8	5
My grandfather(s) usually speak to me in:	83	82	14	4	131	87	8	5
My grandmother(s) usually speak to me in:	95	82	11	7	132	88	9	3
In school breaks, my friends and I usually speak in:	131	3	81	16	202	9	84	6

their peer group. Moreover, many children from linguistic minorities experience racism, and become increasingly conscious of the lower socio-economic status of many ethnic or linguistic minorities they see around them. In their early teenage years most children go through a period of opposition to adults in their immediate environment, and tend to look for psychological security in terms of conformity with the peer group. So adolescents often find it particularly difficult to resist those pressures, which lead them to consider their grandparents' or parents' language and patterns of behaviour as something they do not want to be associated with. Some nevertheless do resist, as the figures show. And this certainly happens with less difficulty in places where the relevant languages are widely used outside as well as inside the home, and when for example the children's languages are in various ways given status in the school, by teachers and the school personnel as a whole.

Language learning

In Bradford just over a fifth out of the 230 bilinguals responding reported that they were currently going to language classes, and a seventh said that they used to go, but did not currently do so. The languages being studied were Urdu, Italian, Panjabi, Ukrainian, Arabic, Spanish and the most common languages previously learned were Urdu and Panjabi. Most of the classes currently attended were community-run, and nine out of ten of the pupils who no longer attended had stopped going by the age of 12.

In Peterborough, more than a quarter of the 153 bilingual respondents were currently attending a class to learn a non-school language – Urdu, Italian, Arabic, Polish, Cantonese, Indian, Panjabi, and Hindi. A further seventh used to attend classes in Italian, Urdu, Gujerati, Panjabi, Chinese, Spanish, or Irish, and of these most had left by the age of 10.

Again, as indicated more fully in Chapter 6 in relation to the MTTD surveys, such figures should not be taken out of context. 'Demand' for and interest in mother-tongue teaching is not to be deduced solely from existing proportion of pupils attending, far less from 'drop-out' figures.

Monolingual and 'mixed route' pupils

From what was reported about their families by those pupils who followed the orange route in our questionnaire, we focus here only on relatives who had grown up speaking languages other than English. In Bradford, about one in seven reported at least one such relative, half of them mentioning one parent and just under a fifth both parents. The most frequently mentioned languages for the first relative were Irish, Italian and German, with smaller numbers of Panjabi, Urdu, Ukrainian, Polish and Welsh. Out of 82 who said the first relative still spoke the language, more than a quarter said they understood most or some of what was said, but nearly 70 per cent only a few words or nothing at all.

In Peterborough about the same proportions reported at least one such relative, with more than two fifths of these mentioning one parent and about an eighth both parents. The most frequently mentioned languages for the first relative were Irish, Italian, Gaelic, German and Welsh, with smaller numbers mentioning French, Polish, Panjabi, Urdu, Ukrainian and Gujerati. Out of 239 who said the relative still spoke the language, again more than a quarter said they understood most or some of what was said, with around 70 per cent understanding a few words or nothing at all.

In both places then, proportions of pupils having contact with languages other than English but who are not themselves fully bilingual are by no means negligible. Everyday contact with other languages is in other words even more widespread than the kind of data represented by the answers to the questions posed in the more narrowly focussed Schools Language Survey might at first suggest. This is surely, therefore, an important part of the data relevant for educational planning.

In addition to the direct contact evidenced above, many of the monolingual pupils were aware of classmates who spoke languages other than English, and of languages spoken in the locality. Table 9.4 shows the most frequently mentioned languages in these categories in the two cities.

There are some differences between the cities which no doubt reflect the different sociolinguistic situations. More interesting than that is the fact that more precise 'language' terms are given more often in the case of classmates' language, while generalised 'ethnic' terms such as 'Indian', 'Pakistani' and 'Chinese' are commoner for the local neighbourhood languages. This may arise from the fact that pupils could confirm the names of languages spoken by others in the class simply by asking them. It should be noted that pupils' use of 'ethnic' labels is a typical reflection of the all pervading monolingual monocultural (racist) majority definition of the situation. Pupils aged 11-13 are hardly likely to welcome being referred to as speaking or indeed being 'Pakistani'.

*Table 9.4 Number of monolingual pupils mentioning the main
minority languages (Qs 43-5, 49)*

Language	Peterborough		Bradford	
	Classmates' language	Local language	Classmates' language	Local language
Cantonese	47	2	29	3
'Chinese'	53	120	14	107
Gujerati	144	16	39	2
'Indian'	103	135	68	103
Italian	572	275	73	59
'Pakistani'	36	185	88	196
Panjabi	173	64	196	51
Polish	49	101	20	59
Ukrainian	-	-	89	11
Urdu	143	73	203	70

Note: Some pupils mentioned as many as four languages in each case.

They may well go through a phase when they want to be dissociated from what they perceive to be widely considered as negative and pejorative.

In Bradford 29 and in Peterborough 15 pupils followed the mixed route, indicating that they had earlier in their lives used a language other than English, but by the time they were filling in our questionnaire used only English. The languages involved in Bradford were Irish, Italian, Hindi, Panjabi, Gujerati, Urdu, and in Peterborough German, Dutch, Irish, Norwegian, Welsh, Italian, and Ukrainian.

Most of these respondents reported that their skills in the minority language were now low. When they answered the questions on the orange pages of the questionnaire, it was clear that most had relatives who still spoke the minority languages, and that these were typically their parents. In both Bradford and Peterborough two-thirds of these pupils said that they could understand the language spoken by the relatives they mentioned.

Languages pupils would like to learn

All the pupils surveyed were asked a question about the languages they would like to learn at school. Most of them mentioned one or more of the traditional school languages, as can be seen from Table 9.5, but it

Table 9.5 Pupils' school language learning preferences

Language	Peterborough			Bradford		
	Bilingual pupils	'Mixed route' pupils	Monolingual pupils	Bilingual pupils	'Mixed route' pupils	Monolingual pupils
'Chinese'	3	–	19	3	–	19
French	6	–	136	40	3	44
German	39	9	731	38	6	146
Greek	–	–	16	4	2	22
Gujerati	2	–	4	1	–	2
'Indian/Pakistani'	–	–	8	–	1	13
Italian	27	5	250	11	6	114
Latin	5	1	58	16	1	31
Panjabi	2	–	1	11	–	2
Russian	2	3	27	5	1	45
Spanish	12	2	201	12	1	101
Urdu	15	–	5	34	–	5

Note: Pupils mentioned up to four languages each.

has to be remembered that at the time of our surveys measures to promote the introduction of minority languages into the LEA school curriculum were in their infancy. It probably did not occur to many of the pupils asked that there might be a real possibility of having their home languages – or those of their classmates –taught in school. As always, the context of the questioning has to be borne clearly in mind: if the DES can in 1983 issue a Consultative Document, entitled 'Foreign Languages in the Curriculum', which devotes itself almost entirely to discussion of the teaching of French, German, Spanish, Italian and Russian to 11- to 14-year-olds, it is hardly surprising that 11- to 14-year-olds themselves may seem unaware of wider options. In fact in Peterborough and Bradford a combined total of over 2,800 pupils produced 194 'requests' for lessons in minority languages such as Greek, Chinese and the various South Asian languages. More interesting still is the fact that 110 of these 194 requests came from pupils who defined themselves as 'monolingual'.

Comparison of SLS and SPS data

We were not in the end able to make many direct comparisons of data on the same pupils obtained by two different methods – through the teachers' mediation in the Schools Language Survey, and direct from pupils' written answers in the Secondary Pupils Survey. Since the administrative arrangements for conducting the two surveys in most places meant that the SLS and SPS data did not derive from exactly the same sets of pupils, we present this comparison only for a single year-group in a single Bradford school. All the third-year pupils present completed the Secondary Pupils Survey, and we also have information on the whole year group from our earlier Schools Language Survey. So, although the two surveys were conducted with different sub-groupings of this same year-group and by different teachers, and although the absentees on the two survey days were inevitably slightly different, the comparisons being made are between essentially the same pupils.

Three hundred and fourteen SPS questionnaires were analysed, of which 84 had been completed by pupils following the bilingual or green route and a further 18 the mixed route. The total of 102 compares with 106 pupils reported in the SLS from the same year group as using a language at home other than English.

The other point of comparison worth attempting is over the particular languages mentioned by the same pupils in the same year group in the two different surveys.

Table 9.6 sets out the information on this.

Table 9.6 Languages reported in SLS and SPS

Languages and language groupings	Number of pupils reported in SLS	Number of pupils reporting* in 'green route' of SPS	Number of bilinguals reporting** in 'mixed route' of SPS
Panjabi	39	40	7
Panjabi (Gurmukhi)	13	4	3
Urdu	28	11	1
Panjabi (Pakistani)	–	2	1
Mirpuri	12	–	–
'Pakistani'	–	2	–
Mixed Urdu-Panjabi	1	–	–
Urdu (Pakistani)	1	–	–
Urdu (from India)	–	1	–
Gujerati	3	6	–
Hindu Panjabi	–	4	2
Hindi	1	–	–
'Indian'	–	2	1
Pushtu	1	4	–
'Pathan'	2	–	–
Bengali	2	1	1
Telugu	1	1	–
'Malaysian'	1	1	–
Indonesian	–	1	–
Akan	–	1	–
Welsh	–	–	1
French	–	–	1
Italian	1	–	–

*   The figures in the middle column are for pupils reporting languages spoken now.

** The figures in the right-hand column are for languages given in answer to Q.1 of the SPS questionnaire by pupils following the mixed route in completing the questionnaire. Since half of these pupils claimed they could understand their minority language quite well, we can only conclude that they had had difficulty in following the routing instructions.

In broad terms the data from the two surveys matches up, although there are problems of detail arising from the different sets of labels used by teachers and by pupils. For example, none of the pupils used the term 'Mirpuri' although it was given by one or two teachers in twelve cases, and Urdu is mentioned more than twice as often in SLS as in SPS. Reported literacy rates, however, correspond remarkably closely, with a figure of 60 per cent from SLS, and a total of 59 per cent of the pupils following the green route in SPS saying that they could read at least a little.

Linguistic awareness in the classroom

We referred earlier in this chapter to the fact that a number of schools had expressed interest in using the illustrated version of the SPS questionnaire as an element in the study of language. Such study takes place in different contexts in the secondary curriculum – sometimes 'Modern Language' time, sometimes as part of Social Studies. And, of course, it may be undertaken at very different levels of sophistication appropriate to different ages and abilities. Since SPS was designed on the principle that all the pupils in a class should take part in the survey, not just the pre-defined bilingual pupils, it made it particularly appropriate for use in most of these contexts.

SPS proved to be a resource for schools in developing and sharing understanding about the attitudes and perceptions of monolingual children. From the perspective of the bilingual children, these attitudes and perceptions were at least as important as the teachers' attitudes. It became evident that the use of the survey questionnaire as curricular material encouraged all pupils and teachers involved to reflect more about the changing linguistic make-up of our society, and the role that language plays in people's daily lives.

There are clearly a number of different aspects of language, language use and language acquisition that can be looked at in a classroom, without necessarily involving formal discussion of the morphological and syntactical features of a language. SPS can help this wider approach to language, starting from the existing linguistic diversity in the classroom.

One aspect of language which is uppermost in a speaker's awareness and which is often referred to in talk about talk is vocabulary. In a sense, it reflects the conceptual system of language and is a good place to look for examples of how languages differ and what they share, as well as how they borrow from each other. Regional varieties of English and creoles also provide good illustrations of variation within as well as between languages. Specialized jargons and registers, along with secret codes and slang can also be a good starting point for looking at language functions and variation in individual speech repertoires.

Moreover, the use of the SPS survey can also generate discussion and classroom activities centred around questions to do with what a survey is, how people conduct surveys, how they decide what questions to ask, who the information is for, and whether there is any difference between what people *say* they do and what they actually do.

Altogether, with imaginative and sensitive treatment by the teachers involved, many schools have already found that conducting a language survey of the kind described in this chapter can be a valuable learning experience. To leave a record of at least one class's use of the material in this way, and as part of its strategy of active dissemination therefore, LINC co-produced a video programme on SPS with the ILEA TV Centre. North Westminster Community school's modern language department was already involved in trying out a foundation course in language awareness for all first-year modern language classes (Garson, 1982), and the filming took place there in December 1981.

The programme, entitled 'Sharing Languages in the Classroom', shows the children and their teacher using the SPS questionnaire. It starts by illustrating the linguistic diversity visible in some London streets, pointing out how vital languages other than English can be for those pupils who use them in their daily life outside school. It goes on to show how a well-prepared teacher introduces the questionnaire in the classroom. Examples of exchanges between pupils and teacher, and among pupils, are shown while the children are completing the questionnaire.

The purpose of the programme is to illustrate two of the possible uses of the questionnaire: as a teaching aid and as a survey instrument. In schools, the programme may encourage other teachers to document linguistic diversity by using the questionnaire in a similar way. It may also serve as a detailed introduction to the use of the questionnaire at class, department, year or school level.

In initial and in-service teacher training the programme may be used in language education and in multicultural education courses, with particular reference to home-school liaison and in discussing the implications of linguistic diversity in the processes of socialisation experienced by each child both inside and outside the home.

The programme may also encourage Education Committees, Officers and Advisers to use the questionnaire as an instrument for surveying different aspects of linguistic diversity in secondary schools on an authority-wide basis (LMS/ILEA, 1983).

10
Epilogue

The main objective of this book has been to put the other languages of England 'on the map' — that is, on the educational and political agenda, rather than on some kind of geographical map, as some of those interested in our research apparently expected when we began.

If the minority languages of England are ever to be seen as more than 'other', and to be acknowledged as important living and developing languages in their new environment, there is an obvious need for widely available information about them. Indeed, a major objective of our work has been to provide a data-base for future research. However, we hope our book has gone beyond the presentation of statistical details of these personal, social and economic resources, and beyond simply proposing ways in which our fragmentary picture can be filled out and developed over time.

Many readers of this book will have been 'home-made' bilinguals (or 'school-made' bilinguals who have survived), who wanted to understand how they could make the acquisition of another language easier for their children. Others may have just been curious about the range of languages used in daily life in England. And there will have been the professionally curious: fellow-researchers in some branch of the social sciences, or practitioners in the health, education or social services. Perhaps we may also have attracted the interest of administrators, policy-makers, politicians or media-workers, who are very influential in shaping the definitions of the situations which we have described.

We hope that we have offered all our readers the opportunity to reflect upon the implications of living in multilingual England, whose linguistic richness derives in large part from a colonial past, and from a particular political definition of contemporary economic needs.

We have tried to help the already bilingual to appreciate the potential contribution of their skills to the development of social and educational policy for all members of our society. We have tried too to convey to monolingual readers something of the intellectual and cultural richness of the world of the bilingual. We may even perhaps have reached the hearts as well as the minds of some readers! That is an essential step if language learners from both majority and minority ethnic backgrounds are to gain the confidence and interest so necessary for effective learning. It is also vital if we are to infuse the less powerful in our society with the confidence to claim their educational rights, and the social recognition of their skills.

By describing some of the characteristics of the newer linguistic minorities in England, we have indirectly reminded the reader of certain fundamental truths. Most of the world's population, and of its school systems, are bilingual or multilingual. It is quite possible for people of all ranges of intellectual ability to learn and use more than one language from an early age. The learning of a second language is helped by building a strong foundation in the first. Bilinguals have the potential for developing specific cognitive and social skills. But in Europe at least these are much more often exploited by upper- and middle-class people. And in most parts of the world bilingualism is all too often valued only with reference to high-status languages. When bilinguals belong to the subordinate sections of society, and there is an imbalance between the status of their two languages, their potential linguistic skills are often lost, and their bilingualism is defined as − and thus becomes − problematic. The bilingual skills of this latter group are rarely acknowledged in the official criteria of achievement established in, for example, school curricula or public language examinations. Dodson has recently expressed the point in these terms:

> Bilingualism is often blamed for a whole range of negative phenomena. However, closer analysis shows that it is not the existence of the individual's two languages that causes this negative behaviour, but a whole range of other social and psychological factors, especially society's view of the status of the languages, its treatment of the bilingual acquiring them, and the self-image which the bilingual develops during this process. (Dodson, 1983)

One of the reasons we have taken a societal approach to bilingualism is that the debate in England has focussed until now on the language development of the individual child, and the responsibilities of the school system in that respect. We did not want to restrict our research to children, nor to LEA schools, since the social meaning of different languages and varieties for their speakers, and for those who develop educational policy and practice, emerges from complex historical, political, economic and social processes in the wider society.

The role of the ethnic majority and minority media is just one of the areas relevant to the educational process which we were not able to deal with adequately in our research. Yet most bilingual children grow up in bilingual families where English medium radio and television has a particular power over the growing child. It provides knowledge and experience which can be shared with others beyond the home. And the media are just one of the unguided means of informal language learning which makes our focus on LEA schools seem rather narrow.

The fundamental source of input for language learning is ultimately the permanent flow of social interaction with other people. We therefore developed different ways of looking at children's language use at home and in their locality, always within a framework of the social constraints on language choice. Because of our limitation to self-report methods, however, we only scratched the surface of sociolinguistic reality. Future research could profitably concentrate on the observed patterns of language use in particular family, peer group, school and workplace settings.

We also focussed on the formal teaching of minority languages, most of which still takes place outside the official school system. Whatever the no doubt considerable educational benefits of this community-run provision, the very existence of these schools tells us much about the marginalisation of minority languages, and about the collective reaction of adult members of linguistic minorities to the policies and practices prevailing in the official school system.

Why is it so difficult for the bilingualism of a large number of pupils in England to be developed as a resource by teachers? A survey of teachers' linguistic resources – another area which could usefully complement our work – might confirm what is all too well known: that is that the overwhelming majority of school staff, even in multilingual areas, is thoroughly monolingual in attitudes and practice. It is likely that such a survey would also show the under-utilisation of existing resources, although there are encouraging signs of interest on the part of a few teachers in their pupils' bilingual skills, and even in learning a minority language themselves. Overall, however, we face a situation in which the needs of linguistic minority pupils are perceived in terms of problems which drain limited resources, and not for what they are – resources which might be used to fertilise the existing rather barren field of language learning. This prevailing view of bilingualism, coupled with vested interests in preserving the status quo, explains why

the bilingual education issue is likely to remain marginal. We have a
graphic illustration of this attitude in the title and scope of the recent
DES consultative paper on school language policy – *Foreign Languages
in the School Curriculum* (DES, 1983).

By carrying out our four surveys in several local areas, we have built
a picture from different perspectives of the various features found in
bilingual settings. Some features, such as code-switching and the non-
reciprocal patterns of language use found in some families, seem to be
particularly common where there are British-born members of the
household. Other features, such as language skills and opportunities to
use different languages, are notably different even within one linguistic
minority in different parts of the country. The main implication for
social and educational policy seems to us to be that policies intended
to foster bilingualism could stop a process of language shift which
might otherwise appear inevitable. We think that such policies should
be implemented. We have not discussed their components in any detail
in this book, because they are many and far-reaching, and because they
were not and could not become the focus of our research. But it should
be obvious from our work that national policies related to professional
recruitment and training, or to curriculum change, will need to have a
built-in responsiveness to local needs and conditions. The role of local
broadcasting, the potential for training community interpreters, or the
strategy for developing bilingualism among children inside and outside
the school, for example, will vary widely. Assessments of different local
initiatives in any one field can help to isolate the main factors which are
essential for the success of specific schemes.

One crucial factor for the success of local initiatives, especially in the
field of education, is the participation of local people. It is our conviction that educational and social research should always be carried out
alongside, and with the active collaboration of the least powerful
sections of the local population. Too often research problems have been
defined by the powerful, surveys have been carried out upon the powerless, and the findings used intentionally or otherwise to preserve the
privileges of the powerful and keep the powerless in their place. In view
of this danger, we developed community-based surveys, so that we
could be made sensitive to the political and sociolinguistic situation of
the local linguistic minorities, and to ensure the greater reliability of
our findings. Developing community-based research strategies also gave
us the opportunity to learn from members of linguistic minorities, and to
assess the most productive ways to disseminate our findings to everyone
involved in the research process. In the case of the school-based surveys

the collaboration with LEAs gave us considerable understanding of the institutional constraints and ingrained attitudes which underlie most policies and practices, as well as of the growing awareness among increasing numbers of educationalists of the inadequacies of traditional approaches. And through our efforts to avoid reinforcing dominant views about bilingual pupils, we were able to develop our instruments into materials which enable teachers to learn without feeling threatened, both from their pupils and from the environment around the school.

We built into our timetable the development of manuals of use and teachers' notes, so that three of our surveys can go on being used, for research and in-service teacher training purposes. Similarly, active dissemination work was built in from an early stage in the research, and should foster the sharing of our findings, methods and experience. Our area of research constantly reminded us that the distribution of cultural and linguistic resources in our society is a reflection of the political and economic imbalançe, to put it briefly, between the dominant monolingual majority and the subordinate, and in many cases bilingual, minorities.

We must admit only limited success in matching our performance to our intentions. For however much we aimed to counter the prevailing view about minority languages and their speakers, our institutional base, and our styles and media of communication were bound to restrict the impact of our research, making it more accessible to the highly educated English-speaking people, and more easily susceptible to manipulation by institutions which have the power to resist change in the status quo. Nonetheless, through our collaboration with a wide range of consultants, fieldwork co-ordinators, teams of bilingual interviewers, minority organizations and mother tongue teachers, as well as LEA teachers, language advisers and local administrators, we have developed alternative outlets for the findings which they helped to establish, and also for the findings of the other surveys carried out in their locality.

The process of research itself proved rewarding to many of the people we worked with. Many interviewers reported the surprise and pleasure of respondents when they realised that someone was interested in their language skills. Often interviewers and consultants were themselves impressed that a university research team wanted systematically to investigate minority language use and attitudes. At the Project's final public conference, the personal and professional response of one Polish interviewer brought home this point quite vividly:

'I was born here in London, my parents were refugees after the war.

They both spoke fluent English, but at home we have always spoken Polish, and we have enjoyed all Polish traditions and celebrations, and . . . kept in touch with people and events in Poland. I went to a Polish Saturday school, I read Polish books, and I wrote to my cousins and uncles and aunts in Poland, in Polish. Of course, at the same time I attended an English school and most of my friends were English, but there was almost complete division between my Polish life and my English life. Perhaps a good illustration of this is the difficulty I have always had in introducing myself to people. If I said I was Polish, I would be asked when I had come here, or I would be told, "No, you are not, you're British!" But I was also told that I had a funny name, that my family ate horrible foreign food, that we spoke a peculiar language, and that we had Christmas on the wrong day.

'I felt very apprehensive about doing the interviews: it seemed like an awful lot to ask people to spend at least an hour out of their evening answering a lot of personal questions. I was sure that most people would refuse, but I need not have worried. In the event I only had two refusals, and the general response was absolutely overwhelming. I always greeted people and explained what I wanted in Polish, and this immediately broke the ice. In fact several people said they would not have invited me in if I had spoken in English. I am quite sure that carrying out the interviews in Polish had a very significant effect on the quality of the data which I obtained. In several cases this was simply because the respondent was not very fluent in English, and would not have understood some of the questions or been able to formulate answers in English. But even with fluent English speakers, there are many aspects of the Polish community's experience and culture which might not be interpreted correctly by an interviewer from a non-Polish background, even if they happened to have learned how to speak Polish. You are all aware of the kind of misunderstandings that can arise, and the important allusions that might be missed when people from different linguistic and cultural backgrounds are trying to communicate. I am sure also that there was greater willingness to answer some of the more personal questions, and to talk at greater length and in more detail about personal histories and attitudes, particularly to express opinions which were critical of British institutions and policies, and even of the Polish community's work. People actually said things like, "I would not say this to an English person, but you know what it is like!"

'The rewards and satisfactions for me of being involved in ALUS have been tremendous, quite apart from all that Polish home cooking and the interviews with very interesting people. One particularly enjoyable and useful aspect was meeting interviewers from other linguistic minorities, and finding that we had a great deal in common: the pleasure and richness in our lives which come from having access to two languages and cultures as well as the problems and frustrations of living in an almost completely monolingual society.

'Above all I welcomed the LMP and the opportunity to be involved because of my particular interest and concerns as a teacher. Firstly, because I have always attached great importance to recognising and supporting children's home language, and I have had a lot of difficulty in convincing some of my colleagues that children from linguistic minorities should be helped and encouraged to maintain and develop their first language, not just for their own benefit but for the benefit of their monolingual friends. Secondly, I am quite sure that no education policy can succeed if it ignores the experiences and aspirations of children's families and communities, especially when dealing with language, which is such a vital part of everyone's life and identity. If we ignore the way in which language is used and the attitudes to language which children encounter in their life outside school, we cannot hope to devise policies which will allow them to use and develop all of their linguistic skills and talents.

'I think it would be a sign of great progress if the kind of labels which exist in North America could become generally accepted in Britain too, so that we could talk about English-British, Polish-British, Chinese-British, Turkish-British, or Bengali-British children in our schools, instead of implying that they must choose to identify with only one language and one culture.'

We will feel that our research has been worthwhile if we have convinced our colleagues that the involvement of bilingual researchers is a necessary development for research in this field. This is particularly the case for the kinds of longitudinal and in-depth sociolinguistic and ethnographic studies which would be an obvious extension of the work of LMP. Bilingual researchers offer not only their linguistic skills and sensitivity to questions of translation and training of support staff: they provide a particular check on the problems of ethnocentrism in research methods and analysis.

Although our research revolved around different kinds of survey work, we hope we have illustrated even in this limited field the advantages of multi-method and interdisciplinary research in complex urban societies, and indeed the necessity for it. Many disciplines are still reluctant to acknowledge the benefits of cross-fertilization, and so many researchers are not trained to use different methods, to develop appropriate strategies, or indeed to work in collective research teams. There were problems, misunderstandings, and information overload within our interdisciplinary team, but the mutual enrichment was invaluable. Because of our origins in different disciplines we were more aware of the need to introduce the language issue into the field of ethnic relations and to illustrate the complexity of the ethnic factor in the field of linguistics. Future academic work in both traditions may have something to gain from our experience.

Within the educational debate we hope we have contributed towards a casting off of the monolingual world-view, and of the practices which help to maintain it. If all pupils had the opportunity to learn and use another language spoken widely in this country, they might experience alternative views of the limited social reality they have known up to now. The kind of bilingual education which aims to develop bilingualism among monolingual and bilingual youngsters, through the use of both languages as mediums of instruction, is one of the most obvious strategies for anti-racist education. This kind of initiative which works to decrease discrimination and prejudice is even more timely for ethnically homogeneous monolingual classrooms in our multilingual society. It is significant that no one in England has yet seriously considered immersion programmes which would allow monolingual English pupils to learn through the medium of a minority language. But it is of course relevant that both these kinds of schemes have been most successful in settings such as Canada, where the status difference between the two languages usually involved is minimal.

This point returns us finally to the social policy implications of our work. We hope that this volume has provided a new framework for research, policy and practice on bilingualism in England. We have raised many more questions than we have answered. If we have managed to convince readers that the educational issue is above all a question of broadening of intellectual horizons, of fundmental values and of social justice, then there is some hope for change.

Appendix 1

Directive 77/486 of the Council of the European Communities on the schooling of children of migrant workers

ANNEX A

No L 199/32   Official Journal of the European Communities   6.8.77

II

(Acts whose publication is not obligatory)

COUNCIL

COUNCIL DIRECTIVE
of 25 July 1977
on the education of the children of migrant workers

(77/486/EEC)

THE COUNCIL OF THE EUROPEAN COMMUNITIES

Having regard to the Treaty establishing the European Economic Community and in particular Article 49 thereof,

Having regard to the proposal from the Commission,

Having regard to the opinion of the European Parliament[1],

Having regard to the opinion of the Economic and Social Committee[2],

Whereas in its resolution of 21 January 1974 concerning a social action programme[3], the Council included in its priority actions those designed to improve the conditions of freedom of movement for workers relating in particular to reception and to the education of their children;

Whereas in order to permit the integration of such children into the educational environment and the school system of the host State, they should be able to receive suitable tuition including teaching of the language of the host State;

Whereas host Member States should also take, in conjunction with the Member States of origin, appropriate measures to promote the teaching of the mother tongue and of the culture of the country of origin of the abovementioned children, with a view principally to facilitating their possible reintegration into the Member State of origin.

HAS ADOPTED THIS DIRECTIVE:

(1) OJ No C 280, 8. 12. 1975, p. 48

(2) OJ No C 45, 27. 2. 1976, p. 6

(3) OJ No C 13, 12. 2. 1974, p. 1

Article 1

This Directive shall apply to children for whom school attendance is compulsory under the laws of the host State, who are dependents of any worker who is a national of another Member State, where such children are resident in the territory of the Member State in which that national carries on or has carried on an activity as an employed person.

Article 2

Member States shall, in accordance with their national circumstances and legal systems, take appropriate measures to ensure that free tuition to facilitate initial reception is offered in their territory to the children referred to in Article 1, including, in particular, the teaching - adapted to the specific needs of such children - of the official language or one of the official languages of the host State.

Member States shall take the measures necessary for the training and further training of the teachers who are to provide this tuition.

Article 3

Member States shall, in accordance with their national circumstances and legal systems, and in cooperation with States of origin, take appropriate measures to promote, in coordination with normal education, teaching of the mother tongue and culture of the country of origin for the children referred to in Article 1.

Article 4

The Member States shall take the necessary measures to comply with this Directive within four years of its notification and shall forthwith inform the Commission thereof.

The Member States shall also inform the Commission of all laws, regulations and administrative or other provisions which they adopt in the field governed by this Directive.

Article 5

The Member States shall forward to the Commission within five years of the notification of this Directive, and subsequently at regular intervals at the request of the Commission, all relevant information to enable the Commission to report to the Council on the application of this Directive.

Article 6

This Directive is addressed to the Member States.

Done at Brussels, 25 July 1977.

> For the Council
> The President
> H SIMONET

Appendix 2
Mother Tongue Teaching Directory survey: Stage 2, List of questions

MOTHER-TONGUE TEACHING DIRECTORY

STAGE 2

List of Questions

(taken from the Stage 2 questionnaire)

History and Aims

1. Please describe the origin and the development of your school.

    e.g. Who started the school? What was the reason for
          establishing it? What changes have there been in
          numbers of pupils and teachers, subjects taught,
          methods used, your financial basis and other problems?

2. What are your present aims?

3. Do you know of any other mother-tongue school/class for
   the same language(s) which was started before your school?

    If so, please write the name and address.

Languages and other Subjects Taught

4. Name the language(s) you teach that are ...

    (a) national or regional language(s)

    (b) language(s) for religious purposes

    (c) language(s) used for other purposes
         Please specify what purposes.

5. Please list all the languages and dialects
   (including English) that your pupils speak at home.

6. Are there other subjects taught in these languages?

Teachers

7. How much is a teacher paid on the average?
   Please add any comments you would like to make.

8. Total number of staff: ____

How many of your staff have ...
(a) a degree in the language(s) taught?
(b) a degree in other languages?
(c) a degree in a non-language subject?
(d) a qualification for teaching the language(s) taught?
(e) a qualification for teaching a second or foreign language?
(f) a general teaching qualification?
(g) teaching experience without formal qualifications?
(h) a general education to secondary school leaving certificate, without teaching qualifications or experience?
(j) other - please specify:

Attendance

9. How many children learn each language, when and what age are they?

Materials and Methods

10. Please give your opinion of the books available by putting one of the following numbers in the boxes below:

> 0 = not used at all
> 1 = not very useful
> 2 = satisfactory
> 3 = useful
> 4 = very useful

- Books published in U.K.
- Books published in home country
- Books published in another country

11. What changes (if any) would you like made to the books and teaching materials you use?

12. How do you decide what class to put your pupils in? Tick more than one if necessary.

(a) according to their age
(b) on the basis of a conversation/ interview with the pupil
(c) on the basis of some written work done by the pupil
(d) some other way
Please explain why:

13.　(a)　If you have pupils of different ages or different levels of knowledge within the same class, how do you organise your teaching? e.g. Do you use different books? Do you divide the class into groups? Do you use pupils as helpers?

　　　(b)　What changes would you like to make if you had the opportunity

14.　Please describe briefly any teaching materials you have developed (and attach examples if possible).

15.　What other teaching materials do you use (besides books mentioned above and your own materials)?

16.　Do you and/or your pupils have access to books in the language(s) you teach from ... (tick where appropriate)

　　　(a)　the school library?
　　　(b)　the mother-tongue school library?
　　　(c)　the public library?
　　　(d)　the local teachers' centre?

17.　Do you have access to equipment and materials? If so, please say what (e.g. charts, tape-recorders, films).

18.　Which of the following do you spend most time on?
　　　(a)　teaching to speak the language
　　　(b)　teaching to read the language
　　　(c)　teaching to write the language
　　　(d)　other
　　　　　Please specify:

19.　Please describe below the methods you use when teaching.

Examinations

20.　Which examinations do you prepare your students for?

21.　If you do not prepare your students for any public examinations, which syllabus do you use in your teaching?

　　　　　(a)　published. Please specify:
　　　　　(b)　teacher prepared
　　　　　(c)　none

22. If you use an examination syllabus, please give your opinion of it. Indicate name(s) of language(s) and tick where appropriate.

   (A) Level of mother-tongue required
   (B) Level of English required to answer examination questions
   (C) Cultural and literary content of examination syllabus
   (D) Balance between oral and written skills required

23. Do you use any other kinds of regular tests in your school/class?

24. What suggestions would you make to improve ...
   -   the range and variety of examinations?
   -   design and content?

Administration and Funding

25. To what extent and in which ways are the parents involved in the school?

26. What are the main problems in running the school?

27. What are the main problems with funding?

28. Have you any other comments to add?

Appendix 3
Adult Language Use Survey: list of questions in English

ADULT LANGUAGE USE SURVEY: LIST OF QUESTIONS IN ENGLISH

The actual questionnaires for each language were all laid out in a bilingual format, with the English version on the right-hand side of the page, and the other language on the left-hand side. (See Figures 4.1, 4.2 and 4.3 for examples.) Here we give only the English version.

'X' = the spoken language of the linguistic minority concerned
'Y' = the written language of the linguistic minority concerned

In the English version below, only the questions themselves are printed in lower case letters. The interviewers were asked to put these questions to the respondents word for word in the appropriate language. EVERYTHING ELSE, WHICH IS PRINTED IN CAPITAL LETTERS, WAS DIRECTED TO THE INTERVIEWERS ONLY AND WAS THEREFORE NOT TO BE READ ALOUD.

1: TOWN IN WHICH INTERVIEW TOOK PLACE: COVENTRY/ BRADFORD/LONDON

2a: NUMBER OF LANGUAGES LISTED IN QU. 4 BELOW
2b: LANGUAGE IN WHICH INTERVIEW WAS BEGUN
2c: LANGUAGE GROUP

3: QUESTIONNAIRE AND CARD NUMBER

SECTION A: LANGUAGE SKILLS AND LEARNING HISTORY

4: Which other languages do you know besides X, including regional languages and dialects?
PLEASE WRITE IN THE LANGUAGE/DIALECT NAMES AND CHECK FOR ENGLISH
(SPACE FOR 8 ENTRIES)

5: When did you last use each of the languages or dialects you have just told me about?
WITHIN ONE DAY/ WEEK/ MONTH/ OVER A YEAR AGO
REFER BACK TO EACH LANGUAGE OR DIALECT LISTED IN QU. 4

6: Did you start speaking X at home? YES/NO

7: Which language or dialect did your mother mostly speak to you when you were a young child? PLEASE WRITE IN:

8: And which language or dialect did your father mostly speak to you when you were a young child? PLEASE WRITE IN:

9: Roughly what age were you when you started speaking X? PLEASE WRITE IN NUMBER OF YEARS:

10: Which country were you in when you first started to speak X? PLEASE WRITE IN:

(FOR LAYOUT OF QUESTIONS 11-24 IN THE BILINGUAL VERSIONS OF THE QUESTIONNAIRE, SEE FIGURE 4.1 IN THE MAIN TEXT OF THE BOOK.)

11: How well would you say you understand X when it is spoken to you? VERY WELL/ FAIRLY WELL/ NOT VERY WELL/ NOT AT ALL

12: How well would you say you speak X? VERY WELL/etc

13: How well would you say read Y? VERY WELL/etc

IF RESPONDENT CANNOT READ AT ALL, SKIP TO QUESTION 18.

14: Did you learn to read Y at home? YES/NO

15: Did you learn to read Y (also) at language classes outside ordinary school times? YES/NO

16: Did you learn to read Y at your ordinary school? YES/NO

17: Roughly what age were you when you began learning to read Y? WRITE IN NUMBER OF YEARS:

18: How well would you say you write in Y? VERY WELL/etc

IF RESPONDENT CANNOT READ AT ALL OR WRITE AT ALL SKIP TO QUESTION 24.

(QUESTIONS 19-22, ABOUT THE CIRCUMSTANCES OF LEARNING TO WRITE Y, WERE DROPPED AFTER THE FIRST STAGES OF THE SURVEY IN COVENTRY, AND ARE NOT INCLUDED HERE.)

23: Which country were you in when you learned to read or write Y? PLEASE WRITE IN:

24: How many years of full-time education have you had? PLEASE WRITE IN NUMBER OF YEARS:

25/26/27: When you went to school which language or dialect was used as the medium of instruction in primary or elementary school/ in secondary or high school/ in college or university?

ONLY X/ ONLY ENGLISH/ ANOTHER LANGUAGE OR DIALECT/ MORE THAN ONE LANGUAGE OR DIALECT/ DID NOT HAVE THIS STAGE OF FORMAL EDUCATION/ NOT APPLICABLE

28/29/30: GIVE DETAILS OF LANGUAGES OTHER THAN X OR ENGLISH GIVEN IN Qs 27-7

(QUESTION 31 WAS DROPPED AND IS NOT INCLUDED HERE.)

32: How well would you say that you understand spoken English? VERY WELL/ FAIRLY WELL/ NOT VERY WELL/ NOT AT ALL

33: How well would you say that you speak English? VERY WELL/etc

34: How well would you say that you read English? VERY WELL/etc

35: How well would you say that you write English? VERY WELL/etc

36: Where did you start to learn English? AT HOME/AT SCHOOL/ SOMEWHERE ELSE

37: If 'SOMEWHERE ELSE', please explain where.

38: Roughly what age were you when you started to learn English? PLEASE WRITE IN NUMBER OF YEARS:

39: Which country were you in when you started to learn English? PLEASE WRITE IN:

(QUESTION 40 WAS DROPPED, AND IS NOT INCLUDED HERE.)

41: Which country were you in when you first used English outside school? PLEASE WRITE IN:

42: Do you ever have someone to interpret for you? YES/NO

IF ANSWER TO QUESTION 42 IS 'NO', SKIP TO QUESTION 45.

When you have someone else to interpret for you:

43: Who is that person? (RELATIONSHIP, NOT NAME) PLEASE WRITE IN:

44: What are the circumstances? PLEASE WRITE IN:

SECTION B: LITERACY

45/46/47: Do you ever see notices in shops/ calendars/ information leaflets written in Y/ written in English? YES/NO
Can you understand them? YES/ NO/ N/A

48/49/50: Do you ever receive personal letters/ formal letters/ bills written in Y/ written in English? YES/NO

Can you understand them? YES/ NO/ N/A

51-55: Do you ever read newspapers, newsletters or magazines/ religious books/ textbooks/ novels/ other books
in Y/ in English? YES/NO

56: Are there any books in Y in the Public Libraries in this city? YES/NO/DON'T KNOW

57: Do you ever use the Public Library? YES/NO

IF 'NO' SKIP TO QUESTION 60.

58: If 'YES', when did you last borrow a book from the Library? WITHIN LAST WEEK/ MONTH/ YEAR/ OVER A YEAR AGO

IF 'NEVER', SKIP TO QUESTION 60.

59: In which languages have you borrowed books? Y ONLY/ MOSTLY Y/ Y AND ENGLISH EQUALLY/ MOSTLY ENGLISH/ ONLY ENGLISH/ OTHER & ENGLISH/ OTHER ONLY/ OTHER MIXTURE OF LANGUAGES

IF 'OTHER CATEGORIES, which languages? PLEASE WRITE IN:

60–67: Do you ever write / lists/ notes in a diary/ messages/ personal letters/ business letters/ notes while listening to someone talking/ notes while reading, e.g. classified advertisements in newspapers/ notes before writing, e.g. a letter or a talk in Y/ in English? YES/NO

68–69: Do you ever write anything else in either of these languages? Please say what:

70: Do you ever write anything else in any other language? YES/NO If yes, please say which language _____ and what _____

SECTION C: HOUSEHOLD LANGUAGE USE

(FOR LAYOUT OF QUESTIONS 71–80 IN THE BILINGUAL VERSIONS OF THE QUESTIONNAIRE, SEE FIGURE 4.2.1 THE MAIN TEXT OF THE BOOK.)

71: How many people live in this household including yourself? PLEASE WRITE IN NUMBER:

I would like to ask you a number of questions about each person in the household in turn:

72: Relationship to respondent, e.g. mother, husband, sister, friend? please write in:

73: Sex of person? MALE/FEMALE

74: How old is this person? AGE IN YEARS:

75: Where was this person brought up (ie spent the first 16 years)? OVERSEAS RURAL/ OVERSEAS URBAN/ OVERSEAS MIXED/ U.K. & OVERSEAS/ U.K. ONLY

76: How is this person employed? WORKS OUTSIDE HOME/ WORKS FOR PAY IN FAMILY BUSINESS ON PREMISES/ WORKS AT HOME FOR PAY/ FULLTIME HOUSEWIFE/ STUDENT OR SCHOOLCHILD/ OTHER

77/78: How well does this person know X/ English? VERY WELL/ FAIRLY WELL/ NOT VERY WELL/ NOT AT ALL

79: When the respondent and this person talk with each other, which language(s) or dialect(s) does the respondent speak in? ONLY OR MOSTLY X/ X AND ENGLISH/ ONLY OR MOSTLY ENGLISH/ OTHER AND ENGLISH/ ONLY OR MOSTLY OTHER/ OTHER MIXTURE

80: When talking with respondent, which language(s) or dialect(s) does the other person speak? ONLY OR MOSTLY X/ X AND ENGLISH/ ONLY OR MOSTLY ENGLISH/ OTHER AND ENGLISH/ ONLY OR MOSTLY OTHER/ OTHER MIXTURE

IF THERE ARE NO CHILDREN OR YOUNG PEOPLE UNDER 21 IN THIS HOUSEHOLD, SKIP TO SECTION E, QUESTION 97.

SECTION D: CHILDREN AND LANGUAGE

81/82/83: In which language(s) or dialect(s) are the following conversations conducted in your household: child to child/ child & mother/ child & father? ONLY OR MOSTLY X/ ONLY OR MOSTLY ENGLISH/ ONLY OR MOSTLY OTHER/ BOTH SPEAKERS X & ENGLISH/ BOTH SPEAKERS X & OTHER/ BOTH SPEAKERS OTHER AND ENGLISH/ ONE SPEAKER X, ONE ENGLISH/ ANY OTHER MIXTURE

84: Is there a child under two years in this household? YES/NO

IF 'NO', SKIP TO QUESTION 87.

85/86: In which language(s) or dialect(s) does the mother/father in this household speak to babies under two years old? ONLY OR MOSTLY X/ ONLY OR MOSTLY ENGLISH/ ONLY OR MOSTLY OTHER/ MIXTURE OF X & ENGLISH/ MIXTURE OF X & OTHER/ MIXTURE OF ENGLISH AND OTHER/ ANY OTHER MIXTURE

87: Has anybody ever taught the children of this household to read and write Y here in the house? YES/NO

88: If 'YES', please say who: (RELATIONSHIP TO CHILD) _____

89: Has anybody in the family taught the children of this household any songs or rhymes? YES/NO

90: If 'YES', please say who: (RELATIONSHIP TO CHILD) _____ and what language did they use? PLEASE WRITE IN: _____

91: Has anybody in the family ever told any stories to the children of this household? YES/NO

92: If 'YES', please say who: (RELATIONSHIP TO CHILD) _____ and what language did they use? PLEASE WRITE IN: _____

93: Do you know of any classes in this city either inside or outside school, where children are taught X? YES/NO

94: If 'YES', please say where and when : WRITE IN _____

95: Have any of the children from this household (BETWEEN 5 AND 18 YEARS OF AGE) been to any of these classes?
WITHIN LAST 7 DAYS/ 4 WEEKS/ 12 MONTHS / YES, BUT OVER A YEAR AGO/ NEVER

IF CHILDREN HAVE BEEN TO SUCH A CLASS WITHIN THE LAST 4 WEEKS, SKIP TO SECTION E, QUESTION 97.

96: Are there any reasons why the children from this household are not going to classes to learn X? PLEASE WRITE IN:

SECTION E: LANGUAGE AND WORK

97: What is your current work situation?
IN PAID EMPLOYMENT/ HOUSEWIFE/ STUDENT/ APPRENTICE/ RETIRED/ UNEMPLOYED/ OTHER
IF 'OTHER', PLEASE EXPLAIN: _____

(THE FOLLOWING QUESTION WAS TO BE ASKED ONLY IF THE RESPONDENT WAS IN PAID EMPLOYMENT OR HAD STOPPED WORKING WITHIN THE PREVIOUS TWO YEARS.)

97a: What is/was your occupation?
WRITE IN AS PRECISELY AS POSSIBLE THE JOB TITLE AND A BRIEF JOB DESCRIPTION

98: What is the occupation of the other people in the household who work?
ATTEMPT TO GET A FULL JOB DESCRIPTION. WRITE IN RELATIONSHIP, NOT NAME.

IF RESPONDENT IS A FULL-TIME HOUSEWIFE OR STOPPED WORK MORE THAN TWO YEARS AGO, SKIP TO QUESTION 115.

IF RESPONDENT IS A FULL-TIME STUDENT, ANSWER THE NEXT TWO QUESTIONS.

IN ALL OTHER CASES, SKIP TO QUESTION 101.

99: Which subject are you studying?
TECHNICAL, SCIENTIFIC, MEDICAL/ COMMERCIAL, BUSINESS STUDIES, ACCOUNTANCY/ ARTS, LANGUAGES, SOCIAL SCIENCES/ OTHER OR MIXED

100: What is the level of your course?
'O' LEVEL OR CSE/ TRADE EXAMS/ 'A' LEVEL OR HND/ DEGREE OR POSTGRADUATE STUDIES/ OTHER

IF RESPONDENT IS A FULL-TIME STUDENT, SKIP TO QUESTION 109.

101: Do you work for yourself or in the family business or for someone else? SELF/ FAMILY/ SOMEONE ELSE

102: What kind of training or qualifications did you need to get this job? NONE/ EXPERIENCE GAINED ON THE JOB/ APPRENTICESHIP OR TRAINING GAINED WHILE WORKING/ PROFESSIONAL OR ACADEMIC QUALIFICATIONS

103: How many hours a week do you work usually? PLEASE WRITE IN NUMBER

104: What kind of organisation or business or industry do you work in? MANUFACTURING INDUSTRY/ TRANSPORT SERVICES/ CIVIL SERVICE OR LOCAL AUTHORITY/ BUSINESS OR COMMERCE/ RETAILING OR CATERING/ OTHER SERVICES (INCLUDING HEALTH)/ OTHER

105: How many people are you responsible for supervising, managing or employing?
FILL IN NUMBER, INCLUDING ZERO WHERE APPROPRIATE

106: Do you need to be able to speak X in order to do your work? YES, IT IS ESSENTIAL/ YES, IT HELPS/ NO

107/108: Do you need to read X / English in order to do the work that you do? YES, IT IS ESSENTIAL/ YES, IT HELPS/ NO

109: How many colleagues, workmates or fellow-students are you in regular contact with during your working day?
PLEASE WRITE IN NUMBER:

110: How many of them can speak X? PLEASE WRITE IN NUMBER:

111: Which languages can the following people at work speak? — UP TO THREE WORKMATES OR COLLEAGUES OR FELLOW-STUDENTS WITH WHOM RESPONDENT WAS IN MOST FREQUENT CONTACT/ FOREMAN OR SUPERVISOR/ BOSS OR MANAGER/ MOST SUB-ORDINATES/ MOST CLIENTS OR CUSTOMERS

112: Which language do you speak to this person at work?

113: Which language does each use when speaking to you? — ONLY (OR MOSTLY) X/ X & ENGLISH/ ONLY (OR MOSTLY) ENGLISH/ OTHER & ENGLISH/ ONLY (OR MOSTLY) OTHER/ MIXED/ DON'T KNOW OR SPEAK/ NOT APPLICABLE

SETION F: LANGUAGE OUTSIDE WORK AND HOME

(QUESTIONS 114 & 116 WERE DROPPED AND ARE NOT INCLUDED HERE.)

115: Outside your home and work, who do you spend most of your time with?
LIST TWO INDIVIDUALS – RELATIONSHIPS, NOT NAMES
Can they speak X? YES/NO
Which language do you actually speak with them? ONLY X/ ONLY ENGLISH/ BOTH/ OTHER/

117/118/119: What about your relatives outside the household who live in the UK/ other friends & acquaintances/ neighbours/: can they speak X? ALL/ MOST/ A FEW/ NONE/ (NO RELATIVES IN THE UK)

Which language do you actually speak with them?
ALL RELATIONS OR FRIENDS ONLY X/ ALL RELATIONS ONLY ENGLISH/ ALL BOTH/ OTHER/ NEVER SPEAK WITH THEM/ X WITH SOME, ENGLISH WITH OTHERS

120: Do you take part in the activities of sports clubs/ religious groups/ hobby groups/ music or dance groups/ literary or other artistic groups/ courses of further study/ political or union activities/ youth or social clubs/ welfare or charitable activities/ informal regular groups/ other groups?
YES/NO (FOR EACH CATEGORY)

121: Of the groups you have mentioned, what are the names of the two where you spend most time?
WRITE IN GROUP-NAMES AT HEAD OF TWO COLUMNS FOR QS 122–126

How many of the members can speak X? ALL/ MOST/ A FEW/ NONE

122: When did you last attend this group? WITHIN LAST: 7 DAYS/ 4 WEEKS/ 12 MONTHS/ OVER A YEAR AGO

123: Have you ever held any office or position of leadership?
YES, STILL DO/ YES, USED TO/ NO
IF 'YES', WHAT OFFICE:

124/125/126: What language is the written business conducted in/ is used for the spoken business at formal meetings/ do you use when chatting informally to other people in the group?
ONLY X/ MOSTLY X/ EQUALLY X & ENGLISH/ MOSTLY ENGLISH/ ONLY ENGLISH/ OTHER/ DO NOT KNOW

127: Do you ever see films in X (include video tapes)? YES/NO

128: When did you last see such a film? WITHIN LAST 7 DAYS/ 4 WEEKS/ 12 MONTHS/ OVER A YEAR AGO/ NEVER

129: Do you ever go to a shop where the shopkeeper or assistants speak X? YES/NO

IF 'NO', SKIP TO QUESTION 131.

130: Which language do you speak with the shopkeeper or assistants?
ONLY X/ MOSTLY X/ EQUALLY X & ENGLISH/ MOSTLY
ENGLISH/ ONLY ENGLISH/ OTHER

131: Do you ever consult a doctor who can speak X? YES/ NO/ DON'T
KNOW

132: Which language do you use with him/her? AS FOR 130

SECTION G: ATTITUDES ABOUT PROVISION OF LANGUAGE
TEACHING

(FOR LAYOUT OF QUESTIONS 133–36 IN THE BILINGUAL
VERSIONS OF THE QUESTIONNAIRE, SEE FIGURE 4.3 IN THE
MAIN TEXT OF THE BOOK.)

(THESE WERE THE INSTRUCTIONS GIVEN TO INTERVIEWERS
FOR THIS SECTION:) 'READ THE INTRODUCTORY STATE-
MENT TO THE RESPONDENT AND THEN READ EACH STATE-
MENT SLOWLY AND CLEARLY AND ASK IF S/HE AGREES OR
DISAGREES WITH THE STATEMENT, AND HOW STRONGLY'

Introduction: Many people think it will be difficult for the X-speaking
community in England to keep up its language over the next generation.
Some people think that the government should help maintain such
languages, perhaps by introducing the teaching of them in schools,
perhaps by supporting the teaching programmes that the communities
have set up already in many areas. We are interested to know your
opinion on these matters, so can you please tell us whether you agree or
disagree (and how strongly) with the following statements which I am
going to read to you.

(ONLY THE 15 STATEMENTS ARE SET OUT HERE: FOR EACH
THE INTERVIEWER HAD TO RECORD THE RESPONDENT'S
OPINION ON A 5-POINT SCALE AS FOLLOWS:–
      strongly agree/ agree/ not sure/ disagree/ strongly disagree)

133: We can maintain the culture and identity of our communities even if
we cease to use our languages.

134: We can keep up the use of our languages over the next generation if
there is proper teaching widely available.

135: We should make every possible effort to maintain the fullest use of
our languages in Britain.

136: The government should provide the teaching of our languages as a
right for all our children in state schools.

137: The use of our languages in school lessons to teach other subjects
would be a great help to our children.

138: Unless we make our children work very hard at learning our
languages they won't be able to keep them alive in Britain.

139: The government should support our communities' efforts and give us money to organize classes for our children to learn our languages.

140: The authorities should produce versions of most official letters, notices, forms and leaflets in our languages as well as in English.

141: Our communities are able to organize all the teaching of our languages that is needed by our children without any help from the government.

142: There is no problem in maintaining our languages; they will not die out in Britain.

143: The maintenance of our languages is the most important of all matters for our communities.

144: The government should employ far more doctors, teachers, social workers, etc. who can speak our languages.

145: Our communities should completely abandon the use of our languages and should adopt the use of English everywhere.

146: More English people should be encouraged to learn our languages.

147: Our children will learn as much of our languages as they need to know from the family without any special teaching.

SECTION H: PERSONAL

IF YOU HAVE ALREADY ESTABLISHED THE ANSWERS TO ANY OF THE REMAINING QUESTIONS IN THE COURSE OF THE INTERVIEW, DO NOT ASK THE QUESTIONS AGAIN. SIMPLY FILL IN THE ANSWERS.

148: Which member of your family was the first to come and live in the U.K.?
RELATIONSHIP NOT NAME _____

149: How many times have you visited a country where X is spoken (during the time that you have been living in Britain)?
WRITE IN NUMBER OF TIMES _____
WRITE IN NAME OF COUNTRY _____

150: How long did you stay there last time? 1 MONTH OR LESS/ 1–6 MONTHS/ 7–12 MONTHS/ OVER A YEAR

151: What is your religion?
BUDDHIST/ GREEK ORTHODOX/ HINDU/ JEWISH/ MUSLIM/ PROTESTANT/ ROMAN CATHOLIC/ SIKH/ OTHER/ NONE

152: How important is your religion in your life?
VERY IMPORTANT/ FAIRLY IMPORTANT/ NOT VERY IMPORTANT/ NOT AT ALL IMPORTANT

153: Are you married?

154: Who is the owner of this house?
RESPONDENT AND/OR SPOUSE/ FAMILY MEMBER/ COUNCIL/
HOUSING ASSOCIATION/ X-SPEAKING LANDLORD/ OTHER
MINORITY LANDLORD/ MAJORITY (ENGLISH) LANDLORD/
OTHER

155: Would you be willing to give us more of your time for a further
interview at a later date? YES/NO

IF 'YES', PLEASE FILL IN CARD A.

156: Do you have any other comments about the questions and issues we
have been talking about?

References

Adelman, C. (ed.) (1981), *Uttering, Muttering: Collecting, Using and Reporting Talk for Social and Educational Research*, London, Grant McIntyre.

Agheyisi, R. and Fishman, J.A. (1970), 'Language attitude studies', *Anthropological Linguistics*, II, pp. 13-57.

Agnihotri, R.K. (1979), 'Processes of Assimilation: A Sociolinguistic Study of Sikh Children in Leeds', unpublished D.Phil thesis, University of York.

Alatis, J.A. (ed.) (1970), *Monograph Series on Languages and Linguistics*, GURT 23, Washington, D.C., Georgetown University Press.

Alatis, J.A. (ed.) (1978), *International Dimensions of Bilingual Education*, Washington, D.C., Georgetown University Press.

Alkan, F. and Constantinides, S. (1982), *Cypriots in Haringey*, London, Haringey Borough Council.

Ambrose, J.E. and Williams, C.H. (1981), 'On the spatial definition of minority: scale as an influence on the geolinguistic analysis of Welsh', in E. Haugen et al. (1981).

Anders, W. (1949), *An Army in Exile: The Story of the Second Polish Corps*, London, Macmillan.

Anthias, F. (1983), 'Sexual division and ethnic adaptation: the case of Greek Cypriot women', in A. Phizacklea (ed.).

Anwar, M. (1979), *The Myth of Return: Pakistanis in Britain*, London, Heinemann Educational.

Arce, C. (1982), 'Language shift among Chicanos: strategies for measuring and assessing direction and rates', *Social Science Journal*, Vol. 19, No. 2, pp. 121-32.

Bain, B. (ed.) (1983), *The Sociogenesis of Language and Human Conduct*, New York, Plenum.

Ball, M. (1981), *Working Papers in Welsh Linguistics*, The Welsh Language Research Unit, University College, Cardiff, and Department of Dialects, Welsh Folk Museum, St Fagans, Cardiff.

Ballard, R (1973), 'Family organisation among the Sikhs in Britain', *New Community*, Vol. 2, No. 1.

Barth, F. (1969), *Introduction to Ethnic Groups and Boundaries*, Boston, Little, Brown.

Baynham, M. (1984), 'ESL and the mother tongue: teaching towards bilingualism', in ESL Publishing Group (eds).

Bellin, W. (1982), 'Determinants of Language Switch in Wales: Applications of Log-Linear Models to Language Census Data', paper presented at the Sociolinguistic Symposium, Sheffield.

Bellin, W.; Harrison, G.; and Piette, B. (1981), *Bilingual Mothers in Wales and the Language of their Children*, Cardiff, University of Wales Press.

Beltramo, A.F. (1981), 'Profile of a state: Montana' in C. Ferguson and S. Brice Heath (eds).

Bender, M.L.; Bowen, J.D.; Cooper, R.L.; and Ferguson, C.A. (1976), *Language in Ethiopia*, London, Oxford University Press.

Bereiter, C. and Engelmann, S. (1966), *Teaching Disadvantaged Children in the Pre-School*, Englewood Cliffs, N.J., Prentice-Hall.

Bernstein, B. (1971), *Class, Codes and Control*, Vol. 1, London, Routledge & Kegan Paul.

Bernstein, B. (1977), *Class, Codes and Control*, Vol. 3, London, Routledge & Kegan Paul.

Berry, J.W.; Kalin, R.; and Taylor, D. (1977), *Multiculturalism and Ethnic Attitudes in Canada*, Ottawa, Minister of Supply and Services.

Bhachu, P. (1981), 'Marriage and Dowry among Selected East African Sikh Families in Britain', unpublished Ph.D. thesis, School of Oriental and African Studies, University of London.

Bhatia, K.C. (1982), 'English and the vernaculars of India: contact and change', *Applied Linguistics*, Vol. III, No. 3.

Bickerton, D. (1975), *Dynamics of a Creole System*, Cambridge, Cambridge University Press.

Blom, J.P. and Gumperz, J.J. (1972), 'Social meaning in linguistic structures: code switching in Norway', in J.J. Gumperz and D. Hymes (eds).

BOTB, British Overseas Trade Board (1979), *Foreign Languages for Overseas Trade*, London, BOTB.

Bourdieu, P. (1970), *Cultural Reproduction*, London, Sage Publications.

Bourhis, R.Y.; Giles, H.; and Rosenthal, D. (1981), 'Notes on the construction of a "Subjective vitality questionnaire" for ethnolinguistic groups', *Journal of Multilingual and Multicultural Development*, Vol. 2, No. 2.

Bradford LEA (1983), *Schools Arrangements for Muslim Children: A Guide for Parents*, Bradford, Directorate of Educational Services.

Bradford M.D. Council (1979), *District Trends*, Bradford, Corporate Policy Unit.

Brah, A.K. (1978), 'South Asian teenagers in Southall: their perception of marriage, family and ethnic identity', *New Community*, Vol. 6, pp. 197–206.

Brice Heath, S. (1983), *Ways with Words: Language, Life and Work in Communities and Classrooms*, Cambridge, Cambridge University Press.

Broadbent, J.; Hashmi, M.; Sharma, B.; and Wright, M. (1983),

Community Languages at 16+, York, Longman, for Schools Council.

Brook, M. (1980), 'The "mother-tongue" issue in Britain: cultural diversity or control?', *British Journal of Sociology of Education*, Vol. 1, No. 3, pp. 237-55.

Brooks, D. and Singh, K. (1979), 'Ethnic commitment versus structural reality: South Asian immigrant workers in Britain', *New Community*, Vol. VII, No. 1.

Bullivant, B. (1981), *The Pluralist Dilemma in Education: Six Case Studies*, London, Allen & Unwin.

Castles, S. (1980), 'The social time-bomb: education of an underclass in West Germany', *Race and Class*, Vol. XXI, No. 4, pp. 369-87.

Castles, S. and Kosack G. (1973), *Immigrant Workers and Class Structure in Western Europe*, London, Oxford University Press.

CEFISEM-CEFREM, Centre de Formation et d'Information pour la Scolarisation des Enfants de Migrants – Centre de Formation pour les Relations entre Ethnies Méditerranéennes (1982), *Expérience Pilote Portant sur l'Enseignement de la Langue et Culture d'Origine d'Enfants Etrangers Fréquentant des Ecoles de la Région de Marseille*, Marseille, CEFISEM-CEFREM.

Chin, W.I. and Simsova S. (1981), 'Information sheets on Chinese readers', London, Polytechnic of North London School of Librarianship, Research Report No. 7.

Ciechanowski, J.M. (1980), 'Poland in defeat, September 1939 – July 1941', in R.F. Leslie (ed.).

CILT, Centre for Information on Language Teaching and Research (1976), *Bilingualism in Britain*, London, CILT.

CILT, Centre for Information on Language Teaching and Research (1983), *Turkish: Language and Culture Guide*, London, CILT.

Clyne, M.G. (1976), 'Aspects of migrant language ecology in Australia', *Talanya*, 3, pp. 75-92.

Colpi, T. (1979), 'The Italian community in Glasgow', *Journal of the Association of Teachers of Italian*, No. 29.

Constantinides, P. (1977), 'The Greek Cypriots: factors in the maintenance of ethnic identity', in J.L. Watson (ed.).

Cooper, R.L. (1980), 'Sociolinguistic surveys: the state of the art', *Applied Linguistics*, Vol. 1, No. 2.

Cooper, R.L. and Fishman, J.A. (1974), 'The study of language attitudes', *International Journal of the Sociology of Language*, No. 3.

Craft, M. and Atkins, M. (1983), *Training Teachers of Ethnic Minority Community Languages*, Nottingham, School of Education.

CRC, Community Relations Council (1981), *Annual Report, 1980-81*, Bradford, CRC.

CRE, Commission for Racial Equality (1980), *The EEC's Directive on the Education of the Children of Migrant Workers*, London, CRE.

Crisp, S. (1980), 'A study of the effects of migration on a South Italian hill village and on the migrants themselves', unpublished Ph.D thesis, University of Cambridge.

Cummins, J. (ed.) (1983a), *Heritage Language Education: Issues and Directions*, Ottawa, Ministry of Supply and Services.

Cummins, J. (1983b), *Heritage Language Education: A Literature Review*, Toronto, Ontario Institute for Studies in Education.

Czaykowski, B. and Sulik B. (1961), *Polacy w Wielkiej Brytanii (Poles in Great Britain)*, Paris, Instytut Literacki.

Dabene, L.; Flasaquier, M.; and Lyons, J. (eds) (1981), *Status of Migrants' Mother Tongues*, Strasbourg, European Science Foundation.

Dale, I. (1980), 'Digraphia', *International Journal of the Sociology of Language*, Vol. 26, pp. 2-13.

Das Gupta, J. (1970), *Language Conflict and National Development*, Berkeley, University of California Press.

Datta, A.K. (1978), 'Languages used by Zambian Asians', in S. Ohannessian and M.E. Kashoki (eds) (1978).

Davies, A. (ed.) (1982), *Language and Learning at Home and School*, London, Heinemann Educational.

Davies, N. (1981), *God's Playground: A History of Poland*, London, Oxford University Press.

De Lange, D.J. and Kosmin, B. (1979), *Community Resources for a Community Survey*, London, Research Unit of the Board of Deputies of British Jews.

Derrick, J. (1966), *Teaching English to Immigrants*, London, Longman.

DES, Department of Education and Science (1965), *The Education of Immigrants, Circular 7/65*, London, DES.

DES, Department of Education and Science (1970), *Statistics of Education Volume 1, 1969*, London, HMSO.

DES, Department of Education and Science (1975), *A Language for Life*, ('The Bullock Report'), London, HMSO.

DES, Department of Education and Science (1981), *Directive of the Council of the European Community on the Education of the Children of Migrant Workers, Circular 5/18*, London, DES.

DES, Department of Education and Science (1982), *Memorandum on Compliance with Directive 77/486/EC on the Education of the Children of Migrant Workers*, London, DES.

DES, Department of Education and Science (1983), *Foreign Languages in the School Curriculum: A Consultative Paper*, London, DES.

Desai, P.B. (1969), 'Language returns of the 1961 Census relating to Gujerati and Languages spoken in Gujerat', in *Language and Society in India*, Simla, Indian Institute of Advanced Study.

De Vries, J. (1974), 'Net effects of language shift in Finland, 1951-1960: a demographical analysis', *Acta Sociologica*, Vol. 17, No. 2, pp. 140-9.

De Vries, J. (1975), *Data Book on Aspects of Language Demography in Canada*, Ottawa, Carleton University, Department of Sociology.

De Vries, J. (1977), 'Explorations in the demography of language: estimation of net language shift in Finland, 1961-1970', *Acta Sociologica*, Vol. 20, No. 2, pp. 145-53.

De Vries, J. (1978), 'Demographic approaches to the study of language and ethnic relations', in H. Giles and B. St. Jacques(eds).

De Vries, J. and Vallee, F.G. (1980), *Language Use in Canada*, Ottawa, Statistics Canada.

De Vries, J. (1981), *Some Methodological Aspects of Self-Report Questions on Language and Ethnicity*, Ottawa, Carleton University, Department of Sociology and Anthropology, Working Paper 81–2.

Dil, S.A. (ed.) (1971a), *Language Structure and Language Use: Essays by Charles A. Ferguson*, Stanford, California, Stanford University Press.

Dil, S.A. (ed.) (1971b), *Language and Social Groups: Essays by John J. Gumperz*, Stanford, California, Stanford University Press.

Dimitropoulos, C.J. (1983), 'Demotic is on the march', *Language Monthly* 2.

Dittmar, N. (1982), 'The unguided learning of German by Spanish and Italian Workers', in UNESCO (ed.).

Dodson, C.J. (1983), 'Living with two languages', *Journal of Multilingual and Multicultural Development*, Vol. 4, No. 6.

Dorian, N.C. (1981), *Language Death: The Life Cycle of a Scottish Gaelic Dialect*, Philadelphia, University of Pennsylvania Press.

Dorian, N.C. (1982), 'Defining the speech community to include its working margins', in S. Romaine (ed.).

Durkacz, V.E. (1983), *The Decline of the Celtic Languages*, Edinburgh, John Donald.

EC, European Communities (1977), *Council Directive on the Education of Children of Migrant Workers*: 77/486, Brussels, EC.

Edwards, V.K. (1979), *The West Indian Language Issue in British Schools: Challenges and Responses*, London, Routledge & Kegan Paul.

Elder, J.W. (1973), 'Problems of cross-cultural methodology; instrumentation and interviewing in India', in Holt and Turner (eds).

Elliot, P. (1981), *Library Needs of Mother-Tongue Schools in London*, London, Polytechnic of North London School of Librarianship, Research Report No. 6.

Enschede (1983), *Bi-cultural Education of Turkish and Moroccan Children in Enschede*, Enschede, Netherlands, Enschede Project.

Entwistle, V. (1979), *Class, Culture and Education*, London, Methuen.

Ervin-Tripp, S. (1968), *Becoming a Bilingual*, Berkeley, University of California, Language Behaviour Research Laboratory, Working Paper No. 9.

ESL Publishing Group (eds) (1984), *Mother Tongue and ESL*, ESL Issues 1, London, ILEA Language and Literacy Unit.

Ferguson, C.A. (1959), 'Diglossia', *Word*, XV, pp. 325–40.

Ferguson, C.A. and Brice Heath S. (eds) (1981), *Language in the USA*, Cambridge, Cambridge University Press.

Fishman, J.A. (1965), 'Who speaks what language to whom and when?', *Linguistique*, No. 2, pp. 67–88.

Fishman, J.A. (1966a), *Language Loyalty in the United States*, The Hague, Mouton.

Fishman, J.A. (1966b), 'Some contrasts between linguistically homogeneous and linguistically heterogeneous policies', in S. Lieberson (ed.).

Fishman, J.A. (ed.) (1966), *Readings in the Sociology of Language*, The Hague, Mouton.

Fishman, J.A. (1967), 'Bilingualism with and without diglossia: diglossia with and without bilingualism', *Journal of Social Issues*, 23, pp. 29-38.

Fishman, J.A. (1971), *Advances in the Sociology of Language*, Vol. 1, The Hague, Mouton.

Fishman, J.A. (1972a) 'Domains and the relationship between micro- and macro-sociolinguistics', in J.J. Gumperz and D. Hymes (eds) (1972).

Fishman, J.A. (1972b), *Language in Sociocultural Change: Essays by Joshua A. Fishman*, Stanford, California, Stanford University Press.

Fishman, J.A. (1980), 'Bilingualism and biculturism as individual and as societal phenomena', *Journal of Multilingual and Multicultural Development*, Vol. 1, No. 1, pp. 3-15.

Fishman, J.A.; Cooper, R.L.; and Conrad, A.W. (1977), *The Spread of English*, Rowley, Mass., Newbury House.

Fishman, J.A.; Ferguson, C.A.; and Das Gupta, J. (eds) (1968), *Language Problems of Developing Nations*, New York, Wiley.

Fried, C. (ed.) (1983), *Minorities: Community and Identity*, Berlin, Springer Verlag.

Furnborough, P.; Jupp, T.; Munns, R.; and Roberts C. (1982), 'Language disadvantage and discrimination: breaking the cycle of majority group perception', *Journal of Multilingual and Multicultural Development*, Vol. 3, No. 3.

Gaborieau, M. and Thorner, A. (eds) (1979), *Asie du Sud: Traditions et Changements*, Paris, Editions du CNRS.

Gal, S. (1979), *Language Shift*, New York, Academic Press.

Garner, M. (ed.) (1981), *Community Languages: Their Role in Education*, Melbourne/Sydney, River Seine Publications.

Garson, S. (1982), 'The role of the language department in a multicultural school', paper given at the conference on inter-cultural education, Nijenrode, Netherlands.

Ghuman, P. (1980), 'Bhattra Sikhs in Cardiff: family and kinship organisation', *New Community*, Vol. VIII, No. 3.

Gibbons, J. (1979), 'U-gaywa: a linguistic study of the campus language of students at the University of Hong Kong', in R. Lord (ed.).

Giles, H. (ed.) (1977), *Language, Ethnicity and Inter-group Relations*, London, Academic Press.

Giles, H.; Bourhis, R.Y.; and Taylor, D.M. (1977), 'Toward a Theory of Language in Ethnic Group Relations' in H. Giles (ed.).

Giles, H. and Powesland, P. (1975), *Speech Style and Social Evaluation*, London, Academic Press.

Giles, H. and Saint-Jacques, B. (eds) (1978), *Language in Ethnic Relations*, Oxford, Pergamon Press.

Giordan, H. (1982), *Democratie Culturelle et Droit à la Différence, Rapport au Ministre de la Culture*, Paris, La Documentation Française.

Gold, G. (1980), 'The changing criteria of social networks in a Cajun community', *Ethnos*, Spring 1980.

Grosjean, F. (1982), *Life With Two Languages*, Cambridge, Mass., Harvard University Press.

Gumperz, J.J. (1962), 'Types of linguistic community', *Anthropological Linguistics*, 4, pp. 28-40.

Gumperz, J.J. (1964), 'Hindi-Punjabi code switching in Delhi', in H.G. Lunt (ed.).

Gumperz, J.J. (1970), 'Verbal strategies in multilingual communication', in J.A. Alatis (ed.).

Gumperz, J.J. (1982a), *Discourse Strategies*, Studies in Interactional Sociolinguistics 1, Cambridge, Cambridge University Press.

Gumperz, J.J. (ed.) (1982b), *Language and Social Identity*, Studies in Interactional Sociolinguistics 2, Cambridge, Cambridge University Press.

Gumperz, J.J. (1983), 'The communicative bases for social inequality', in C. Fried (ed.).

Gumperz, J.J. and Hymes, D. (eds) (1972), *Directions in Sociolinguistics: the Ethnography of Communication*, New York, Holt, Rinehart & Winston.

Gumperz, J. and Wilson, R. (1971), 'Convergence and Creolization: a case from the Indo-Aryan/Dravidian border', in Hymes, D. (ed.).

Hall, S. (1978), *Policing the Crisis*, London, Macmillan.

Halliday, M.A.K. (1978), *Language as a Social Semiotic*, London, Edward Arnold.

Haugen, E. (1966), 'Dialect, Language and Nation', *American Anthropologist*, 68, pp. 922-35.

Haugen, E. (1969), *The Norwegian Language in America: a Study in Bilingual Behavior*, Bloomington, Indiana, Indiana University Press.

Haugen, E. (1972), *The Ecology of Language: Essays by Einar Haugen*, selected and introduced by Anwar Dil, Stanford, California, Stanford University Press.

Haugen, E. (1981), 'Language fragmentation in Scandinavia: the revolt of the minorities', in E. Haugen et al. (eds).

Haugen, E.; McClure, J.D.; and Thomson, D. (eds) (1981), *Minority Languages Today*, Edinburgh, Edinburgh University Press.

Hawkins, E. (1981), *Modern Languages in the Curriculum*, Cambridge, Cambridge University Press.

Hebdige, D. (1979), *Subculture: The Meaning of Style*, London, Methuen.

Hechter, M. (1975), *Internal Colonialism: The Celtic Fringe in British National Development 1536-1966*, London, Routledge & Kegan Paul.

Henry, S. (1984), 'Bilingual teachers in adult education', in ESL Publishing Group (eds).

Hewitt, R. (1982), 'White adolescent Creole users and the politics of friendship', *Journal of Multilingual and Multicultural Development*, Vol. 3, No. 3.

Holt, R.T. and Turner, J.E. (eds) (1973), *The Methodology of Comparative Research*, New York, Free Press.

Houlton, D. and Willey, R. (1983), *Supporting Children's Bilingualism*, York, Longman, for Schools Council.

Hsu, Raymond S.W. (1979), 'What is Standard Chinese?', in R. Lord (ed.).

Hudson, R.A. (1980), *Sociolinguistics*, Cambridge, Cambridge University Press.

Husband, C. (1977), 'News media, language and race relations: a case study in identity maintenance', in H. Giles (ed.).

Husband, C. (ed.) (1982), *'Race' in Britain: Continuity and Change*, London, Hutchinson University Library.

Husband, C. and Saifullah Khan, V. (1982), 'The viability of ethnolinguistic vitality: some creative comments', *Journal of Multilingual and Multicultural Development*, Vol. 3, No. 3.

Husen, T. and Opper, S. (eds) (1983), *Multicultural and Multilingual Education in Immigrant Countries*, Oxford, Pergamon.

Hymes, D. (ed.) (1971), *Pidginization and Creolization of Languages*, Cambridge, Cambridge University Press.

Hymes, D. (1974), *Foundations in Sociolinguistics: An Ethnographic Approach*, Philadelphia, University of Pennsylvania Press.

ILEA, Inner London Education Authority (1979), *Report on the 1978 Census of those ILEA pupils for whom English was not a first language*, London, ILEA.

ILEA, Inner London Education Authority (1981), *1981 Language Census*, London, ILEA.

ILEA, Inner London Education Authority (1982), *Bilingualism in the ILEA: The Educational Implications of the 1981 Language Census*, London, ILEA.

ILEA, Inner London Education Authority (1983), *1983 Language Census*, London, ILEA.

Illich, I. (1981), 'Taught mother language and vernacular tongue', in D.P. Pattanayak (1981).

Isaac, J. (1954), *British Post-War Migration*, Cambridge, Cambridge University Press.

James, A. and Jeffcoate, R. (1982), *The School in the Multi-cultural Society*, New York, Harper & Row.

Jones, P.R. (1983), 'Vietnamese refugees in the UK: the reception programme', *New Community*, Vol. X, No. 3.

Kalendarz Dziennika Polskiego (The Polish Daily's Diary) (1984), London, Dziennik Polski.

Kelly, L.G. (ed.) (1969), *Description and Measurement of Bilingualism*, Toronto, University of Toronto Press.

Khlief, B.B. (1980), *Language, Ethnicity and Education in Wales*, The Hague, Mouton.

Khubchandani, L.M. (1979), 'A demographic typology for Hindi, Urdu, Panjabi speakers in South Asia', in W.C. McCormack and S. Wurm (eds).

King, R. (1979), 'Italians in Britain: an idiosyncratic immigration', *Journal of the Association of Teachers of Italian*, No. 29.

Kloss, H. (1968), 'Notes concerning a language-nation typology', in J.A. Fishman et al. (eds).

Labov, W. (1966), *The Social Stratification of English in New York City*, Washington, D.C., Center for Applied Linguistics.

Labov, W. (1972), *Language in the Inner City*, Oxford, Blackwell.

Ladbury, S. (1977), 'The Turkish Cypriots: ethnic relations in London and Cyprus', in J. Watson (ed.).

Ladefoged, P.; Glick, R.; and Criper, C. (1972), *Language in Uganda*, London, Oxford University Press.

Lambert, W.E. (1972), *Language, Psychology and Culture: Essays by W. E. Lambert*, edited by A.S. Dil, Stanford, California, Stanford University Press.

Lambert, W.E. (1983), 'Deciding on languages of instruction: psychological and social considerations', in T. Husen and S. Opper (eds).

Lambert, W.E. and Tucker, G.R. (1972), *Bilingual Education of Children: the St Lambert Experiment*, Rowley, Massachusetts, Newbury House.

Lavandera, B. (1978), 'The variable component in bilingual performance', in J.E. Alatis (ed.).

Lawton, D. (1968), *Social Class, Language and Education*, London, Routledge & Kegan Paul.

Leeuwenberg, J. (1979), *The Cypriots in Haringey*, London, School of Librarianship, Polytechnic of North London, Research Report No. 1.

Leith, D. (1983), *A Social History of English*, London, Routledge & Kegan Paul.

Le Page, R.B. (1978), *Projection, Focussing, Diffusion, or Steps Towards a Sociolinguistic Theory of Language*, Society for Caribbean Linguistics, Occasional Paper No. 9.

Le Page, R.B. et al. (1974), 'Further report on the sociolinguistic survey of multilingual communities: survey of Cayo District, British Honduras', *Language and Society*, 3, pp. 1-32.

Le Page, R.B. and Tabouret-Keller, A. (1982), 'Models and stereotypes of language and ethnicity', *Journal of Multilingual and Multicultural Development*, Vol. 3, No. 3.

Leslie, R.F. (ed.) (1980), *The History of Poland since 1863*, Cambridge, Cambridge University Press.

Levine, J. (1981), 'Developing pedagogies for multilingual classes', *English in Education*, Vol. 15, No. 3.

Lewis, E.G. (1978), 'Bilingualism in education in Wales', in B. Spolsky, and R. Cooper (eds).

Lieberson, S. (1966), 'Language questions in censuses', *Sociological Inquiry*, 36, pp. 262-79.

Lieberson, S. (ed.) (1966), *Explorations in Sociolinguistics*, Indiana, IJAL Publication No. 44, Indiana University.

Lieberson, S. (1969), 'How can we describe and measure the incidence and distribution of bilingualism?', in L.G. Kelly (ed.).

Lieberson, S. (1970), *Language and Ethnic Relations in Canada*, New York, Wiley.

Linguistic Minorities Project (1983), *Linguistic Minorities in England*, Report for the DES, University of London Institute of Education, London, Tinga Tinga for Heinemann Educational.

Little, A. and Willey, R. (1981), *Multicultural Education: The Way Forward*, London, Schools Council.

LMP/LINC (1983), *The Schools Language Survey: Summary of Findings from Five LEAs*, London, LMP, University of London Institute of Education, Working Paper 3.

Lord, R. (ed.) (1979), *Hong Kong Language Papers*, Hong Kong, Hong Kong University Press.

Luke, K.K. and Richards, J. (1982), 'English in Hong Kong: functions and status', *English Worldwide*, Vol, 3, No. 1.

Lunt, H.G. (ed.) (1964), *Proceedings of the Ninth International Congress of Linguists*, The Hague, Mouton.

McCormack, W.C. and Wurm, S. (eds) (1979), *Language and Society*, The Hague, Mouton.

McKinnon, K. (1977), *Language, Education and Social Processes in a Gaelic Community*, London, Routledge & Kegan Paul.

Majid, S. (1984), 'Bilingual teaching with Asian (Pakistani, Indian, Bangladeshi) students who have the same mother tongue as the teacher', in ESL Publishing Group (eds).

Martin-Jones, M. (1984), 'The newer minority languages: literacy and educational issues', in P. Trudgill (ed.).

Meillet, A. (1921), *Linguistique Historique et Linguistique Générale*, Paris, La Société Linguistique de Paris.

Merdol, Y. (1982), *Turkish Women*, Stockholm, Statens Invandrarverk.

Michaelson, M. (1979), 'The relevance of caste among East African Gujeratis', *New Community*, Vol. VII, No. 3.

Miller, J. (1983), *Many Voices: Bilingualism, Culture and Education*, London, Routledge & Kegan Paul.

Milroy, L. (1980), *Language and Social Networks*, Oxford, Blackwell.

Ministry of Education (1963), *English for Immigrants*, London, HMSO.

Mobbs, M.C. (1981), 'Two languages or one? The significance of the language names "Hindi and Urdu"', *Journal of Multilingual and Multicultural Development*, Vol. 2, No. 3.

MOTET, Mother Tongue and English Teaching Project (1981), *Summary of the Report*, Vols 1 and 2, Bradford, School of Education, The University.

Moys, A. (ed.) (1984), *Foreign Language Examinations: the 16+ Debate 1980–83*, London, CILT.

Mullard, C. (1980), *Racism in Society and School: History, Policy and Practice*, London, Centre for Multicultural Education, University of London Institute of Education, Occasional Paper No. 1.

Nagra, J.S. (1979), 'Asian Supplementary Schools and the Attitudes of Asian Children and Parents towards the Teaching of the Mother Tongue', unpublished M.Ed. thesis, University of Birmingham.

NCLE, National Congress on Languages in Education (1982), *Report of the Working Party on the Languages of Minority Communities*, London, CILT.

Neale, B. (1974a), 'Kenya's Asian languages', in W.H. Whiteley (ed.).

Neale, B. (1974b), 'Language use among the Asian communities', in W.H. Whiteley (ed.).

New South Wales (1980), *Survey of Students from Non-English Backgrounds*, Sydney, New South Wales Department of Education.

Nixon, J. (ed.) (1981), *A Teacher's Guide to Action Research*, London, Grant McIntyre.

Norst, M. (1982a), *Ethnic Schools: Report with Recommendations*, Canberra, Commonwealth Schools Commission.

Norst, M. (1982b), *Ethnic Schools: Data Digest*, Canberra, Commonwealth Schools Commission.

NUT, National Union of Teachers (1982), *Linguistic Diversity and Mother Tongue Teaching*, London, National Union of Teachers.

Oakley, R. (1970), 'The Cypriots in Britain', *Race Today*, 2, pp. 99-102.

Oakley, R. (1979), 'Family, kinship and patronage', in V. Saifullah Khan (ed.).

O'Bryan, K.G.; Reitz, J.G.; and Kuplowska, O.M. (1976), *Non-official Languages: a Study in Canadian Multiculturalism*, Ottawa, Ministry of Supply and Services.

Ohanessian, S.; Ferguson, C.A.; and Polomé, E.C. (1975), *Language Surveys in Developing Nations: Papers and Reports on Sociolinguistic Surveys*, Arlington, Va., Center for Applied Linquisitics.

Ohannessian, S. and Kashoki, M.E. (eds) (1978), *Language in Zambia*, London, International African Institute.

OPCS, Office of Population Censuses and Surveys (1980), *Classification of Occupations and Coding Index*, London, HMSO.

Open University (1982), *Ethnic Minorities and Community Relations*, Milton Keynes, Open University Press.

Pal, Animesh K. (1969), 'Bengali speech community and its neighbours', in *Language and Society in India*, proceedings of a seminar, Simla, Indian Institute of Advanced Study.

Palmer, R. (1977), 'The Italians: patterns of migration to London', in J.L. Watson (ed.).

Parkin, D.J. (1974a), 'Status factors in language adding: Bahati housing estate in Nairobi', in W.H. Whiteley (ed.).

Parkin, D.J. (1974b), 'Language shift and ethnicity in Nairobi: the speech community of Kaloleni', in W. H. Whiteley (ed.).

Parkin, D.J. (1974c), 'Nairobi: problems and methods', in W. H. Whiteley (ed.).

Pattanayak, D.P. (1981), *Multilingualism and Mother Tongue Education*, Delhi, Oxford University Press.

Patterson, S. (1977), 'The Poles: an exile community in Britain', in J.L. Watson (ed.).

Pearson, R. (1983), *National Minorities in Eastern Europe 1848-1945*, London, Macmillan.

Pedraza, P. and Attinasi, J. (1980), *Rethinking Diglossia*, Language

Policy Task Force Working Paper No. 9, New York, Center for Puerto Rican Studies, City University.

Phizacklea, A. (ed.) (1983), *One Way Ticket: Migration and Female Labour*, London, Routledge & Kegan Paul.

Polomé, E.C. (1982), 'Sociolinguistically oriented language surveys', *Language in Society*, Vol. II, No. 2.

Polomé, E.C. and Hill, P.C. (eds) (1980), *Language in Tanzania*, London, International African Institute.

Poplack, S. (1979), *'Sometimes I'll start a sentence in English, y termino en Español': Toward a Typology of Code Switching*, Language Policy Task Force Working Paper No. 4, New York, Center for Puerto Rican Studies, City University.

Poplack, S. (1984), 'Intergenerational variation in language and structure in a bilingual context', in C. Rivera (ed.).

Pradelle de Latour, M.L. (1983), 'Identity as a complex network', in C. Fried (ed.).

Pride, J.B. (1979), *Sociolinguistic Aspects of Language Learning and Teaching*, London, Oxford University Press.

Proudfoot, M.J. (1956), *European Refugees 1939–52: a Study in Forced Population Movement*, Evanston, Illinois, Northwestern University Press.

Rampton, M.B.H. (1981), 'The English of UK Ethnic Minority Schoolchildren of South Asian Extraction', unpublished MA Dissertation, University of London Institute of Education.

Rampton Committee of Enquiry into the Education of Children from Ethnic Minority Groups (1981), *West Indian Children in Our Schools* (Interim Report), London, HMSO.

Reid, E. (1984), 'The newer minorities: spoken languages and varieties', in P. Trudgill (ed.).

Reid, E. (ed.) (1984), *Minority Community Languages in School*, London, CILT.

Reuter, M. (1981), 'The status of Swedish in Finland in theory and practice', in E. Haugen et al (eds).

Rex, J. and Moore, R. (1967), *Race, Community and Conflict: A Study of Sparkbrook*, London, Oxford University Press.

Rex, J. and Tomlinson, S. (1979), *Colonial Immigrants in a British City: A Class Analysis*, London, Routledge & Kegan Paul.

Rivera, C. (ed.) (1984), *An Ethnographic/Sociolinguistic Approach to Language Proficiency Assessment*, Bristol, Multilingual Matters.

Romaine, S. (1981), 'Problems in the sociolinguistic description of communicative repertoires among linguistic minorities', in L. Dabene et al (eds).

Romaine, S. (ed.) (1982), *Sociolinguistic Variation in Speech Communities*, London, Edward Arnold.

Romaine, S. and Dorian, N.C. (1981), 'Scotland as a linguistic area', *Scottish Literary Journal*, Language Supplement 14, pp. 1–24.

Rosen, H. (1973), *Language and Class: A Critical Look at the Theories of Basil Bernstein*, Bristol, Falling Wall Press.

Rosen, H. and Burgess, T. (1980), *Languages and Dialects of London School Children*, London, Ward Lock Educational.

Russell, R. (ed.) (1982), *Urdu in Britain*, London, Urdu Markaz.

Saifullah Khan, V. (1976), 'Existing provision by linguistic minorities for language maintenance', in CILT, 1976.

Saifullah Khan, V. (1977a), *Bilingualism and Linguistic Minorities in Britain*, London, Runnymede Trust.

Saifullah Khan, V. (1977b), 'The Pakistanis: Mirpuri villagers at home and in Bradford', in J.L. Watson (ed.).

Saifullah Khan, V. (1979a), 'Work and network: South Asian women in South London', in S. Wallman (ed.).

Saifullah Khan, V. (1979b), 'Ethnic identity among South Asians in the U.K.', in M. Gaborieau and A. Thorner (eds).

Saifullah Khan, V. (ed.) (1979), *Minority Families in Britain*, London, Macmillan.

Saifullah Khan, V. (1980a), 'The "mother tongue" of linguistic minorities in multicultural England', *Journal of Multilingual and Multicultural Development*, Vol. 1, No. 1, pp. 71–88.

Saifullah Khan, V. (1980b), 'Old themes, new tensions: a comment on the contemporary mother tongue teaching debate', in *Mother Tongue Teaching*, Conference Report, Commission for Racial Equality and Bradford College.

Saifullah Khan, V. (1981), 'Some comments on the question of "the second generation"', is *On Immigrant Children and Youth in Norway*, Oslo, Ministry of Local Government and Labour.

Saifullah Khan, V. (1982a), 'The role of the culture of dominance in structuring the experience of ethnic minorities', in C. Husband (ed.).

Saifullah Khan, V. (1982b), 'The dynamics of ethnic relations', in Open University, 1982.

Saifullah Khan, V. (1983), 'Language dominance and discrimination in multilingual England', Institute of Linguists, Threlford Memorial Lecture, *The Incorporated Linguist*, Vol. 22, No. 3.

Sayer, S. and Bajpai, A. (1984), 'The Importance of Bilingual Teachers in ESL Issues 1', in ESL Publishing Group (eds).

Schmidt-Rohr, G. (1963), *Mutter Sprache*, Jena, Even Diederichs Verlag.

Schools Council (1970), *Teaching English to West Indian Children: The Research Stage of the Project*, London, Evans Methuen Educational.

Shapiro, M.C. and Schiffman, H.F. (1981), *Language and Society in South Asia*, Delhi, Motilal Banarsidass.

SHAPRS, Spitalfields Housing and Planning Rights Service (1981), *The Spitalfields Survey*, London, SHAPRS.

Shuy, R.W. and Fasold W. (eds) (1973), *Language Attitudes: Current Trends and Prospects*, Washington, D.C., Georgetown University Press.

Simons, H. (1979), *Mother Tongue and Culture in Bedfordshire*, EC Pilot Project, First External Evaluation Report, Cambridge, Institute of Education.

Sinclair, J.M. and Coulthard, M. (1975), *Towards an Analysis of Dis-*

course: The English Used by Teachers and Pupils, London, Oxford University Press.

Singh, R. (1978), *Sikhs in Bradford*, Bradford, Bradford College.

Sivanandan, A. (1982), *A Different Hunger: Writings on Black Resistance*, London, Pluto Press.

Skutnabb-Kangas, T. (1984), *Bilingualism or Not? The Education of Minorities*, Bristol, Multilingual Matters.

Skutnabb-Kangas, T. and Toukomaa, P. (1977), *Research Report No 26*, Tampere, Finland, Dept of Sociology and Social Psychology, University of Tampere.

Smith, D.J. (1977), *Racial Disadvantage in Britain*, Harmondsworth, Penguin.

Smith, G.P. (1982a), *Locating Populations of Minority Language Speakers: An Example of Practice from the Coventry Languages Project*, LMP Working Paper No. 1, London, University of London Institute of Education.

Smith, G.P. (1982b), *The Geography and Demography of South Asian Languages in England: Some Methodological Problems*, LMP Working Paper No. 2, London, University of London Institute of Education.

Smith, G.P. (1984), *Sampling Linguistic Minorities: A Technical Report on the Adult Language Use Survey*, LMP/CLE/LINC Working Paper No. 4, London, University of London Institute of Education.

Spolsky, B. and Cooper, R. (eds) (1978), *Case Studies in Bilingual Education*, Rowley, Mass., Newbury House.

Sponza, L. (1980), 'Per una storia dell' emigrazione Italiana in Gran Bretagna nell '800', *Journal of the Association of Teachers of Italian*, No. 20.

Stewart, W.A. (1966), 'A sociolinguistic typology for describing national multilingualism', in J.A. Fishman (ed.).

Stone, M. (1981), *The Education of the Black Child in Britain: The Myth of Multiracial Education*, London, Fontana.

Sutcliffe, D. (1982), *British Black English*, Oxford, Blackwell.

Tambs-Lyche, H. (1980), *London Patidars*, London, Routledge & Kegan Paul.

Thomson, N. (1983), 'The community directive, 77/486/EEC: origins and implementation', *Journal of Multilingual and Multicultural Development*, Vol. 4, No. 6, pp. 437–58.

Tolstoy, N. (1977), *Victims of Yalta*, London, Jonathan Cape.

Tolstoy, N. (1981), *Stalin's Secret War*, London, Jonathan Cape.

Tosi, A. (1979), 'Mother tongue teaching for the children of migrants', *Language Teaching and Linguistics Abstracts*, Vol. 12, No. 4.

Tosi, A. (1982a), 'Between the mother's dialect and English', in A. Davies (ed.).

Tosi, A. (1982b), *The Development of Italian in the Young Italo-Australian Child*, Oxford, Oxford Polytechnic and Catholic Education Office of Victoria.

Tosi, A. (1984a), *Immigration and Bilingual Education: A Case Study of Movement of Population Language Change and Education within the European Community*, Oxford, Pergamon.

Tosi, A. (1984b), 'Materials for mother-tongue teaching in the context of second language learning – criteria for design and evaluation', in E. Reid (ed.).

Trudgill, P. (1974), *The Social Differentiation of English in Norwich*, Cambridge, Cambridge University Press.

Trudgill, P. (1975), *Accent, Dialect and the School*, London, Edward Arnold.

Trudgill, P. (ed.) (1978), *Sociolinguistic Patterns in British English*, London, Edward Arnold.

Trudgill, P. (ed.) (1984), *Language in the British Isles*, Cambridge, Cambridge University Press.

UNESCO (ed.) (1982), *Living in Two Cultures: The Socio-Cultural Situation of Migrant Workers and their Families*, Gower, The Unesco Press.

Voegelin, C. F. and Voegelin, F.M. (1977), *Classification and Index of the World's Languages*, Oxford, Elsevier.

Waggoner, D. (1981), 'Statistics on language use', in C. Ferguson and S. Brice Heath (eds).

Wallman, S. (1978), 'The boundaries of "race": processes of ethnicity in England', *Man*, Vol. 13, No. 2.

Wallman, S. (ed.) (1979), *Ethnicity at Work*, London, Macmillan.

Wallman, S. (1983), 'Identity options' in C. Fried (ed.).

Wallman, S.; Dhooge, Y.; Goldman, A.; and Kosmin, B. (1980), 'Ethnography by proxy: strategies for research in the inner cities', *Ethnos*, 1980, 1–2.

Watson, J.L. (1975), *Emigration and the Chinese Lineage: The 'Mans' in Hong Kong and London*, Berkeley, University of California Press.

Watson, J.L. (ed.) (1977), *Between Two Cultures: Migrants and Minorities in Britain*, Oxford, Blackwell.

Weinreich, U. (1953), *Languages in Contact*, The Hague, Mouton.

Wells, G. (1981), 'Describing linguistic development at home and at school', in C. Adelman (ed.).

Wells, G. (1982), *Language Learning and Education*, Bristol, Centre for the Study of Language and Communication, University of Bristol.

Werbner, P. (1981), 'Manchester Pakistanis: life styles, rituals and the making of social distinction', *New Community*, Vol. IX, No. 2.

Whiteley, W.H. (ed.) (1974), *Language in Kenya*, London, Oxford University Press.

Wilding, J. (1981), *Ethnic Minority Languages in the Classroom? A Survey of Asian Parents in Leicester*, Leicester, Council for Community Relations.

Wiles, S. (1984), *Working with Young Bilingual Children*, London, ILEA Learning Resources.

Williams, G. (1978), *Social and Cultural Change in Contemporary Wales*, London, Routledge & Kegan Paul.

Williams, G. (1982), 'Bilingualism, Class Variety and Social Reproduction', paper presented at the Sociolinguistic Symposium, Sheffield.

Williams, G. and Roberts, C. (1983), 'Language, education and reproduction in Wales', in B. Bain (ed.).

Wilson, A. (1978), *Finding a Voice*, London, Virago.

Winchester, S.W.C. (1974), 'Immigrant areas in Coventry in 1971', *New Community*, Vol. 4, No. 1.

Wright, J. (1982), *The World in a City: Bilingual Learning Materials*, London, ILEA Learning Materials Service.

Young, M.F. (ed.) (1971), *Knowledge and Control*, London, Collier Macmillan.

Zengel, M.S. (1962), 'Literacy as a factor in language change', *American Anthropologist*, No. 64, pp. 132-9.

Index

For Product Safety Concerns and Information please contact our EU
representative GPSR@taylorandfrancis.com
Taylor & Francis Verlag GmbH, Kaufingerstraße 24, 80331 München, Germany

www.ingramcontent.com/pod-product-compliance
Lightning Source LLC
Chambersburg PA
CBHW050555270326
41926CB00012B/2066